CONTEMPORARY ENTREPRENEURS

Profiles of Entrepreneurs and the Businesses They Started, Representing 74 Companies in 30 Industries

Including Biographical Information, the Origin of
the Venture, Revenues, How Business Growth Was Managed,
Business Obstacles Faced and How They Were Overcome,
and Personal Perspectives on Keys to Success, Future
Vision, and the Lessons Gleaned from Experience

Edited by

Craig E. Aronoff, PhD.
Dinos Distinguished Chair of Private Enterprise
Kennesaw State College, Marietta, Georgia

and

John L. Ward, PhD.
Ralph Marotta Professor of Free Enterprise
Loyola University, Chicago, Illinois

Omnigraphics, Inc.

Penobscot Building • Detroit, Michigan 48226

Craig E. Aronoff and John L. Ward, Editors
Mary Boswell Cawley, Project Manager

Library of Congress Cataloging-in-Publication Data

Contemporary entrepreneurs : profiles of entrepreneurs and the businesses they
started, representing 74 companies in 30 industries : including biographical information
... / edited by Craig E. Aronoff and John L. Ward.
    p.   cm.
    Includes bibliographical references and index.
    ISBN 1-55888-315-0 (lib. bdg. : acid-free paper)
    1. Businessmen—United States—Biography. 2. Business enterprises—United
States—History. I. Aronoff, Craig E., 1951- . II. Ward, John L., 1945- .
HC102.5.A2C66   1991
338'.04'092273—dc20
[B]   91-7637
                                                                        CIP

Omnigraphics, Inc.

* * *

Frank R. Abate, *Vice President - Dictionaries*
Eric F. Berger, *Vice President - Production*
Laurie Lanzen Harris, *Vice President - Editorial Director*
Peter E. Ruffner, *Vice President - Administration*
James A. Sellgren, *Vice President - Operations & Finance*

* * *

Frederick G. Ruffner, Jr., *Publisher*

The information in this publication was compiled from the sources cited and from
other sources considered reliable. While every possible effort has been made to
ensure reliability, the publisher will not assume liability for damages caused by
inaccuracies in the data, and makes no warranty, express or implied, on the accuracy
of the information contained herein.

Printed in the United States of America

Table of Contents

Introduction

"The highest manifestation of life consists of this: that a being governs its own actions. A thing which is always subject to direction of another is somewhat of a dead thing."

—*St. Thomas Aquinas*

Since the beginning of American history, our society has admired risk-takers. Well we should, for our nation was created by those who faced the unknown, men and women who embarked on perilous journeys into unfamiliar territories. Our present was wrought by those relative few who challenged what was with what could be. They urged our freedom, forged our government, expanded our frontiers. They were risk-taking visionaries; they were the first, the ultimate, American entrepreneurs. To this day, entrepreneurs continue to be our heroes. They are the business people who fuel our private enterprise economy, create vast numbers of our jobs, and ease our lives with new goods and services. They assume the risks and they earn the profits. Yet, in a larger sense, we all profit.

The Scope of the Book

Jeffrey A. Timmons, one of the leading and most insightful scholars of entrepreneurship, has argued that "once you know how winning entrepreneurs think, act and perform, you can establish goals to practice emulating those actions, attitudes, habits and strategies—and consider in a more intelligent way if the loneliness of entrepreneurial life is for you" (*The Entrepreneurial Mind*, p. xii). This book shows entrepreneurial actions, attitudes, habits and strategies—the realities of the entrepreneur's life.

Contemporary Entrepreneurs contains biographical sketches on 74 current business men and women. Selected for entrepreneurial achievement during the last decade or so, the business people included here represent about three dozen industries, 27 states in all regions of the country, and a wide range of backgrounds. When they started their businesses, they ranged in age from 18 to 62. They tended to be younger, however, with almost three-fourths aged 40 or less and 13 under 30. In slightly more than a decade, some have guided their companies through phenomenal growth and generated enormous profits. A few have failed. But their lives, their experiences and their visions contain lessons for those who would "assume risk for profit."

Some profiled here succeeded by identifying and exploiting a previously undiscovered market niche. Others have achieved by applying technology or commercializing sophisticated research. In some cases a home-grown skill or recipe has been developed into a thriving business. Not surprisingly, computer manufacturing, software and retailing provided the most entries in this volume (16). But basic businesses related to food (10), clothing (7) and building (8) are represented too. The list is almost equally divided between manufacturing and service.

Success and "happiness-ever-after" are not the end of each of these tales. Some of the ventures chronicled here have failed, others continue to struggle. Some will become legacies in business families, others will be converted to cash. All, however, demonstrate hard work, discipline, perseverance and an element of luck.

The Organization of the Volume

Each entry begins with a listing of factual data about the entrepreneur(s) and the company, including birth date(s), marital status, and number of children, if any; the nature of the business venture; the company name, address, and telephone number; the date the company was founded; current revenues; the number of employees; the amount of the original investment; and the current value of the company. In a few cases, some of this information was unavailable.

Later sections of each sketch, which often draw heavily on quotations from the entrepreneur(s), include revealing and often inspiring comments on early experiences, the origin of the venture, how business growth was managed, and how business obstacles were overcome. Each case offers the entrepreneur's perspective on keys to success, future vision and any lessons gleaned from his or her experience. Closing each sketch is a list of references for further reading.

An index to the entrepreneurs, company names, geographical locations, and types of industries follows the text.

Audience

This book is intended for students in high school and undergraduate and graduate business courses who wish to find a starting place for their case studies, investors who wish to find information on areas of economic growth, and entrepreneurs themselves, who may find in these 74 brief biographies the inspiration they need to make their dreams of entrepreneurship a reality.

Acknowledgments

We want to express our appreciation to a number of people who made this volume possible. Mary Cawley at Business Owner Resources spent long hours coordinating all aspects of the project from its inception to its final production by Omnigraphics, Inc. In her capacity as project facilitator, she was sometimes a researcher, sometimes a writer, and often an editor.

She was ably assisted by Robbie Hunt Stinneford of Writers' Warehouse in Atlanta. Ms. Stinneford not only wrote several profiles, but through her own entrepreneurial company also provided many writers: Mary J. Beaulieu, Shelly Browne, Edward Crowell, Leah E. Perry, Anne DeHoff Kraft, Bruce Miller and Laura Raines. Authors' initials follow each profile.

Other writers who contributed profiles include Alison Allen, Terence Allen, Cathy A. Coburn, Donna Espy, Kelly S. Miller and Faye M. Smith. Debra Underwood and Glenda Wills contributed research materials, and Lara Aronoff provided editorial suggestions.

Finally, we thank the business men and women included in this volume. Many provided enlightening corporate materials—annual reports, product descriptions, news releases and clippings. Those entrepreneurs profiled here who generously took time from their busy schedules to talk with our writers and to share their thoughts and lessons deserve special mention. These are all men and women who have left valuable blueprints for future generations of entrepreneurs.

Craig E. Aronoff, Ph.D.
John L. Ward, Ph.D.
Editors

The Editors

Craig E. Aronoff, Ph.D., holds the Dinos Distinguished Chair of Private Enterprise and is professor of management at Kennesaw State College in Marietta, Georgia. The oldest son of a wholesale clothing business family, Aronoff created and directs Kennesaw State College's Family Business Forum, which is, according to *Family Business Review*, the nation's premier model of college-based educational programs for family businesses. Founding president of the Association of Private Enterprise Education and winner of two Freedom Foundation Leavy Awards for Excellence in Private Enterprise Education, Aronoff was named one of the top two post-secondary business educators in the nation by the National Federation of Independent Business Foundation in 1989. He has participated in two business start-ups and serves on the boards of three entrepreneurial ventures.

John L. Ward, Ph.D., initiated and serves as the Ralph Marotta Professor of Free Enterprise at Loyola University of Chicago. He teaches strategic management and business leadership at Loyola's Graduate School of Business. Ward is the author of *Keeping The Family Business Healthy*, a leading book in the family business field. His research findings have been featured in many respected business and academic publications. Ward is a visiting lecturer on family business at the International Institute for Management Development, in Lausanne, Switzerland, and the Instituto de Estudios Superiores de la Empresa, in Barcelona, Spain. In addition to speaking to more than 30 trade and professional audiences yearly, Ward has an active consulting practice focusing on family business succession, outside boards of directors and strategic planning. A founder and partner in three business ventures, he currently serves on the boards of six companies.

Drs. Ward and Aronoff edited the three-volume series *The Future of*

Private Enterprise, as well as *Initial Public Offerings Annual: 1989* and *Family Business Sourcebook.* As contributing editors for *Nation's Business,* they co-author a monthly column. They serve as frequent resources to national media.

Larry C. Addington

Addington Resources, Inc.

Larry C. Addington: Born 1936. Married, three children.
Venture: A corporation that mines and markets bituminous coal in Kentucky, Ohio and West Virginia.
Company: Addington Resources, Inc.; Route 180 Big Run Road; Ashland, KY 41101; (606) 928-3433
Founded: 1981. Incorporated in Delaware, 1986.
Revenues: $220 million as of June 1989.
Employees: 1,000 plus.
Original Investment: $3,200.
Value: $67 million net worth, according to published reports (June 1989).

Founder

Larry Addington grew up on a farm in Elliott County, Kentucky with five brothers and sisters. The family struggled financially, but believed in the value of a good education. Both parents and grandparents were teachers at various times. "By some standards we were poor. But we were taught to work hard and I always had a burning desire to succeed," says Addington. Larry's father also had a dream to succeed in business and opened a lumber mill and plant in the 1950s. He suffered a setback when a customer reneged on a $1,000 payment, and later abandoned the business.

Larry Addington has also seen setbacks and some tough battles with land owners and regulatory agencies, but they have never stopped him. He is known in the industry as a shrewd but fair bargainer.

Class president for four years at Sandy Hook High School, Addington served in the U. S. Army from 1957 to 1959, then studied civil engineering at Morehead State University and the University of Kentucky from 1959 to 1963. He worked as a construction engineer until 1967 when he started his own company, Addington Engineering.

Addington family members have played strong roles in Larry's successful ventures. Brothers Robert and Bruce also attended Morehead State University. Robert taught school for seven years before joining Larry at Addington Engineering, while younger brother Bruce went to work at Addington Brothers Mining in 1974.

Larry Addington is the driving force behind the business. "He has the vision and he's the damndest doer I've ever seen," says Lowell Hughes, a former state senator and part-owner of Addington's first coal company. He often works 10 to 14 hours a day and is involved in several other businesses besides Addington Resources.

"Addington has a unique ability to maintain control over fifty different projects at once and remain up-to-speed. He has marvelous powers of retention, a lot of patience and he's never been afraid to take risks," says Mark Merritt, the company's sales and marketing manager.

Business Origin

The idea to start a coal company grew out of Larry Addington's experience as an engineer and his own construction business. He noticed that when companies made large highway cuts, they were throwing away the coal they exposed. He saw an opportunity to start a company which he thought would have growth potential and would allow him to stay close to his home in eastern Kentucky.

By 1972, Addington Brothers Mining was in business. Larry and Robert pooled enough capital to begin leasing properties, then convinced Walker Equipment Company to lease them a million dollars worth of new equipment and allow them 75 days to make the first payment.

Larry Addington describes that as the "best sales job" he has ever done. At the time many coal companies were fly-by-night operations with reputations for not paying bills. Addington showed that he was different.

"We figured we could make $1 a ton on coal which was selling for about $6 a ton back in 1972. We shipped 10,000 tons that first month and made $1.15 a ton," says Addington.

They mined and shipped 600,000 tons the following year.

"Addington picked an excellent time to get into the coal business," says Merritt. The OPEC oil embargo and a United Mine Workers strike caused the price of coal to jump from $6 a ton in 1973 to $40 a ton in 1974.

While most companies were selling their coal on the spot market for the highest price, Addington made the decision to sell coal to utility companies through long-term contracts for about half the going rate. That strategy made the company's fortune when the price of coal plummeted a few years later.

Addington has also bought long-term contracts from his competitors, and still believes that is the only stable way to run a coal company. The formula is to buy a long-term contract at a price that gives the utility a lower price on coal and still brings in a profit. "It was the long-term contracts that gave the company a base from which to grow," affirms Merritt.

The Addingtons sold Addington Brothers Mining to Ashland Oil Inc. in 1976 for $51.5 million. Two years later they started Pyramid Mining Company in Western Kentucky, and sold that company to First Mississippi Corporation for $32.5 million in 1981.

Addington wanted to move back to eastern Kentucky and concentrate his business in low-sulfur coal reserves. Low-sulfur coal burns cleaner, causing less air pollution. Because of new and pending environmental regulations, he felt that the demand for low-sulfur coal could only increase.

"Low-sulfur coal is going to be valuable for the long term, especially as new technology is being developed to make it cleaner burning. Thanks to Addington's foresight, we feel that we're prepared for any eventuality," says Merritt.

Business Growth

Larry and Robert began the businesses which led to Addington Resources, Inc. in 1981. The company was incorporated in 1986 and continued to expand through acquisition of new coal reserves. To pay off some of its debt, it offered 1,700,000 shares of common stock to the public in July 1987, netting $29,718,936. Originally selling for $19.50 per share, the stock has split once and trades over-the-counter (NASDAQ). The Addington brothers retain 66.5 percent.

Larry Addington is president and chief executive officer, Robert is vice-president of operations and research/development, while Bruce is vice-president of operations. "The three have different strengths, but have always worked well together. Larry is the ultimate administrator and decision maker, Robert is an ideas man and Bruce is the driving force behind day-to-day operations," says Merritt. Recently a fourth brother, Stephen, joined the company after pursuing his studies in mining engineering at the University of Kentucky.

Addington Resources, Inc. is a major Eastern coal producer, operating seven surface coal mines in Kentucky, Ohio and West Virginia. It sold nearly 6.5 million tons of coal in 1988.

The company holds long-term contracts with the Tennessee Valley Authority, East Kentucky Power Cooperative, Consumers Power, Cincinnati Gas & Electric, Appalachian Power Company, the South Mississippi Electric Power Association and Duke Power Company.

In 1988, Larry Addington predicted the company would reach $500 million in annual revenues in five years. Merritt says that figure is "entirely possible," but that the growth would not come solely from coal, which as an industry has grown slowly in recent years.

To spur revenues, Addington Resources has diversified its holdings to include other material-moving operations such as gold mining, sanitary landfill development,highway construction and related contracting.

The company recently sold a gold mine in Colorado, netting $20 million in pre-tax revenues. "The sale of Addwest Gold fulfills our strategy of focusing more fully on developing our core businesses in coal mining and sanitary landfill operations," Addington announced to his stockholders. Although temporarily out of the gold-mining business, Merritt states that the company continues to look for other gold reserves and is always open to new acquisitions.

The Green Valley Environmental Corporation, a subsidiary of Addington Resources, plans to open the first phase of a 937-acre landfill in Greenup County, Kentucky. The landfill site is just part of a 22,000 acre parcel that Addington bought from American Electric Power Company for $4 million. Addington, who plans to put a race track, mall and perhaps a theme park on the remainder of the property, describes that purchase as "one of the greatest deals we ever did." With so many landfills approaching capacity and solid-waste tonnage growing, Addington sees landfill development as a growth opportunity. "I want to build the safest landfill ever built; the best facility possible. I plan to put in a clay and a synthetic liner. We will raise the level of this landfill to state-of-the-art and reclaim it better than any surface mine," says Addington. Addington's coal mines have been examples of environmental responsibility, having won reclamation awards in three states.

Business Obstacles

"Obtaining dependable markets has been and will always continue to be the biggest problem in the coal business," says Merritt. The Addingtons have faced that problem by aggressively going after utility companies and locking them into long-term contracts whenever possible. As other companies have seen the value of this strategy, competition for long-term contracts has increased in recent years.

Keys to Success

"Most of our success comes from innovative management and just plain hard work. We haven't reinvented the wheel when it comes to coal mining methods, but we have brought old methods such as blast casting to a new level of technology using state-of-the-art mobile equipment," says Merritt. In an interview in *Coal,* Addington concurred. When asked if he thought he brought the Midas touch to his company's management, Addington responded, "I don't think so. I think more we're a company that brought innovation into the board room as well as into the mine site."

Efficiency is the overriding objective behind Addington Resources' operations. The company mines most of its coal through the mountaintop removal method, a highly-efficient surface mining technique. By refining the mining process, the company can ship 99 percent of its coal "run of mine," which means that Addington coal has few impurities. This eliminates the costly washing that many coal companies use, giving the company a competitive edge.

Addington also markets his product farther afield than most of his competitors. Transportation by river barge makes long-distance delivery possible. "Putting coal on the river system proved to be an efficient way of getting coal to market and one of the company's most valuable assets," says Merritt. Approximately 90 percent of Addington's coal is delivered by water. Addington also controls costs by acquiring coal reserves located near its three barge-loading facilities on the Ohio and Green rivers, so that product can be shipped economically.

"We attribute much of our efficiency to a highly-motivated, non-union labor force," says Merritt. Employees have turned down union attempts to organize in the past. "There is very little turnover in our people. Our benefits are superior to most union employees and they get more work days than most union coal companies offer their workers," Merritt adds.

"Addington Resources is different from most coal companies in its ability to respond quickly to new situations and to grasp new opportunities," says Merritt. He believes much of that is due to Larry Addington's confidence and his ability to see "the big picture." In Merritt's opinion, Addington's implementation of long-term contracts and barge transportation were perfectly timed, and some of his most controversial acquisitions have paid off handsomely. "If he were convinced a project was worthwhile, even though advised to the contrary, he would bet the company on it again," says Hughes.

Future Vision

Addington Resources will continue to be a major coal producer, but is focusing more attention on its landfill development operations. "Landfills are recession-proof. People throw away about 1,600 pounds per person per year," says Addington.

Landfill development could become 30 percent of the corporate revenues within five years, says Merritt. "Larry has become very interested in the concept of resource recovery and recycling. He really likes the idea of taking something that is a cost to society and turning it into something productive. We're already working on a refuse-derived fuel to sell to our customers," Merritt relates.

Entrepreneurial Lessons

Larry Addington's achievements indicate he strongly supports the theory that the best place to find success is in one's own backyard. Combining an acknowledged bit of luck and the natural resources of his home state with engineering, salesmanship and sheer determination, Addington has built one of the fastest-growing coal companies in his home state of Kentucky.

He is also a man who feels a debt to his community and wants to give something back. In 1988, Addington donated $500,000 to help rebuild a Grayson, Kentucky elementary school that had been destroyed by fire (one of many charitable contributions, says Merritt). Addington says simply, "If you can afford to do it, you should. I feel you are rewarded for the good deeds in life."

References

"Addington Had Record Revenues Last Year." *Lexington Herald-Leader*, April 1, 1989.

Addington Resources, Inc., Annual Report, 1988.

Addington Resources, Inc., Third Quarter Report, 1989.

Daykin, Tom. "Low-Sulfur Coal Turns High Profits for Addington." *Lexington Herald-Leader*, September 26, 1988.

Hershberg, Ben Z. "Larry Addington Driven to Succeed Along Sometimes Bumpy Coal Road." *Louisville Courier-Journal*, September 11, 1988.

Malloy, David E. "Witnessing the Birth of an Empire." *Huntington Herald-Dispatch*, July 10, 1988.

Sanda, Arthur P. "Addingtons' Success." *Coal*, April 1989.

——L. R.

Alan C. Ashton
Bruce W. Bastian

WordPerfect Corporation

Alan C. Ashton: Born 1942. Married, eleven children.
Bruce W. Bastian: Born 1948.
Venture: The founding of a company to develop a word processing program for the city of Orem, Utah.
Company: WordPerfect Corporation; 1555 North Technology Way; Orem, UT 84057; (801) 222-4000
Founded: 1979.
Revenues: $452 million (1990), according to company sources.
Employees: 2,700.
Original Investment: Not available.
Value: $28 million, according to published sources.

Founders

Alan C. Ashton, president and co-founder of WordPerfect Corporation (WPCorp), graduated magna cum laude in mathematics from the University of Utah in 1966 and earned his Ph.D. in computer science there four years later. After graduation, Ashton was a full professor of computer science at Brigham Young University (BYU) for 14 years.His enjoyment in working with students on advanced-degree projects resulted in his selection by BYU's graduating computer science class as "Outstanding Professor of the Year" in 1986. Ashton continued to teach computer science classes until 1987, when he left BYU to assume full-time responsibilities as president of WPCorp.

In 1987, Ashton received the Entrepreneur of the Year Award from the Small Business Association of Utah.

Bruce W. Bastian, co-founder of WPCorp, is chairman of the board and president of the International Division. After receiving a masters degree in computer science from Brigham Young University in 1987, Bastian turned down numerous job offers from prestigious companies including Hewlett-Packard and Texas Instruments, choosing instead to join forces with Ashton in an entrepreneurial venture.

Ashton conceived what became WPCorp as a graduate student at the University of Utah. He developed plans for two areas of research—one involving music, the other word processing. He was awarded funding for the music research, not knowing that word processing would ultimately become his major focus. Nine years later he revived his second idea and, with Bruce Bastian, developed a best selling word processing program.

Ashton and Bruce Bastian met at BYU when Ashton was a professor of computer science and Bastian was a graduate student in music and director of the school's marching band. Interested in automating the band, Bastian took a course on computers and music taught by Ashton. Ashton persuaded him to earn his master's degree in computer science rather than music with the idea that the two would go into business together when he graduated.

Business Origin

After an initial joint venture between the two failed, Bastian took a job as a programmer for Eyring Research to develop a word processing program for Orem, Utah. Ashton and Bastian reached an agreement with Eyring that Bastian would work extra hours and Ashton would work for free in his spare time in return for rights to the program. The program was designed for a Data General minicomputer in Orem's city offices.

When the program was completed in 1979, Bastian left Eyring and with Ashton founded Satellite Software International (SSI) to polish and market the program. Ashton believes their partnership was a natural "since both Bruce and I are musicians. There is a lot of information a musician needs to have on paper. So when we put our talents to another field, such as word processing, we were accustomed to thinking how we wanted the thing to turn out."

Business Growth

After forming SSI and perfecting their program working nights and odd hours on Orem's computer, the co-founders incorporated the company and began selling word processing systems. The revenues enabled them to hire additional personnel and bring in Peter Peterson as executive vice president. "Pete Peterson came in with the business acumen and really was able to take over the business duties," says Ashton. "This left Bruce and I to take care of the technical duties. We are really programmers and designers."

When International Business Machines (IBM) introduced the personal computer (PC), SSI immediately began to adapt their word processing system to fit the PC. Their initial goal was to target everyone, rather than selecting a particular niche market. According to Ashton, "word processing is the best application for personal computers that exists because everybody needs to write, everybody needs to communicate. We saw that people in large corporations need all the capabilities of a general word processing system, even though a particular individual may not use all of the features."

Since perfecting its IBM-PC version, WPCorp has adapted the program for computers manufactured by Apple, Tandy, Texas Instruments and other companies, and has introduced simpler, less-expensive formats such as "WordPerfect JR" and "Student WordPerfect."

The company's revenues have doubled each year since 1980, the first full year in operation. WordPerfect's share of the word processing market jumped from 35 percent in June 1988 to nearly 65 per cent by the end of 1989.

Numerous companion products have joined WordPerfect—WordPerfect Office LAN, an office automating package for networks; WordPerfect Office PC, a desktop organization program; and DataPerfect, a database management program. In early 1990, WPCorp released DrawPerfect, adding a presentation graphics package to its line of business software.

In 1990, WordPerfect ranked third in overall personal computer software sales with over four million end-users worldwide. It was the top selling word processing program for the PC. The product received *PC Magazine's* Product of the Year Award and *Info Magazine's* World Class Award in 1986, 1987 and 1988.

WPCorp is represented throughout the world by 44 offices and distributors serving 89 different countries. Its programs are available in 16 different languages and development in others is underway.

Business Obstacles

Adapting their program for the IBM PC was far less difficult for the company than overcoming the drawback of being an unknown company from the unfamiliar Utah town of Orem. "That was really hard to overcome. Just having a good product is not enough," Bastian said. Computerland would not even talk to them, so they began to approach the chain's major stores with the WordPerfect program. The back-door approach worked, and by 1983, dealers were asking Computerland to carry the product.

WordPerfect was late with its word processing system for Apple Computer Inc.'s Macintosh, enabling Microsoft to grab 85 percent of that market. "We are sitting back and watching," says Ashton.

Analysts say another mistake occurred when WPCorp enraged feminists with a thesaurus listing "handmaiden" as synonymous with women and "breadwinner" as synonymous with men.

Keys to Success

WPCorp's success has been built upon WordPerfect's ease of use, its flexibility and its ability to combine text and graphics. The product is so versatile, says Ashton, that "people can extend WordPerfect and actually create a number of special functions for their particular use."

The founders think WPCorp distinguishes itself from other companies by its willingness to listen and respond to customer needs. It continues to offer toll-free customer support for the United States and Canada while most of its competitors have discontinued such services. Although the service costs the company more than $12 million a year, and many of the calls are not WordPerfect questions, Ashton says, "Rather than turn those calls away and have people go elsewhere for those answers, we generally just answer them. Because we've done that, the customers have a very warm feeling toward WordPerfect." More than 500 employees (almost one-third of the total number) work in customer support.

WPCorp has found an additional benefit of the toll-free number—market research. The company finds customers are more inclined to talk when they are not paying for the cost of the call. Comments, requests and suggestions that come in on the toll-free number are filed in a computer and reviewed by programmers when upgrading products. Two WordPerfect program features (the Speller and Thesaurus functions) were both callers' suggestions.

The company makes available upgraded versions of WordPerfect for approximately one-fifth of the price charged by its leading competitor, believing that once you have a customer, it is important to keep him. Through practices such as these, the company has had remarkable success in retaining customers in an industry where buyers are quick to defect when a better product comes along.

High-calibre, loyal employees (WPCorp has been able to draw upon graduates of Brigham Young) play a role in corporate success. The company aggressively nurtures loyalty and performance in a number of ways. Four WPCorp research vice presidents began as programmers, illustrating the corporate commitment to promoting from within. And when the company passed $100 million in sales, approximately 300 employees were rewarded with vacations for two in Hawaii. As a result of such policies, turnover is minimal—only two of more than 200 programmers have left the company since its founding.

Future Vision

The privately-held company is debt free. The two founders are not interested in selling the company or going public. "We like our freedom too much," says Ashton. Bastian adds, "I think our independence has bred a lot of the success of the company."

WPCorp's chief goal is continued diversification from word processing products, which now account for 85 percent of sales. The company's executives believe that DrawPerfect will take the number one spot in the $100 million market for which it was created. "There's no huge, predefined leader," says Bruce Bastian. Since graphics and word processing often work together, "we could dominate graphics," adds Ashton.

"The future is very exciting for us because we have such good developers with expertise that's unequalled," Ashton says. As a company grows, information becomes important. As more documents such as spread sheets need to be presented with solid graphics, the word processor will become more presentation-oriented.

"There are some exciting things coming with images and computer movie-type information, sound, high-resolution displays, faster CPUs, voice," Ashton adds. "It's a multimedia environment where people can communicate information and dial up services to investigate and learn new things and do comparisons."

Bastian sums up the future: "Our goal is to be one of the top software program producers in the world."

Entrepreneurial Lessons

"The public is very aware. We listened to the needs and wants of consumers," Ashton says. "We succeeded by giving them what they wanted, not what we thought was best for them."

References

Atchison, Sandra D. "A Perfectly Good Word for WordPerfect: Gutsy." *Business Week*, October 2, 1989.

Bolton, Guy. "Word-processing Pair Makes Sweet Music." *Lake City Tribune*, August 31, 1986.

"An Interview with Alan Ashton." *Micro Center Flyer*, Winter 1989.

WordPerfect Corporation Company Profile, March 1990.

WordPerfect Corporation Company Profile, August 1991.

WordPerfect Corporation Corporate Report, January 1990.

"WordPerfect Corporation's CEO Alan Ashton on: Taking Giant Steps." *Personal Computing*, March 1988.

——A. D. K.

Neil Balter

California Closet Co., Inc.

Neil Balter: Born 1960. Single.
Venture: Closet installation contractor and franchisor.
Company: California Closet Co., Inc.; 1700 Montgomery St.; Suite 249; San Francisco, CA 94111; (415) 433-9999.
Founded: 1978. Incorporated February 27, 1981.
Revenues: $12.5 million projected sales fiscal 1990, according to a company financial statement (August 2, 1989).
Employees: 100.
Original Investment: $1,000.
Value: $1.1 million net worth (1989), according to published reports.

Founder

Growing up in Los Angeles, Neil Balter says that he never considered running his own company. "I wanted to be a trial attorney," he remembers. "I was aggressive and always into things, but I didn't think about building a company."

Balter showed business instincts at an early age, however. At age 10, he turned a profit by hiring neighborhood children to deliver the newspapers on his two paper routes. As a high school senior, Balter hosted a party for 500 guests while his parents were on vacation, and he charged a dollar per person to get in.

Balter's parents say that their son developed a "bad attitude" as a teenager and paid little attention to his schoolwork or other responsibilities. Reportedly the party incident was the "final straw" that pushed them to demand

18

that he change his behavior or leave their home. At age 17, Balter moved into his own apartment.

Balter admits that he was a "rowdy 17-year old," but he believes that he was no more mischievous than others his age. "I just got caught a lot more," he says.

Business Origin

Balter graduated from high school and began studying at Pierce Community College in Los Angeles. On his own by then, Balter had to find a way to support himself. He began working as a carpenter, doing "odd jobs" for people he knew.

Balter says that he "backed into" custom designing closets, an activity that has grown into the multi-million dollar enterprise he runs today. When a friend's father asked him to build closet shelves, he built the shelves in a way that utilized the closet space more efficiently. The improved closet worked so well that fellow students in his apartment building began asking Balter to re-design their closets.

"At first, it was just a way for me to make a living—I didn't see any real business potential. I was a kid who had some talent as a carpenter," Balter said. "I needed money, and people wanted me to re-organize their closets."

Balter borrowed the money he needed to buy tools and began operating his "closetology" shop out of the back of a van. In 1981, one of his marketing professors advised Balter to leave college and concentrate on his fast-growing business. At the time, Balter was generating annual sales of $100,000.

Balter quit school and hired several carpenters. He also asked his parents, who had moved to Idaho, to return to California and join his new company.

When he heard about his son's venture, Balter's father remembers asking, "What's a closet business?" His mother says that she "was just glad he was working."

Balter's parents invested $15,000 for a 49 percent stake in their son's business. Balter asked his father to become the company's vice president of sales. "Neil handed me an old briefcase and took me out for three or four days to show me how to design closets," his father told *Sales and Marketing*

19

Management magazine in 1984. Together, the Balter family incorporated California Closet Company Inc. and began growing their new joint venture.

Business Growth

California Closet Company has continued to offer the same type of service that Balter provided as a one-man operation. For a fee, the company sends a "closet consultant" to a client's home to evaluate the customer's closet space and storage needs. Using an assortment of multilevel rods and shelves, wire mesh baskets drawers and racks, the consultant produces a closet arrangement designed to maximize existing space.

In the early days, customer referrals were the company's major source of business. Balter decided to advertise after a couple of years, hoping to reach a wider audience of potential customers. Using the money his parents had invested and a bank loan, he bought advertising space and hired a public relations agency to promote the company.

California Closet's first advertisement in the *Los Angeles Times* drew a huge response. "That's when I knew this was really going to be big. The public reaction was overwhelming—business began to rush in. It was as if we had taken the plug out," Balter recalled.

Balter branched into franchising in 1982. He continued to provide services directly to customers, but he saw franchising as a way to grow the business. Balter named the franchised operation "Creative Closets" because he feared the name "California" would evoke an image of a "flaky" company outside of his home state.

Both as a contractor and a franchisor, California Closet grew rapidly over the next few years. In 1987, the company had revenues of $4.2 million, including franchise sales, royalties, company store sales and merchandise sales. In December 1987, California Closet became an international business when Balter sold franchise rights to Daido Keori, a leading Japanese apparel maker. By 1988, the company had designed more than 650,000 closets and its client list included celebrities and other well-known people.

California Closet's 1989 revenues grew to more than $9 million and the company projects fiscal 1990 sales of $12 million. Balter's company operates outlets across the United States, and in Japan, Canada, Australia, Norway and New Zealand. "We're the McDonald's of closets," Balter says.

Business Obstacles

At age 30, Balter is a successful executive with 12 years' experience running his own business. While he says that youthful energy is an asset, Balter admits that people have often refused to take him seriously because of his age. "When I started out, many people wouldn't listen to my ideas or believe I was committed to making this work. I think many of them were jealous," Balter says. "To some people who had been in business for many years, I was a kid who hadn't 'paid my dues.' Many people still don't take me seriously," he adds.

Balter recognizes that his role as "boss" to his parents is unique, and he says that the arrangement has its advantages and drawbacks. "It's tough at times. After all, they are still my parents and I respect them as 'Mom and Dad.' But ultimately, I am the guy in charge of the business," he says. "I'm glad to have them with me, though. They have the courage to tell me things that others won't say."

This young executive acknowledges that he has learned to run a business through "the school of hard knocks. This has been a true case of on-the-job-training. I gain more confidence as I go along," he says.

Keys to Success

Once Balter had introduced the concept of closet re-organization, he found a public eager to take advantage of the service. As higher construction costs and property values made it impossible for people to move in search of more space, they were willing to pay to make the most of their current square footage. California Closet marketed its services to upwardly-mobile, white-collar professionals who had money to spend on reorganizing and redecorating.

"At the height of the recession, we really built the business," Balter says. "People were hanging on to low-interest homes and choosing to improve them instead of moving. We helped them by creating new space out of existing space, eliminating waste."

Balter calls messy closets, "America's least-talked about problem," but he says that once a customer inquires about his service, a sale generally results. "If someone invites you into their house to look at something as personal as their closets, you've already got them," Balter says. He adds that after customers have one closet re-organized, "they can't bear the sight of others in disarray."

As the popularity of closet remodeling grew, so did Balter's competition. An influx of remodeling stores entered the California market in the mid-1980s and cost Balter's company market share. However, California Closet has remained an industry leader.

"We were the innovators of this business, and we've developed the concept in a more sophisticated way," Balter says. "We also offer customized, personal attention to our customers, and they appreciate it. Here, integrity, quality and pride are more than just words—they're deeds. That's what sets us apart."

Balter credits his employees for the company's success. "It's my responsibility to select the best people, offer them training and growth opportunity, and motivate them to best serve our customers. If I can do these things well, we will be successful," Balter says. His relationship with California Closet franchisees is also critical to the company's success. Balter reports that he spends much of his time talking with franchise owners, asking questions and listening to their concerns. "I'll often ask them, 'if you could wave a magic wand and be granted one wish, what would it be?' And then I try my best to make the wish come true," Balter explains. "I really want these people to do well. Like any business, we want to make money, but we are a family too. When a prospective franchiser calls McDonald's, all he gets is a canned sales pitch. When he calls here, he talks to my mom."

Future Vision

California Closet's next step is into "whole-house organization," according to its founder. "People keep accumulating possessions but their space doesn't grow—this creates a fabulous opportunity. Our company will continue to be productive and successful as we help our customers organize all of their living space," he says.

Balter intends to be an integral part of that future. "I'll keep doing this as long as I enjoy it. It has been fun so far. Like most people, I have days when it seems that 'the grass is greener' somewhere else, but I really don't have the desire to do anything else right now," Balter says. "I like being the 'closet king.'"

Entrepreneurial Lessons

Balter believes that young entrepreneurs often fail because "they go into business undercapitalized and thinking that they will become millionaires at the end of six months. You have to be optimistic but realistic," he cautions. "People tend to have grandiose dreams about the money they're going to make, but they don't realize that you have to work hard, and you will face setbacks. The key is to keep pushing to overcome obstacles."

Balter adds that he has learned to share responsibility with those around him. "I used to run the business by myself, but now I run the people who run the business," Balter says. "My role is to motivate others to do their best. I've never pretended to know everything, and I am very willing to leave what I don't know to others."

Although building a business is hard work, Balter says that the rewards can be great. "It's been very exciting for me to travel the world and see my concept grow. I have seen places I never dreamed I'd visit. It is also very rewarding to be able to motivate people to get excited about this business and offer them the opportunity for growth and success."

References

"Can't Find a Thing in That Pandora's Box You Call a Closet? Summon Spacemaker Neil Balter." *People*, August 13, 1984.

Morrison, B. "California Closet Expects $1.5 Million in Sales Here." *St. Louis Business Journal*, May 15, 1989.

Quinones, S. "Never Enough Space." *Idaho Statesman*, June 14, 1986.

Schlax, Julie. "The Closet as Status Symbol." *Forbes*, May 30, 1988.

Spencer, M. "$15 Million Business Grows out of Odd Jobs, Messy Closets." *News and Observer*, October 17, 1985.

——M. J. B.

Edward R. Beauvais

America West Airlines

Edward R. Beauvais: Born 1936. Married, five children.
Venture: An air carrier for passengers and cargo with a hub and spoke route network concentrated primarily in the western United States.
Company: America West Airlines; Sky Harbor International Airport; 4000 East Sky Harbor Boulevard; Phoenix, AZ 85034; (602) 894-0800
Founded: September 1981. Incorporated in Delaware, 1981.
Revenues: $1.3 billion (1990), according to company sources.
Employees: 14,000.
Original Investment: Raised over $25 million for pre-operating and start-up costs through public stock offerings and subsequent equity transactions.
Value: $836 million in assets (year end 1989). $192 million market value (year end 1989).

Founder

A native of Pueblo, Colorado, Edward R. Beauvais graduated from Regis College in Denver with a degree in accounting and economics. Before founding America West, Beauvais was a principal partner in an air transportation consulting firm from 1970 to 1981, providing analysis, research, forecasting and route development studies for major U. S. cities and airlines. He began his aviation career in 1960 as a senior staff account-ant for Frontier Airlines. In 1963, he joined Bonanza Airlines as director of budgeting and cost control. From 1966 to 1970, he served as assistant vice president of research and development for Bonanza, which merged with two other carriers in 1968 to become Airwest Airlines.

As founder of America West Airlines, Beauvais conceived its route system, developed the initial business plan and assembled the management team in 1981. He is directly responsible for company policy, management practices and corporate development. The airlines' capital formulation, route development, pricing, marketing, corporate communications and advertising all fall under his direction. Beauvais participates in a variety of public relations activities as primary spokesman for the airlines.

Beauvais credits his success to his father. "My father was a real role model for me," he notes thoughtfully. "He never went to college, and he worked in middle management for 42 years and made a major contribution to his company. He was an inspiration to me because he took real pride in his work."

"I believe the extent of my experience in the airline industry and my personality traits have helped contribute to the success of the airline," Beauvais states. "I am an optimist, and that helps a lot."

Business Origin

After airline industry deregulation in 1978, Beauvais saw the opportunity to begin an airline that served the West and catered to the business traveler as well as to the leisure passenger. Incorporated in 1981, the carrier began business on August 1, 1983 with three Boeing 737 aircraft and 280 employees.

"America West was born through my professional expertise," Beauvais declares. "An opportunity presented itself (deregulation) and I took advantage of it." Known in the airline industry as a numbers man who has the ability to also look at the big picture, Beauvais wasn't afraid to take a risk. America West began service to five U. S. cities—Colorado Springs, Kansas City, Los Angeles, Phoenix and Wichita. Two months later, he added service at Albuquerque and Ontario, California.

Business Growth

Beauvais cites the selection of a top-notch management team as his most important milestone in leading America West Airlines. "This is not a one-man show—we have a talented management team and each member contributes to the success of this company," Beauvais notes. One of his most valued management members is Michael Conway, president and

CEO of America West. Conway was lured to the company by Beauvais at its inception, and has been responsible for the major corporate financial development, aircraft acquisition and the comprehensive benefit and compensation package that was designed to tie the employees' success to the success of the company.

America West implemented a plan whereby employees purchase stock equivalent to 20 percent of their first year's annual base pay. A profit sharing program, under which 15 percent of pre-tax profit is distributed among employees, is part of the program as well as anniversary incentive stock options to attract and retain highly-qualified employees. Beauvais believes the "ownership attitude" created by the compensation plan provides a necessary commitment to quality service and encourages employees to keep operation costs low. Employees currently own 35 percent of America West.

Beauvais attributes much of America West's growth and success to employee ownership. Beauvais says, "As employee owners, we enjoy the advantage of working together as a unit, sharing a common goal and achieving excellence. Our people have a deeper commitment to succeed, and thus, a performance record that cannot be equaled." America West's on-time performance is consistently the best in the industry.

Beauvais' market surveys have led America West to begin service to smaller airports all along the California coast as well as to major ski resorts in Colorado. On July 1, 1985, the airline initiated air cargo service. The airline company carried 13.4 million passengers in 1989 to 56 cities throughout the United States and western Canada through hubs in Phoenix and Las Vegas. Its fleet of 88 aircraft includes two Boeing 747s, ten Boeing 757s, 70 Boeing 737s and eight de Havilland Dash 8s. The carrier has made firm aircraft purchase commitments and options which will nearly double its fleet.

Revenues of $993.4 million for 1989 were up 28.1 percent from revenues of $775.7 million in 1988. Net income of $20.0 million in 1989 was up from a net gain of $9.4 million in 1988.

Business Obstacles

Beauvais remembers the major obstacle he encountered in founding America West was raising $20 million in capital for its start-up. "It took two years to raise the money, and you must raise more than you need," Beauvais recalls. "I suppose the difficulty in raising capital was because of the high failure rate of new airlines." While he thinks people enjoy talking about entrepreneurs, he maintains "most people don't really understand or empathize with them."

Many of those from whom he sought funding responded that his venture was too risky or too difficult. He was asked why he could do it when the bigger airlines weren't pursuing that market. "You have to do a very hard sell, and it's a very difficult environment in which to justify your existence," Beauvais remarks.

America West faced a serious setback in 1987 when it lost $62 million because it doubled its size in just one year to keep pace with the competition. While many analysts were writing the airline's epitaph, Edward Beauvais says he and his management team were "moving forward with a high degree of faith in a five quarter stretch." By the company's sixth anniversary, it had put together five consecutive profitable quarters during which it netted a total of $38.8 million, almost entirely from operations. "I think we've passed the survivability test," Beauvais maintains. "That challenge is behind us."

Beauvais points out that tough times turn into useful memories in the day-to-day job of management. "You have to be prepared to deal with those difficult situations, but it causes you to do a better job of managing," Beauvais says. "You remember those tough times and develop an important instinct. If it [the business endeavor] came easy, decision-making won't come that same way."

One of those "tough times" came in June 1991, when Beauvais sought protection for his company under Chapter 11 of the bankruptcy laws. He cited unforeseen rises in fuel costs brought about by continuing unrest in the Persian Gulf region as well as a national recession, both of which "caused a serious drain on our cash reserves." Shortly thereafter, the company announced a $100 million cost reduction program. Conway reassured customers there would be no change in service. "It will be business as usual," he said.

Keys to Success

What factors contributed to the growth of America West in such a competitive industry? "We set out to create the kind of company we wished we could have started in," Beauvais says, adding his years of experience in airline consulting paved the way to avoid problems other airlines have encountered. "We have a clear perception of our market

27

niche, adequate capitalization, modern and efficient aircraft and a highly productive workforce. Also, if you offer a meaningful career and create jobs that are effective for people, you'll be successful."

Beauvais practices what he preaches. To create an interesting and challenging work environment, the company has a unique cross-utilization position called Customer Service Representatives (CSRs). A fully-trained CSR may work as a flight attendant, reservations, gate or ticket counter agent, or load baggage when assigned to ramp duties. CSRs may apply for management positions in 16 different areas. Pilots and technicians participate in voluntary cross-utilization programs.

The market niche key to America West's success has been the concept of the "Superhub system," a Beauvais brainchild. Phoenix and Las Vegas gateways allow America West to dominate the Southwest with two good-weather, modern airports offering convenience and fewer delays. America West is more than doubling its Phoenix gates with a new terminal, and recently opened its own hangar and technical support facility at its headquarters. Designed to feed passengers to and from the lucrative California market, its system has been expanded to include New York, Boston, Baltimore and Honolulu. The company is seeking permission to serve Tokyo and Sydney.

Beauvais recognizes Michael Conway's contributions. "It has been a major benefit for me to have Mike working alongside me day in and day out," Beauvais says. "He's had a critical role in our success. Starting a business is often too hard for just one person—he has been essential to making it work." Indeed, Conway was so essential that when Beauvais stepped down as CEO, Conway was elected to fill the position, on the recommendation of Beauvais.

Future Vision

Beauvais wants to run the best airline in the world and believes he has the ingredients in America West Airlines to do just that. "We want to take advantage of the opportunities available," Beauvais says. "No one can foresee the future, but we must be adaptable to industry changes." To be the best, says Beauvais, requires a modern fleet (America West's average fleet age is 6 years); a productive workforce; a solid financial position; and a constant view toward strengthening the company's market niche.

Beauvais sees the future embracing a globalized airline industry. Flying beyond U. S. borders with effectiveness and efficiency will be of utmost importance. Already flying to Hawaii and Canada and with plans to serve Japan and Australia, Beauvais thinks Mexico and other countries are viable service areas, "but we must address the cost of doing business there." He has no fears of growth in both routes and employees. "We're creating a management tradition that becomes clearer the more we employ it. It should be workable no matter how large the company is," he says. Beauvais does not envision America West as a takeover candidate. "We have grown as an independent company and a sellout would not be a good step for us," he says, emphatically reiterating that 35 percent of the company is owned by employees who would not profit from "a quick sale."

Entrepreneurial Lessons

Edward Beauvais defines an entrepreneur as "a person who identifies a market, makes the decision to go after it, and takes the risk." He sees himself as a "visionary" to some extent—but he believes every entrepreneur must be. "You have to see the big picture no matter what your background is, and you must understand your market niche."

He believes his 11 years as a partner in an air transportation consulting firm primed him for his current position as founder and chairman of the board of America West. "But the major issue is that I am an optimist—and I believe in what I'm doing," Beauvais says.

A successful entrepreneur, he explains, must get emotionally involved. Surround yourself with loving, supportive persons, he suggests. "It can become a very good experience, but both you and they will be tested. Starting a business can consume you, but the rewards can be significant."

References

America West Airlines Corporate Report, 1989.

Beauvais, Edward R. "Cleared for Take-off." *Executive Excellence,* October 1989.

Henderson, Danna K. "Rolling the Dice in the Desert." *Air Transport World,* December 1989.

Hopkins, Harry. "The Fastest Airline in the West." *Flight International,* May 20, 1989.

Hosansky, Anne. "A Near Miss." *Venture,* May 1989.

O'Toole, James. "The Spirit of Phoenix." *Business Month,* October 1989.

Ragle, Dwight. "Success in a World of Deregulation." *Rolls Royce Magazine,* March 1989.

——D. E.

Steven D. Bedowitz

AMRE, Inc.

Steven D. Bedowitz: Born 1942. Married, two children.
Venture: Siding, cabinet refacing and countertop laminating contractor.
Company: AMRE, Inc.; 4949 West Royal Lane; Irving, TX 75063; (214) 929-4088
Founded: 1980. Incorporated February 26, 1987.
Revenues: $277.1 million in fiscal 1991, according to company sources.
Employees: 1,800.
Original Investment: $6,000—$3,000 from Bedowitz and $3,000 from company co-founder Troy Dale.
Value: $16.8 million net worth (1989), according to published reports.

Founder

"I think I learned the personality of a sales person from my mother," says Steven Bedowitz. After his father's death, his mother sold Stanley Home products door-to-door to support him and his sister. "My mother was proud and didn't want welfare. I learned that a person can accomplish what they have to." As a youngster, Bedowitz helped support the family selling newspaper subscriptions and baby furniture, and delivering groceries.

After high school, Bedowitz joined the Air Force, then earned a business education degree from Husson College in Maine. He worked in the New York garment district for a couple of years before moving to Texas. There he sold insurance and houses, later opening his own advertising agency in Austin.

Business Origin

Approached by friend Troy Dale for business advice in 1980, Bedowitz recommended starting a home improvement company. He saw home improvements as an industry that would withstand the ups and downs of the economy. To help Dale get started, Bedowitz matched his friend's $3,000 stake and the two men founded American Remodeling. While Dale handled construction, Bedowitz marketed the business. He would cruise residential neighborhoods in the evenings, looking for potential customers and pitching the fledgling company's services.

American Remodeling was struggling in 1981 when Bedowitz decided to put all his efforts into making it a success. He sold his ad agency, mortgaged his home and put the proceeds—$125,000—into the business. Research showed Bedowitz that although hundreds of companies installed siding, few sold more than $1 million annually. He reasoned that the $3 billion siding industry could yield high profits if he applied sound business principles.

Business Growth

American Remodeling sold and installed everything from new kitchens to exterior siding at first, with Bedowitz continuing personally to market its services. Wanting to accelerate the company's growth, Bedowitz asked a competitor for advice. The owner of the largest siding company at the time told the entrepreneur to stop spending his time selling and concentrate on growing the business. "I stopped selling right then and started building a sales force," said Bedowitz. He vowed to break the invisible ceiling and turn American Remodeling into a big-time operation through direct consumer marketing.

After applying for the local Sears licensing rights for siding, a local gutter repairman offered to subcontract the installation work to American Remodeling once the deal was set. Bedowitz and Dale decided instead to go after the Sears contract themselves. They got it in 1981.

One by one, the company won the right to Sears' territories in other Texas cities, Oklahoma and Louisiana. By 1986, the company had 15 sales offices and total revenues of $72 million.

AMRE moved corporate headquarters to its best market, Dallas, changed the company's name to AMRE, Inc., then went public in February 1987.

Troy Dale, unhappy over changes within the company, resigned in 1987. He sold his AMRE stock for $18 million.

Presently, AMRE, Inc. sells and installs siding and does kitchen furbishing work from 62 sales offices in the U.S.

Business Obstacles

Bedowitz knew that his greatest obstacle lay in achieving legitimacy. His company inherited the siding industry's reputation for shoddy work and fly-by-night con men. "This has always been a downtrodden industry," Bedowitz said in an interview with the *Fort Worth Star Telegram* in 1987, "full of slick, blue-suede-shoe types. We wanted to run it like a real business." The Sears name gave AMRE a measure of credibility.

Bedowitz believed the key to maintaining that reputation would be instituting and enforcing strong quality control over subcontractors who installed the siding. According to the company's 1989 annual report, AMRE requires subcontractors to deposit 10 percent of each labor contract (up to $1,000 maximum) into a service reserve fund that is to be used to correct defective workmanship.

As the company began to grow, AMRE experienced cash flow problems. In 1982, Bedowitz hired Robert Levin, a CPA with a background in home improvements, to be his vice president of finance. After installing new cash management practices, Levin was able to win better terms from suppliers, pay bills on time and make payroll. Levin took over day-to-day operations, with Bedowitz handling the marketing programs.

Not all of AMRE's efforts have been successful. The company closed down its outdoor deck sales and manufacturing division in 1989 and took a $13 million write-off.

In January 1991, the Securities and Exchange Commission (SEC), after conducting a private six-month investigation into AMRE's accounting policies and revenue recognition practices, expanded the investigation after the company admitted that financial statements for fiscal 1988 and 1989 were inaccurate. Bedowitz and Levin resigned from their positions, with Bedowitz remaining as an AMRE employee and keeping his seat on the board of directors and Levin being retained as a consultant. As a result of the investigation, AMRE later submitted to an SEC consent decree to avoid litigation, and restated financial information for fiscal 1987-1990. AMRE did not "admit or deny the allegations of the complaint."

Keys to Success

AMRE has a sales force of 637, which Bedowitz claims is one of the strongest and most professional sales groups in the country. "It's one of the hardest professions. We don't go out and tell customers we're going to put their house in *Life* magazine," he said.

Bedowitz looks for salespeople who close on 20 percent of their calls—a figure one-third higher than industry averages—or tells them to move on. On average, AMRE salespeople come close to meeting Bedowitz's goal. According to figures in the 1989 annual report, approximately 17.2 percent of all presentations result in sales.

Bedowitz says he is willing to sacrifice some of his own ways of doing things for the sake of growth. He believes the company has benefitted from his decision to professionalize its management. He admits to his weaknesses in the administrative area, and compensated by hiring people with strengths that complement his marketing abilities.

Future Vision

By gaining Sears licensing in cities across the U. S. for its cabinet refacing division, AMRE plans to repeat its success with exterior siding. Cabinet-front and countertop installations are expected to make up for the somewhat seasonal nature of the siding end of the business and provide steady, year-round cash flow.

Entrepreneurial Lessons

Bedowitz believes in recognizing his own weaknesses and compensating for them. "Professional managers are used to writing things down, documenting what happens. They drive entrepreneurs crazy," Bedowitz says. "But I have to determine *what's* right, not *who's* right, for the company. This may be right for the company even though it's not right for me personally."

For him, taking risks also played a significant role. "People tend to want to live within a comfort zone. I think an entrepreneur is never afraid to go look at the unknown."

In the beginning, Bedowitz put in 16-plus hours each day, seven days a week. In 1985, he cut his workweek to five days. But he concedes the strain of building a business contributed to the end of his second marriage. "I put everything into the business at first. I often think about why I was lucky—but I really had nothing else in my life at the time. I had been divorced, my children lived with their mother in another city, I was married but not happily—so the company became my baby. There was nothing more important to me."

The poverty of his childhood motivated Bedowitz and taught him to believe in the rewards of hard work. He paid himself no salary during AMRE's first 18 months in operation, but by 1990, he took home $414,300 annually. He later sold a small percentage of his AMRE stock for $4.8 million.

Financially comfortable, Bedowitz could indulge in his biggest passion outside of business—fishing. But he isn't ready to retire to the old fishing hole yet. "If somebody said to me 'Steve, let's do $250 million a year forever,' I'd say 'Fine' and leave. I believe God put us on earth to accomplish something—and I'm not done yet."

References

AMRE, Inc., Annual Report, 1989.

Blumenthal, Karen. "AMRE, Ex-Officers Agree to Settlement of Holder Lawsuit." *Wall Street Journal*, November 12, 1991.

Hyatt, Joshua. "The Inc. 100 Portfolio." *Inc.*, May 1988.

Jaffe, Thomas. "Tinny Story?" *Forbes*, April 30, 1990.

Schnurman, Mitchell. "AMRE Says It Will Agree to SEC Injunction." *Fort Worth Star-Telegram*, August 7, 1991.

"The Siding of America." *Dallas Morning News*, December 6, 1987.

Smith, Sarah. "AMRE Inc." *Fortune*, May 28, 1988.

Staton, Tracy. "AMRE Investors Cite Ex-Officer Pay." *Dallas Business Journal*, August 16-22, 1991.

"The Vinyl Men." *Fort Worth Star-Telegram*, October 23, 1988.

Welles, Edward O. "Tin Men." *Inc.*, October 1990.

——S. B.

Michael Benziger

Glen Ellen Winery & Vineyards

Michael Benziger: Born 1951. Married, three children.
Venture: Winery & vineyard.
Company: Glen Ellen Winery & Vineyards; 1883 London Ranch Rd.; Glen Ellen, CA 95442; (707) 935-3000
Founded: 1980.
Revenues: $80 million (1989 estimated sales).
Employees: 300 (500 during peak harvest season).
Original Investment: $750,000.
Value: Unknown.

Founder

Michael Benziger's introduction to the wine business was through his late father, Bruno, part owner of Park-Benziger, a wine and liquor importing and distribution business in New York. In 1975, after graduating from Holy Cross College in Worcester, Massachusetts, he worked for two years with Beltramos, a major California wine retailer. Wanting to learn the marketing side of the business, he then worked with his father at Park-Benziger. Next he took an apprenticeship in wine-making at Stoney Ridge Winery. There Benziger met his future partner, Bruce Rector, a University of California-Davis graduate in fermentation arts who trained him in wine chemistry.

Bruno, who had grown tired of his business and had always wanted to pursue his horticultural interests, was interested in his son's plans. "If you ever stumble upon the right piece of property, I could be interested,"

Bruno Benziger told his son. "That stuck in the back of my mind like glue," Michael recalls.

Business Origin

While at Stoney Ridge, Benziger spent his weekends searching the countryside for property. For two years he drove from San Diego to Mendicino, ultimately discovering Glen Ellen, a hundred-acre ranch in the Napa Valley. Benziger describes his first visit. "I had this vision—it was almost like a mystical experience. I knew that this was the place where it was going to happen. I knew that if I didn't get this place, I wasn't interested in doing this anymore. This was the place where the Benzigers were going to succeed."

Within two weeks his dad came out. Two weeks later Bruno quit his job and they started a partnership. Father and son sold all their investments to finance the business and to purchase the $1 million property. Bruno's wife, Helen, and his three other sons joined the fledgling business as partners.

Business Growth

The original idea was to concentrate on expensive wines as a small, "boutique" winery. "My dad figured his sons would make a few thousand cases of wine and then he'd call up some friends to unload the stuff," recalls Michael. The plans were modified when their wine won some awards and was all sold within three months. "My Dad had nothing to do and he'd hang around and drive us crazy. To keep him busy we went out and found him some inexpensive lots of surplus cabernet and chardonnay to sell." The sons jokingly referred to the surplus wine as Bruno's "Cashflow Red" and "Cashflow White."

Bruno noticed a huge price gap in the market between $3.00 jug wines and $8.00 premium wines. Labelling the wines "Proprietor's Reserve," he marketed them in the $4.00 to $7.00 range. The wine tapped a new market of wine drinkers ready to move up from red and white jug wines to single-grape "varietals" like chardonnay. Glen Ellen gave birth to a new category in the industry—"fighting varietals."

"It started out as Bruno's 'Cashflow Red' and 'Cashflow White' to get him off our backs, and ended up being the 'Proprietor's Reserve' Cabernet and Chardonnay," says Michael. " Within two years, that was the wine that was calling the shots at Glen Ellen." Wineries producing their own grapes and wine were upset by the Glen Ellen practice, but dealers eagerly stocked the product. The Benzigers had the market to themselves for 18 months before the other vintners followed. In 1982, almost 6,000 cases were shipped; by 1990, annual sales had reached 3 million cases, a quantity their competitors took 20 years to achieve.

By 1985, Glen Ellen was using all the bulk wine available, so the Benzigers started to buy grapes. The winery established short and long-term contracts with 240 growers throughout the state. Each grower's grapes were kept in separate lots through each stage of the production process. After the harvest, the wines would be categorized according to maturity and flavor. Glen Ellen developed a complex blending system to bottle wine of varied regions and flavors to a consistent taste.

Taste is also controlled by working directly with the farmers to grow for specific flavors. Most growers never get to taste the fruits of their efforts. Since Glen Ellen keeps each grower's product separate as it matures, the farmers gain direct feedback to apply to next year's crop.

Business Obstacles

Glen Ellen's first major obstacle has become something of a legend. The family's first grape crush came before construction was completed. The Benzigers ran 200 feet of extension cord to Bruno's house to operate the crusher. With auto headlights for illumination, they worked all night crushing grapes into an old double-tank milk truck, one side for sauvignon blanc, and the other chardonnay. Those two wines placed first and second out of 479 Sonoma County wines, an unequaled accomplishment.

The notoriety put the winery on the map, but also caused the second major challenge—physically managing growth. The bottling facility measured just 16 by 31 feet. In a two-year period, the Benzigers were able to ship three million cases from that one room by working 18 hours a day, six days a week.

After the success of Bruno's value-priced wines, the Benzigers "went through a lot of soul searching regarding image and what they wanted [Glen Ellen] to be," Michael recalls. Most wineries establish their name with premium wines and then market down with lesser-priced varieties. The "Glen Ellen" label on the winery's premium estate wines confused customers who associated the name with inexpensive wines. In 1986 they changed the label on their high-priced estate wines to "Benziger."

Another major obstacle was the quick turn-around they had to achieve as they switched from 98 percent of their production purchased as bulk wine to 98 percent purchased as fresh grapes. "With grapes you don't know 100 percent what you're purchasing," Benziger explains. "With finished wine, that's the end product."

Keys to Success

"Bruno saw an opportunity," explains competitor Michael Mondavi, of the Robert Mondavi Winery. "He filled a void and beat us to the punch." Michael Benziger describes the opportunity as "millions of gallons of cabernet and chardonnay that were sitting in tanks around the state of California." He continues, "In those days it was not the thing to do to sell cabs and chard for less than $10 and taboo to sell wines that you didn't produce yourself. Glen Ellen came onto the scene, but had no idea what convention was. We purchased these really great cabernets and chardonnays at a price that was ridiculous, and we could easily make a buck and sell them for under $5.00 a bottle. Instantaneously, we captured America's palate."

From the beginning Glen Ellen had decided that its philosophy would be "not to own." The Benzigers realized there were more grapes and production capacity available in the region than the industry needed. In addition to contracting with growers, the winery rents or leases seven production facilities near the grape growing areas that are supervised by Glen Ellen staff. Avoiding vertical integration and capital investment enables Glen Ellen to react swiftly to the changing marketplace. It is also able to maintain quality by choosing grapes from the areas that had the most successful harvests.

Bruno's experience in wholesale distribution and three of the sons' retail experience brought new marketing expertise to the industry. Another partner, Tim Wallace, holds a Harvard business degree. "We worked from the shelf backwards," Michael Benziger explains. Distributors and retailers served on tasting panels from the very beginning, helping to determine blending, price, and promotion. "We took their advice to heart," he says. "Those distributors and retailers are now our biggest supporters."

Future Vision

"We're running under the footsteps of the elephants," explains Benziger. "Glen Ellen now competes with Grand Metropolitan, Allied Lyons, Seagrams, E. J. Gallo, and Nestle—all billion dollar companies. From 1981 to 1987 we were a very small company that operated from around a kitchen table. Since 1988 we've had to bring on a lot of people and inject more management and structure into our company because we've had to compete with these big guys." The retail environment has changed as well. "Due to leveraged buy-outs, retailers are working on the shortest of margins," he explains. "Big chains looking for short term profit are not willing to take chances. They want to go with brands that the consumer recognizes and want companies that can do most of the work for them when it comes to selling, marketing, and merchandising that product in their store."

According to Benziger, only the strongest brands will survive in the nineties. "With the scanning information that the big chains have," he explains, "they can tell you on Friday how many bottles of wine you've sold. With that kind of power, there's no more shucking and jiving anymore. Either you're hot and you sell, or you're not and you're out of there."

Entrepreneurial Lessons

"The biggest thing I learned is that it's got to be fun on an everyday regular basis, especially when you work as hard as we do," says Benziger. "This is a business that's not only work, but it's a lifestyle, a hobby, and everything else all rolled into one. Unless you find ways to keep it fun, there's no way you can be successful at it."

"Our success in the future," he continues, "will not be based on managing our growth, but on keeping that magic, that down-home family feeling that Glen Ellen has. That's the reason why our distributors and the retailers like to do business with us. Because we're honest, they get quick decisions, they see family members, and they see the enthusiasm that we have in doing business—and they automatically relate it back to our product." Mike Benziger's enthusiasm is captured in the company's mission statement: "Going beyond the expected and having fun doing it."

References

Galvin, Andrew. "The Impossible Dream: A New York Family Moved West to Start a Winery and Made a Success of It." *Beverage World*, November 1989.

Sheeline, William E. "Fighting Varietals." *Fortune*, September 12, 1988.

Turner, Jim. "The Benzigers of Glen Ellen." *The Wine News*, August/September 1991.

Weisman, Katherine. "Mike Benziger's Fighting Varietals." *Forbes*, February 19, 1990.

——B. M.

David Bing

Bing Steel, Inc.

David Bing: Born 1943. Single, three children.
Venture: Steel service company that provides wholesale steel and fabricates custom parts from steel strip, primarily for the auto industry.
Company: Bing Steel, Inc.; 1130 W. Grand Blvd.; Detroit, MI 48208; (313) 895-3400
Founded: 1980.
Revenues: Approximately $30 million for fiscal 1991, according to published reports.
Employees: 60.
Original Investment: $80,000 from Dave Bing's personal savings, plus $250,000 line of credit.
Value: $1.1 million net worth (1989 published reports).

Founder

Dave Bing, one of the greatest guards in professional basketball history, always viewed sports as a means to an end because he wanted to become a businessman. An All-American at Syracuse University, he earned his B.A. degree in economics and marketing in 1966. For the next 12 years he played professionally with the Detroit Pistons (1966-75), the Washington Bullets (1976-77), and the Boston Celtics (1978). Among his athletic honors: National Basketball Association Rookie of the Year (1966), top scorer (1968), and Most Valuable Player of the All Star team (1976).

During his peak basketball years, Bing was already preparing for his eventual transition to the business world. He relates, "During the off-season I worked eight years for the National Bank of Detroit and learned everything there was to know about money, financing, and the banking industry."

Just before he left basketball, proprietors of Paragon Steel (who were also part-owners of the Detroit Pistons) offered him a public relations job. Bing declined. He wanted a more meaningful position. "I wanted to find out about the meat and potatoes of the steel industry," he explains. Paragon offered Bing a two-year training position to learn the business from the bottom up. "I worked in the warehouse with inventory control, in the plant getting a basic knowledge of the product, and in shipping and receiving. On the inside I started in the accounting area, then on to credit, purchasing, sales, and marketing," explains Bing. Bing traveled with Paragon executives throughout the U. S., Europe and South America gaining additional valuable insight.

Dave Bing also donates time to community groups. He serves on the boards of directors for Children's Hospital of Detroit, the Michigan Association of Retarded Children and Adults, the Black United Fund, the Detroit Urban League, and the March of Dimes. Ever mindful of the help he received in making the transition from athlete to businessman, Bing has joined forces with other retired NBA stars to form a retired players association to help active players develop careers.

Business Origin

Bing was able to make an unusually smooth transition from athlete to entrepreneur. "I realized that an athlete's playing life is short-lived and fragile," he explains. After he left the Celtics, Bing met with the accounting firm of Coopers & Lybrand, which helped him develop a business plan. He started Bing steel with his savings and a $250,000 line of credit from his old employer, the National Bank of Detroit. In July 1980, Bing started with four employees in an inner-city Detroit warehouse.

Business Growth

Bing buys domestic steel and then cuts, bends and reshapes it before sending it to customers who fabricate the steel into their own products. When Bing Steel opened in July 1980, the company had only a few small contracts. Initially, he had no equipment so he acted as a broker, putting companies that needed processed steel in touch with the steel processors. With the promise of a General Motors contract, Bing invested $500,000 from his NBA savings along with capital from several other sources for the necessary equipment to operate a steel plant. General Motors started giving Bing larger contracts once they recognized that he could deliver. This enabled him to purchase steel-cutting equipment to help the company expand. "The steel business is very capital-intensive," he explains. "You're talking about very expensive equipment. The inventory costs are unbelievable."

The company grossed $1.8 million in its first fiscal year, but operated at a loss. By 1982 the company was profitable, grossing $4.2 million. This growth continued with $11.2 million in 1983 and by 1985 the company was grossing $45 million. Much of this growth was attributable to an upturn in the auto industry as well as acceptance of Bing Steel in the marketplace. In 1984 the Reagan Administration recognized Bing as the National Small Businessperson of the Year. In 1990, he was presented with the Celebrity Business Owner Recognition Award in Detroit. He thanked the presenters but said, "I am not in business to win awards. I'm in business to make money."

With 53 customers in seven Midwest states, Bing supplies steel for automobile inside panels, door hinges, and other parts. "Nearly 60 percent of our business is auto related," says Bing, "but we also provide steel to farm implement people (John Deere), air-conditioning (Carrier) and construction companies (Barton-Marlow)."

Business Obstacles

Dave Bing had two major obstacles in starting his business. First, he was black, and second, he was an ex-athlete. Of the 1,400 steel service centers in the U.S., Bing Steel was the first to be black-owned. "Most folks don't think blacks understand economics of scale, big business, and big dollars," he relates. "Being an athlete was a negative because we are viewed as idiots." Compounding the problem, Bing started the business during the worst downturn in the U.S. steel industry since the Great Depression. America was awash in cheap, imported steel. Plants were being closed and steel workers were being laid off.

"The first six months we lost $90,000 and I was scared to death," recalls Bing. "I thought I was going to bleed to death. I couldn't appreciate the phrase 'Black is Beautiful' until my second year. All of a sudden instead of red marks at the bottom of my financial statement, I started to see some black."

While many competitors in the industry struggled to survive, Bing trimmed his operating costs. He bought cheap inner-city buildings for his facilities. Rather than hiring a contractor to renovate the buildings, the former NBA star decided to do the work himself. As a youth, Bing learned to lay bricks, finish concrete, and do carpentry work from his father, who was a building contractor. Bing also hired non-union workers, each of whom could perform multiple jobs in the plant. In addition, he followed the "just-in-time" method of manufacturing rather than stockpiling inventory. He was able to turn over inventory twice as often as competitors.

Bing's big break was the contract to provide steel to General Motors' Fisher Body plant in Detroit in late 1980. "It took a good seven months of constant badgering and persistence to get GM to do business with me," he says.

Keys to Success

The key to Bing's marketing strategy was to capitalize on his visibility as a former NBA star. He signed on as a radio commentator for Michigan State basketball games, providing name recognition and exposure throughout his midwestern market. Bing also did commentary for the Detroit Pistons. When he goes after a contract, his potential customers are already familiar with him. Bing also credits his sports experience for his ability to build team effort in the corporate arena. "It doesn't matter if you're the executive vice-president or one of my hourly workers, you're going to get respect from me. Team effort is important here," he explains.

While being black was a handicap in starting the business, it proved to be an asset once the company was established. As a minority-owned firm, Bing often garners business from corporations, primarily in the auto industry, that seek minority-owned vendors to fulfill government contracts.

Future Vision

The auto industry is particularly vulnerable to the fluctuations of the economy. To weather the next recession, Bing has been diversifying his business. Drawing on his experience as a youth helping his father in the construction business, he has started Heritage 21, a construction company that specializes in renovations. He also runs a fiberglass insulation distributorship. "My ambitions," he says, "don't stop with Bing Steel."

Entrepreneurial Lessons

Dave Bing has found the lessons of the basketball court to be useful in the competitive marketplace. He explains, "I'm very competitive and want to be the best. I learned discipline on the basketball court. My whole approach was never to underestimate my opponent. And I don't do that in business."

References

Bishop, Morin. "Ex-pro Basketball Star Dave Bing Now Scores His Points in Business." *Sports Illustrated*, April 8, 1985.

Blood, Katherine. "Steel Star." *Forbes*, February 25, 1985.

Deck, Cecilia. "Slowdown Puts Squeeze on Minorities, Bing Says." *Detroit Free Press*, October 3, 1990.

"Former Basketball Star Heads $40 Million Steel Firm." *Jet*, May 13, 1985.

Gite, Lloyd. "Scoring with Steel." *Black Enterprise*, January 1985.

Henderson, Tom. "Dave Bing's Best Turnaround." *Corporate Detroit Magazine*, October 1991.

Hyatt, Joshua. "Basketball Player Dave Bing Goes for the Steel." *Inc.*, May 1985.

Telander, Rick. "Life Lessons From a Man of Steel." *Sports Illustrated*, August 19, 1991.

——B. M.

Steven R. Bostic

American Photo Group
Delphi Partners, Ltd.

Steven R. Bostic: Born 1943. Married, three children.

Venture: Started the American Photo Group (APG), which became the second-largest photo processing company in the country. Sold to Eastman Kodak for a reported $45 million in September 1987. Started Delphi Partners, Ltd., in 1988 to manufacture and distribute automated photo machines.

Company: American Photo Group and Delphi Partners, Ltd.; 1117 Perimeter Center West; Suite N415; Atlanta, GA 30338; (404) 396-1119

Founded: American Photo Group in 1981. Delphi Partners, Ltd., in 1988.

Revenues: Approximately $78 million in 1986 for APG. None published for Delphi Partners, Ltd.

Employees: 2,350 for APG at time of sale, 65 for Delphi Partners, Ltd.

Original Investment: $250,000 for APG, and $40 million for Delphi Partners, Ltd.

Value: Not released.

Founder

Steve Bostic grew up in the small town of Peru, Indiana, where his father worked for the railroad and later owned a sporting goods store and restaurant. Bostic learned his first business lessons in the family business. The first in his family to attend college, he received a degree in marketing and economics from Indiana University in 1964. He married the girl he met in kindergarten and dated in high school. He describes his wife as "the most influential person" in his life.

Bostic's dream was to own his own business, but his first attempt failed miserably. With financial backing and encouragement from his father-in-law, he opened two Burger Chef franchises in Florida at the age of twenty-one. In a 1989 interview for *Inc.* magazine he describes that first venture.

"It was terrible. I was thrown into two weeks of training at a hamburger school, and I didn't understand anything. We were in a shopping center that was under construction and there was a big economic crisis. Interest rates shot through the roof. So they stopped building the shopping center and shut down the road in front of us. The whole thing was a disaster," Bostic recalls.

He and his father-in-law lost $70,000 in the deal, but Bostic learned from it. "Had I been knowledgeable, I would have avoided the situation altogether. There were half a dozen warning signals out there that I didn't know to look for," he adds. Bostic decided that he needed some experience in the real business world, and he turned to corporate America to get it.

He says that his first job with American Hospital Supply Corporation taught him how to sell. At 27, he was marketing vice-president of PepsiCo's North American Van Lines, and left five years later to become president of the photo-processing division of Berkey Photo, Inc.

Bostic expected to take over the presidency of the company when aging founder, Ben Berkey stepped down. But a falling-out with Berkey and a failed take-over attempt propelled him into a position as president of Nimslo Corporation, a start-up company that had developed a 3-D camera. Bostic put together a world-wide business strategy and raised $60,000,000 equity for the young company, but when the corporation went public, Bostic felt his opportunities were limited and liquidated his interest.

"I started APG because there was nothing left for me to do. I'd been fired twice, so I didn't consider it any riskier than working in a large corporation," says Bostic.

Bostic does not consider himself an entrepreneur. By his definition an entrepreneur is a risk-taker, someone who operates on "instinct or gut feeling, with no planned approach." Rather, he calls himself "an enterprising individual" and defines that concept in his interview with *Inc.*

"When I talk about enterprising individuals, I mean people who take a rational and orderly approach to business. They usually come out of big corporations. Most of the ones I know have been fired. They've said, 'Look, I'm not going back into that corporate environment. I've got severance pay; I've got knowledge; I'm going to take what I've got and leverage it into getting control of my own destiny.'"

Business Origin

The idea for American Photo Group came out of Bostic's unsuccessful bid for control of Berkey Photo. "Transamerica Phone Service, a contact from my days at Berkey, asked if I was interested in buying their photo processing business," says Bostic.

With $250,000 in severance pay and a loan from General Electric Credit Corporation, Bostic bought Transamerica Film Service Corporation with the intention of building a major company. He had seven years experience in the photo processing industry, understood the market and had made valuable contacts he could recruit to his new company.

Business Growth

Bostic's strategy was to acquire regional companies in trouble and combine them into a national processing company with national economies of scale. He made 10 acquisitions in rapid succession.

In each case, he kept his own capital investment small, borrowing about 90 percent against the acquired company's assets. He would increase the profit margin within six months by reducing inventory and selling off superfluous buildings and equipment. "We cut overhead by centralizing financial and marketing services. We renegotiated contracts with vendors to buy supplies in bulk. Achieving such tremendous economies of scale, we could offer our product cheaper. It was not a new strategy—other companies had tried it," explains Bostic.

It worked because he paid well for the businesses he bought and treated former owners with dignity, inviting them to serve on the company's board of advisors and paying their way to trade shows. He also earned a reputation for making improvements in the facilities, employee benefits programs and marketing concepts of acquired companies.

He taught his managers to think of themselves as a marketing rather than a processing company, and to help their customers (drugstores, stationers and photo outlets) earn higher profits. Bostic created a marketing plan built on quality and diversity. He offered photographers the assurance of Kodak materials, and a full range of products including different-sized prints, double prints, photo posters and jigsaw puzzles. "I used a maxim I'd learned from Ben Berkey—'Quality and Service are paramount'," explains Bostic.

Through these strategies, Bostic was able to grow APG by 52,244 percent in five years and achieve sales of $78 million in 1986. He had 20 plants and outlets in every state but Hawaii. In 1987, he was at the top of *Inc.* magazine's list of 'America's Fastest-Growing Private Companies.'

Soon after, Bostic sold his company to Kodak, who had recently acquired Fox Photo, Inc. and had begun cutting into APG's profits. Bostic maintains that selling to Kodak had been a major possibility in his game plan all along. "I compare my business plan to building a rocket ship. Before you design it, you have to know where you are going, so that you can build in the capability to get there. And, you also have to plan for a return trip. It's on the return that you cash in," says Bostic.

Knowing that selling the company to Kodak made sense and that foreign companies were also interested in buying APG, Bostic was able to negotiate from strength. He sold the processing business, but retained rights to new technology that would serve as the basis for his next company. "We sold out so that we could start again with a new paradigm, a new space ship," says Bostic.

Business Obstacles

"Putting deals together with the bank that you could live with and finding enough capital to keep control of the company was an ongoing obstacle," admits Bostic, who often felt that he was financially out-on-a-limb, but refused any transaction that would not allow him to maintain control.

Another challenge was putting the marketing programs in place so that the company could grow internally, especially after the company grew too large for Bostic to be in all places at once. "That's when you have to have good people and make sure that everybody is working according to the same plan," says Bostic.

He surmounted that obstacle by developing and implementing Q-Plan Systems, a corporate planning system that pulls people from all levels of the company together to work on various projects. "I'm opposed to the vertical organization of most companies. I like to put people from different sections together, tell them the game plan, then turn them loose to solve the problem," relates Bostic. "It's kind of a perpetual motion, project-solving system, an atmosphere that creates rapid growth in profits and sales. It's also a great way to evaluate employee performance," he adds.

Keys to Success

"Good timing was a major key to our success. We came into the industry during a time of turmoil and were able to make a major impact," says Bostic. He correctly assessed that the photo industry was going through a transition and was ready for consolidation.

Photo processing had become big business. Competition and new technology caused the price of prints to decrease, while the cost of supplies was increasing. For smaller processors there was little profit. "It was a tough business and a lot of second- and third-generation owners were looking for a way out. We were able to take a bad situation and turn it into something good," says Bostic.

Recognizing the right time to sell was also an advantage. Kodak was the correct choice, says Bostic. "Because we'd been buying Kodak products and had a good rapport with them, we were able to cut a fair deal and maintain a good relationship. One problem with entrepreneurial companies, is that the owners lose their objectivity about the business and get past the point of no return. They end up in places the business was never designed to go."

Having a great management team and a system in place so that you can grow at a fast rate and keep control is also crucial, Bostic believes. But APG's growth would never have happened without Bostic's vision and his ability to translate that vision to a working, understandable plan. "I believe that what you see is what you get. You can't just have a dream, you have to be able to see how to make it work, all the steps involved. Then you put it in writing. That is what separates successful individuals from the crowd," Bostic maintains.

Future Vision

Bostic's new company, Delphi Partners, Ltd., plans to revolutionize photo processing by eliminating the need for clerks. He will manufacture and market automated photo machines to be placed in supermarkets, office buildings and other high-traffic areas. Through an interactive screen (similar to bank teller machines) and robotic technology, customers will be able to drop film off and pick it up the next day. The machine will allow them to pay by cash or a credit card, and even makes change. "We are looking at other applications also. In the future, they might sell insurance, air line tickets or dispense promotional coupons," explains Bostic.

Bostic will still offer quality service and use Kodak products. He has entered into an agreement with IBM to manufacture 10,000 machines under the R. Stevens Express brand name, with $46 million backing from various investors. So far, the machine has been test-marketed in Charlotte, North Carolina, with good results.

"We're very excited about this venture and especially Kodak's and IBM's involvement. We're hoping that 'Big Blue' (IBM) and 'Big Yellow' (Kodak) will turn into big green," he jokes.

Bostic admits that his dream is someday to own a billion dollar company, and Delphi Partners may or may not be it.

He is also investing heavily in a company called Delphi Health and Science, which under the direction of clinical psychologist Dr. Mogens Jensen, is developing an interactive workstation to identify and help correct learning disabilities. Bostic hopes to market the technology to schools and thereby greatly reduce the number of learning-disability problems in the classroom.

Entrepreneurial Lessons

"Without planning—real focused, front-end planning—you can't create opportunity or control your own destiny. So first of all you have to know what you want. Then you have to really understand your own skills and range of experience and how that translates into the real world," says Bostic.

After that, you have to understand your market. "You have to know what your customer requirements are now, and what they'll be in the future. You have to understand the economics and the technology of the industry," he adds.

Bostic found the corporate environment an excellent ground to acquire a business education. He advises young people to get a wide range of experience by actively seeking new positions and skills. "Once you've learned what you need to know, and formed a detailed plan, then you're ready to step out and try it on your own," affirms Bostic.

References

Gendron, George, and Bo Burlingham. "Thriving on Order." *Inc.*, December 1989.

Greyard, Harry. "IBM-Backed Firm Tests Automated Photo Machines." *The Charlotte Observer*, August 17, 1991.

Hartman, Curtis. "Photo Opportunity." *Inc.*, December 1987.

Herndon, Keith. "Kodak Now Owns Local Firm at Top of *Inc.* List." *Atlanta Journal*, November 28, 1987.

Mangelsdorf, M.E. "Local Heroes." *Inc.*, March 1988.

Welch, M. "Entrepreneur Steve Bostic Jumps Back Into Business with New Photo Technology." *Atlanta Business Chronicle*, August 14, 1989.

——L. R.

James Edgar Broyhill

Edgar B. Furniture Company

James Edgar Broyhill: Born 1954. Married, three children.
Venture: Establishment of a decorating center (wall coverings, paint, brushes) in Winston-Salem, North Carolina. The original venture evolved into the present catalog furniture sales company.
Company: Broyhill, Inc.; d/b/a Edgar B. Furniture Company; 3350 Highway 158; Clemmons, NC 27012; (919) 766-7321
Founded: 1978.
Revenues: Approximately $16 million (1990), according to a company source.
Employees: 70.
Original Investment: $150,000.
Value: $2.7 million equity (1988), according to published reports.

Founder

"My grandfather built an entire industry, my father was a powerful United States Senator. It's easy to lose your identity in a family filled with achievers. I didn't want that to happen, so I had to create something of my own," reflects J. Edgar Broyhill, grandson of furniture magnate J. E. Broyhill. "I wanted to compete," he explains. "More importantly, I needed to establish an identity of my own."

While Broyhill refused to accept an executive position in the Broyhill Furniture Industries empire, he never strayed far from his roots. He opened a home decorating center the day after receiving his M.B.A. He built a 10,000 square foot building, staffed it, stocked its showroom with paint, wallpaper and brushes, and opened the doors for business.

The first few years, the store consistently lost money on sales of roughly $500,000 per year. Even into late 1980 Broyhill found he was "spending a dollar to make a dollar sale." Expanding locations or sales staff would take a major investment and be extremely risky since the local economy was suffering from its share of the national recession. Since Broyhill could find no way to make his business profitable, he knew he needed a new direction.

"In January of 1981, I spent four or five hours working with a troublesome customer to make a $200 wallpaper sale," recalls Broyhill. "Afterward, I realized I was working for less than $10 an hour. It wasn't what I wanted to do." On that day, Broyhill settled on one of the personal rules that would guide his business in the future.

"I decided it wouldn't take any more time to make a large sale (or a sale with a high margin) than it does to make a small one. I looked around my showroom, and began to understand that the majority of the products I was selling were small, low-cost items. I would have to sell tremendous amounts of them to make any money."

Business Origin

The one line of products Broyhill was selling that had high-margin, large-sale potential was furniture. Ed Broyhill began contacting some of the finest furniture manufacturers in the country. In just a few days the home decorating center became Edgar B. Furniture.

Edgar B. sold only high-margin, top-quality furniture, but its area market (especially in Winston-Salem) was relatively small. Even if Broyhill captured 100 percent of the market, the high-priced quality of the pieces he was selling meant that repeat sales would be years apart.

Broyhill decided the only way to make enough of even the high-margin sales he was targeting was to do something no other furniture store had done—mail order sales across the entire nation.

"I placed my first ad in *Washingtonian* because I had heard there were a lot of people from Washington driving down to North Carolina to buy furniture, and because I figured it was only a few hours away, so we'd be able to deliver." The results of the half-page, black and white advertisement convinced Broyhill that the sales technique would work.

The first call came from northern Virginia, and resulted in the sale of six bar stools. In all, more than $100,000 worth of orders came in from the $2,800 ad. "I took all the orders myself," says Broyhill, "I was the only one that knew anything about the furniture." Edgar B.'s next ad was a four-state buy in *Better Homes & Gardens.* The company began selling its first catalog, at three dollars a copy, the same year.

Business Growth

By 1982 Edgar B. advertisements were running in magazines throughout the country. "I just advertised in every shelter-related magazine I could find," Broyhill remembers. "It was a haphazard way to go, but it was working."

From annual sales of just over $500,000 as a home decorating store, Edgar B. posted sales of more than $20 million in 1989, with an average sale of more than $3,000 per customer. Deliveries are made by professional movers, not freight shippers, and a small army of counselors and decorators are available to assist customers over the phone. The mailing list and sales of the company catalog grew at rates of more than 30 percent a year. The company now produces two editions of its catalog annually (along with smaller supplements throughout the year) and sells it to more than 300,000 subscribers nationwide.

Business Obstacles

In 1984, furniture sales exceeded $10 million, but Edgar B. still wasn't turning a profit. "I was selling all this furniture and losing my shirt," he states. The company suffered with administrative and managerial problems, as well as with technical problems surrounding the switch from manual to computerized systems. Broyhill sought professional help.

Turning to his company's accounting firm, Broyhill "basically signed away the management of Edgar B." for several months while a team of consultants took control. Over time the consulting team implemented a series of administrative and management reforms, and helped recruit the firm's first professional administrator. They also helped instill a new attitude in Edgar B.'s owner.

As more and more consumers are entering local showrooms armed with an Edgar B. catalog (which usually offers competitive prices the showrooms can't meet), retailers across the nation are beginning to refer to the company as "The North Carolina Problem."

The formerly disjointed furniture industry is consolidating through corporate takeovers, and manufacturers are increasingly tightening restrictions on retail outlets (and on Edgar B.'s mail-order operation). To counter mail-order furniture retailing, major manufacturers are opening single-brand showrooms, and many no longer sell to Broyhill.

In September 1989, Broyhill and several North Carolina retailers formed the American Retail Furniture Corp. (ARFC) to market their own line of furniture at reduced prices. Commenting on the restrictions imposed on retailers and the ARFC, Broyhill told the *Greensboro News & Record,* "We've tried to create a program that is, one, not subversive in any way. It's intended to complement the galleries. And, two, it provides a transition to those retailers that have lost a lot of out-of-state business, because, well, their faucets have been cut off."

Keys to Success

While driven by his desire to compete and to pioneer the mail-order furniture industry, success only came, says Ed Broyhill, after he developed a strong commitment to make money.

With the help of his consulting team and his new vice president of operations, Broyhill set out to build a management team that could do all the things he could not. "I learned to know my strengths and my weaknesses," he says. "I bring to the company an ability to give direction, to create opportunities and to instill a sense of urgency." For administration and management, Broyhill now looks to his professional staff.

The commitment to professional managers is working. Edgar B. broke even for the first time in 1986, and has been increasingly profitable since. Today, the company mailing list includes roughly 20 percent of the top-quality furniture market.

Future Vision

If necessary, Edgar B. is preparing to carry on without major manufacturing firms. The company is featuring a growing number of "Signature Series" items—high quality pieces made for Edgar B. by nearby North Carolina craftsmen. The idea is to build customer loyalty, not to an Edgar B. supplier, but to Edgar B.

In the past, Edgar B. has been at the "end" of the sales process, according to

Broyhill. Traditionally, a customer would decide what pieces of furniture to buy, perhaps after visiting a local store, and then contact Edgar B. to get a better price. By carrying products under its own labels, and by making decorators and furniture consultants available by phone, Broyhill hopes to change that tradition. "We want to get to the front of the sales transaction," he explains. "We want to be involved in the entire process, even in the educational steps at the very beginning."

Entrepreneurial Lessons

Ed Broyhill points out that axioms such as "the type of product really doesn't matter," "keep it simple," and "don't build the business around a single customer or supplier" are really valuable guides. To them Broyhill adds advice from his own experience—"make a commitment to make money."

Broyhill recommends that every business keep five basic goals in mind—quality, value, shopping convenience, product variety, and reliability. Those five, he says, are the difference between a failing company and one that is succeeding.

References

Altany, David R. "Broyhill's Rebel Spirit Lives." *Industry Week*, March 9, 1987.

Cutler, Ivan S. "Discounter Group Seeking National Retailer Base for Alternative Line." *Furniture Today*, October 8, 1990.

Garrett, Echo Montgomery. "My Catalog Is My Showroom: J. Edgar Broyhill II Built a $20 Million Business on His Name and Good Timing." *Venture*, November 1988.

Horyn, Cathy. "Ed Broyhill: Innovator Broke Tradition with Mail-order Furniture." *Virginian-Pilot*, May 12, 1985.

Montgomery, Mike. "Catalog Company Designed for Upscale Furniture Sales." *Times-Picayune*, July 9, 1988.

Sutter, Mark. "Retailers' Group Finds Alternative." *Greensboro News & Record*, June 4, 1990.

Wojahn, Ellen. "Going Against the Grain: J. Edgar Broyhill's Mail-order Business Is the Bane of Retail Furniture Stores." *Inc.*, November 1985.

——E. C.

Thomas H. Bruggere

Mentor Graphics Corporation

Thomas H. Bruggere: Born 1946. Married, two children.
Venture: Started Mentor Graphics to build computer-aided engineering (CAE) workstations. Mentor is now the world's leading supplier of electronic design automation (EDA) software and systems.
Company: Mentor Graphics Corporation; 8005 S.W. Boeckman Rd.; Wilsonville, OR 97070; (503) 685-7000
Founded: 1981.
Revenues: $435 million (1990 annual report).
Employees: 2,400.
Original Investment: $10,000 in personal savings and $1 million in venture capital.
Value: $1.1 billion market value, according to company figures (June 1990).

Founder

Thomas Bruggere grew up in Berkeley, California. His father was one of nine children and had to drop out of school early to help support the family. "We were a modest-income family, but everyone worked hard so that the next generation could succeed," says Bruggere, the first and only member of his family to attend college.

Bruggere earned a B.S. in mathematics from the University of California at Santa Barbara in 1968. He then enlisted in the army with the intention of becoming a career officer. A year in Vietnam led him to consider other career possibilities. A computer programming course taken in his senior year spurred him to graduate work in that field.

59

In 1972, he earned an M.S. degree in computer science from the University of Wisconsin, Madison. As a software engineering manager for Burroughs Corporation in Pasadena, California, he earned an M.B.A. at night from Pepperdine University.

Bruggere believes strongly that access to education should be one of the country's most crucial concerns in the next decade and century. He serves on the Oregon State Board of Higher Education, is chairman of the Oregon Centre for Advanced Technology Education and the Ed-Net Commission. Ed-Net is a two-way video link between all Oregon school systems, which offers programing to students in all areas of the state.

In 1977, Bruggere moved to Beaverton, Oregon to join Tektronix, Inc. His M.B.A. course encouraged him to think about a company of his own. "In 1980, I felt it was time to get out of the stands and onto the playing field," Bruggere recalls. While most people start with an idea or a product, Bruggere went looking for the right people.

"It didn't matter to me what the technology was. I wanted to go through the experience of starting a company, getting it going, and making it successful," Bruggere relates in the account of his company's history, *The Mentor Graphics Story*.

"I began asking around Tektronix to find out who were the best engineers, the best marketing managers, the best financial people. I was also looking for people who were willing to take a risk, who were hardworking achievers, . . . who basically wanted to change the world," recalls Bruggere. Many of them he had never met. But he approached them individually and convinced most to join him in an enterprise that had no name and no structure. "I think all successful people have to have a good sales component in their make-up," he adds.

Bruggere's judgment of people and his ability to sell his vision were to prove two of his greatest contributions to the company. Bruggere started business with eight co-founders—Jack Bennett, Gerry Langeler, Dave Moffenbeier, Rick Samco, Charlie Sorgie, John Stedman, Steve Swerling, and Ken Willett. "I give them a lot of the credit. All have made strong contributions to the company and after ten years, all are still working for Mentor Graphics," states Bruggere proudly.

Business Origin

His team had enormous potential, but no product and no funding, so Bruggere devoted himself to research and planning. He called on numerous 'future' customers in the technical fields, gleaning all the information he could about problems, trends and new products in the marketplace. From that information, the group collectively chose a product—computer-based workstations that would automate the electronic designer's job. The idea was revolutionary for engineers who were used to designing their circuitry on pieces of paper.

Software applications for designing and for simulating electronic circuitry already existed, but the programs were disjointed and not applicable to a wide range of engineering uses. Mentor's goal was to build a schematic, and simulate the circuitry on a single computer using a common database. Mentor's workstation would be "interactive," allowing the engineer to control simulation, stop it and make changes where needed. It was to be a useful set of automated tools which would allow engineers to design and test circuits faster and with less expense.

A great idea, but could it be done? Many outside the company said no. "We were naive. We didn't know enough to know that it couldn't be done. We felt like we had good vision and we were willing to try," says Bruggere.

Business Growth

To design tools that would make an engineer's job easier became the common cause that united all nine of the founders. 'The product' was the overwhelming focus of the company until June 1982, when they unveiled the new system at the Design Automation Conference in Las Vegas. Their product was the talk of the show and quickly exceeded Bruggere's financial projections. His original business plan had projected sales of a little less than $25 million by 1985. In fact, the company went over the $25 million mark before the end of 1983.

Once the first products were shipped, employees expected things to slow down to a manageable pace, but in truth there has never been a slowdown at Mentor Graphics. "There is no finish line," says Bruggere. Continuously pushing the technological limits, creating additional products and expanding into new markets has kept the company growing rapidly.

In the early years, Mentor invented the computer-aided engineering (CAE) industry along with two major competitors, Daisy Systems Corporation and Valid Logic. Thanks to some early management decisions, Mentor has long since surpassed those two companies in sales and market share. "Our product line has always been customer-driven. It wasn't enough to create state-of-the-art technology—it had to be useful, to solve real problems that our customers had," Bruggere relates.

"Too many companies in this industry are in a rush to be the first to introduce a product. It means that products get sold before they are really ready to be on the market. Our standards are different. We're not always first, but our products get the highest marks in the industry for quality and reliability. In the long run that has paid off," says Bruggere.

The company also decided to concentrate on major accounts and to enter the international marketplace almost from the beginning. "We knew that our kinds of products would have worldwide applications and that we needed to participate in marketing abroad," says Bruggere. "I felt strongly that for our foreign customers to trust us, we couldn't just sell through distributors. We took the long-term approach of setting up wholly-owned subsidiaries, so that we were there for sales and service," Bruggere explains. Roughly 50 percent of the company's sales come from international markets, and that percentage is growing.

The company has 66 sales and support offices around the world. And with 1990 revenues of $435 million, the company is the world's leading supplier of EDA (electronic design automation) systems. Mentor is more than twice as large as its nearest competitor.

About 80 percent of Mentor's growth was internal, achieved through broadening its product base and increasing its markets. Mentor now manufactures and sells a wide range of computer tools to allow hardware engineers and designers to design, analyze, test, package and document complex integrated circuits, printed circuit boards, and electronic systems and subsystems.

In 1984, an initial stock offering generated $55 million in new capital. A second stock offering in 1985, netted $52 million and allowed Mentor to weather a brief downturn in the industry. The NASDAQ stock split two for one in 1989, and Mentor Graphics was the only company in its industry to pay a dividend.

Approximately 20 percent of the company's growth has come from the strategic acquisition of smaller companies to acquire new software technology. In March 1990, Mentor acquired Silicon Compiler Systems, a leader in the growing integrated circuit (IC) segment of the EDA market. By far Mentor's largest acquisition, it reflects the continuing consolidation and shakeout of EDA companies and Mentor's strong determination to maintain its lead in the industry. "In other acquisitions we mostly acquired technology. With Silicon we are getting 200 engineers and a fully-developed distribution and management system as well," says Bruggere.

Besides being the leader among EDA corporations, Mentor is also the fourth-largest supplier in the design automation industry. Bruggere's sights are on the top spot, now held by IBM.

Business Obstacles

"In the early days, our biggest problems centered around getting the products out before the venture capital ran out. The products always proved to be more complex than we had anticipated, and the money never lasted as long as we had expected," says Bruggere.

Rather than cut corners on software, Bruggere managed to borrow additional funds and raise money by selling company stock. "We knew that we wanted to go public at some point because it would give us added visibility and marketing advantages. In 1984, we saw an opportunity to do a public offering and took it," Bruggere remembers.

"Today our biggest problems are people issues, because we have grown so large and are so spread out," says Bruggere. Mentor works to keep the same entrepreneurial spirit and excitement that existed in the beginning in its present day-to-day operations.

"We try to decentralize, so that small groups have responsibility for the creation and marketing of one product line. We want to push down the decision-making to the appropriate level. At the top, we measure and guide the progress of the various departments and try to keep bureaucracy to a minimum," he explains.

With every product diversification, Mentor gains new competitors. Each department is responsible for knowing its competition and for developing the strategy to beat it. "The company is too large and too successful to be completely driven by one person anymore," Bruggere notes.

Keys to Success

"There are three keys to our success," notes Bruggere. "First, we had a consistent and clear vision. Everyone was working toward the same goal. Second, we made certain that we took care of the day-to-day technical problems as they arose. We saw a lot of companies shoot themselves in the foot by ignoring something that seemed small at the time. Third, we provided a company culture that didn't allow anyone to become dissatisfied, so we didn't lose our top talent. Working at Mentor is fun and challenging and people can take pride in being part of a winning team," says Bruggere.

Recognizing the need to maintain an inventive edge, Mentor rewards employees for taking risks. Bruggere operates on what he terms a 'Jesuit' principle of management. "I tell employees that it's easier to ask forgiveness than to ask permission. A person could grow old waiting for permission. If they have a new idea, I'd rather they just go off and do it. If they fail, then they can always ask forgiveness," he maintains.

Future Vision

"Mentor Graphics has always been the kind of company that attracts and retains the best people in the industry. We want to maintain and improve on that," Bruggere says.

Because the EDA industry has become increasingly complex, the possibility of major new competition entering the field has grown slimmer. "There haven't been any significant new entrants into the market in five years, because it is a very difficult market," says Bruggere. His first software product contained about 100,000 lines of code, his latest has 5,000,000 lines of code. Small niche companies emerge who do one thing well, but most don't grow much past $10 million in revenues before they are absorbed. Bruggere predicts that further consolidation in the marketplace is still to come.

Mentor's immediate concerns are to solidify the recent acquisition of Silicon Compiler Systems and to bring to market its newest product, Release 8.0. According to its 1989 annual report, "With Release 8.0, Mentor Graphics will do something that has never been done before in the history of the design automation business. We will deliver a full second generation, state-of-the-art technology software system that runs on our customers' existing hardware, protects their investment in databases, and is free to those on support contracts. It will be an exceptional accomplishment."

Bruggere also has definite long-term goals for Mentor Graphics. "We'd like to be in the *Fortune 500* by the end of 1991, and have a billion dollars in revenues by the mid 1990s. And, we want to set the industry standards for concurrent engineering," he says. Concurrent engineering is a new methodology for designing a product which allows the designer to work on all phases of it simultaneously. Designers can create products with dramatically increased reliability faster than ever before.

Entrepreneurial Lessons

"My best advice to people with a new idea is to go do it. The most important thing is to take that first step," says Bruggere.

He believes that the risk is never as great as people think it is. "The worst-case scenario is that you will fail and have to go back to what you're doing now—but with a lot more experience and wisdom. When you stop and consider that the downside is that you'll learn something, that alone is worth the risk."

References

Anderson, Michael A. "Mentor Graphics Bets Growth on Hardware." *Business Journal* (Portland), March 4, 1985.

Brandt, Richard. "Mentor Graphics Becomes 'The Big One'." *Business Week*, May 30, 1990.

Manning, Jeff. "Mentor's Steady Growth Doesn't Satisfy Its Execs." *The Business Journal* (Portland), June 22, 1987.

Mentor Graphics Corporation Annual Report, 1988, 1989.

The Mentor Graphics Story. Beaverton, OR: Mentor Graphics Corporation, 1988.

"10 Top U.S. Executives." *Electronic Business*, September 3, 1990.

"Thomas Bruggere of Mentor: The Value of Starting Anew." *Electronic Business*, June 15, 1985.

Wilkerson, Jan. "Mentor Streaks Toward Fortune 500." *Business Journal* (Portland), March 24, 1988.

——L. R.

Donald C. Burr

People Express Airline, Inc.

Donald C. Burr: Born 1941. Married, four children.
Venture: Bargain airline that offered "no frills" service and low fares.
Company: People Express Airline, Inc.; Newark International Airport; Newark, NJ
Founded: October 1980.
Original Investment: $350,000.
Value: Sold to Texas Air Corporation for $125 million in September 1986. Merged with Texas Air subsidiary Continental Airlines in January 1987.

Founder

Donald Burr's fascination with airplanes began early. As a boy growing up in South Windsor, Connecticut, he often coaxed his parents to make weekend trips to the nearby Hartford Airport where he would spend hours watching planes take off and land. "I always liked aviation. It's romantic," Burr told the *Hartford Courant* in 1984. "It's the moon, the beyond, it's questing. It's not making toilet paper. In aviation there's the hidden promise that there's something better out there somewhere," he said.

Burr also developed a keen eye for business as a child, and he often visited local merchants to watch how they ran their stores. "The local grocer was my hero—I figured he had to be the smartest man in the world," Burr recalls. "I knew from an early age that I wanted to run my own business, but I didn't think I'd ever be smart enough."

Burr grew up in what he calls an "inspirational and motivational" atmosphere. "My parents were very religious and taught us to believe that people were basically good and honest," he says. At the family's church, Burr's father was choirmaster, his mother taught Sunday school, and Burr headed a youth fellowship organization.

Burr was also active in school. He played saxophone in his high school band, competed in varsity basketball, baseball and soccer, and was treasurer of his senior class. In a 1985 *Business Week* article, Burr reflected on his adolescence this way: "The concept of good and evil was a distant drum. The papers could have said there was a war, but it would not have been real to me. I was having fun and partying. I suppose it sounds naive . . . but I didn't begin to grow up until I was in my thirties."

Burr attended Bowdoin College in Brunswick, Maine, transferring after a year to Stanford (California) University, where he earned a bachelor's degree in economics in 1963. Two-years later, Burr graduated from Harvard Business School and began working as a securities analyst for National Aviation Corporation, an investment company that specialized in aerospace industry securities. At age 31, he was named the company's president.

In 1973, Texas International, a regional airline in financial trouble, asked Burr to join the company. Burr orchestrated a financial turnaround of the airline by introducing low-cost "peanut" fares. Under Burr's leadership, Texas International gained a reputation as one of the most aggressively marketed airlines of the 1970s. He was named Texas International's chief operating officer in 1976 and company president in 1979. During that period, the company's net income rose from $2.5 million in to $41.4 million.

Business Origin

Burr left to start a new airline after just six months as Texas International's president. The Airline Deregulation Act of 1978 had phased out federal regulation of the industry, making it possible for new carriers to enter the market. Venture capitalists were eager to fund upstart airlines looking to take advantage of the loosened restrictions. It was the perfect opportunity for Burr to fulfill his dream of starting a business. Two Texas International executives joined Burr a day after he resigned. The three pooled savings of $545,000 and applied to the Civil Aeronautics Board for permission to form a new airline. Burr funded People Express Airline, Inc. with $24 million in venture capital raised on the public market in October 1980. He used the money to purchase 17 used Boeing 737 jets. On April 30, 1981, People Express made its first scheduled flights from Newark, New Jersey to six U.S. cities.

People Express introduced the concept of "bargain" air travel, offering deeply discounted fares and flying to cities not serviced by major carriers.

To keep overhead costs low, Burr established the airline in an abandoned terminal at the Newark Airport and flew refurbished and repainted jets. People Express passengers enjoyed none of the amenities provided by the other carriers—no reserved seating, no free food or beverages, no free luggage checking. Tickets were sold on board the planes.

Burr created a different type of corporate organization within People Express. Disenchanted with the way Texas International operated, Burr believed that "there had to be a better way for people to work together" within American companies. "The single, predominant reason that I cared about starting a new company was to try to develop a better way for people to work together," he says. Burr's goal was to establish a "humanistic" company where every employee had an elevated role as an owner-manager.

"My business experiences had clashed dramatically with the beliefs I was taught as a child. I had a 'mental model' of people as all good, and when I went to work, I saw that [my] model didn't conform with the realities of the work-a-day world. Instead, I saw people who were greedy and suspicious, systems that were hierarchical, and poor value structure throughout organizations. It gave me a great deal of pain," Burr says.

"When I started People Express, I had the desire to build an organization that trusted people and gave them the freedom to do their best. This was my chance to implement my beliefs with my own organization," he explains.

Burr established a flat corporate structure that eliminated "boss/worker" distinctions. At People Express, employees were "customer service managers" and pilots were "flight managers." Burr required all employees, with the exception of flight managers, to be trained in a variety of jobs including selling tickets, unloading baggage and a range of office duties. He insisted that all employees buy at least 100 shares of People Express stock at discounted prices, and he offered no-interest loans to finance the purchases.

Business Growth

People Express became the fastest-growing airline in aviation history. In just four years, the airline grew to be the ninth-largest in the United States, reaching $1 billion in annual revenues. The company was in the black in 1982, earning a small profit on revenues of $139 million. In response to growing customer demand, Burr purchased 20 additional used planes and leased a jumbo jet. By early 1983, the airline serviced nineteen cities in the United States, and expanded service to London. In July 1983, People Express stock rose to $50 per share and split two-for-one. By 1984, the airline had grown from 250 to 4,000 employees, expanded its fleet of planes from three to 70 and was carrying a million passengers a month to 39 U.S. cities and to London.

While revenues more than doubled from 1983 to 1984, profits began a steady decline. After enjoying seven consecutive profitable quarters, the company lost more than $10 million for the last three months of 1984. People Express stock dropped to a low of $8 per share. By cutting expenses and abandoning plans for expansion, the company was able to post profits again in 1985.

However, Burr's cost-cutting measures were not enough, as increasing competition from major carriers offering low fares and full service continued to threaten People Express. Burr then broadened the airline by buying several smaller carriers. People Express declined again in 1986, losing $56 million in the first quarter alone. The company was also losing customers, filling only an average of 60 percent of available seats, down from a high of 84 percent.

Burr sold People Express to Texas Air Corporation for approximately $125 million in January 1987, and he left the company in April of that year.

"I will grieve about People Express all of my life," Burr told *FW* magazine. "It was one of those really rare, rare things. You get a shot once in your lifetime, and if you blow it, you never get over that."

Business Obstacles

Many people have speculated about what went wrong at People Express. To Burr, the answer is simple: "The competition got smarter and figured out how to beat us at our own game," he says. "The industry developed a more efficient way of designing, delivering and servicing the product that essentially outmoded People Express' product. They came up with a computerized reservation system that allowed them to match our prices—and they offered full service as well. This was the first time that information technology had been used as a competitive weapon to revolutionize an industry, and we couldn't compete. They left us in the dust."

Critics agreed. Airline Analyst Louis Marckensano told *Venture* magazine in 1988, "The only advantage they had was low fares. So when the majors finally woke up and realized they were losing market share, it was the beginning of the end."

Some have commented that People Express' growth was the key to its failure. In a 1986 article, *The Economist* commented, "The flaw in Mr. Burr's formula is that for profits to grow from low-priced tickets, the airline has to grow—and the more it grows, the more it exposes the weaknesses of an inexperienced staff and an inadequate reservation system." Observers said that while the original People Express formula worked well on short trips to unpopular airports, Burr could not compete directly with the larger, more powerful carriers. Beginning in 1984, industry analysts began to speculate that People Express would not generate enough new customers to fill its expanded capacity. In addition, passenger complaints to the U.S. Department of Transportation about delayed flights, lost luggage and overbooking were growing. The problems earned the airline the nickname "People Distress."

As People Express' profits continued to decline, Burr's organizational structure was widely criticized. James S. Carey of Airline Economics, Inc., told *Venture* magazine in 1988 that People Express' lack of management structure caused the company's problems. "When People Express started, Burr had this vision of free, unstructured management," Carey said. "It was his strength in the beginning, but in the latter days, when the airline was growing so fast, management was unable to match it and the airline fell into general disorganization."

Burr insists that organizational structure was not the problem. "The reason People Express didn't roll on had nothing to do with its people systems. What happened had everything to do with information technology," he says. "In fact, I believe that we had more trouble convincing people within the company that our system would work early on than when business started to take a downturn," Burr adds. "By that time, employees had seen that the system could work and they were sold on the idea. They enjoyed their jobs and believed in the company."

Burr says that people outside of the company were his harshest critics.

"The same people who said I was crazy in the beginning were quick to say 'I told you so' when things started to go bad. When we stumbled, they were sure it was because our organization was flawed."

Burr admits that the company's phenomenal early success created high expectations. "People Express [had] a mystique; we couldn't do anything wrong," he says. "The expectations [were] colossal and self-generated. We went around telling everybody that we were going to be great, do great and conquer the world. "

Burr concedes that he could have better managed the business for long-term success. "I failed to look into the future to see where we needed to be. We didn't modernize our product mix or look for fresh approaches. My theory was, 'hey, if it isn't broken don't fix it.' That was a huge mistake."

Keys to Success

When Burr introduced his "bargain airline" in 1981, the market was ready to embrace the concept. Burr had correctly theorized that lower fares would entice people to fly instead of riding in cars, buses and trains. The airline's average passenger load was 84 percent during its boom years versus 60 percent for any other carrier. Because operating costs were low, the airline could afford to charge passengers 50 percent less than its competitors. Passenger volume was so high that the airline was more profitable than the major carriers.

With customers flocking to People Express and profits rising, the airline captured the attention of the public and the press. Articles focused more on the way Burr ran the company than on the public's acceptance of "no frills" air travel. Several business schools used the People Express corporate model as a case study.

Burr clearly articulated his organizational vision, outlining the goals or "precepts" that drove the company. Burr's first priority was promoting service, growth and the development of people. Last on his list was maximizing profits. In 1985, he told *Time* magazine, "This is not some old company refurbishing itself, it's a brand-new idea in brand-new clothes. This is not a social experiment. It's a hard-driving capitalist business," he said. "We want to maximize profits, but we can find a better way to do it, a way that's more friendly and more conducive to people getting out of life what they're trying to get out of it. You just don't want to make a buck. You want people to become better people."

While many People Express employees earned less than their counterparts at the larger carriers, they joined the airline for reasons other than salary. Many were recent college graduates or people looking to change careers. Some were attracted by the chance to own stock in a growing company. Comments from members of the People Express team during the airline's early years indicate that for many employees, working for People Express was more than a job. As one pilot said, "It's very stimulating and exciting. I never thought I would have this much fun." Another employee called working at People Express, "my road to self-actualization."

"Our people were more likely to say, 'wow it's Monday,' than 'thank God its Friday,'" says Burr. "Our way of treating people worked so well because it is honestly and truly more consistent with human nature and the way people want to work. It really does create an environment where people are free to excel." In a recent comment to *FW* magazine, Burr appraised his style of flexible management. "That was the most successful part of People Express," he said.

Burr views the airline's greatest contribution as its "people systems." "We were one of the first to say, 'people don't care about profits.' The workplace is where people get their identity. People need something to believe in; they'll kill for something they believe in. So we tried to set big goals for our people," he says.

As the company's top executive, Burr reflected the company's value system in both words and actions. At new employee orientation sessions, Burr often told newcomers that one of the objectives of the company was "to make a better world."

Having set profits at the bottom of his list of precepts, Burr paid himself a fraction of what his fellow CEOs were making. In 1983, when the company had a profit of $10.2 million on sales of $292 million, Burr's pay was only $95,000, including a $35,000 bonus. He often relinquished his office for staff meetings and, like everyone else at People Express, Burr didn't have a secretary.

Burr let employees make decisions about how the company should be run. When his colleagues called for a policy against employees taking airline snack foods without paying for them, Burr refused. He said that because the workers were owners of the airline, they should decided whether snacks would be free.

Although People Express ultimately failed as a business, Burr believes that the company left an important mark on the airline industry. "People Express was one of the early innovations, and it was a very successful one. Our success fostered the development of computer technology by our competition. Computer technology was the innovation the old-line carriers came up with to outgun us."

Future Vision

Burr is currently writing a book on the People Express experience. "It is interesting to take a step back and see if there is any wisdom in all this. While I was running the company, I didn't have the time to reflect on what was happening," he says. "Now, I can look and see what we did right and where we went wrong."

He speaks at colleges, universities and to private groups interested in the People Express story. He continues to watch the airline industry for future business opportunities, and he doesn't rule out the possibility that he may someday launch another airline. "If I were to start another company, I would put in place exactly what People Express had. And there are people who would come banging on the door to get back in," he says.

Entrepreneurial Lessons

"When I started out, 'entrepreneur' was a dirty word," Burr says. "My mother wanted me to be a doctor or a lawyer. In those days, a business person was not looked on with great respect. Today's business culture is different—now our entrepreneurs are heroes."

Burr encourages others to take advantage of current opportunities. He proudly reports that his oldest son had started three businesses by the time he was 25 years old. "The first step is to figure out what you want to do—to set a vision and a purpose," Burr says. "That's often easier said than done. It is difficult for many people to determine what they really want to create—to understand what 'gets them up in the morning.'

"What mattered most to me was trying to help people do good things within organizational settings," he says. "I wanted to create a place where people could do satisfying work and motivate and inspire them."

Burr believes that to be successful in the future, all companies must look closely at what motivates people and look for creative ways to incentivize employees. "When the windows of opportunity are open, people don't wait, and its the best and smartest people that are the first to jump.

Companies that just stick with what they know will get stuck with bad talent," he says.

"Once you know what you what to do, you have to create a plan for doing it. Then you have to go for it with all arms and legs flying," Burr says. "It takes passion and commitment to turn ideas and dreams into realities. If you work hard and believe in what you are doing, you can translate your ideas into successful businesses. The key to entrepreneurial behavior isn't thinking up some incredible idea. It is leadership."

References

Barrett, Amy. "The Last Romantic." *FW*, May 14, 1991.

Burr, Donald. "Coming of Age." *Inc.*, April 1989.

"Burr, Donald Calvin." *Current Biography Yearbook*, 1986.

Dubin, Reggi Ann. "Growing Pains at People Express." *Business Week*, January 28, 1985.

"The Fall of People and the Rise of the Oligarchs." *The Economist*, June 28, 1986.

Freeman, D. "People Express Founder to Be Leaving Texas Air." *Houston Post*, April 11, 1987.

Friedrich, Otto. "Seven Who Succeeded." *Time*, January 7, 1985.

Garrett, Echo M. "Plane Talk from People's Founder." *Venture*, May 1989.

Gendron, George. "Bitter Victories." *Inc.*, August 1985.

Glassman, J.K. "Arrant Burr." *The New Republic*, October 6, 1986.

Lang, J. "Donald Burr's Economy Class." *Hartford Courant*, July 22, 1984.

Silver, A. David. "Donald C. Burr." *Entrepreneurial Megabucks: The 100 Greatest Entrepreneurs of the Last 25 Years and How They Did It.* New York: Wiley, 1985.

——M. J. B.

Victoria B. Buyniski

United Medical Resources, Inc.

Victoria B. Buyniski: Born 1951. Married, two children.

Venture: Establishment of a company to serve as a third party administrator (TPA) of employers' self-funded medical, dental and other benefit plans.

Company: United Medical Resources, Inc.; 2343 Auburn Avenue; Cincinnati, OH 45219; (513) 651-3737

Founded: 1983.

Revenues: $6 million projected sales (1991), according to a company source.

Employees: 130.

Original investment: Not released.

Value: Not released.

Founder

Victoria Buyniski, president and CEO of United Medical Resources (UMR), fondly remembers her association with the Junior Achievement program in high school. The JA program instilled in her a knowledge of business and a strong desire to run a company of her own. Before embarking on a career, she studied business and data processing at Indiana University.

She began her career with National Cash Register (1969-1973) in computer operations and software sales. A stint in sales for Acme Visible Records preceded a move to managing data processing for a management consulting company serving the health care industry. From 1977 to 1983, she served in executive positions at organizations dealing with review of medical credentials.

In 1984, Buyniski was a member of Leadership Cincinnati and has served on its steering committee. A board member of Junior Achievement of Greater Cincinnati, she serves on the Emerson North Hospital Community Advisory Board and is active in the Cincinnati Chamber of Commerce, which in May 1991 named her Small Businessperson of the Year. She was also recently honored by the local YWCA chapter with a Career Women of Achievement Award.

Business Origin

In 1982, through her involvement in the Cleveland Business Coalition, Buyniski was approached by a Stouffer Corporation executive who was dissatisfied with the third party administrator of Stouffer's self-insurance plan. When asked if she would be interested in running the plan, Buyniski recalls she told him she would be back to him in 30 days.

Buyniski formed a partnership with Dr. James L. Armitage, a Cincinnati physician, to begin UMR. Each put up personal assets as collateral to obtain bank funding. The company's original site was a carriage house which they worked in while renovating a building. Nine months after UMR was founded, Stouffer Corporation signed a two-year contract. At that time, Buyniski quit her job to devote her energies to UMR.

Business Growth

As a TPA, UMR constantly reviews claims against its customers' plans, spotting inconsistencies in billing, unnecessary or inappropriate treatment, duplicate billings and billings for services not received. This careful evaluation of claims saves customers 10 to 50 percent more than the competition.

UMR's services are enhanced by the use of powerful technological tools. The company's sophisticated software keeps track of each company's existing programs and expenses by employee and local plan as well as total expenses. These figures are made available to the company in a series of reports. The client is then able to assess the strengths and weaknesses in its plan and make changes to improve it.

UMR requires second opinions for 17 commonly abused medical practices, differing from other plans by requiring that the doctor meet personally with the patient. Other plans require only that the second physician review the records, make an evaluation and send a report.

Employers quickly accept UMR as a TPA because it decreases the amount of time required to process a claim, paying doctors and employees more quickly. The company has also established a toll-free phone number so employees can call with health care questions. UMR believes that this service helps place responsibility on the employee.

First year revenues of $380,000 increased by 55 percent in the second year and 73 percent the third year. Since 1987, growth has been a steady 37 percent annually. UMR does very little marketing; its growth is the result of customer referrals. Buyniski says the company "has grown in healthy, manageable increments." Grown so healthy, in fact, that she had to turn away new customers in the first quarter of 1991. "We were getting stressed out and decided to focus on retention instead of growth," she told *The Cincinnati Post.*

Business Obstacles

To obtain a bank loan to found UMR, Buyniski and her partner were asked to furnish proof to the local bank that they actually had a client. The company's potential client (Stouffer Corporation) did not want to sign a contract with UMR until the company had definite funding. This impasse was finally resolved when Stouffer agreed to furnish the bank with a letter of intent for a two-year contract, contingent on UMR receiving the necessary financing.

Less than two years after starting UMR, Buyniski was approached by Nestle Foods Corporation, Stouffer's parent company, regarding a potential buyout. Nestle submitted a contract to purchase UMR for a half million dollars. If UMR refused to sell, Stouffer would cancel their contract when it expired six months later. Since Stouffer was UMR's main client, the company would be out of business. Buyniski says, "It was a very tense time." Nestle was ultimately convinced that it was a food business, not a third party administrator, and decided not to go through with the deal.

Keys to Success

Buyniski gives a great deal of credit for her success to her training in Junior Achievement. She says, "Most people who start businesses have a narrow perspective of what they need to do. When you spend time in Junior Achievement, you get the perspective of what makes a business tick—of balancing all the different aspects of the business to produce a profit."

Victoria Buyniski goes on to say, "One of the main reasons for UMR's success is that I believe it is my responsibility to teach my managers how to make business decisions that are in the best interests of our clients and are based on the values we have established as a company." The organization's philosophy is based on customer satisfaction. Internal correspondence at UMR is headed with, "Quality is not an endpoint. It is the excellence you bring to each moment in time. It is a choice you make again and again." Each person knows what they are supposed to do and does it. Buyniski takes the time "to explain the reasoning behind decisions, rather than just making automatic decrees."

When UMR signed a contract with its first client, Stouffer Corporation, it prepared a plan for one Stouffer location. After signing the contract, it was faced with preparing plans for Stouffer's operations in 23 states. UMR's continued success is based on its ability to adapt its services to individual customers' needs. Everyone on the staff is trained to listen carefully to the customer and keep priorities focused on the customer.

Her company is successful, says Buyniski, because its services save customers money. She illustrates by revealing that after contracting with UMR, Stouffer's insurance plans costs dropped $1.6 million in the first year.

Future Vision

UMR was one of the first third party administrators to offer cost control services. Buyniski believes the market for this service is virtually untapped, leaving the company open for unlimited expansion. However, she plans to proceed cautiously, aware that rapid growth can bring enormous problems. Only by managing growth, she thinks, can the company continue to properly train employees and service customers.

As part of her five-year plan, she intends "to increase revenues and the number of clients served while continuing to deliver premium service. Our management team is currently refining a plan for controlled growth, . . .

which revolves around carefully reviewing progress to date and then using a cookie cutter style approach to replicate our ideal business units. The ideal business unit will be a flat organization that keeps the decision makers close to our customers and constantly delivers premium customer service."

Since the majority of employees at UMR are women, Buyniski believes some of the jobs at UMR will eventually be shared.

Buyniski is currently researching the possibility of marketing UMR's services in international markets.

Entrepreneurial Lessons

Victoria Buyniski believes it is extremely important to plan for future needs. The main thing UMR must have to fulfill client needs is sufficient staff. She hires people before they are actually needed. By doing this, the staff is always kept at, or above, the level required to properly service customers.

Buyniski commented that she does not encounter problems as a woman in business. She says, "I don't think about being a woman in the business world. If you don't make an issue of it, other people don't either."

She says that small businesses frequently get so "wrapped up in day-to-day activities that they overlook employee training." Buyniski says that "she learned the hard way how important it is to spend the money required to train people properly." She goes on to say, "If you don't spend the money to train people, you'll spend it another way, because the employee will either leave to work for another company or they won't perform up to their potential. You might as well teach them properly in the beginning."

Buyniski feels it is important for entrepreneurs in a service industry to give service to the community. She says, "People should not do it for rewards and should only contribute in a way that they really want to, but eventually it does come back. People do become aware of you."

References

Buyniski, Victoria, and Donald C. Flagg. "Using a TPA to Find Cost Savings." *Personnel Administrator*, June 1985.

Conlan, Maureen. "Women of Achievement." *The Cincinnati Post*, May 4, 1991.

Gordon, Richard L. "Mt. Auburn Business Administers Company-Funded Health-Care Plans." *The Cincinnati Post*, May 1988.

Griesmeyer, Cathy. "Overseer Trims Stouffer's Waste." *Cleveland Business*, July 1985.

Kent, Jennifer. "United Medical's Pulse Robust." *The Cincinnati Post*, May 8, 1991.

McQuaid, Kathy. "UMR Keeps Medical Costs Healthy." *Concise*, February/March 1989.

Schor, Adam. "A Turning Point: The Firm She Started Can Now Run Without Her." *The Cincinnati Inquirer*, April 18, 1988.

"Victoria Buyniski." *Ohio Business*, February 1, 1988.

——A. D. K.

Joseph R. Canion

Compaq Computer Corporation

Joseph R. Canion: Born 1945.
Venture: Design, develop and manufacture portable and desk-top personal computers.
Company: Compaq Computer Corporation; Box 692000; Houston, TX 77269-2000; (713) 370-0670
Founded: 1982.
Revenues: $3.6 billion (1990), according to company sources.
Employees: 11,300 worldwide.
Original Investment: Not available.
Value: $815 million, according to published reports.

Founder

Joseph Rodney (Rod) Canion describes his childhood as typical "Americana," the son of a salesman and elementary school teacher. Raised in Houston, Canion's fondest memories include boyish antics such as scaring girls with "gross" bugs and frogs. However, Canion's other memories center around what family members called an "annoying habit"—tinkering.

Cars, appliances or toys—nothing was safe from Canion's inquisitive mind. His desire to know "how things worked" led him to destroy countless items. His passion was cars, particularly hot rods. Even the fear of punishment seldom stopped the youth.

Canion worked his way through high school and college. He attended the University of Houston, taking courses in math and physics. He decided to study engineering after another student convinced him that the field was "where the real stuff was." In 1967 he earned a masters degree in electrical engineering. He decided to pursue his doctorate in the field, but became disillusioned with the education he was getting. Hands-on business experience seemed the next logical step.

In 1968, he joined Texas Instruments as a staff engineer designing computer printers. During his 13 years with the company he was promoted several times, eventually to senior management. While the promotions were nice, he was not happy in the working environment. Canion became frustrated with what he termed the "bureaucracy and paperwork." Before quitting, Canion and two other Texas Instrument managers discussed ideas for the entrepreneurial venture that became Compaq computer.

The success of Compaq computers has not changed this low-key computer pioneer. Canion still lives in Houston, only minutes from his boyhood home. He prefers living in the suburbs, rather than the "glitzy" locales where Texas' oil barons reside. When flying, Canion prefers to ride coach. Industry analysts say Canion's lack of "dramatics" is a primary factor in his success in Silicon Valley.

Business Origin

When Canion, Jim Harris and Bill Murto left Texas Instruments in 1981, they knew they wanted to continue working together. "We wanted to combine the discipline of a big company with an environment where people felt they could participate in success," says Canion. "We wanted the best of both worlds. And we wanted to do it right." The band of would-be entrepreneurs came up with several ideas, including owning and operating a chain of Mexican restaurants. Another idea was to "capitalize on the hoopla surrounding the new IBM (International Business Machines) Personal Computer."

Their idea was simple: a 5.25-inch hard disk drive which would be compatible with the IBM-PC. They presented the idea to Benjamin Rosen, president of a local high-tech venture capital firm. He was impressed with Canion and his comrades, but less impressed with their idea. He suggested they try again.

They did, this time deciding to produce a complete IBM compatible personal computer, what the industry refers to as a "clone." Most computers of the day were large and difficult to move. Canion wanted to condense the personal computer, make it more "luggable." Canion recalls the development of the idea: "We set up a meeting . . . with an industrial designer. We went to a pie shop across the street and sketched on a paper placemat what we wanted the portable to look like. That drawing went into our business plan." This time Rosen was so impressed that he not only funded the venture but signed on as chairman of the board.

Before long, Compaq introduced its first products: the Compaq Portable and the Compaq Plus. During that first year, Compaq became the fastest growing start-up in the history of the computer industry. While profits were "modest," revenues were in excess of $110 million. Compaq was soon the nation's third largest personal computer supplier behind IBM and Apple Computer.

Business Growth

Compaq's plan was to offer complete compatibility with IBM's personal computers, but with added power and features. The plan appeared to be working. Compaq beat IBM to market with a computer using the faster and more versatile Intel 80386 microprocessor. In 1987, Compaq announced that it could not build enough computers to supply demand. To cope with demand, the company opened new manufacturing plants in Singapore, Scotland and Houston.

Business Obstacles

In 1988, IBM took a second look at the industry standard MS-DOS (Microsoft Disk Operating System). Microsoft was considered the leader in disk operating system development. The disk operating system is a collection of programs that allows a computer to control its operations as well as controlling the computer's input and output functions. IBM had no exclusivity with Microsoft, thus the MS-DOS program was widely distributed to other computer companies, including Compaq. As "clones" gained in popularity, IBM was losing market share.

To counter, IBM developed a new line, Personal System/2, which relies on a relatively new technology called the Micro Channel. The PS/2 does not accommodate older "add-on" equipment, thus the peripherals of clones like Compaq will not work with the newer PS/2. IBM's argument is that "few customers actually use old cards with new computers." Canion disagrees, and is "leading an industry effort to build computers with PS/2 capability but using 'standard architecture' that allows users to plug in their old peripherals."

In November 1989, Compaq introduced its first computer system based on standard architecture. According to Canion, EISA, Extended Industry Standard Architecture, will "help Compaq's personal computers handle the more demanding and sophisticated jobs required in the coming decade, but will still allow customers to use their existing software and hardware products."

Reaction is mixed regarding IBM's introduction of the PS/2. Says Canion, "We've been telling people that they don't gain anything from switching. And from our growth, its obvious they've been listening." One industry analyst was quoted as saying that while IBM is getting the PS/2 off the ground, "Compaq will sell the daylights out of its current products." However, another analyst claims that when considering the strong marketing capabilities of IBM, "Compaq will be forced to conform."

Keys to Success

The changing face of computer technology has made some computer dealerships "particular" about those with whom they deal. Sensing this, Canion found a way to endear Compaq to computer dealers, by selling exclusively through them. Other companies have extensive sales teams which compete with the computer dealerships. "You can't put a price tag on the goodwill we have established," reflects Canion.

Becoming "yesterday's news" can be instant death in the fast-paced computer industry. Therefore, Compaq continues to lead the industry with products that incorporate the latest technology. Once the commitment is made to develop a new product, the work is done simultaneously rather than in stages. Doing so allows Compaq to introduce the product in six to nine months, rather than the 12 to 18 months of other companies. Said Canion, "the blistering pace enables [Compaq] to get late-breaking technology into the marketplace ahead of [the] competition."

Future Vision

After a board meeting in October 1991 that lasted 14 hours, it became clear that Compaq and Joseph Canion no longer had a future together. Canion was replaced as president and CEO by COO Eckhard Pfeiffer, one day after the company announced a $70.3 million quarterly loss (the first ever) and the layoff of 1,400 employees, 12 percent of Compaq's workforce. Canion told a reporter he was surprised, but "I have to take a realistic view. It was the board's decision." Some industry analysts were surprised too, noting that Canion had started to take action to counter the company's loss of market share during what was acknowledged as an overall downturn in the industry.

Canion hopes Compaq will "evolve by remembering how we naturally worked as a small company. We learned to make efficient use of every resource we had . . . to only work on the most important things that need to be done." Canion also adds, "I have also told our people many times that if we can simply keep our culture in place, we can successfully compete with any company in the world."

Entrepreneurial Lessons

According to Canion, the best advice he can give entrepreneurs is to seek out and take the advice of others. Seeking the opinions of others is the cornerstone of a business philosophy he calls "the process." Top executives meet once a week for a discussion session, while Canion meets once a quarter with corporate employees. Canion says "the process" allows people to speak up and let him know when something is not working, one reason he believes Compaq has avoided certain pitfalls.

"The process was really just a formalization of getting a lot of advice," Canion explains. "I make a lot of mistakes myself. By getting advice, a better decision could be made."

References

Catalono, Frank. "Joseph R. Canion: A Compatible Game Plan." *Electronic Business,* April 1, 1986.

Gannes, Stuart. "America's Fastest-Growing Companies." *Fortune,* May 23, 1988.

Guterl, Fred V. "Take That, Goliath." *Business Month,* December 1987.

Hayes, Thomas C. "Compaq Ousts Its Legendary Chief." *New York Times,* October 26, 1991.

Ivey, Mark, Deidre A. Depke, and Thane Peterson. "Compaq's New Boss Doesn't Even Have Time to Wince." *Newsweek,* November 11, 1991.

Kindel, Stephen. "Rod Canion: Compaq Computer." *FW,* April 5, 1988.

Kotkin, Joel. "The Smart Team at Compaq Computer." *Inc.,* February 1986.

"Managing." *Fortune,* August 15, 1988.

Pauly, David. "A Genius for Sales." *Newsweek,* October 2, 1989.

Richards, Evelyn. "Compaq Ousts President Who Founded Firm." *Washington Post,* October 26, 1991.

"10 Top U.S. Executives." *Electronic Business,* September 3, 1990.

Thomas, Les. "Rod Canion." *Southern Living,* June 1990.

——R. H. S.

Laura Chenel

Laura Chenel's Chèvre

Laura Chenel: Born 1949. Single.
Venture: Established first commercial plant in the United States to manufacture chèvre, a French-style goat cheese.
Company: Laura Chenel's Chèvre; 1550 Ridley Avenue; Santa Rosa, CA 95401; (707) 575-8888
Founded: September 1981, a sole proprietorship.
Revenues: The privately-owned company releases no financial information. Last reported sales (1986) were $400,000.
Employees: 9.
Original Investment: Approximately $20,000.
Value: Undetermined.

Founder

A California farm girl, Laura Chenel learned early that she could do whatever she wanted—so she did. After a couple of years in California universities, she opted for a taste of life in New York City. While there she worked as a waitress and married. Returning to Sonoma County, she and her husband managed a restaurant on Chenel's parents' farm.

The eldest of three children, Chenel credits her parents for her adventuresome spirit. During her childhood, her parents left their original careers to buy and run their own farm. The couple later became restauranteurs. Chenel says that the couple's determination to follow their dreams impressed her more than the success or failure of their ventures.

"Our parents taught us that we should never be afraid to try," Chenel recalls. "I took ballet lessons and piano lessons. I worked on the farm. I studied in Europe. Throughout my childhood, my parents gave me a strong sense of the security of family, and although I have tried many new things in my life and moved from place to place, I have always felt grounded by that security."

By the mid 1970s, Chenel and her husband owned and ran their own small farm in Sonoma County. Chenel tended their dozen or so goats, but the herd was producing far more milk than the couple could consume. She had two choices: get rid of some goats or find a way to use the surplus milk. Her solution was to organize a goat milk co-operative to contract with a manufacturer, the Sonoma Cheese Factory, to make Monterey Jack-type cheese.

Her efforts to keep all of her goats eventually led to the business she operates today.

Business Origin

Chenel built Laura Chenel's Chèvre her own way—by tenaciously following her instincts and intuition. She began making cheese not in response to a market need, but as a way to fill a need of her own.

When she started selling goats' milk to the Sonoma Cheese Factory, she also began delivering the co-op's resulting cheese to local cheese shops. Chenel quickly points out, however, that her cheese distribution was on a volunteer basis. She had no plans to create a business of her own. Her reward was in "meeting people who knew so much about cheese. I wasn't interested in making money," she says. "In fact, any profits I made from the milk were barely enough to support my goats. It was more fun than anything else."

During one of those deliveries, a local shop owner gave Chenel her first taste of chèvre. "The French cheese was wonderful, and once I tasted it, I knew I had to learn how to make it myself," she recalls. "I asked everyone I could think of, but no one in the United States knew how to make it."

As Chenel describes it, she became "passionately interested" in learning to make chèvre. Recently divorced, in 1979 she decided to go to France in search of a teacher. Leaving the goats in the care of friends, she set off to France for three months of intensive, hands-on training as an apprentice cheese-maker.

She returned to Sonoma County with a wealth of knowledge, bought a house and immediately began producing chèvre in her basement. She found eager and grateful customers in wine and food stores, restaurants and gourmet shops. A one-woman cheese business, she made the cheese, tended her dozen goats, harvested the goats' milk and distributed cheese to local customers. Because her operation was small and generated little profit, Chenel worked two waitress jobs to pay the mortgage on her house.

Stress and overwork caught up with her and she became ill. She had never before considered that she might need help, but, she remembers, "When I got sick, I knew I couldn't go on working that way any longer. Something had to give." In January 1981, Chenel "got serious about making cheese."

Over the next eight months, she sold her house, sold her goats, and located her company in what had been an escargot processing plant in Santa Rosa, California. Using the profit from the sale of her house and several thousand dollars loaned from friends, she scraped up enough money to buy the plant and bring it up to state health standards. She designed cheese-making equipment using materials from France. Chenel then gave her company a nâme, designed its logo and package labels, and hired her first employee. In September 1981 Laura Chenel's Chèvre opened for business.

Business Growth

Without a long-term plan, Laura Chenel's Chèvre operated under what its founder describes as a "seat of the pants" approach to management. As obstacles presented themselves, Chenel followed her instincts to make critical decisions about the size and scope of the business. The company's continued growth is a reflection of Chenel's growth as a businesswoman and manager.

Chenel first hired friends to help in the factory, but as the business grew, she realized she needed to take a more organized approach to hiring, work schedules and management. After three years, she hired a general manager to help oversee day-to-day operations. The two hired a team of six employees. This was Chenel's first real experience with hiring and training, and it was the first time that she had to delegate responsibility and share control of the business that had been all hers.

With professional management on-site, Chenel was freed from non-stop cheese production and able to pursue activities outside of the factory. She co-authored her first cookbook, *Chèvre! The Goat Cheese Cookbook* (Peaks Pike Publishing Co., 1983), with friend and cooking enthusiast Linda

Siegfried. As the two traveled the country promoting book sales, Chenel got a welcomed break from the intensive rigor of cheese-making while spreading the word about her product. Chenel and Siegfried produced a second book, *American Country Cheese* (Addison-Wesley Publishing Co.), in 1989.

Once she became less involved in everyday operations, Chenel focused greater attention on business management. Eventually, she decided that the business was running well enough for her to consider bringing in outside investors. While she had contemplated investors before, she believed that she needed to understand her business better and to turn a larger profit before accepting partners.

In 1986, Chenel met two female MBAs who approached her at what she says was the "right time." They excited Chenel about the possibility of raising capital for expansion, and together wrote a business plan to attract venture capital. Chenel traveled around the country presenting the proposal. Each venture capitalist rejected the offer, telling her that the business was not making enough money to be an attractive investment.

"I learned so much from that experience—it was the first time I had thought at all about planning and projection," Chenel declares. "I learned that for the company to continue to grow, I'd have to focus my attention inward again and find ways to run a more efficient and profitable operation. I resolved to take a hard look at my business, to 'clean out all the corners' and get things in top shape. That meant learning more about my product, the market, production and the financial implications of managing a business," she explains. "I was confident that if I did the necessary work, I could attract investors when the time was right."

Over the last two years, Chenel has learned as much as possible about her business and made significant operational changes. She hired a professional production manager with a background in dairy science to help reorganize the plant's manufacturing process. She read as much as she could about cheese-making and visited other cheese plants. And she learned for the first time about financial management, including the ins and outs of collections, accounting and cash flow projections.

In 1990, Laura Chenel's Chèvre was the largest of 50 producers of specialty goat cheese products in a small but growing U.S. industry. With less than 10 employees, the company hand-crafts 14 varieties of fresh and aged cheeses—such as a *crottin* with a mold-ripened surface and a *chabichou* preserved in olive oil and herbs—all made from 100 percent pure goats' milk. The company's products are found in gourmet food shops, specialty food sections in grocery and department stores, and a number of the nation's leading restaurants.

Chenel says that she is now ready to take Laura Chenel's Chèvre into its next phase of operation. "My goal is to move the company into a period of planned growth. I know my product as well as I ever have, and I am confident that the business is on solid ground. I see that the market is expanding, and I'm excited about where we can take this thing."

Business Obstacles

Chenel freely admits that while blind determination and perseverance were her greatest assets in making her dream a reality, her naivete about running a business presented the greatest obstacle, especially in the early days. "With what I know now, I sometimes look back on how the business ran for so many years, and wonder how it survived," Chenel muses.

"I knew I wanted to make cheese—and I was determined to produce the best chèvre that people had ever tasted," she states. "What I lacked was a plan, a strategy, goals, any idea of the size of the market or how to promote my product. I learned by making costly mistakes."

In the beginning, Chenel bought milk from eight local producers and made as much cheese as the milk would yield. Some weeks she would end up with more cheese than customers and had to throw much away. She soon hired a local distributor to help her bring the product to market.

Chenel also had initial product quality problems. "Because I was so new at making chèvre, I didn't always get the process right. I didn't understand the chemistry of the cheese, and I would sometimes get unacceptable or even contaminated product," she confesses. "My errors created interruptions in the process and caused problems with customers. Mainly through trial and error, I learned the best way to make the cheese."

Reflecting on the past, Chenel remarks, "People ask me if I was ever afraid I'd fail. I honestly never worried about failure. I just went ahead and did what I wanted to do. It has occurred to me," she continues thoughtfully, "that I may have been afraid of success, though."

Keys to Success

Chenel's sheer determination to make a high quality product and her love of cheese-making have been the most important contributors to the small company's survival and growth. She has never been afraid to make changes if she or one of her employees discovered a better way of doing something.

While she cites no formal mentors, Chenel says that she has learned valuable lessons from people in all walks of life. "I talk to anyone and everyone—asking questions, listening to their experiences. Many of my friends and associates are fellow cheese makers, wine makers, owners of small businesses. I get so many ideas by comparing notes with them," she maintains.

Chenel believes her role as a pioneer has given her a continued edge over fellow American cheese makers in an industry dominated by French producers. Laura Chenel's Chèvre products are highly-acclaimed and figure prominently in the menus of fine restaurants across the country. Her story has captured the interest of restaurant and food industry trade publications, and magazines and newspapers around the country. The company's Santa Rosa plant is highlighted in regional guide books as a "must see" for tourists visiting Northern California. All of this attention has encouraged the spread of goat cheese enthusiasm and earned Chenel's chèvre a reputation as a superior product. The company today boasts a more extensive range of cheeses than any of its competitors.

Future Vision

Just as she could not have predicted that her love of goats would grow into a successful business, Chenel says she cannot be sure where her company is headed. She stresses, however, that she has a clearer vision than ever before of what she wants for the business. Having set the American goat cheese industry in motion, Chenel is determined that she will share in that growth. Her plan is for Laura Chenel's Chèvre to gain as large a share of the market as it can. Change has already begun. With professional managers in place, the little company is no longer the same as it was a decade ago. Even the Santa Rosa plant has expanded to meet the needs of a more sophisticated business. Chenel is considering third-party investors as a possible way to achieve her growth goals.

"I'm finally confident that we're producing an excellent product, the business is strong, and I've got very talented and capable people working with me," she states. "Now, I'm concentrating on what the future holds for the business and me."

Chenel plans to try distancing herself from her demanding job occasionally to benefit herself and the company. "The best way to enjoy your work is to take time away from it, but that's often difficult, if not impossible, especially when you're building the business. I recall so many times when it seemed to me that I'd have to work around the clock just to keep the company afloat. I'll try this year to keep myself away from work more often so that I can do a better job when I'm there."

Entrepreneurial Lessons

Although Chenel has built her business largely by intuition, she doesn't recommend a purely intuitive method. In fact, she says that if she had it to do over again, goal-setting would be one of her top priorities.

"I wouldn't encourage anyone starting a business venture to follow exactly in my footsteps. I made too many mistakes because I didn't understand what I was doing or why. Certainly everyone makes mistakes, but you're less likely to make the same errors over and over again if you have a plan."

Chenel believes her venture taught her a great deal about herself. "At each stage of the business, I have become more aware of who I am and what motivates me. As a result, I'm a far different person than I was ten years ago. I'm pleased that I've been able to take my ideas and follow them through to completion, whether it was becoming a professional cheese maker, writing books, understanding financial management or learning to manage people." She sees self-awareness not only as a desirable personal goal, but also as a great business asset.

Chenel advises prospective entrepreneurs to thoroughly understand their market and their product before going into business. "When I began, I knew how to make goat cheese, but I didn't know the product well enough to be able to correct problems quickly when the cheese was less than up to standards. Now I can see how those early troubles could have been resolved in a fraction of the time and cost."

Finally, Chenel offers this advice to would-be entrepreneurs: "Make certain to pay attention to the world around you and be open to new ideas. The death of any business can come when management becomes myopic.

As markets change and your customers change, you have to be able to adjust your business. Ask, listen, and learn . . . it has worked wonders for me."

References

Chenel, Laura, and Linda Siegfried. *American Country Cheese*. Reading, MA: Addison Wesley, 1989.

———. *Chèvre! The Goat Cheese Cookbook*. Santa Rosa, CA: Peaks Pike, 1983.

Jones, Evan. "New American Cheesemakers." *Gourmet*, January 1985.

Reichl, Ruth. "The Making of an Entrepreneur." *Working Woman*, August 1984.

Wallace, Bill. "Farmstead Cheeses of Northern California." *Bay Foods*, August 1991.

———M. J. B.

James H. Clark

Silicon Graphics, Inc.

James H. Clark: Born 1944. Married, two children.
Venture: The design, manufacture, marketing and service of high-performance computers capable of producing three-dimensional graphic images.
Company: Silicon Graphics, Inc.; 2011 North Shoreline Blvd.; Mountain View, CA 94039; (415) 960-1980
Founded: 1981.
Revenues: Approximately $550 million in fiscal 1991 (1991 annual report).
Employees: 2,500.
Original Investment: $800,000.
Value: $650 million, according to published reports (1989).

Founder

James Clark, founder and chairman of Silicon Graphics, received B.S. and M.S. degrees from the University of New Orleans and a Ph.D. in computer science from the University of Utah. After completing his education, Clark's career as a university professor took him to the University of California at Santa Cruz, the New York Institute of Technology and the University of California at Berkeley before he was hired by Stanford University. While working as an associate professor of engineering at Stanford, he led the research team that developed the "Geometry Engine," which Clark patented. Along with several graduate students from the University of California at Stanford, Clark founded Silicon Graphics in 1981.

He received the Research Society of America's Annual Gold Medal in physics in 1970, the Annual Computer Graphics Achievement Award in 1984, and the Arthur Young & Company and *Venture* magazine's Entrepreneur of the Year award in 1988. He is the author of numerous articles on special-purpose graphics and Computer-Aided Design (CAD) systems. He shares his experience and knowledge by lecturing throughout the world at universities and conferences. Clark is an active supporter of the arts in the San Francisco Bay area.

Business Origin

In 1969, while still a graduate student, Clark invented the graphic architecture which has become the basis for 3-D computer technology. Later, while a professor at Stanford University, Clark patented the "Geometry Engine," a large semi-conductor chip that made 3-D computer images possible.

Clark's discoveries forced him to reevaluate his career, and he finally concluded he was not a true academician. "I had always seen myself as a senior professor at a university," Clark told a reporter in 1988. "But I think I learned that my strength is making things that work, rather than writing papers." With a new set of goals, Clark began Silicon Graphics in 1981 to develop and market the 3-D technology he invented at Stanford.

Business Growth

After patenting the "Geometry Engine," Clark had to decide whether Silicon should license the design for his microchips, or manufacture the machines which would use the microchips. Concluding most people would not know how to properly use the microchips, Clark concentrated on developing the technology for a 3-D workstation to house the chips. In 1983 he raised $4.5 million to begin production of the workstation, which the company began selling in 1984.

The 3-D workstation contains the elements of a conventional computer workstation with the addition of sophisticated hardware that allows the computer to draw geometric shapes on the computer screen. With the workstation, designers and other specialists can create and move realistic 3-D images almost instantaneously. The computer-produced three-dimensional images allow for more accurate prototype development.

The computers have a variety of other applications. Among key customers are a number of the nation's largest defense and aerospace contractors, who use the workstations to train jet pilots and tank personnel.

To respond to a maturing graphics and 3-D market, in 1988 Silicon introduced the "Iris, " a moderately priced workstation which retained many of the capabilities of higher priced models. The introduction of the $13,000 "personal Iris" pierced a price barrier and broadened the market for 3-D computers. At the same time, Silicon also introduced several high-end workstations to maintain its upper end market share. "Silicon is not terribly interested in the high-end market, but it is important because it relates to a family of products," says Clark.

Revenues have doubled every year, growing from $5 million in 1984 to approximately $550 million in fiscal 1991. The dramatic growth can be attributed to sales increases resulting from new products, sales force expansion, and continuing development of the 3-D graphics market. Silicon currently controls more than 50 percent of the 3-D market and ranks fourth in the graphics supercomputer market.

In 1991, Silicon teamed up with Compaq Computer. Compaq acquired 13 percent ownership in Silicon and provided R&D funds while Silicon shared 3-D and workstation technology with Compaq.

Business Obstacles

In the rapidly changing world of computer technology, designs quickly become obsolete. To survive, Clark feels computer manufacturers must constantly develop new products or improve existing ones. In 1984, Clark felt his management team was not responding fast enough to changes in the marketplace, and the company was losing valuable market share. To put Silicon back on track, Clark made one of the most difficult decisions of his career, and replaced his entire management team. Clark's move was not popular with staff members, and he was strongly criticized.

But the decision stood well with industry analysts. Said Morgan Stanley & Co. analyst Rick Ruzkun, "These aren't just young kids running a hot company. This team is capable of building a company well beyond the $500 million mark." With new management came fresh ideas and Silicon began regaining lost market share. Since that time, Clark regularly evaluates his management team and does not hesitate when changes are necessary. "There's a lot of me tied up in this company," Clark says. "I like to think that when I do stir the pot it's for the right reasons."

Keys to Success

Silicon's initial success may be attributable to Clark's creative genius, but Clark believes the company's continued prosperity is due in no small part to his decision to put strong management in place and step aside. The founder allows the experienced executive team to manage the company while he concentrates on creating and inventing. Forest Baskett, vice-president of research and development and a highly regarded computer architect, acts as a communications bridge between Clark and Edward McCracken, president and CEO.

Head of the new managerial team brought in by Clark, McCracken is known as an outstanding entrepreneurial CEO. He believes in "letting each individual in the organization play a major role in deciding what they can do in the overall plan." McCracken is credited with being the prime nurturer of the company's close relationships with software developers who bring Silicon's products to life.

Silicon receives high marks from customers for responsiveness to their needs. If a company has a problem with any Silicon product, Silicon personnel are instantly available to help.

Clark believes in sharing company profits. All employees own stock in Silicon.

Future Vision

Clark believes three-dimensional computer graphics will grow to become a $30 billion industry during the 1990s and he expects his company to share in that growth. While 3-D computers no longer occupy a niche market, Silicon remains the leader. Clark states that, "the company must continue to prove it can hold its own in a highly competitive environment."

Silicon plans to remain competitive by developing lower priced workstations. In 1991 Silicon introduced a computer with 3-D capabilities that sold for under $10,000. The company believes that this model will help bring 3-D computers to such price-sensitive areas as architecture, interior design and landscape analysis. Clark predicts that 3-D computers will eventually be as common as personal computers.

Silicon also hopes to develop more integrated programs for all its products. Doing so, says Clark, will involve designing a hardware platform that "talks to the equipment associated with other steps in the design. The designer, analyzer and person working on materials would have the same platform to deal with."

To remain the leader in 3-D graphics, Clark stresses that Silicon must avoid "looking over its shoulder to see what the competition is doing." When a company begins to do that, he says, "it becomes a follower, not a leader. It is important to focus on what the customer needs, not what the competition is doing."

Entrepreneurial Lessons

Clark's personal philosophy in building Silicon is a morally based policy of fairness. "If you treat people with a lot of respect and give them opportunities to grow with the company," he believes, "you create a positive environment." Clark says Silicon Graphics is "a great company that everyone feels good about."

Clark cautions against getting "to the point where you're responding to what the competition is doing rather than what the customer needs," or becoming "one step removed from the customer by virtue of following the competition." He believes the leading company in any field must "develop its own instinct and vision, and follow that direction. To do this, it must understand what the customer needs and innovate to answer that need."

References

Clark, James H. "Guest Commentary—Three Dimensional Computing: An Emerging Design Tool." *Design News*, February 27, 1989.

Gengo, Lorraine. "Silicon Graphics Poised for Huge Surge in Sales." *San Jose Business Journal*, September 26, 1988.

Kaufman, Steve. "3-Dimensional Workstations: A Fight Looms." *San Jose Mercury News*, July 18, 1988.

Koland, Cordell. "Graphics Firm Leader Combines Technical, Management Talents." *San Jose Business Journal*, December 14, 1987.

———. "Silicon Graphics Heats Up Battle in Workstation Market." *San Jose Business Journal*, February 22, 1988.

"Silicon Graphics Teams with Microsoft, Compaq." *Newsbytes News Network*, April 3, 1991.

Silverthorne, Sean. "Price of 3-D Could Open New Markets." *Palo Alto Peninsula Times Tribune,* October 4, 1988.

Tharp, Joan. "The Pioneering Silicon Graphics Can't Stop Now." *Palo Alto Peninsula Times Tribune,* July 13, 1987.

——A. D. K.

Michael Coles

The Original Great American Chocolate Chip Cookie Company, Inc.

Michael Coles: Born 1944. Married, three children.
Venture: Retail cookie sales with company and franchise cookie stores in shopping malls.
Company: The Original Great American Chocolate Chip Cookie Company, Inc.; 4685 Frederick Drive; Atlanta, GA 30336; (404) 696-1700
Founded: May 1977.
Revenues: $100 million in sales as of March 1990.
Employees: 72 in the corporate offices.
Original Investment: $8,000.
Value: Not released.

Founder

Michael Coles says his Great American Chocolate Chip Cookie Company probably was not the best idea he ever had for a business, but it was the one he decided to quit dreaming about and make happen.

The son of first-generation immigrants from Russia, Coles says he learned to work hard from his father, who left school at age 12 to help support a family of 11. The youngest of three children, Coles went into sportswear manufacturing at 20. By 1976 he was president of Male Slacks and Jeans, and formed two successful clothing companies of his own.

In 1976, he sold his company intending to write and photograph children's books. "I had written a children's book and was going to work really hard on publishing it," says Coles. An avid photographer, he wanted to devote time to developing his art.

Coles owned three bicycle shops in Atlanta for a time, reflecting his interest in cycling. For the past 10 years he has biked across the U. S. three times on regular bikes and once on a record-breaking four-man team riding a recumbent bicycle.

He co-founded a Marietta, Georgia bank which he terms "very entrepreneurial." Coles' interest in the environment and U.S./Soviet relations led to his participation in trout fishing and conservation efforts in both countries.

Business Origin

Coles got the idea for the cookie company on a trip to California where he saw similar shops. His friend and co-founder Arthur Karp got the same idea simultaneously. The partners tested recipes in Karp's garage until they were satisfied. As the partners debated which recipe to use, Arthur's wife Susan baked a batch from her own recipe—and the question was settled.

The "Original" recipe for chocolate chip cookies is one passed down to Susan Karp from her great-great-grandmother, a Blackfoot Indian from West Virginia. Coles believes the recipe may predate the famous "Toll House" recipe. "We think it's probably the oldest recipe for chocolate chip cookies," says Coles.

The first Original Great American Chocolate Chip Cookie Company store opened in Perimeter Mall in Atlanta against the advice of the mall's management. Although the partners knew nothing about baking, they counted on their marketing experience to pull it off. "Our lack of knowledge about the cookie industry allowed us to be more daring," Coles remarks.

Business Growth

The founders thought the cookie company would be only a side business, with one or two stores. The third store opened before a year had passed; there were 10 at the end of the second year and 20 by the third year of business. "The growth started out slow, although it seemed aggressive at the time," says Coles.

"The hardest thing in growing a business is the first five years. You have to make decisions that are going to take you past that crucial sixth year into the future," he says. "All you're doing is running around putting out fires. The last thing you think about is putting in a sprinkler system. In time and with experience, you learn to put out the fires *and* put in the sprinkler system."

Relief came when the partners were able to hire a director of operations. They couldn't afford to pay the top salary that the kind of person they needed was worth, but looked for someone who could take the company to 100 stores. "We had to convince them that they would wind up with a very good job and make a lot more money than they'd probably ever make [elsewhere]."

Top personnel helped them avoid the mistake of making decisions too quickly because of time pressures. "As you get more successful and make more money, you tend to make decisions in a minute," Coles declares.

"You have to still analyze things and agonize over them like you do in the beginning. If you make a mistake, you don't have as much latitude, because the overhead is so much greater."

Coles focuses on finance, product development and marketing. Karp handles franchise sales and legal matters. "My partner makes the company grow and my job is to keep it from dying," laughs Coles.

Part of the Original Great American Chocolate Chip Cookie Company's success comes from running lean and mean. "We don't have all those levels of management," says Coles. "With fewer layers, we have more direct communication with on-line people. We run very efficiently and are careful that we don't duplicate information."

Another part of that success undoubtedly comes from the company's corporate philosophy, which Karp revealed in an interview in *Shopping Center World.* "We finally came up with four building blocks that have been the cornerstone of the company. They are easily stated, but can be talked about endlessly: pride, fairness, responsibility, responsiveness and profitability."

By 1990, one hundred company stores and 200 franchises produced annual sales reaching $100 million.

Business Obstacles

Coles faced a major setback shortly after the first store opened. Riding home from work on his motorcycle, he ran into a telephone pole. Doctors told him he'd never walk again. Sheer determination and bicycle riding therapy helped him prove them wrong.

Coles went on to ride across the United States four times and competed in cycling, fishing and other sports events internationally. The accident made him stronger. "I've learned there is no goal too high or a setback too hard to overcome," he says.

At the same time, the young company faced a major problem. "We wanted to ship our cookie batter refrigerated, but the technology did not exist to do it. We could either ship the dry ingredients and add the wet ingredients at the store level, or ship the batter frozen. Neither appealed to us," said Coles.

Through trial and error the partners developed the way to package, seal, and refrigerate the dough. They considered themselves lucky to do it in the six months before the first store needed the dough.

The second obstacle was convincing landlords to lease space. Cookie stores compete with other types of shops for the entertainment dollar, including record stores and other restaurants.

Originally, 95 percent of the stores were franchised, but the company bought back several stores and opened many in key markets, although Coles says, "we never open a store deliberately to become a company store."

"We've learned how to test market products through experience. We don't do control testing—we just put it out and see how it sells," says Coles.

One flop, the granola brownie, was "probably the best product we ever had," says Coles. "At some point we may bring it back. We even changed the name to the oatmeal raisin brownie, hoping that would be enough to make it sell—but I guess people aren't looking for something healthy when they visit our store."

Keys to Success

Because of their background in retailing, Karp and Coles understood their customers. "Maybe that comes first even before understanding your business," says Coles.

"The easiest way to succeed in business is to figure out how to operate less expensively—then you don't have to sell one more cookie."

"We think we are best. We are one of best operating fast food businesses that I know of. We do not have any illusions about our business itself. What we have is a product that on a retail level costs more than the most expensive steak you could buy in a grocery store. That approach makes customer satisfaction top priority."

The company focused franchise sales on investors rather than mom and pop owners. "We went after strong business people who wanted multiple stores, who would be committed to expanding their operations," states Coles.

Future Vision

Coles foresees a continuing weeding out of cookie stores. With fewer mom and pop operations, there will be more spaces available in malls. He expects more huge malls, able to support two cookie shops. "We have stores in malls where Mrs. Fields has stores," says Coles. "We like competing with them."

"We have the potential in the next five years to double the size of the company in the U. S. and possibly be as big as we are today in 10 years internationally. We will continue doing what we've been doing, growing at 15 to 20 percent a year."

With two stores in Guam open, the company is negotiating its first international contracts with four countries. Australia or Japan is expected to become the first international licensee.

Entrepreneurial Lessons

"When you're an entrepreneur, you literally are a risk taker. I think building a business is like playing a poker game. You basically are betting the company almost from the beginning. But at some point you have to learn how much of the company to bet, and to build a solid base to grow on."

"If you want to do something, you have to do it," says Coles. "A lot of people spend a lot of time doing research and thinking about companies, but you have to do it. When the cookie business idea crossed my mind, I just decided I would do it no matter what."

Coles believes people should never be afraid of failing. "There is a lot more to be learned in failure than in success. When you succeed, everything goes right and it's hard to look back at what you did and then do it again. Rather than blame failure on extraneous things that happened around you, try to find out what your responsibility is and learn from it."

References

Baker, N. *Nation's Business*, March 1990.

Butler, V. "Cookie Store Chain Magnate a 'Good Guy' to Feminists." *Cobb Extra* (Georgia), September 25, 1986.

"Cookie Business Booms for Pair." *The Sunday Sun*, October 20, 1985.

Cornish, Kathy. "Two Smart Cookies Concoct Recipe for Success." *Shopping Center World*. May 1991.

McNamara, V. "That's the Way the Gourmet Cookies Crumble." *Houston Business Journal*, June 19, 1989.

Rice, Faye, and Katharena Leanne Zanders. "How to Succeed at Cloning a Small Business." *Fortune*, October 28, 1985.

——S. B.

Finis Conner

Conner Peripherals, Inc.

Finis Conner: Born 1943. Married, two children.
Venture: The design, development, manufacture and marketing of 3.5-inch disk drives for computers.
Company: Conner Peripherals, Inc.; 3081 Zanker Road; San Jose, CA 95134; (408) 433-3340
Founded: 1985.
Revenues: $1.7 billion in sales in 1991, according to published reports.
Employees: 10,000 worldwide.
Original Investment: $12 million was invested by Compaq Computer Corporation in 1986.
Value: Conner Peripherals had a net worth of approximately $201 million at the close of 1989, according to published sources.

Founder

Finis Conner was born in rural Alabama in the middle of World War II. He grew up in a variety of places in Alabama, Texas, and Florida, and left it all behind in 1961 to seek his fortune in California.

Conner went to California with a high school education, $50, and not much else (he started with $100, but lost half of it in a poker game on the trip west). "I was just a naive country boy," he recalls. Once in California, however, country boy or not, he quickly got down to work.

In California, Finis Conner found the motivation to go with the energy and intelligence he has always possessed. By his own admission, his high school years consisted mainly of "going to the beach almost every day."

107

Still, Conner quickly enrolled in San Jose State University, joining the school's industrial management program. Shortly after enrolling, he took his first Silicon Valley job—as a clerk/typist for IBM.

During his short tenure with IBM, Conner got his first opportunity as an entrepreneur. A friend of his had started a small firm to design circuit boards and asked him to join the company. He agreed.

"The first thing you learn about starting a company is that employees expect to get paid every week," Conner says recalling his early experience. "I learned that nobody works cheaper than the owner."

The experience was not all bad, however. The background it provided helped him land a position with semiconductor-maker Stewart Warner Microcircuits shortly after he graduated from San Jose. For $850 a month Finis Conner was a professional salesman. He was scared to death.

More than anything else, Conner remembers feeling self-conscious about his Southern accent, afraid it would label him as ignorant, or "some kind of hick" in the high-tech world of Silicon Valley. He discovered his fears were unfounded and learned an important lesson—"the customer has as much to fear as you do."

Eventually, Conner moved on to the Memorex Corporation, where he met Alan Shugart, then vice president of developmental engineering. Conner became Shugart's "gopher" and the two developed what turned out to be a mutually profitable relationship. Shugart liked Conner's energy and insight and involved him in projects linked to the newly developing world of personal computers. One project in particular fired the imaginations of both men —floppy disk drives for desktop computers.

The two tested their idea in an unusual manner that would eventually become a Conner trademark. They went to a computer industry trade show in 1972 and talked with people they met about their product. While the product did not exist, the positive responses were incredible. Both Conner and Shugart were convinced the market and timing for their floppy disk drive was right.

Armed with their conviction and the results of their "marketing study," the two men asked Memorex to commit greater resources to creating the new product. Memorex refused, not because it did not believe their research, says Conner, but because "it was a peanut-sized deal to them."

But Conner and Shugart saw the future and a fortune in both the product and the market. They decided to act on their conviction even if their employer would not. The two formed Shugart Associates, a floppy disk drive company, and raised part of their start-up capital from a nearby venture capital fund call the Sprout Group.

A former general partner of the Sprout Group, Ed Glassmeyer, remembers his earliest impressions of the two entrepreneurs, especially Finis Conner. "He had high energy," says Glassmeyer. "He also had a lot of knowledge about his product and the market. He was the kind of person that one would gravitate to."

Shugart Associates proved Conner and his partner were right about their product. The company grew and prospered to the point where Xerox Corporation bought it in 1978. Conner stayed with the firm until 1979 and then left to explore for new challenges.

A brief association with International Memories, Inc. convinced Conner that the next challenge would be found in building another company. At International Memories Conner was involved in the development of a 5.25-inch hard disk drive and became convinced that it was the wave of the future. Conner left International Memories and called Al Shugart. They went to see Ed Glassmeyer again.

Conner, with his eye for marketing, and Shugart, with his development and engineering expertise, made "an outstanding team," recalls Glassmeyer, whose Oak Investment Partners became the lead investor in Shugart Technology (later renamed Seagate Technology, Inc.).

Seagate achieved more than either partner expected. Shugart's products and Conner's marketing were perfectly tuned to the needs of the industry. In just a few years Seagate was the leading manufacturer of 5.25-inch hard disk drives and was providing them to every major U.S. manufacturer.

But by 1984, Conner began to feel that Seagate had lost its innovative edge. "Seagate focused on market share and was very aggressive with respect to pricing," remembers Glassmeyer. "Finis wanted to move to a higher capacity, higher value product that would earn higher margin."

Conner points out that by 1984 at least one competing firm, Maxtor Corporation, was producing a hard disk drive that could store 100 megabytes "but we [Seagate] could only get to 40 megabytes."

Feeling that he could no longer influence the product strategy of the company, Conner left Seagate in 1984. He was now a wealthy man, with no financial need ever to work again. Since his first child was born about the same time, Conner decided to relax and enjoy his success. He spent time with his family, played golf (on the pro-am circuit) and spent plenty of hours sailing his yacht.

Business Origin

Only 42, Finis Conner was not ready to retire. Even before he knew what product he would manufacture, he formed Conner Peripherals in 1985. Then he watched and waited, certain he would find a product for his new company to make.

It did not take long. In December 1985, John Squires, who had founded and recently left a disk drive company called Miniscribe, came looking for his former competitor.

What Squires had was the product Conner wanted—a 3.5-inch hard disk drive. What John Squires wanted was the money to build it.

Business Growth

Through a business relationship between Conner and Compaq Computers, Inc., Conner Peripherals got the financial support it needed and now supplies disk drives to all leading computer manufacturers, including the Japanese, both for desktop machines and the increasingly popular laptops. But Finis Conner makes it clear that he understands the company's growth will continue only as long as the firms stays responsive to the consumer.

"My grandmother always said that God gave you two ears and one mouth for a reason," he says, "I learned that it works better to listen to what the customer wants and have the technical base ready to supply it."

According to Squires, Conner's vice president of engineering, the success of Conner Peripherals has a lot to do with the man who gave the company its name. "A lot of people don't understand Finis' direction," he says. "But he's willing to try something crazy to see if it works. He's capable of dreaming up outrageous things, but at the same time, he's very conservative."

Squires also praises Conner's above-board manner in dealing with customers and employees. "Finis is tough, but he's always fair," he says.

Business Obstacles

Nineteen-eighty-five was "exactly the wrong time" to launch a new disk drive venture. "The success rate of disk drive start-ups was not exactly high, and financial community made it clear that it was not going to fund any new disk drive companies," recalls Squires.

But Conner was not looking at the way things were. He was focused on the way they would soon be. Conner realized that Squires' 3.5-inch drive was the perfect mate for a new microcomputer design that allows microprocessors to handle more data at faster speeds. If Conner could produce the new drive it would have an even greater impact on the computer industry than had the Seagate drive.

Unfortunately, not everyone shared Conner's vision for the new drive's potential. Even Ed Glassmeyer and his partners refused to get involved. "Finis and I spent about two months talking about the Conner Peripherals deal," he recalls. "But the disk drive industry was under a lot of pricing pressures, and while Finis had a great track record as a marketeer, he hadn't yet run the day-to-day operations of a company."

Conner faced a seemingly impossible situation. The disk drive industry was in a slump, and he and Squires' had a product that was certain to breathe new life into the market, but no one would risk funding it because the market was so slow. In the midst of this frustration Conner turned to an old friend for advice.

Joseph (Rod) Canion had come to Finis Conner years earlier when he and some friends were trying to get a company of their own started. Conner had provided good advice and support, and Canion and his associates had gone ahead with their plans. Their start-up was called Compaq Computers, Inc.

When the two met at the Comdex trade show in the spring of 1986, it was Conner looking for advice. What he got from Canion was $12 million.

"Rod needed a smaller disk drive product, and we needed money," recalls Conner. By the time Conner finished explaining his new product, Canion was convinced. He not only arranged for Compaq to take a stake in Conner Peripherals but also became the new company's first customer. Compaq bought 90 percent of Conner Peripherals first year production.

The relationship was "win-win" for Compaq and Conner. The only losers were the venture capitalists, who were now unnecessary. "I went back to

Glassmeyer and said, "I've got good news and bad news. The good news is that we've got a customer. The bad news is he's also our investor."

The arrangement worked. In 1987, Conner Peripherals surpassed even Compaq's first-year sales record with revenues of $113 million; in 1988, Conner reached $256 million, and in 1989, the skyrocketing company sold more than $700 million worth of product. That growth has made Conner Peripherals the undisputed leader in the hard disk drive industry and, according to *Forbes*, the fastest-growing company in computer industry history.

Keys to Success

When pressed about the secret to his own success, Conner insists that it is really simple. "A lot of people could have done what we've done," he says. "Maybe we saw something a little sooner, maybe we've pushed a little harder."

If there is one single key to Conner's success it is his willingness and ability to be customer drawn—rather than create a product and then find customers for it. Perhaps the best example of this philosophy is seen in a disk drive made for Compaq.

When Compaq decided to create a 6-pound or less PC that could fit into a briefcase, it needed a special disk drive. Conner suggested that Compaq use a 2.5-inch drive that it was then developing. Compaq vetoed the idea and asked for a 3.5-inch drive that would meet its needs. Conner Peripherals responded with a secret project called "Stubby" which, in only eight months, developed a lightweight, low-power 3.5-inch drive that met Compaq's needs. "Stubby" is still built exclusively for and sold only to Compaq.

Future Vision

For the moment, Conner's future vision is wrapped up in the future of Conner Peripherals. While his firm is currently the undisputed leader of its industry, others are starting to fight for a piece of the pie. Most notably, one of the other firms Conner founded, Seagate, is determined to win a share of the 3.5-inch drive market.

That's all right with Conner though, because he's convinced that his current firm can keep its technological edge. "We're the most innovative company in the business," he claims, "and we're going to stay that way."

Entrepreneurial Lessons

The most important lesson to Finis Conner is one he tries to teach his staff every day—listen to what the market wants—don't try to tell it. "It's why we're where we are," he explains, "and why we will stay ahead of everyone else." Conner points out that as important as the research and development of new technology is to his firm (Conner Peripherals has introduced a new generation of hard disk drives every year of its existence), creating the products the market needs, not trying to convince people that they need what Conner creates, is the key to continued expansion.

References

Bertrand, Kate. "Conner's Japanese Success Drive." *Business Marketing*, December 1991.

Garrett, Echo M. "Experience Shows." *Venture*, May 1989.

Kupfer, Andrew. "America's Fastest Growing Company." *Fortune*, August 13, 1990.

Leone, Genevieve. "Finis Conner: The Fast Track from Success to Success." *San Jose Business Journal*, May 29, 1989.

"Pick a Fast Horse." *Success*, September 1990.

Pitta, Julie. "The Survivor." *Forbes*, July 8, 1991.

Rebello, Kathy. "Conner Revels in Lifestyle of Fortune 500." *USA Today*, March 9, 1990.

Shepherd, William. "Short Cycle Play." *FW*, April 19, 1988.

Zachary, G. Pascal. "Conner Peripherals Could Claim Title of Fastest Growing Manufacturing Firm." *Wall Street Journal*, October 23, 1989.

——E. C.

Joel Cooper
Michael Tomson

Gotcha Sportswear, Inc.

Joel Cooper: Born 1953. Single.
Michael Tomson: Born 1954. Married.
Venture: A casualwear manufacturer whose clothing styles reflect current surfer fashions.
Company: Gotcha Sportswear, Inc.; 17871 Von Karman; P.O. Box 19511; Irvine, CA 92713; (714) 222-4444
Founded: December 1979.
Revenues: $125 million (1990), according to a company source.
Employees: 200 plus.
Original Investment: $10,000.
Value: Not known.

Founders

Joel Cooper and Michael Tomson used what they knew—clothing manufacturing and surfing—to launch what is now a $100 million company specializing in surfwear.

Both grew up around the beaches of Durban, South Africa, an area recognized for its challenging waves. They met at the University of Natal (S.A.), where Cooper earned a business degree and became the country's youngest certified public accountant. Tomson also earned a business degree, concentrating on marketing and finance.

After graduation, Cooper worked in his family's clothing manufacturing business for two years in preparation for "making a living in the business," he says. Tomson headed for the beach and professional surfing. He eventually ranked fifth in the world, but realized he needed a career after surfing. He recalls, "On the circuit I was doing fairly well, but I was thinking to myself that it was time to start looking toward a longer view. So I considered the opportunities and looked at my strengths."

After assessing what he knew—"I had a reasonable understanding of the surf market"—the surfer met with the accountant. They combined complementary backgrounds, and began manufacturing beachwear.

Maintaining surf authenticity is important to both men. Gotcha sponsors surfing events regularly, and a major event yearly in Hawaii. They also back up-and-coming surfers, like 1990 world champion Martin Potter, whom they've sponsored since his teens. Additionally, Tomson surfs often and retains his world-class reputation. In August 1990, he took first place at The President's Heat at Malibu Beach, an event showcasing the surfing prowess of the presidents of the top surfwear companies.

Business Origin

Gotcha, the name, was inspired by the series of Gillette razor commercials popularizing the phrase. "You know the Gillette commercial where the guy cuts himself while shaving and yells 'Gotcha'?" Tomson asks. "Well, I watched that and was fascinated by the abbreviation of the English language in American advertising. So when we were trying to come up with the name, it was as simple as writing down a few names, asking Joel what he liked, and settling on Gotcha."

Gotcha, the business, evolved out of the contemporary surf culture. Tomson articulated, "Surfing sells. It's an outdoor culture with a certain mystique to it. That leads to a certain sort of style that leads from the water to the man." Tomson and Cooper aimed to embody that "mystique" in beachwear, while cultivating the youthful surf market. "We are very much a surfwear company with a surf commitment," confirms Tomson.

With the surfing lifestyle as its foundation, the company started in 1979 in a house in Laguna Beach, California. An asymmetrical surf trunk and a walk short designed by Tomson made up the first clothing "line." Tomson and Cooper got a distributor and considered themselves in the clothing business.

Business Growth

Cooper is the firm's business voice, overseeing expansion and licensing ventures. Tomson is in charge of design and advertising, which both agree played an important role in establishing Gotcha's image and contributes to its current success. "Our ads really convey the Gotcha image, but they also focus on the unique aspects of [our] products," says Tomson. Their advertisements have been called provocative and "on the cutting edge." Says Tomson, "Our advertising has set a standard of innovation in the industry." According to Cooper, Gotcha was first to use female models in "sexual poses" with male models. Cooper makes clear their diversity saying, "We're always changing our ads and our products, trying something new to see what works."

Ever a company in touch with its market, Gotcha's marketing director frequently takes ads and product samples down to the beach to generate feedback from the "authentics." Says Cooper, "It's key to know your market here. You have to be true to your roots." Tomson, the marketing expert, agrees: "Be aware of consumers. What do kids think? How are they acting? What are their favorites?" He also stresses the importance of researching, "your own market, the pop culture trends, [and] the rest of the world." Cooper concludes, "The only way a company stays on top is by always reassessing the marketplace and reacting quickly to the changes."

Quickly reacting has increased Gotcha's sales from $500,000 in 1979 to over $100 million in 1990. Its once two-item clothing line is now a 300-item collection of swimsuits, t-shirts, walk shorts, clamdiggers, and other "beachy" men's sportswear.

Gotcha introduced a line of junior swimwear in 1987, a line of women's swimwear, which accounts for ten percent of sales, and has expanded into kidswear. Gotcha's clothing can be found in leading department stores, as well as in surf specialty shops. A new line of surfwear on the label MCD (More Core Division), designed for the active surfer, is sold exclusively in surf shops.

Business Obstacles

In 1979 surfing as a sport was 25 years old, but the surfwear market was relatively young, dominated by Quicksilver and Ocean Pacific (OP). Gotcha sold its first line of surfwear in local surf shops, and worked with a few distributors who shared their vision. The industry did not initially embrace the "Gotcha" guys. Tomson explains, "When we first started, people were not interested in carrying our line. We had to convince them that this is what people wanted and that they would sell well." Enter advertising. Cooper explains, "Before us, advertisers in our market just used pictures of dumb guys on surfboards." Gotcha's "sexually-charged" ads attracted attention and criticism, and were effective. The ads now vary from the sexual to the surreal.

Keys to Success

Gotcha gained its number three market position not by unmatched business savvy—they admit they worked out the business details as they went along—but because their clothing embodies the surfing lifestyle. Their designs not only cater to the changing tastes and styles of surfers, but also shape trends. Cooper explains, "When we first started, Ocean Pacific had been around for a long time, and they had really carved out the surfwear industry. Gotcha filled the gap that was left when [OP] began losing touch with the growth of the market and the ever-changing tastes of the people on the beach." Tomson adds, "We are very close to the surf scene, the 'authentics,' and yet our clothes embody what we think is a major fashion statement." Their growth is fueled by three energies: style, attitude, and performance. Tomson spells it out, "Our clothing defines surf style. Our ads give us attitude. Our business expertise gives us performance."

It is that understanding of the surf culture and Tomson's underriding creativity that keep the company moving ahead. Gotcha strives to keep the spirit of creativity in marketing and design, employing young—under thirty—surf-oriented people. "In our company, the designers, those in marketing, in advertising—they're all surf people," Tomson says.

Future Vision

Expansion is the watchword. Gotcha tapped the Japanese market in 1985, licensing Chori, the largest trading company in Japan, to manufacture and distribute their line. The label has also expanded into the northeast and midwest regions of the United States, and in overseas markets like Europe. Tomson and Cooper believe European youths will be receptive to their style because the clothing is authentic and directed toward the average person, unlike the more abstract styles of European designers.

To introduce inland youth to Gotcha, the company has been advertising on MTV, a music video network.

Gotcha is also trying its hand at movie-making, with the $400,000 production of *Surfers, the Movie*. The movie, explains Paul Holmes, vice-president of marketing for Gotcha, "covers the spirit of surfing. It's about competition, about the Zen, the soulful experience of surfing, along with the changes, and dangers of big wave surfing." Explaining the impetus for such a venture, he says, "The company has to be authentic, to be true to surfing. Gotcha has been doing well, so when we got to the point where we had the available resources, we felt it was about time surfing had a real surf movie." Tomson sees the film as a tribute to surfing—the sport and the lifestyle. The film's limited-engagement cross-country tour began in California and worked its way to New England. Following that has been *Surfers Take-Two*, a 90-minute documentary that features top female and male surfers. Tomson has been quoted as saying that while the projects were not expressly meant to make money, he hopes to recoup costs by releasing both films on videocassette.

Entrepreneurial Lessons

Tomson spells out Gotcha's philosophy, saying, "Try and operate with integrity, and look for the long run rather than the short run. Never try to repeat yourself. Always try to do it first, but first do it right." How do you get started? "Belief is all you need," he concludes.

References

Ballen, Kate. "Joel Cooper." *Fortune*, October 27, 1986.

Cole, Benjamin Mark. "Gotcha's Swimwear Rides Wave of Popularity on Both Sides of the Pacific." *Los Angeles Herald Examiner*, June 2, 1985.

Kuhns, Lynn. "Gotcha: Beachwear." *Groundswell*, August 1990.

Leivenberg, Richard. "They've Gotcha in a Social Revolution." *Men's Look*, December 1987.

Stanton, Russ. "Riding the 2nd Wave." *The Orange County Register*, April 23, 1991.

——A. A.

Michael Dell

Dell Computer Corporation

Michael Dell: Born 1965. Married, one child.
Venture: Mail order sales of IBM personal computers, Dell-manufactured IBM clone computers, and peripherals.
Company: Dell Computer Corporation; 9505 Arboretum Boulevard; Austin, TX 78759; (512) 338-4400
Founded: The company began in 1983 as a part-time business run from Michael Dell's college dormitory room and was incorporated in 1984.
Revenues: $546.2 million for fiscal 1991, according to company sources.
Employees: 2,300.
Original Investment: $1,000 of personal savings.
Value: $75 million estimated net worth (1989), according to published reports.

Founder

The son of a well-to-do orthodontist father and stockbroker mother, Michael Dell says he could have lived a comfortable life regardless of the profession he chose. His parents hoped he would go into medicine when he got to college. Instead, he went into retail when he got to second grade.

"When I was in second grade I was selling candy at school," Dell recalls. "My teacher told me then I was going to be an entrepreneur." The teacher was right. Dell followed his candy venture with a nationwide mail order business trading stamps and baseball cards. He made more than $2,000 by the age of 12.

During his high school years, Dell got his first taste of computers. With money he had made from his stamp trading business, he purchased an Apple II computer—and promptly took it apart. This became a ritual for the next several machines he owned. "I always wanted to see what was inside," explains Dell, noting that he also always put the machines back in working order—usually with extra components and features added.

Still in high school, Dell found that he could buy a basic model personal computer, add a variety of components and sell the rebuilt machine at a profit. "I knew where to get parts for a good price," he says. Without being familiar with the term, he became a value-added reseller. That concept would stick with him through high school, and would figure prominently in his future success. In the meantime, he was making his main income in another endeavor.

Dell had gone to work selling papers for the *Houston Post*, but rather than taking a paper route he devised his own way to market subscriptions. Using one of his computers for record-keeping, Dell obtained and maintained lists of everyone who moved into, or got married in the *Post's* marketing area. He then mailed each identified person or couple an offer for a free two-week subscription to the paper, conducting follow-up calls to solicit regular subscriptions later. Dell earned nearly $20,000 from his efforts, and used the money to buy himself a fully loaded BMW—as soon as he was old enough to drive.

In 1983, Dell graduated from high school, and went off to college at the University of Texas at Houston (UT). The idea, as far as his parents were concerned, he recalls, was for Michael to study pre-med, and eventually become a doctor, just as his older brother had done. It did not work out that way.

Business Origin

To this day, Dell claims he really intended to study medicine, but not long after he arrived at UT, his love of marketing overshadowed his freshman studies.

In high school, the buying and selling of computer parts had been a sort of hobby—now it became a growth industry. In his dormitory room at UT, Dell set up the same type of resale business he had run at home, only this time on a greatly expanded level. Other students were soon working for Dell, making buying trips to retailers throughout the state, and shipping parts across the country—all coordinated from the freshman's dorm.

Dell was soon averaging $30,000 a month in sales. That amount of business could not be hidden for long, so about halfway through his freshman year, Dell made his business activities known to his parents and worked out a deal with them. They agreed that Michael would run his enterprise through the summer break. If the business proved to be successful, he would continue. Otherwise, he would drop it and go back to school.

The last month Dell was enrolled as a freshman at the University of Texas, his dormitory-based firm netted approximately $80,000. Michael Dell did not go back for his sophomore year.

Business Growth

With his parents' approval, Dell devoted all of his efforts to his fledgling business. Dell Computer was incorporated in 1984, and Dell ran the business from his home until he opened a storefront under the name of PC's Limited later that year. The store picked up where Dell's home-based business left off, selling a small portion of its products to walk-in customers, but concentrating on mail-order sales for most of its volume.

Dell admits the results surprised him. By early 1985 the company had more than 30 employees and was adding one new employee every week. Though other companies were entering the discount mail-order market for "gray-market" IBM computers, Dell was already establishing the PC's Limited name as a national leader in the fast growing field. For him, however, this was not enough.

In July 1985, less than two years after he made his first sale on the University of Texas campus, Dell's young company introduced its own computer, the Turbo PC . That September, Dell introduced his 286/8. New models followed the next April and August, and in each case, the new line outsold the one introduced before.

During this time, Dell's family played an important role. Wholly owned by Dell, the company needed money to finance its continued expansion and the development of new products. Family members lent the firm more than $500,000, enough to see the fast-growing firm through its first major expansion phase. The loans were repaid by the end of 1986 as PC's Limited sales expanded to more than $30 million.

But Dell Computer's growth had just begun. After one early manufacturing error, the company received excellent reviews on its products from computer magazines. Dell invested heavily and consistently in both R&D

and advertising. In addition, Dell began to use the market information gathered by his direct sales and telemarketing staffs for planning. That information allowed Dell to stay in close contact with the marketplace.

Coupling the timeliness of his market information with state-of-the-art assembly facilities, Dell Computer began to emerge as a manufacturing leader. Michael Dell constantly sought and used systems that worked—such as his own version of Japanese "just in time" materials procurement—and used those systems to draw closer to his goal of building each machine on a made-to-order basis. By manufacturing only machines that were already sold, Dell planned to keep overhead low while maintaining the pricing advantage that made continued rapid growth possible.

In addition to developing and adopting cutting edge production techniques, Dell sought out the right people, including outside investors. In 1987 he completed a $21.5 million private placement. An initial public offering in June 1988 raise more than $32 million. The value of Dell's remaining personal holdings in the company was more than $107 million. These capital infusions gave the company the means to expand once again to meet still growing demand.

Sales reached nearly $70 million in 1987, $150 million in 1988, and figures for fiscal 1991 showed the company moving more than $546.2 million of product, making Dell one of the top ten computer manufacturers in the nation. But what about those other nine? "I don't think for a second that our competitors are going to sit around and keep doing what they're doing, because it's clearly not working," Dell told *Business Week*.

Business Obstacles

The most notable potential obstacle to the firm's growth came with the introduction of Dell's first PC's Limited-brand computer. In a rush to bring his own line of machines to the market, Dell manufactured computers that violated FCC regulations regarding radio wave emissions. Before long, customers as well as the government noticed the problem and brought it to the company's attention.

Dell calls the incident a potential disaster because this was the firm's first attempt at making a computer, and competitors were quick to blame the problem on what they claimed was his youth and naivete. If the company's reputation was tainted, its market could potentially disappear. Few people, Dell points out, will buy from a mail-order company with a reputation for shoddy workmanship. His response to the situation, however, saw the company through, and even enhanced its reputation.

The firm paid a small fine to the FCC for its violation and quickly corrected the production error. It then intensified quality assurance and testing. Today, if even a few calls are received regarding some defect in the firm's products, customer service personnel can take the information directly to the engineering or manufacturing unit responsible. As a result, an error that creeps into the design or manufacturing process can be corrected quickly, often within a day of its discovery. The system has gained Dell a reputation for quality and responsiveness that the founder sees as a major key to his firm's future success. "[Our] strategy puts us extremely close to our customer," said Dell in a *Fortune* cover story.

Keys to Success

Along with citing his commitment to quality and responsiveness, Dell is quick to credit timing and the policies of at least one competitor with contributing to his firm's growth. "IBM's sales policies really set me up in business," he says. That, coupled with the fact that the personal computer industry was still in its infancy in 1984, are the two factors Dell says were most important to his early success.

Others at the firm, however, are more likely to credit Dell himself—especially his ability to make correct business decisions almost instantly. "Michael can assimilate in an hour what might take you or me a semester," says one vice president. "He has a remarkable faculty for getting to the nub of the problem quickly," says president and chief operating officer E. Lee Walker.

Dell told *Nation's Business*, "One of the things I benefited from when I started this business was that I didn't know anything. I was just instinct with no preconceived notions. This enabled me to learn and change quickly. . . ."

As far as his continuing success is concerned, the founder credits the company's intense dedication to the development of both its product line and its telemarketing operation. "We are the distribution channel of the future," he insists. "In the 1990s and beyond, this will be the way it's [computer sales] done." Dell is taking a step in that direction. His company has signed an agreement with Staples, Inc., to ship to the office superstores a line of low-profile desktop and notebook computers. Dell points out that such stores are a "high-growth segment of the market for office equipment" and that both companies share a dedication to customer satisfaction.

Future Vision

Dell's vision of the future is clear—and concise. His first goal is to build Dell Computer into a one billion-dollar company (annual sales) by the time he is thirty. His next is to keep on leading the firm after that. "My goal," he explains simply, "is to be CEO for 60 years."

Entrepreneurial Lessons

When it comes to lessons he has learned from building Dell Computer, Michael Dell focuses clearly on the need to trust his own instincts when making business decisions. For an example he points to his decision to quit school and found PC's Limited. "Everything was wrong—we didn't have the money, the people, the resources," he says. "But I had a gut feeling that drove me to start this company."

References

Anderson, Stephanie. "PC Slump? What PC Slump?" *Business Week*, July 1, 1991.

Angrist, Stanley W. "Entrepreneur in Short Pants." *Forbes*, March 7, 1988.

Deutschman, Alan. "America's Fastest Risers." *Fortune*, October 7, 1991.

Goldstein, Mark L. "An Industry Legend—at 21." *Industry Week*, April 20, 1987.

Green, Tim. "Backyard Battlers." *Austin Business Journal*, March 6, 1989.

Kelly, Kevin. "Michael Dell: The Enfant Terrible of Personal Computers." *Business Week*, June 13, 1988.

Kotkin, Joel. "The Innovation Upstarts." *Inc.*, January 1989.

Landendorf, Kirk. "Fast Track Phenomenon." *Austin American-Statesman*, June 26, 1988.

Lary, Banning Kent. "An 'Instinct' for Computer Success." *Nation's Business*, April 1991.

Nichols, Don. "Young Man in a Hurry." *Texas Business Magazine*, November 1986.

Pope, Kyle. "Dell Computer Experiences Growth Pain." *Austin American-Statesman*, January 29, 1989.

Richman, Tom. "The Entrepreneur of the Year. " *Inc.*, January 1990.

Tyson, Kim. "To Be Young, Rich, and Michael." *Austin American-Statesman*, June 26, 1988.

——E. C.

Anthony DeSio

Mail Boxes Etc.

Anthony DeSio: Born 1930. Married, two children.
Venture: Franchisor of neighborhood postal, business and communication service centers.
Company: Mail Boxes Etc.; 5555 Oberlin Drive; San Diego, CA 92121; (619) 452-1553
Founded: Incorporated May 19, 1980.
Revenues: $30.3 million in fiscal year 1991 (1991 annual report).
Employees: 100 in the corporate offices.
Original Investment: $100,000.
Value: $7 million net worth (1990), according to published reports.

Founder

After 25 years in corporate America, Tony DeSio left a successful career as a big-company executive to start his own business. DeSio was nearing retirement when he decided to "do something for myself before it was too late." He went on to found one of the fastest-growing franchisors in American business.

DeSio grew up in the Bronx section of New York City, leaving home after high school to attend the University of Connecticut. He worked his way through college and graduated in 1958 with a degree in electrical engineering.

DeSio began his career as an electrical engineer with Lockheed Aircraft Corporation in Sunnyvale, California. He moved into Lockheed management and remained with the company until 1971. DeSio then spent two

126

years in Washington D.C. as a member of a presidential executive exchange program. From 1972 until 1979, he held executive positions with General Electric and Western Union Corporation.

Business Origin

"I had often considered starting a business of my own, but I was always too busy to do it," DeSio says. "As I approached my 50th birthday, I figured that I had better do it then, or I wasn't going to do it at all. I decided it was time to stop tying my future to big companies. I wanted to feel more in control of my own destiny," he says. "I believed that since I had years of management experience, I could successfully manage my own operation. And by that time I had a financial base to get me started."

Having decided to enter the world of entrepreneurship, DeSio looked for a business opportunity. He recognized that many busy Americans like himself had "become impatient with the Postal Service's long lines, short hours and limited services," and he wondered if private business could offer a solution. "I saw that companies like Federal Express and DHL had become successful by offering alternatives to the post office, and I thought the same alternatives could work for retail postal services."

In 1979, DeSio and four partners each invested $100,000 to open a store called "U. S. Mailboxes," in LaCosta, California. Like the post office, the store rented post office boxes, sold stamps and shipped packages. It also offered services that the post office did not, such as 24-hour access to boxes, suite-number addresses for small businesses, and call-in service to customers wanting to check on their mail and packages.

Business Growth

Soon after U. S. Mailboxes opened, DeSio expanded the store's offerings and began supplying such business support services as printing, copying, and telephone messages. DeSio later introduced telegram, fax and telex service as well. "The public loved the idea from the beginning," DeSio reports.

Spurred by the business' popularity, the partners looked for funding to expand. "We believed we had a viable concept, and we took our plan to venture capitalists and banks," DeSio said. "They wouldn't listen to us—

some even laughed at our idea. I think it was too new and different for them."

DeSio and his partners were determined to raise the money they needed, and they decided to franchise the business as a way to raise capital. They opened the first Mail Boxes Etc. (MBE) franchise in Solana Beach, California in November 1980. Three additional San Diego-area stores soon followed. "We then expanded to Florida when a San Diego resident who was moving there wanted to open a store," DeSio remembers. "People saw this as an idea whose time had come."

In 1983, DeSio and one of his partners bought out the other co-founders. In 1984, the company recorded its first annual profit on sales of $1.1 million. Revenues rose to $2.2 million in 1985.

DeSio took the company public in 1986, raising $5.1 million and boosting the company's total assets to $10.25 million. By April of that year, MBE had 266 franchises.

The company earned revenues of $9.4 million in 1987 and $12.5 million in 1988. By 1988, MBE had grown to 572 franchises and expanded into the Canadian market. In 1989, the company established its first Japanese outlet and posted sales of $19.3 million. The company has also been recognized as a top franchise by *Black Enterprise, Entrepreneur* and *Success* magazines.

Today, 1,500 Mail Boxes Etc. franchises operate in 48 states, Puerto Rico, Canada, Japan and Mexico, with Master Licenses awarded to open centers in Jamaica and Spain. The company is the country's largest supplier of postal, business and communications services and is five times the size of its closest competitor. DeSio reports a new MBE franchise opens each business day.

Business Obstacles

DeSio and his partners struggled to attract customers to their first store. "The people who came in gave us rave reviews, but many people had no idea we were there," DeSio says. "We didn't have much money to spend on promotion, so we had to be creative. We knocked on doors, hung flyers and handed out leaflets. We depended on word of mouth for a lot of our business," he says.

"I was working 80-hour weeks, and we were just getting by," DeSio recalled. "It was long and exhausting work, and the business didn't seem to be going anywhere. I certainly gained a fast appreciation for what it takes to be out on your own."

DeSio calls his 1983 buyout of his partners "one of the scariest decisions I've ever made. By 1983, we had about 100 units but we were still just breaking even," he said. "There were months we took little or no salary and some of the partners got discouraged and wanted out." To come up with the money he needed to buy the business, DeSio signed a personal guarantee on everything he owned, including his wife's jewelry.

"This was a turning point in my life and my career. I was risking the nest egg I'd built over almost 30 years. If I didn't have a wife who believed in me, I could not have done it," he says.

While the decision was difficult, DeSio says that he never considered abandoning MBE. "I had invested three years of my life in the business, and I truly believed the concept was a good one. The risks were great, but together my wife and I made the decision to go forward. Neither of us really knew what would happen, but we weren't going to let go of our dream."

Keys to Success

DeSio saw an opportunity to provide a service that the Postal Service could not offer. He bet correctly that people would visit a store that offered an alternative, and he found a public eager to embrace his idea.

From the beginning, DeSio has insisted that he is not in competition with the U. S. Postal Service. "We see ourselves not as competitors, but as retail centers in partnership with the Postal Service. They really do provide good service. But customers today are primarily looking for convenience," he says. DeSio reports that the Postal Service has attempted to copy some of MBE's concepts. "They've come into our centers and taken photos with our permission. They see what we're doing and they're interested in learning how to improve the quality of their service," he says.

DeSio has successfully tailored MBE services to meet customer needs. "Although the initial concept was a hit, we realized that we had to expand our service mix to keep people coming back," he says. "Our customers were small business people, consultants, manufacturers' representatives, multi-level marketing types and other people who didn't need an office, but needed a base from which to operate. We gave them the services they needed," he says. DeSio calls today's MBE "the 7-Eleven of postal services. We're a one-stop office service center," he says.

The company's most significant growth step was the decision to franchise, DeSio says. "The venture capitalists' refusal to fund our growth was actually a good thing because it forced us into franchising. We originally did it to raise money, but it became clear that this business was made for franchising. It worked like a dream."

DeSio is committed to helping his franchisors succeed. Owners attend training courses at "MBE University" in San Diego and receive ongoing business assistance from MBE corporate. "A good franchisor has to have the drive and motivation to promote the store because promotion is the lifeblood of this business. You have to be willing to go out and meet people and sell yourself. If you wait for customers to come to you, you will be beaten by the competition," DeSio says.

MBE's president says that his company's size keeps it ahead of the competition. "We have developed a national reputation that our competitors simply can't match," he says. "We have proven that our concept can be duplicated and we now can take advantage of the economies of scale that our international network of franchises offers."

Future Vision

DeSio believes that the public's appetite for MBE's services will continue to grow. "Social trends are escalating demand for what we offer. As more women enter the worldwide workforce, and as people lead busier lives, fewer people have the time to socialize in post office lines," he says. "People today are more willing than ever to spend disposable income on convenience, and they are placing a higher premium on time."

DeSio foresees a shrinking number of players in the offices services market. "Today there are a lot of mom-and-pop stores and a few small chains offering what we do. Eventually the market will be pared to two or three big chains." DeSio is confident that MBE will be one of them. "We want to capture the lion's share," he says.

"We intend to become the 'Federal Express' of our business," he adds. DeSio expects to have 5,000 franchises by the year 2000. "Someday there will be a Mail Boxes store on every corner," he says.

Entrepreneurial Lessons

Working for himself has brought different demands and rewards than those DeSio experienced while working for others. He says that his entrepreneurial experiences have taught him lessons about business, and about himself.

"The fact that this business is mine has given me a much higher interest in my work," DeSio says. "I feel in control of my own destiny, and I see clearly how my performance will result in the success or failure of the whole. You definitely work harder when you work for yourself. I used to play a lot more golf when I was working for someone else," he says. "As a manager, I think I am more frugal. I think less about appearance and more about results—it all hits closer to home."

DeSio encourages others who want to start a business to look for a marketable opportunity. "I hear people say that there aren't any ideas left for new businesses, but I see a world of needs out there. The key is to find something that the public wants and supply it." DeSio cautions would-be entrepreneurs that dedication and commitment are essential to success. "Once you decide what your business will be, you have to build it with a positive attitude. You have to keep telling yourself that you will be successful, and you must be willing to make the necessary sacrifices."

References

"Annual Francise 500." *Entrepreneur*, January 1991.

Bonasia, J. "The Check is in the Mail for Local Resident." *The Del Mar Citizen and LaCostan*, August 5, 1987.

Garrett, Echo M. "Mailbox Missionary." *Success*, March 1990.

Gibson, D. "Mail Boxes Etc. Leads Burgeoning Private Mail Industry." *Investor's Daily*, August 23, 1989.

Greco, G. "Addressing the Demands of a Pressured Public." *Entrepreneur*, September 1987.

"Keys to Ensuring Success in Your New Franchise Operation." *Business Opportunities Journal*, June 6, 1987.

"Mail Boxes Etc. Expands into Spain." *The San Diego Union*, April 16, 1991.

"Straight Talk About Competition and Alternate Delivery." *Postal Life*, October-November 1989.

"SUCCESS Survey Winners—The Top 10 Business Service Francishes." *Success,* March 1991.

Thompson, Kevin D. "Breaking New Ground." *Black Enterprise,* September 1990.

——M. J. B.

Samuel Edelman
Louise Edelman

Sam & Libby, Inc.

Samuel Edelman: Born 1952.
Louise Edelman: Born 1954. Married, three children.
Venture: Started a company that markets a line of women's leather shoes.
Company: Sam & Libby, Inc.; 1123 Industrial Rd.; Suite C; San Carlos, CA 94070; (415) 598-9211
Founded: 1987.
Revenues: $100 million projected sales (1991), according to a company source.
Employees: 85.
Original Investment: $350,000 plus.
Value: $1 million net worth, according to 1990 published reports.

Founders

The shoe business seems to run in the Edelman family: Sam Edelman is the third generation of his family to work in the industry. After graduating from college, Edelman rose to vice president-sales at Lighthouse Footwear, the family business, and served in a similar capacity at Horse Shoes, Inc. Next he stepped up to executive vice president of Kenneth Cole before becoming president of the shoe division of Esprit. There he hired his wife Libby as his merchandise manager.

Louise B. "Libby" Edelman earned a B.A. in journalism and was a model editor for *Harper's Bazaar* as well as a fashion editor for *Seventeen Magazine*.

She worked for Calvin Klein as director of public relations before joining Esprit.

The couple met in New York in 1978 and married in 1980. While working together at Esprit, the Edelmans became involved in all phases of the shoe business. Together they built Esprit's shoe division sales to $55 million. In 1987, they decided to go it alone. Sam & Libby, Inc. was born.

The Edelmans' three children are included in the business in many ways. When possible the couple takes one or all of them on business trips. The children are included in personal appearances and appear on posters and ads. The Edelmans combine shoes with image, and that image includes working and playing with their children. Says Libby, "People immediately see we're a working couple, we have a family. I think we typify what's happening."

Business Origin

Sam and Libby Edelman brought many years of experience as well as a reputation for success to the creation of Sam & Libby shoes. The personal success and exposure they gained during their careers at Esprit proved to be extremely valuable to the couple when they launched their own business. Footwear designer Kenneth Cole explains, "Sam and Libby are both very close to the consumer, attentive to her. What they have brought to the industry is a responsiveness to the market place that apparently was very badly needed."

To get their business started the couple literally put everything on the line, selling their Porsche, a prize show horse, and some property to raise $350,000. The Edelmans used that money to design their first collection of shoes in Italy, buy a used computer software system, rent office space and furniture, set up an office in Brazil where some of their shoes are manufactured (others are made in Taiwan), and hire a production person and an assistant.

Business Growth

In the company's infancy, Sam was fearful. He played the role of the pragmatist and lost a great deal of sleep worrying that they would lose the company as well as their possessions. Libby was the optimist, never doubting success. Success came quicker than either Sam or Libby imagined, however. First year sales hit $7 million. The company was profitable from its first year and enjoys a 15 percent operating margin. Sam believes, "First year sales could have been more than $14 million if we hadn't spent so much time raising money." In 1989 sales reached $40-$50 million.

Within a year of its inception, Sam & Libby shoes were being shipped to every major city in the country. The company's shoes were being sold in many fine department stores including Macy's, Bloomingdale's, Burdines, Belk, Nordstrom and Dayton Hudson. Bloomingdale's even created a special Sam & Libby boutique in its flagship New York store. Many of these stores are now also featuring Sam & Libby children's shoes. Immediately successful, the children's line generated sales of over 100,000 pairs to 100 accounts in a few months.

In just two years, Sam & Libby, Inc. made an impressive mark on the contemporary footwear market. It has combined innovative shoe designs, quality and affordable style to achieve its success. Although the company has relied on department store business for growth, promotional campaigns that began in 1990 have also been aimed at the independent stores. Promotion and marketing have been the key to growth at Sam & Libby.

Business Obstacles

The Edelmans' biggest business problem was raising necessary capital in the beginning stages of their venture. Underestimating the capital needed to keep the business running, Sam and Libby quickly learned that many bankers were not interested in backing a "husband-and-wife" business. Smith-Barney's venture capital group warned the couple that they would never see $7 million in annual sales. "The story was the same with each of them. Because we were a couple, we were not considered a good risk," Sam recalled. "Our rejection has made me very critical of the venture capital community for not viewing married couples as possessing an enormous amount of potential." In Sam's opinion, the couple made a real mistake by not starting a banking relationship earlier. Eventually they found a bank that agreed to a small loan against the company's receivables. Ultimately Sam and Libby had to turn to Sam's parents for a loan "in six figures." Sam & Libby, Inc. was then truly on its way.

Keys to Success

The quick success of Sam & Libby, Inc. seems due to several significant factors. The Edelmans themselves have very different business abilities, and possess complementary strengths. Sam is adept at sales and finance, while Libby is strong in design, marketing and public relations.

The Edelmans feel another secret to their success is a shared vision for their business. Sam says, "We're doing something we really believe in and people believe in us." Libby agrees, "We have our differences, but when it comes to making important decisions, we find that we share the same goals and tastes." She finds occasional disagreements healthy and necessary for improvements and a better run business. During the shaky early months of their business, Libby's optimism and belief in their success served to balance the fears that haunted Sam. That balance was an important factor in their journey toward success.

The Edelmans view entwining their children in their business life as not only important, but advantageous. They don't feel the need to shelter their children from business discussions since business is their life and including their children is necessary and beneficial.

Another key to making it work is the Edelmans' ability to keep quality up and cost down. The shoes are made in Brazil and Taiwan where low-cost labor and high-quality leather are plentiful. "Because of how and where we manufacture, there's no difference in longevity or quality between a $35 pair of our shoes and anyone else's $80 pair, and at our prices, women can afford to be daring," explains Sam.

While Sam and Libby head the company, they credit their employees with being the energy behind it all. Sam told *Footwear News*, "Libby and I were ready to take the gamble to start our own company, but the people in our company really make it work." He later added, "The best thing about Sam & Libby is the energy of the people. When you walk into Sam & Libby everyone's running around with a smile on their face. The people who work for us believe in our vision."

Future Vision

At Sam & Libby, "We have only scratched the surface," Sam Edelman says. Men's shoes were introduced in August 1990. The Edelmans also plan to accessorize body parts other than feet. Sam & Libby, Inc.'s products will be expanded to apparel, hosiery, handbags, belts, jewelry and watches. Athletic products are also contemplated. As Libby puts it, "I guess we just want to do everything."

Entrepreneurial Lessons

Sam Edelman believes the biggest single mistake an entrepreneur can make is blindly listening to other people. "If somebody says you're going into the worst business in the world, don't believe them. Find out for yourself," he told *Entrepreneur*.

In Sam and Libby's opinion, their time at Esprit contributed to their own company's success. Esprit, says Libby, gave them the opportunity to learn about style, service and relating to other people. It also gave them a chance to make mistakes and learn from them so they would not be repeated. The Edelmans feel fortunate to have worked for great entrepreneurs before going off on their own.

As Sam told *Footwear News*, "To have a business, you have to either involve the family or divorce the family, so the whole family is involved." Libby added, "The best thing about working together is sharing the same concerns, knowing the same people and making the same sacrifices."

The relationship Sam and Libby share is a vital part of their successful business. "What I've learned from our enterprise about our relationship is as enriching and as important as any financial gains we might get from it," Sam explained in *New Age Journal*. "Libby and I have more belief and more loyalty for each other than just 'best friends,' and that's what keeps us going."

References

"Cheap Thrills from Sensible Shoes." *People*, Spring 1990.

Rottman, Meg. "Sam & Libby." *Footwear News*, November/December 1989.

Silverman, Dick. "At Sam & Libby It's All in the Family." *Footwear News*, August 12, 1991.

Slovak, Julianne. "Sam & Libby California." *Fortune*, April 9, 1990.

Turk, Rose-Marie. "'Thirtysomething' Fits Shoe-design Couple." *Los Angeles Times*, May 20, 1988.

"Unlimited Partners." *New Age Journal*, March/April 1989.

Weinstein, Bob. "An Entrepreneurial Couple Breaks the Mold When It Comes to Mixing Love, Marriage and Business." *Business Week Newsletter For Family Owned Business*, July 1990.

———. "Beyond the Boardroom." *Entrepreneur*, July 1990.

Bruce L. Engel

WTD Industries, Inc.

Bruce L. Engel: Born 1940. Married, five children.
Venture: Starting from a single sawmill, Engel created WTD Industries, Inc., a wood products holding company engaged in the manufacture and sale of softwood and hardwood lumber and by-products.
Company: WTD Industries, Inc.; 10260 S.W. Greenburg Road; Suite 900; Portland, OR 97223; (503) 246-9570
Founded: Founded 1982. Incorporated in Oregon, 1983.
Revenues: $243.9 million in net sales in fiscal 1991, according to company sources.
Employees: 1,200 plus.
Original Investment: $3,000 and the assumption of a $2 million debt.
Value: $40 million, according to published reports (February 1990).

Founder

Engel grew up on a farm outside of Alsea, Oregon. The family was never wealthy and his father eventually had to sell his land. The first family member to attend college, he graduated from Portland's Reed College in 1961 and the University of Chicago School of Law in 1965.

Turning down offers from several eastern law firms, he returned to Portland to start a corporate law practice. Bored with law after practicing for over 17 years, he decided to change careers. "When you're a business lawyer, you have frustrations that your clients don't really want business advice and they make mistakes. That was a major factor in getting me into business," says Engel.

In 1982, after representing three of the six owners of a troubled sawmill in Glide, Oregon, Engel bought the mill as an investment. Believing he could succeed where others had failed, he planned to sell the mill when the market improved. "I was going to do what none of my clients ever did—sell mills when times are good. But two things happened. First, good times never came, and second, what we were doing worked so well that we continued to expand the company," Engel explains.

A basic tenet of Engel's business philosophy goes back to his farming roots. "Every time I get involved in something, I want to grow it," he says.

Business Origin

Engel incorporated WTD Industries, Inc. in January of 1983, and proceeded to buy struggling or bankrupt mills at advantageous prices during a serious recession in the timber industry. Over 100 Oregon mills were closed, causing 10,000 workers to be out of jobs. "Have you ever heard the expression 'the best of times is the worst of times, and the worst of times is the best of times'?" Engel asks. For Engel, entering the timber industry's recessionary environment proved wise. Because the status quo wasn't working, the time was right to take risks and to learn. "You'll do things in the worst of times that you wouldn't ever think of doing in the good times," asserts Gerard R. Griffin, the company's vice-president of corporate development.

Creative financing was crucial to business growth. On some early loans, Engel convinced bankers to accept a share of the mill's lumber production in lieu of monetary debt service payments. He used his cash to service additional loans and buy more mills.

An important early decision was to concentrate the business in second-growth timber (younger and smaller logs). He viewed old-growth timber as the sunset portion of the industry. Most of Engel's mills are set up to convert second-growth timber and logs that other competitors are not equipped to process. As a result, the company has more flexibility in the kind of log it buys, and can usually find supplies even when timber is scarce.

When access to capital continued to be a problem, Engel took the company public in 1986. He sold 42 percent of the company for $24 million. Engel now owns about 40 percent of the stock. The NASDAQ-traded stock earned $1.40 per share in 1989, the seventh straight year of earnings increases. "Going public moved us from being an entrepreneurial start-up company, towards a well-financed corporation," Griffin maintains.

Business Growth

With 14 mills operating in several states, WTD markets and sells its products through its completely-owned subsidiary, Treesource, Inc. Treesource sells to all major U.S. markets and Canada, and is expanding into Europe, Australia and the Far East. Having a centralized distribution system keeps delivery problems and costs to a minimum.

"We began WTD with the premise that productivity, attendance and safety in the work place, coupled with reasonable capital cost of operating assets and rational purchasing of raw materials would work to make us a strong and viable player in the industry," says Engel.

Business Obstacles

"Engel's greatest obstacle in the early days was lack of capital, so he learned to do without. When it began to impede growth, he took the company public," Griffin recalls. Older timber executives caution that Engel is carrying too much debt for the long haul, but neither Engel nor his corporate development specialist agree. "The company carries a high debt, because it has been oriented to building a large base of capacity. If we wanted to, we could pay it off in three years," Griffin believes.

Engel also faced stiff criticism from tradition-bound industry giants, who called his methods unorthodox and short-sighted. Griffin disagrees with those who label Engel a maverick, however.

"He's not just bucking the system. He is a man who is seeking to succeed by the most timely and cost-effective means. He chose not to do it like everyone else has done it, because he believed in his method," says Griffin.

The nature of the timber business itself presents problems, sensitive as it is to changes in the economy and federal and state environmental policies. High log prices and scarce timber are currently squeezing WTD's margins. A controversy over the northern spotted owl, which environmentalists claim cannot exist outside of the old-growth forests of Washington and Oregon, has caused the government to issue a ban against commercial log harvesting in some public areas. While WTD buys approximately 70 percent of its logs from the open market and not from old-growth public lands, the log shortage resulting from the ban impacts on the company indirectly.

"As the woodbasket shrinks on public lands, more companies are now competing with us for open-market timber, thus driving up the price and narrowing the profit margins," explains Griffin. With environmentalists pushing for even greater protection of public lands, analysts are expecting some shake-out of higher-priced producers in the timber industry.

"It is the company's only goal to be the low-cost and best producer in the industry, and we're getting very close," says Griffin. To do that, WTD is adjusting its strategies away from expansion and towards internal restructuring.

A setback occurred in January 1991, when WTD filed for protection under Chapter 11 bankruptcy laws. In September 1991, a Plan of Reorganization was filed. Engel cited "extreme adverse conditions in our industry combined with severe weather conditions" as the reason the company failed to meet debt covenants. *National Home Center News* quoted a WTD employee as saying, "WTD was started with a long-term view. We haven't closed up shop."

Keys to Success

"The key ingredient to WTD's success has always been in finding and fitting the right people to the organization," says Griffin. "Engel has the ability to ferret out the winners in the industry and to get them to join the team. Then he creates an atmosphere in which an individual can do his best. If you do that, all else falls into place," Griffin adds.

From the beginning, Engel's business practices have been non-traditional. He attributes the phenomenal growth of WTD to three basic strategies. First, he maintains margins by purchasing logs and converting them immediately into lumber that he can sell profitably on the open market. Other industry giants carry substantial log inventories or lock themselves into long-range buying contracts because timber shortages could cause plant shut-downs. By buying cheaper logs on the open market (usually no more than a two-three week supply), Engel can sell his lumber for less and still make a profit.

"Engel came up with the just-in-time inventory concept out of necessity. It was the only one that fit our needs. We couldn't afford to own a lot of timber land or buy high-priced logs," says Griffin. "The lumber business should be geared to the short-term. Prices can change dramatically in 30 days, requiring flexible production practices," asserts Engel.

Engel's second principle is using leverage to acquire new production capacity at reasonable capital costs. While his competitors move into the high-tech world of computers, Engel only upgrades facilities in the proportion to which the improvements will upgrade profits. He believes strongly that workers, not electronic gadgets, make a company productive.

His third principle is to increase productivity through employee incentive plans. Engel's mills are non-union, but he says that his workers make more than union workers when bonuses (averaging $3 an hour) are included.

When WTD Industries buys a mill, Engel does not change the name of the company. He wants the workers to think of it as their mill, to take pride in ownership and to make it work. "In many ways, Engel views business as a game, with himself as the coach," Griffin explains. "He welcomes employees as part of the team. We're working with narrow margins and we need turned-on labor to win." So seriously does Engel take the teamwork concept, that he expects every mill to field a softball team and take part in an annual corporate tournament each summer. "He really believes that the way a person plays on the ball field is an accurate reflection of how they work or live," adds Griffin.

One of his trademarks is to fly from mill to mill, and personally to hand weekly bonuses to shift-workers based on attendance, safety and higher-than-expected productivity. Managers, clerical staff and salaried personnel also receive bonuses based on monthly profits from their mill or region.

Some have criticized Engel's labor-management program for its lack of long-term benefits like a pension plan. A 1987 research report by the brokerage firm of Piper Jaffray & Hopwood, Inc. found that WTD "employees exhibit a high degree of enthusiasm, and turnover has been quite low." In some mills, production jumped by over 50 percent per shift once WTD took over.

Future Vision

Griffin notes that WTD Industries will be changing its focus in the next couple of years to adapt to major changes in the industry. With 1.9 billion board feet of capacity, the company will no longer be looking to acquire new properties. "Instead we'll be staffing up the company, making some capital improvements and working on getting the most product from our raw materials before we think about expanding again," says Griffin.

WTD plans to concentrate on recovery, overrun and productivity as the cornerstones for producing the most lumber at the least cost.

They plan to use thinner saws, and change the way a log is cut, to "recover" more lumber from each log. Decreasing the time a log must travel through the mill will also increase productivity and profits.

The company reached its eighth consecutive year of sales increases in 1990 ($460 million), but future earnings could go down, due to dramatically changing times.

"The plan we are working out will contribute to the first fiscal year in WTD's history that earnings will not exceed the prior year. But these moves will position the company for improved earnings . . . ," says Engel.

Eventually, WTD plans to construct a $450 million pulp mill at Port Westward, Oregon which would convert wood chips (one of the company's by-products) to bleached kraft market pulp for the export market. WTD is in the process of acquiring the necessary permits and a joint-venture partner for the project.

Entrepreneurial Lessons

Griffin describes Engel as being naturally inquisitive and "someone who is driven to divining the secret of what makes something work." It is a trait that has led him into a host of other ventures besides WTD Industries. In 1988 he took control of the troubled American Guaranty Financial Corporation. He has also owned radio stations, bowling alleys, small technology businesses, financed a recording of the Oregon Symphony and attempted to buy the Seattle Mariners baseball team.

He is often asked to speak to the question of what makes a person successful, says Griffin. "Engel tells audiences that . . . 'Life is simple. You read, you observe and you do. Then you practice and practice until you get it right'," Griffin relates. He is a confirmed sportsman and intense about winning.

On a recent trip to New York, Engel saw a sign in an office that he admired. Running down a large poster board, the lines read, 'It can't be done . . . It can't be done . . . It can't be done . . . It can't be done . . . It's done!' "I'd say that attitude summarizes the man," says Griffin.

References

Arnold, David. "Risky Business." *The Sunday Oregonian Magazine*, August 21, 1988.

Engel, Bruce. "Why the All-Star Mills?" *The Millwriter*, Summer 1989.

Gauntt, Tom. "Engel Seizes Control of American Guaranty." *The Portland Business Journal*, August 15, 1988.

Hill, Robert L. "Mr. Fix-It." *Oregon Business Magazine*, June 1987.

Kadera, Jim. "Attorney Cutting It in Lumber." *The Oregonian*, November 23, 1987.

MacKenzie, Bill. "WTD Plans to Build Kraft Pulp Mill Near Clatskaie." *The Oregonian*, August 20, 1988.

Major, Michael J. "The Return of Paul Bunyan." *OTC Review*, January 1989.

Northman, Tod. "WTD Reports Seventh Consecutive Year of Record Earnings and Sales." *Western Investor*, Summer 1989.

Ruderman, Gary. "Fast Rise of Lumber Producer Leads to Speedy Decline." *National Home Center News*, August 5, 1991.

Willoughby, Jack. "Paul Bunyan in Pinstripes." *Forbes*, April 6, 1987.

WTD Industries, Inc., Annual Report, 1989.

——L.R.

Debbi Fields

Mrs. Fields' Cookies, Inc.

Debbi Fields: Born 1956. Married, four children.
Venture: Establishment of a chain of fresh-baked cookies and baked goods stores in shopping malls.
Company: Mrs. Fields' Cookies, Inc.; 333 Main St.; Park City, UT 84060; (801) 649-1304
Founded: 1977.
Revenues: $118 million in 1989, according to company sources.
Employees: 5,000 plus.
Original Investment: $50,000.
Value: $44 million net worth, according to published reports.

Founder

Growing up in East Oakland, California, Debbi Fields remembers wanting to stand out instead of being just the youngest of five sisters. Never an outstanding student, she found satisfaction in making the best chocolate chip cookies around. Fields never dreamed she would sell her cookies throughout the U.S., Canada, Japan, Hong Kong, and Great Britain.

As a teenager, Fields discovered work as a way to feel good about herself. Her first job, ball girl for the Oakland A's, helped her feel comfortable in front of crowds. At 15, Fields worked at Mervyn's department store part time, earning recognition for her customer-pleasing efforts and organization of her department.

Fields graduated high school with the intention of skiing every possible minute and working when she ran out of money. She met her husband,

Randy Fields, in the Denver airport after a ski trip and they married in 1975.

Randy was a child prodigy, a whiz with stocks and bonds by age 12. He graduated from Stanford with a M. A. in political science at age 21 and worked as a consultant to *Fortune* 100 companies.

The Fields firmly believe businesses should return something to the community. Mrs. Fields' Cookies is one of the major corporate supporters of research to find a cure for cystic fibrosis, giving millions over the past several years.

Business Origin

Mrs. Fields' Cookies began out of Debbi's need to do something with her life. At 19, she needed more than part-time classes and serving her warm cookies during Randy's important meetings. Although executives would call ahead to make sure Debbi would be baking cookies that day, they unanimously pooh-poohed her idea of selling them in a store.

"It'll never work," said marketing specialists, her family, Randy's family, and her friends. Bankers rejected the idea and refused to loan the couple money. Finally their home mortgage banker made the loan, although he thought the business would flop. "At least you'll know where she is every day," the banker consoled Randy. "And it'll be a terrific tax shelter."

Debbi opened Mrs. Fields' Chocolate Chippery in Liddicoat's, a revamped arcade of specialty shops in Palo Alto, California in 1977. Her cookies were much larger than people were used to, and were served warm from the oven on a napkin. They cost twenty-five cents—because of the high-quality ingredients—at a time when cookies usually sold for nine cents each.

Her first day almost became her last. Randy had bet her that she wouldn't have fifty dollars in the till by the end of the day. At noon, not one cookie had been sold.

Determined, Fields called a friend to work in the store and went out on the street looking for customers. She gave away all her unsold cookies and went back to bake more. Soon those people came looking for her and bought cookies. At the end of the day, Fields had exactly fifty dollars in the till.

Business Growth

The little cookie store developed loyal customers. Fields insisted that everyone be greeted, complimented or asked a question, and walk away with a smile.

A few months after opening, she was offered a spot in a new shopping mall in San Francisco by a devoted customer. Fields declined, not wanting to expand. A year later, the Pier 39 agent called again to say they were still holding a spot for her. "Pier 39 was holding out for *my* business," wrote Fields in her autobiography, *One Smart Cookie.*

Her employees wanted to open the new store, to give them a chance for more responsibility and increased salaries. To deny them the chance would have "ruined the business," she decided.

A few weeks after opening, the Pier 39 management demanded that Fields do something about the crowds around her store. "At this point, if I hadn't had Randy, I would have had to invent him," says Fields. "But there he was, one of the best business consultants in the world who also just happened to be my husband."

Although busy with his own businesses, Randy developed the computerized management system that allows Fields to maintain centralized control of all the stores. The system, called Retail Operations Intelligence (ROI), won the 1991 Optimas Award in the Innovation category, annually presented by *Personnel Journal* (*PJ*). So successful was the system that Fields Software Group Inc. was formed to market ROI. "We have used technology to free employees to be with customers," Randy told *PJ*.

Fields resisted franchising her business. "Mrs. Fields Cookies was not created specifically to make a profit. I can't imagine a franchisee buying into it for any other reason," she says. The caring and love she puts into the business couldn't be duplicated by franchisees who would be looking at the bottom line. "Debbi's been a genius at getting people to care and own and represent the quality of that which we put out on the front counter. . . . That's what led to the brand name," Randy told *Bakery Production and Marketing.*

Business Obstacles

With three stores running and more in the works, Fields "hit the wall." "I was twenty-two years old and working sixteen hours a day, rushing madly from store to store, trying to keep everything going right and under control. The cookie business had become a monster, demanding and demanding, slowly sapping my energy," she remembers.

Desperate for help, she offered half the business to a friend, then told Randy. He vetoed the plan. "Don't do it," he told her. "We'll find a way to survive."

They had to open new stores because the opportunity and demand for her cookies wouldn't wait. Going into more debt meant visiting more bankers who perceived soft cookies as a soft business. The Fields decided to sell the rights to Mrs. Fields Cookies outside California—but no one would buy. Now they're glad no one took them up on it.

Slowly, with the help of talented employees, the burdens became easier. By 1981, there were 14 stores. Trying to break into the big league shopping centers, the Fields built a $90,000 prototype store and gave away $8,000 worth of cookies at a 1983 convention. Landlords and development companies were converted, opening doors for Mrs. Fields' Cookies into new malls across the country.

In 1988, according to *Forbes*, the company closed 97 stores and posted a $19 million net loss for the year. Stores in locations that did not do well were closed.

"We made the decision to focus on bakeries as our strategy going forward" says Fields. The company turned around to profitability the next year, and opened 35 stores in 1990.

Annoying rumors dog the company: that the Fields are going bankrupt, that they are getting a divorce, that Debbi is dying, or that the company cheated a customer after promising to sell her the recipe for chocolate chip cookies. The story is impossible, Fields says. No one knows the recipe for her famous cookies except Debbi herself.

Keys to Success

Her early work experiences taught Fields that people crave service and attention, and respond by purchasing something. She began to develop her philosophy of making excitement behind the sales counter as a way to entice customers into coming back for more.

Whether it's a contest to see who can give the most cookies away or a round of "Chippety-do-dah," employees are supposed to make Mrs. Fields a fun place to be.

The products continue to be made of the best and often most expensive ingredients, no matter what the current price of raisins, macadamia nuts or butter. Cookies more than two hours old are donated to charity.

Mrs. Fields employees are chosen for their enthusiasm, winning personalities and love of fun. A corporate accountant may find himself working with the construction crew or flying to Florida to bake cookies for a few days on one of Fields' safaris. "I like corporate employees to work in the stores, so they get to know what's happening there and what it all means," says Fields.

Each store sets a daily sales goal, just like Fields did her first day in Palo Alto, pitting employee vs. employee and store against store. Sales data is transmitted to Utah headquarters each evening where it is analyzed and downloaded back to field supervisors at 8:00 A.M. the next day. The sales leader will receive a congratulatory call from Fields or another manager, along with encouragement to do even better.

The store computer uses sales histories to decide what kind of cookies should be made and sold each quarter hour. It tells the manager how much sales help he will need. The manager must update the computer with what's happening at the cash register each hour, forcing him to be aware of how sales are doing.

Future Vision

"We plan to continue to grow," says Fields. "We never want to grow to be biggest, we just want to do what we do best. Our focus will be on quality and customer service." That commitment to quality and customer service has now been carried over to TCBY Frozen Yogurt outlets through an agreement placing Mrs. Fields Cookies in several hundred TCBY stores.

She foresees continued growth in the cookie business as well as in neighborhood bakeries. The retailer of the future has to discover how to spend more time with each customer, although there will be fewer service people to take care of customers. Through its computerization, Mrs. Fields is building the technology to allow greater efficiency.

"In merchandising and packaging, we see tremendous opportunities to take fresh quality products and serve and sell them in a way that is fun, festive, and creates a happy, feel-good feeling," says Fields. "We intend to initiate a birthday club and a kids' pack, something special just for kids."

"It is not our intention to change our recipes, but it is our intention to build products that customers want. Those will be great tasting and some will have to be good for you."

Entrepreneurial Lessons

Fields looks for a lesson in every failure, whether it is with an employee promoted beyond his or her capability or a new muffin recipe that bombed. She believes that failures can lead to course corrections that ultimately lead her closer to her goals.

She discovered that trying out your ideas can be a lonely challenge. "Once you find something you want to do, people will say you can't—and it will be an overwhelming response. Your friends and family will say 'do something safe,' like work for somebody else."

Finding what you love to do makes success possible. Fields says she did not set out to make lots of money, but to make the best cookies she could.

References

Fichtner, M. "Debbi Fields Has Turned a Beloved American Institution into a $70-Million-a-Year Business." *Miami Herald,* November 21, 1986.

Fields, Debra. *One Smart Cookie.* New York: Simon & Schuster, 1987.

Filipowski, Diane "1991 Optimas Awards: Innovation." *Personnel Journal,* January 1991.

Garrison, Bob. "Transition Team." *Bakery Production and Marketing,* April 24, 1990.

Kerwin, Kathleen. "Blowing the Lid Off Mrs. Fields." *Detroit Free Press,* April 13, 1987.

"Mrs. Fields Automates the Way the Cookie Sells." *Chain Store Age Executive,* April 1988.

"Mrs. Fields, Yogurt Concern in License Agreement." *Milling & Baking News,* September 17, 1991.

Schember, Jack. "Mrs. Fields' Secret Weapon." *Personnel Journal,* September 1991.

Silver, A. David. "Debbi Fields." *Entrepreneurial Megabucks: The 100 Greatest Entrepreneurs of the Last 25 Years and How They Did It.* New York: Wiley, 1985.

Stein, J. "The Chips Never Seem to Be Down for the Smiling Founder of the Multimillion-Dollar Food Empire." *Los Angeles Times,* October 16, 1987.

Walkowitz, R. "Whipping Up Quite a Cookie Business." *The Atlanta Journal and Constitution,* July 13, 1990.

Weisman, Katherine. "Succeeding by Failing." *Forbes,* June 25, 1990.

Austin O. Furst, Jr.

Vestron, Inc.

Austin O. Furst, Jr.: Born 1943. Married, three children.
Venture: Home video and motion picture production and distribution. Also owned video cassette rental stores.
Company: Vestron, Inc.
Founded: 1981.
Original Investment: Unknown.
Value: Sold to Live Entertainment in 1990.

Founder

Austin O. Furst, Jr., was a 1966 graduate of Lehigh University in Bethlehem, Pennsylvania, where he majored in economics and marketing. His career path first took him to Procter and Gamble as a staff assistant in promotion development. After short stays with Compusamp and Metromedia, he took a position with Time, Inc. as circulation manager for *People* magazine in the early 1970s. The next 10 years with Time took him to the company's other subsidiaries, notably Home Box Office and Time-Life Films, of which he became president.

Business Origin

Time's film division was losing money, and the job of shutting it down fell to Furst. The last assets to be sold off were the home video rights to their collection of films. Time, Inc. was certain that the future lay in cable and pay TV. When Furst approached them to buy the home video rights for a

153

relative pittance, Time was happy to unload what seemed to be dead weight. Furst got the rights for 20 years on a contingency basis. Most of the more than 200 titles were never released. Some notable films—*Fort Apache-the Bronx* with Paul Newman and *They All Laughed* directed by Peter Bogdanovich—were included. The purchase required Furst to take out a second mortgage on his home and to use his personal savings. The risk paid off as millions of Americans wanted prerecorded videos for their new VCRs.

Furst was 37 at the time. He hired 34-year-old Jon Peisinger from the music industry to be his president and second in command. In the first year Vestron earned $2.2 million on revenues of $12 million. The Time rights accounted for 78 percent of the company's income.

Furst spent months on the phone convincing producers to work with his new distribution company. Furst's big break came when Vestron bought the rights to a collection of Orion Picture's major films for $10 million. Vestron would later pay up to $5 million for a single film's rights.

Business Growth

In 1983, Peisenger's music industry connections enabled Vestron's deal, the *Making Michael Jackson's Thriller* video cassette. With *Thriller*, Vestron practically invented the made-for-home-rock video market. The best-seller brought in over $12 million of that year's $45 million revenue.

Revenue more than doubled again in 1984. By 1985 Wall Street was impressed. With home video gross rentals rivaling movie theater revenues, Vestron announced its initial stock offering. The 1985 offering of 5.4 million shares raised $64.4 million, $31.9 million going to the founding shareholders.

When the video cassette market began to sag in late 1985, Vestron entered the production end of the motion picture business with Vestron Pictures. The company produced a dozen films with budgets of $2 million to $6 million in 1987. One of those films, *Dirty Dancing,* provided the next major break at a time when the company was losing money. By mid-1988 the film grossed $175 million and generated two hit albums, a TV series, and a touring show. *Dirty Dancing* was shot with a non-union crew in right-to-work states for $5.2 million. The major gamble was whether to invest another $6 million to release the film nationally. The gamble paid off.

In its first year in the production business, Vestron received over 5,000 scripts. Most product comes from the castoffs of the major studios. When a project being developed by a studio stalls, it goes into "turnaround." *Dirty Dancing* was among the films produced by Vestron that were picked up from the majors.

Business Obstacles

Vestron's large library of "B" movies eventually began to lose value with a public hungry for top box office films. Two of these top films, *Platoon* and *Hoosiers*, became the focus of a bitter lawsuit when Helmdale Films, the producer, reneged on a deal with Vestron and delivered the films to HBO Video for more money.

Competition heated up as movie producers became aware of the increasing value of videocassette rights and decided to get into the distribution business themselves. Companies like Orion, which had sold rights to Vestron, now held on to them. Prices skyrocketed and Vestron got caught paying too much. The box-office disaster, *Shanghai Surprise* with Madonna, cost Vestron $5 million for the home video rights.

This changing climate set the stage for Vestron's entry into motion picture production as Vestron Pictures. The company reasoned, why pay $5 million for a questionable product when it could produce its own films for the same money? "I always intended to build a distribution company, but I didn't realize that I would have to build a production company to feed it," Furst acknowledged.

In 1985, Furst decided to offer the public 10.8 million Vestron shares at $16 to $19 a share, roughly 25 times the previous year's earnings. Since half of the shares would come from his own holdings, he stood to pocket more than $130 million dollars from his four-year-old company and still own 70 percent.

Forbes described the valuation as "fantasy." *Manhattan, inc.* published a story titled "Burnt Offering" that put Furst's potential windfall at $500 million. Experts questioned how much confidence the founder had in the future of his own company if he planned to cash in immediately. Furst was forced to withdraw his own shares and to cut the price of the stock to $13 for his offering to be acceptable to investors.

An investment banker pointed out, "Unlike the major studios which can fall back on real estate, tours, libraries, or television, Vestron has no ready source of cash flow. There's no margin for error."

This was proven true in October 1988. After Vestron had received a tentative commitment of a $100 million loan from California's Security Pacific Bank, the bank cancelled the loan and Vestron sued. "Our tragic mistake was that we chose the wrong bank to deal with," Furst told *Newsweek*. Vestron could not secure financing after the Security Pacific pullout.

By October 1990, Vestron, "one of the earliest and most important players in the homevideo industry" according to the trade paper *Variety*, was deep in debt. Live Entertainment, a video distributor, proposed acquiring Vestron and the company accepted. Furst took what remained after the acquisition—the lawsuit against Security Pacific—and formed a company called Infovision, whose sole purpose was to reinstate a line of credit and seek compensatory damages.

What went wrong? Furst believes the cancellation of Vestron's $100 million bank loan led to financial problems and to the ultimate sale of his company. However, industry insiders point to other reasons for Vestron's downfall, including the acquisition of a videostore chain that drained assets from the company, acquiring and producing many pictures that were without "legs" (box office staying power), and the inability to get a sequel to *Dirty Dancing* made.

Keys to Success

Vestron's strategy was to budget movies at a maximum of $6 million to avoid expensive mistakes. They also produced a number of under-$2 million quickies as part of their "low budget" division. Vestron shared 25 percent or more of its production costs through limited partnerships that were sold through large syndicators. The investors were largely well-to-do people who wanted to be involved in the "glamour" of the film business.

Austin Furst, Jr., is known to be a shrewd businessman who runs with a streak of luck. By his own admission, "If I'm driving around the block looking for a parking place, it seems like just as I pull up in front of where I'm going, there's always a parking place waiting for me right where I want to be."

The parking place that opened for Austin Furst was the home video revolution. Being in the right place at the right time was a key to success, but keeping that momentum alive was a constant challenge in the volatile film business. "He doesn't sit back and let life happen to him. He's always in there helping to make things happen," his wife Leslie remarked.

"I am highly competitive," says Furst, "I am afraid I am impatient at times, which is not a virtue, but I don't believe in standing around and issuing a lot of orders. I believe in asking a lot of questions."

Furst is an unconventional CEO. He returns his own phone calls and makes his own appoinments. This style is reflected in company traditions, most notably "the gong." As Furst explains, "It is rung by someone why has done a great deed in the company . . . it could be any significant task. The person's colleagues sort of coerce him into ringing the gong, then everybody who hears it immediately wants to know why the gong rang and who did this great thing."

Future Vision

Austin Furst is presently chairman and CEO of his new company, Natural World, Inc. in Connecticut. According to company literature, Natural World "was founded to develop naturally inspired, environmentally responsible consumer products." As he told the *Fairfield County Business Journal*, "We call ourselves a cross between Mary Kay [cosmetics] of environmentally sound skin care and household products with a Land's End catalog approach." Natural World's 90-plus products are ordered by customers through an 800 number or by mail. Field representatives distribute catalogs and answer customer questions.

Furst says that with Natural World, he can combine both work and leisure, adding that his five-year goal for the company is about 10,000 independent sales representatives and hundreds of environmentally safe products.

Entrepreneurial Lessons

For nearly a decade, Austin Furst, Jr. has been willing to go against the odds—a willingness to risk it all. "I like being an entrepreneur, " he said. "There are moments of loneliness and fear and terrible frustration involved with being an entrepreneur, but there are also moments of exhilaration and pride and fun that go with it that are hard to find in normal jobs."

References

Alexander, Max. "Requiem For a Vid Heavyweight." *Variety*, August 1, 1990.

Alexander, Max, and Marc Berman. "Dying Vestron Says 'I Do' To Live Proposal." *Variety*, October 8, 1990.

"Croesus Unbound." *Forbes*, October 7, 1985.

Garr, Doug. "Risky Business." *American Film*, October 1987.

Gubernick, Lisa. "Where's the Payoff." *Forbes*, July 25, 1988.

Hall, Peter. "Austin Furst's Thriller Diller." *FW*, November 27, 1985.

Hammer, Joshua. "The Crash of a Moviemaker." *Newsweek*, September 4, 1989.

"Hitting It Big by Going Out on Your Own." *U.S. News & World Report*, October 21, 1985.

Mathews, Shirley. "Luck Keeps Furst from Being Last." *Stamford Advocate*, October 30, 1988.

Stableford, Joan. "Natural World's Personal Care Line Takes Its Cue From the Environment." *Fairfield County Business Journal*, July 1, 1991.

Video Week, September 2, 1991.

——B. M.

O. Gene Gabbard

Telecom USA, Inc.

O. Gene Gabbard: Born 1940. Married, three children.
Venture: The founding of a company to develop and market fiber optics telecommunications. The original company, SoutherNet, merged with Teleconnect Company in 1988 to become Telecom USA, Inc., the fourth-largest communications company in the United States.
Company: Telecom USA, Inc.; Atlanta, GA
Founded: 1983.
Original Investment: $1 million.
Value: Sold to MCI Communications Corp. in 1990.

Founder

Gene Gabbard, former chairman and chief executive officer of Telecom USA, holds a B.S. degree in electrical engineering from the University of Kentucky (1961) and an M.S. in engineering from the University of Pennsylvania (1965).

His experience in telecommunications began in 1965 with COMSAT Corporation where he oversaw the design and development of digital communications equipment. While employed by COMSAT, Gabbard served on INTELSAT (the organization that represents all U. S. communications companies at the international level) technical committees and worked with International Post, Telegraph and Telephony (an international organization of communications companies) on INTELSAT's worldwide satellite system.

Before founding SoutherNet, Gabbard was founder and vice president of Digital Communications Corporation and vice president of M/A-COM, a major provider of microwave components and assemblies and fiber optic systems. M/A-COM also manufactured microwave radio equipment, satellite communications equipment, CATV equipment and data communications equipment.

In 1983, Gabbard founded SoutherNet, Inc., a regional telecommunications company. In 1988, SoutherNet merged with Teleconnect Company. The new company was incorporated in 1988 under the name of Telecom USA.

Gabbard is a former chairman of National Telecommunications Network (NTN), and serves as a director of Wegener Corporation, DCA Inc., and Health Images, Inc. During his career in the telecommunications industry, Gabbard has acquired numerous patents and published a number of articles in trade and professional publications.

Business Origin

In the early 1980s, when many companies were still focusing on the potential of microwave and satellite technology for long-distance communications, Gene Gabbard realized the industry's future would be in digital transmissions over fiber optics cable. The digital signal is much clearer, and a single hair-thin strand of fiber-optic cable can carry more information than a standard telephone cable containing 16,000 copper wires.

In 1982, Gabbard left M/A-COM to develop fiber optic technology for use in the telecommunications industry. In 1984, joined by two partners who invested a total of $1 million, he founded SoutherNet in Atlanta, Georgia.

Business Growth

To build SoutherNet, Gabbard focused on mid-sized businesses in the southeastern region of the United States. His goal was also to bring fiber optic technology to businesses in medium-sized cities. The majority of the growth effort was aimed toward the acquisition of small long-distance brokers.

In 1986, SoutherNet completed laying 2,200 miles of fiber optic cable. Thirty-eight acquired firms had become part of SoutherNet by 1988.

Although revenues grew rapidly (from $16 million in 1983 to $228 million in 1987), the company incurred losses from 1983-1986, due to expansion costs. However, the company bounced back in 1988, netting $8.7 million.

Recognizing the importance of a toll-free long-distance network, SoutherNet sought a provider of that service. In 1988, Gabbard merged his firm with Teleconnect Company to create Telecom USA, the fourth largest company in the telecommunications industry.

Business Obstacles

Telecom USA encountered few real obstacles during its growth. Determining a market, then focusing on ways to develop that market resulted in success. The most critical decision Telecom made was to avoid direct competition with industry leaders AT&T, Sprint and MCI. While the big corporations focused their marketing efforts on major metropolitan cities, Telecom targeted medium-sized cities and built a loyal, growing client base.

Keys to Success

Telecom offered customers a unique combination of service, product, technological superiority and price.

Costs were kept to a minimum. For example, SoutherNet laid cable when local utilities did, splitting costs with the local company. The resulting per mile cost was less than half that of competitors. Another factor which helped control cost was the acquisition of additional companies by stock swaps rather than straight buyouts.

SoutherNet's technology gave it a competitive edge. A technological leader throughout the 1980s, the company was one of the first to use fiber optics and digital transmission.

Superior service and customer satisfaction were Telecom's main goals. The company's research group constantly reviewed customers' needs. Each new customer received Telecom's "Customer First Guarantee," which promised that if the customer was not completely satisfied, Telecom would reconnect the company to its former long distance system at no charge. The guarantee was seldom used. Telecom's customer attrition rate was less than 1.1 percent.

Telecom offered customers a unique combination of services not provided by competitors. The Telecom credit card furnished customers with an unprecedented assortment of features and options including Voice News Network (VNN), which provided the card holder news, weather and stock information, updated every fifteen minutes. Speed dialing, message storage and forwarding were other available credit card options.

The company was the first long distance company to offer residential customers a personal 800 hotline. Telecom stressed the importance of operator assistance, and (unlike many carriers who use third-party operators), Telecom's customers were assisted by Telecom operators.

Future Vision

In June 1990, Telecom USA shareholders approved the acquisition of the company by MCI Communications Corporation. By July 1990 the acquisition had met all federal regulations, and it was finalized in August 1990. While the name Telecom USA may have disappeared, Gabbard did not. He was made executive vice president and chief financial officer of MCI.

Gene Gabbard says the deal was "a merger of choice, certainly not a merger out of trouble." He comments, "We have certainly combined forces with one of the big guys," further explaining that he views the merger as the next step in the consolidation of the industry. "We've seen some 1,000 companies shrink to about 200 since 1962," he said. "Now we will begin to see even fewer—but stronger—entrants in the marketplace."

Entrepreneurial Lessons

Gabbard's business approach at Telecom was straightforward, emphasizing efficiency, quality and service. Just before the merger was complete, a Telecom spokesperson explained the company philosophy. "Stick to your initial stated strategy, then strive to be the best at what you're doing. Enhance the business offerings to customers, but remain very tightly focused. Be sure everything the company does makes sense and fits into the overall picture."

Telecom's founder puts it this way: "It's really a question of listening to the customer and then moving fast."

References

Caenevale, Mary Lu, and Rick Christie. "MCI to Acquire Telecom USA for $1.25 Billion." *Wall Street Journal*, April 10, 1990.

Shields, Michael J. "Long-Distance Operator." *Georgia Trend*, January 1990.

Turner, Melissa. "Telecom USA Buyout Would Transform Long-Distance Industry." *Atlanta Constitution*, April 10, 1990.

——A. D. K.

David Geffen

David Geffen Co.

David Geffen: Born 1943. Single.
Venture: Originally a record producer, the company also produces motion pictures through Geffen Films, Inc., and co-produces Broadway musicals.
Company: David Geffen Co.; 9130 Sunset Blvd.; Los Angeles, CA 90069; (310) 278-9010
Founded: 1980.
Revenues: $225 million estimated 1989 sales, not including revenues from Broadway shows.
Employees: 110.
Original Investment: Unknown.
Value: *Forbes* estimated David Geffen's total investments to be worth nearly $900 million in late 1990.

Founder

David Geffen was born in Brooklyn, the second son of Russian Jewish parents. He failed at two universities, but faked a college degree so he could pursue his dream of becoming a movie producer. He entered the industry through a job in the mailroom at the William Morris Agency, a large talent management company.

In 1970, he left the agency to start his own record company, Asylum Records. Joni Mitchell, Jackson Browne, and the Eagles achieved stardom on the label. Asylum also featured Linda Ronstadt, and Crosby, Stills, Nash, & Young. Bob Dylan was also under contract for a short time. Geffen sold Asylum in 1972 to Warner Communications for "the biggest number I could think of, $7 million," Geffen says. "Warner made it back on the next Eagles record," he admits.

Geffen ran the combined Asylum/Elektra labels for Warner for three years. He then was made vice-chairman of Warner Brothers Pictures, a job he sought, but soon discovered he didn't like. "I hated it. That was the first time I really felt like I had a job. I wasn't in control of my situation." One of the pictures he approved for production was *Oh God*, with George Burns.

After being misdiagnosed with cancer in 1976, he left the film studio and was absent from the entertainment scene for four years while he concentrated on eliminating stress and tension from his life. He took part in "est" training, a self actualization movement popular in the late 1970s. The "est" philosophy had a powerful influence and helped shape his management style when he returned to the entertainment industry. During this same period, Geffen gave lectures on the music business at UCLA and Yale.

David Geffen is a noted art collector, an interest kindled when he used to eat lunch at the Museum of Modern Art early in his career. His extensive collection includes works by modern artists Magritte, David Hockney, Edward Ruscha and Ferdinand Leger. The competitive Geffen once got in a bidding war at an art auction with a show-business foe. He won, but only after paying an exorbitant price for the work.

Business Origin

In 1980, after four years of semi-retirement, he called Warner Communication chairman, Steve Ross, and Warner Records head, Mo Ostin, and told them that he wanted to start a record company. Within two days they gave him the money to start in exchange for distribution rights. Geffen had no grand plan at the time. He explains, "When I started, all I knew was that I was going to have a record company."

The business began as a "boutique" label that served as a home for older pop stars trying to make their comebacks. Among the first artists he signed were Elton John and Donna Summer, but the key deal that thrust the label center stage, was the signing of John Lennon and Yoko Ono after Lennon emerged from retirement. Every record company had bid on Lennon, who signed with Geffen for less money than other record labels offered.

Business Growth

The David Geffen Co. is an umbrella organization for Geffen Records and Geffen Films. The record producer represents diverse talent ranging from long-established pop stars to rising newcomers. The company contracts with the talent and packages all the creative and marketing elements that become part of a musical recording. Physical manufacturing and distribution of the records, cassettes, and compact discs are handled by outside concerns. A separate motion picture production company, Geffen Films, Inc., produces pictures distributed through Warner Brothers Pictures.

Geffen Films' first solid success was the teenage hit, *Risky Business*. Every major film studio had rejected the screenplay before Geffen decided to produce it. The film grossed $52 million in its first two months. Other films produced by Geffen include *Lost in America*, *Little Shop of Horrors*, and the cult favorite, *Beetlejuice*.

Geffen has also had considerable success on Broadway, most notably the long-running *Cats*, which he co-produced. Other Broadway hits include *Dreamgirls*, *Little Shop of Horrors* and *Miss Saigon*.

Even though David Geffen has produced for stage and screen, he is most at home in the music industry. "The stakes are much smaller in the music industry, so there's much less panic and desperation," he explains. "In the movie business people can lose their jobs over one picture. I thought the record business was cutthroat until I got involved with film, which makes the music industry look like Disneyland."

Geffen doesn't sign acts any more, yet he is still the guiding force in the company. The hallmark of his approach is to stress solid relationships with the artist. According to one employee, "At every record company there's one department that holds the real power. In most places it's sales or promotion—here its A&R."

A&R, or "artists and repertoire," is a creative management function that puts together talent, music and style into a single package that will sell. A&R executives sign their own acts and essentially run their own operations under the Geffen label. While one A&R executive specializes in heavy rock, another handles more mainstream pop performers, and yet another has an ear for emerging groups. Each A&R executive has the style and personality best suited to that specialty. Geffen's team is considered the best in the industry.

The company will line up musicians, studios, and crew, oversee the recording session and provide artistic direction to the album's concept and design. Until 1990, the actual distribution of product was handled through Warner Records. Warner distributed Geffen's records and the two shared the profits. Warner also got a distribution fee and made profits manufacturing cassettes. In 1989, estimates placed Warner's profits from the deal with Geffen at $30 to $50 million.

The record industry is healthy as sales of more profitable compact discs gain on records and tapes. With strong sales across a variety of musical categories from jazz to rap, and a hefty return on investment, the big six record companies have been scrambling for several years to buy up smaller labels, often bidding up prices sharply.

Geffen entered the fray in early 1989 with an attempt to buy the artist roster and master tapes of floundering Chrysalis records. He was stymied by the British company Thorn-EMI, which bought half of Chrysalis plus an option for the whole. Nonetheless, Geffen tripled the $6 million he invested in the deal.

As Geffen's contract with Warner neared its end in 1990, he found his own company in the center of a bidding war. Geffen's strong history of discovering hit groups would be a tremendous asset to a bigger company, especially since U. S. rock music continues to gain in the world market.

Thorn-EMI reportedly offered Geffen $700 million, half in cash and half in stock. The figure, nearly three times sales revenues, caught many in the industry by surprise. The deal did not go through because of tax problems.

Business Obstacles

While Geffen's original intent was to start a record company, as early as 1976 he had a strong interest in film production. He gave writer Carol Eastman (*Five Easy Pieces*) $100,000 to write a screenplay with nothing more than a handshake. Six years later she submitted the script for *Man Trouble*, which starred Jack Nicholson and Diane Keaton.

Geffen's first film release, *Personal Best*, received positive reviews but it performed poorly at the box office. Adding to this burden, the film's director, Robert Towne, sued Geffen for $155 million, claiming that Geffen had interfered with his film and had boasted that he would "completely destroy" Towne. They eventually settled out of court.

Geffen's infant label had a strong start with Lennon/Ono's *Double Fantasy* and the debut album from the group Asia reaching number one. However, the company that had its start with established pop stars did not produce any major hits through the mid-1980s. Its salvation came in the late 1980s with successes by heavy metal groups such as Aerosmith, Whitesnake, and Guns n' Roses.

The boost from heavy metal allowed the company to diversify into more varied acts, including Peter Gabriel, the New Bohemians, Don Henley, and Cher. By 1989 the company had three records simultaneously in the top five of *Billboard's* album chart, and in early 1991, Bart Simpson's rap single "Do the Bartman" was number one on British charts, the first time a Geffen act had made that position since John Lennon 10 years before.

Keys to Success

Geffen believes the company's success is the result of the quality of product, quality of staff, and quality of the thought that goes into marketing. While his success may also include a mix of luck, business savvy and hustle, David Geffen does have an eye and ear for what will attract the public. "Somehow I tap into what people like. I haven't a clue why. But it seems to work," he admits.

The ability to discover new talent is just part of the equation. The other is his skill in building close working relationships with the artists and nurturing their careers. One close associate of Geffen explains, "When David talks to artists, he always makes them feel as if they are the center of the universe."

A prominent entertainment attorney explains the financial side to Geffen's finesse with people, "David's secret is that no matter how tough the negotiations get, he always makes sure his partners make their money as soon as he does. That way he gets a lot of people who want to be his partner."

Irving Azoff, a powerful rock manager, describes the flip side to Geffen's charm, "If he's your friend, he'll do anything for you. But if he's your enemy, he'll. . . . Let's just say he's a formidable adversary."

Like most successful entrepreneurs, Geffen is driven to succeed. He's on the phone from wake-up until bed. A rival record executive puts it succinctly, "That's all he ever wanted to be—successful."

Future Vision

In March 1990, MCA bought Geffen Records for $550 million in stock. David Geffen became MCA's largest shareholder, with a stake equivalent to 12 percent of the company but with limited voting power. He said in *Newsweek*, "My bet on MCA has turned out to be a very lucrative bet."

Music industry analysts see Geffen as one of the last significant music acquisitions available. MCA, say the analysts, sorely needed greater product flow to compete with the other major record companies. The deal gave MCA-Geffen more pop album titles on *Billboard*'s 1989 chart than any other company.

MCA executives believe the huge investment is justified. The music business is an industry in which a single, crucial individual can help generate huge profits. Geffen will continue to run Geffen Records and retains ownership of Geffen Films.

In January 1991, Geffen's MCA stock was turned into $670 million (mostly in cash) when MCA was bought by the Japanese electronic company Matsushita, which also signed Geffen up to a four-year contract to run Geffen Records.

Entrepreneurial Lessons

Geffen's understated approach to doing business may be a key to his success. His casual manner and dress, his modest office and scruffy chair, are all reflections of his belief that the foundation of success in business lies at the personal level.

Geffen's recent deal makes him one of the richest men in America. But in an interview a few years back, he tried to put his success in a more modest perspective, saying, "There's a cleaner and there's a butcher, and there's a plumber and there are people who make paintings. Everybody does what they can, and this is what I can do."

References

Conant, Jennet. "Doesn't David Geffen Know the Eighties Are Over?" *Gentlemen's Quarterly*, March 1991.

Coopman, Jeremy. "Bart Conquers U.K." *Variety*, March 4, 1991.

Fabrikant, Geraldine. "Talking Deals, Music Producer Faces Big Choice." *New York Times,* March 8, 1990.

———. "The Record Man With Flawless Timing." *New York Times,* December 9, 1990.

"Forbes 400." *Forbes,* October 23, 1989.

Goldstein, Patrick. "Geffen: From Minor to Mogul." *New York Times,* December 12, 1982.

Gubernick, Lisa and Peter Newcomb. "The Richest Man in Hollywood." *Forbes,* December 24, 1990.

Oppel, Pete. "Hagar, Quarterflash Prove Geffen Genius." *Dallas Morning News,* February 28, 1982.

Rea, Steven X. "Whatever He Touches Turns into a Success." *Philadelphia Inquirer,* October, 18, 1983.

Ressner, Jeffrey. "Geffen's Coming of Age." *Rolling Stone,* July 13, 1989.

Schwartz, John. "Geffen Goes Platinum." *Newsweek,* December 10, 1990.

Stevenson, Richard W. "Pop Impresario Strikes Gold in $550 Million Sale to MCA." *New York Times,* March 15, 1990.

———B. M.

John F. Geisse

The Wholesale Club, Inc.

John F. Geisse: Born 1920. Married, ten children.
Venture: A group of membership warehouses with outlets in several states.
Company: The Wholesale Club, Inc.
Founded: May 1982.
Original Investment: Unknown.
Value: Sold to Sam's Club in 1991.

Founder

John Geisse's business career is peppered with retail start-ups. He co-founded the Target Stores division of the Dayton-Hudson Corporation in 1962. Six years later he moved to May Department Stores in St. Louis, where he established the Ventures Stores division. In 1976, Geisse became the CEO of Ayr-Way Stores, an Indianapolis-based discount chain. Two years later, he left Ayr-Way to establish a retail consultancy that he still maintains.

Geisse graduated from Annapolis Naval Academy with engineering training. He says that training has been a plus to his business endeavors. "Having an engineering background gives me the mind to solve business problems. You would be surprised at the obtuse way people go about solving simple business problems," he says.

Business Origin

When he decided to start The Wholesale Club in Indianapolis in 1982, Geisse was motivated by several factors. First, he had a desire to serve the public. Then, he admits, he was lured by the challenge. He says, "I wanted to be on the cutting edge. I was fascinated by the distribution end of the wholesale business. Plus, I wanted the privilege and the challenge of being in the forefront." Finally, The Wholesale Club allowed Geisse to realize one of his greatest dreams—"starting a business from scratch and taking it public"—when it made its initial public offering in 1985.

The Wholesale Club was a self-service cash-and-carry membership wholesale warehouse. Warehouse clubs like it operate by merging the self-service aspect of wholesaling and the discount aspect of retailing. They are successful because merchandise is carefully selected among popular brand names; merchandise turnover is much greater than regular discount and department stores; and operating costs are kept much lower than those of merchandisers and retailers.

Membership was divided between individual consumers and small wholesale customers, who could not be serviced efficiently by large wholesalers. Wholesale customers paid an annual membership fee, while individuals were charged five percent over members' costs. Merchandise included food, personal goods, electronics, automotive accessories and miscellaneous items.

Business Growth

Geisse's first Wholesale Club opened in February 1982. His second store opened the next year in Cleveland. Since then the Club has grown to 25 locations in six midwestern states. Three stores are planned in the near future. Geisse targeted the midwest as his initial market because, he says, "I'm from the area, and I think it's a growing, progressive, outstanding community."

The Club was experiencing 19 percent sales growth for the third straight year in 1990. Although there are many other warehouse clubs—Sam's Club (owned by WalMart's Sam Walton) and the industry leader, Price Club—The Wholesale Club had enjoyed several years with minimal or no competition in several key markets.

In February 1991, however, all 27 Wholesale Club stores were merged with Sam's Club; Geisse was retained as a consultant to the company.

Business Obstacles

Within a year after opening The Wholesale Club, Geisse had to make major adjustments to spur sagging sales. "We thought all we had to do was get people in here and they would see we've got the lowest prices in town," Geisse explained, but he learned firsthand that the legendary "discriminating Midwest shopper" required more. He had to increase his inventory, cut the office supply merchandise in half, stock more apparel and hire an apparel buyer to help move the clothing out of the store.

Geisse also had to diversify his inventory to match his customers' purchasing strategy: he learned that they preferred lesser known brands at cheaper prices over better known brands that were more expensive. He illustrates, "We had Kelly Springfield tires at a seven percent markup. There was no way to sell them less. . . . What we found is . . . our shoppers are looking at price first. The name doesn't matter until you get to the Michelin level." Subsequently, B.F. Goodrich tires, priced 20 percent to 30 percent cheaper, were stocked and tire sales rose dramatically.

Even after fine-tuning his operation, Geisse found the first several years difficult and unprofitable. While the optimum shopping period for Club members is once every two weeks, "instead we [found] they only [came] about once every five weeks," he says. He couldn't count on the return business essential for a successful warehouse club. "We opened West Allis [Wisconsin]," Geisse says, "and had a fabulous grand opening, but people didn't come back. I don't think we did our homework well. This was only our third unit." After relentless telemarketing to sign new businesses and to renew memberships, plus the unwavering effort to pinpoint wanted and unwanted products, the Club was profitable from 1985.

Keys to Success

Geisse's thirty years of experience in the retail/wholesale industry, in addition to a solid understanding of his shoppers, have paid off with a thriving enterprise. "Our member is a very intelligent consumer. You'd better have the right item at the right time, the best price and make sure it's presented properly," he explains.

Geisse believes that his employees must share his goals and enthusiasm for both to be successful. He states, "You must have a firm belief in the basic business, and believe in what you're doing. You must teach your employees how to care about your business—bring them along so that they can have an abiding respect for your business."

Geisse also believes that a combination of good fortune and knowledge contribute to a winning business strategy. "Being in the right business at the right time is one of the best ways of being successful, but understanding why people need you is the greatest key to business success," he concludes.

Future Vision

Geisse's future plans are very simple; he intends to continue on his present course, but he wants to "do it better," perhaps lending his expertise to one of his sons should they decide to start their own wholesale business. He says, "This business is pretty entrepreneurial. There are no textbooks written about it."

Entrepreneurial Lessons

Extending from his extensive experience and technical training, Geisse's business philosophy centers on having a thoughtful, knowledgeable approach. He counsels, "My message to people hot after this business is to be careful. It's not like rolling off a log. You've got to know what you're doing. Be research-minded. Draw from your experience and make reasonable decisions."

Finally, modesty is important to Geisse. "The most successful people in business are usually modest. They realize how important they are, but they also know that the world will go on without them," he says.

References

Diggle, Raymond H. "The Wholesale Club." *Indiana Business Magazine*, October 1989.

Dinnen, S. P. "Wholesale Clubs Join Wal-Mart." *Indianapolis Star*, February 3, 1991.

"Geisse Finds 'Club' Is a New Ball Game." *Discount Store News*, November 14, 1983.

"No-Frills Warehouse Stores Growing Fast, Spurred by Sales to Thrifty Customers." *Atlanta Journal and Constitution*, June 3, 1990.

"Proxy Corner." *Indianapolis Business Journal*, May 29, 1989.

Stavig, Vicki. "No Minnesota Magic." *Corporate Report*, February 1, 1988.

——T. A.

C. Michael Gooden

Integrated Systems Analysts, Inc.

C. Michael Gooden: Born 1946. Married, two children.
Venture: Engineering services company specializing in defense systems for the U. S. Navy.
Company: Integrated Systems Analysts, Inc.; 2800 Shirlington Rd.; Suite 1100; Arlington, VA 22206; (703) 824-0700
Founded: 1981.
Revenues: $41 million in sales for 1990, according to company sources.
Employees: 550.
Original Investment: Unknown.
Value: $7.4 million (1989), according to company sources.

Founder

C. Michael Gooden enlisted in the Navy as a teenager in 1963 and was commissioned through the Navy's Enlisted Scientific Education Program (NESEP) in 1972. As an engineering duty officer, Gooden's naval career focused on the operation, maintenance, and design of integrated combat weapons systems. These systems integrate data from ships, planes, and missiles to coordinate a variety of weapons systems during combat. During his 17 years of active duty, Gooden obtained a B.S. degree in applied science from Miami University, his M.S.E. in computer science from the University of Pennsylvania, and did graduate work in business at the Wharton School, University of Pennsylvania.

Gooden also served in the Naval Reserves for eight years, retiring as a commander in 1988. He is involved in several trade organizations, serves on the United Negro College Fund Advisory Board, and is active in the Advent Lutheran Church.

Business Origin

During his years in the Navy, Gooden amassed considerable insight into the Navy's needs and decided to start a systems engineering firm which focused on addressing those needs. "I'm certainly a good advertisement that the service is a good place to get your start," he acknowledges. "Most of my experience in the Navy was concentrated on learning naval weapons systems," Gooden continues. "I started out as a systems operator, moved on to systems maintenance, and finally went into systems design and integration. Over the course of time I saw quite a bit of the acquisition process for weapons systems."

In 1981, Gooden enlisted the aid of fellow Navy veteran, Ronald Cornelison, and founded Integrated Systems Analysts, Inc. (ISA). "The two of us started the business in an efficiency apartment, doing documentation and engineering work for the government," says Gooden. "It took a lot of personal sacrifice in terms of savings invested and second mortgages."

Business Growth

Initially ISA was hired as a minor subcontractor on major government projects. In 1982, the company was certified as an "8(a)" contractor by the Small Business Administration, a minority-owned designation that made the company eligible for direct government contracts. Since then, 90 percent of the company's contracts have come from the Navy. ISA grew quickly to 650 employees in eight offices during the defense build-up of the 1980s. That growth has placed ISA in *Black Enterprise* magazine's "Industrial/Service 100" ranking, a list of the largest black-owned companies in the U.S.

ISA's work for the Navy is in three major areas: improving fleet maintenance, enhancing communications, and developing advanced surveillance systems. ISA generally acts as the prime contractor, or agent, of the Navy, assisting with the development of a major program. ISA develops the design specifications which the Navy then assigns to major prime contractors for actual manufacturing. ISA then follows up with testing and operational assessments. "We play a vital role in helping the Navy keep its operational and weapons systems current and capable of combating threats to the nation's security," Gooden explains.

Programs include maintenance planning for naval vessels, corrosion control on ships, performance evaluation of ships and submarines, acoustic engineering, and Arctic research. Through its analysis of ice formations and tests on underwater acoustics, ISA helped develop communications equipment to provide transmissions and detect vessels through layers of ice. The firm is also providing logistical planning to outfit aircraft and submarines to operate effectively in the Arctic cold.

Business Obstacles

When the company was founded in 1981, the combat systems engineering field was dominated by major aerospace firms like Boeing, TRW, and McDonnell Douglas. "There was tremendous resistance to minority firms in the defense marketplace," Gooden recalls. "I was trying to create a niche for ISA that would be unique among small and minority businesses in order to minimize competition in our early stages." Gooden identified combat systems integration as his niche. ISA plugs the communications gaps between the many data gathering systems the Navy uses in combat.

The company's involvement with the government's 8(a) program gave the firm a boost. However, according to Gooden, the company has also had to pay a price. "There's a strong connotation that an 8(a) firm is a little bitty company without the wherewithal to do anything meaningful or significant," he says. "This is an interesting marketplace. You're either small or large. There's no middle ground. It is important to get through that medium range as fast as possible."

In 1987 the company graduated from the 8(a) program, a change which required ISA to compete without the benefit of minority set-asides. The early years of the defense build-up were a time of high inflation and ISA was forced to sustain its growth by borrowing much-needed capital at interest rates as high as 20 percent. In addition, the seed money for new defense systems often came through budget cuts on older systems. "Many defense systems that seemed to have endless futures were arbitrarily zeroed in favor of the newest technology," says Gooden.

"Competition for talent to keep abreast of a dynamic defense market was keen," he continues. "Legislative and regulatory initiatives affecting companies in the defense sector were continually changing in scope. ISA survived this dynamic market because we learned to stay abreast of the issues and adjust operations to absorb the impact."

Keys to Success

With his first-hand military experience, Gooden started the firm with a solid background in the intricacies of naval weapons systems. Similarly, Gooden recruits Navy veterans as his top managers. "We were trying to minimize the learning curve, the time it takes to learn the Navy jargon, the way the systems operate," says Gooden. Sixty-five percent of his managers once worked for the Navy, some having well over 25 years of experience.

The company has steered clear of controversial programs like the MX missile and the B1 bomber due to the close scrutiny these programs receive and the likelihood of funding cut-offs. Instead, ISA pursues more stable, long-term contracts like maintenance planning. By keeping close contact with the latest vessels in the fleet, the company insures a long-term source of business. Gooden also tries to make sure that the company constantly works on numerous projects, as many as 65 or more.

Future Vision

Given the fundamental change in East-West relations, congressional scrutiny of defense spending, and the country's desire to reduce the national debt, Gooden expects U.S. defense spending to be reduced in the foreseeable future. "Substantial cuts in the defense budget assuredly will have some impact on us," says Gooden. "However, ISA does not subscribe to the 'extinct dinosaur' mentality which the media has painted for defense contractors." He explains, "The average annual budget cuts are expected to be in the 2-3 percent range." Gooden feels that the impact on ISA will be minimized by the fact that most of its contracts are for sustaining existing defense systems, rather than for building new ones.

He has also planned for the expected budget cuts, and looks to diversification outside of defense to sustain the company's growth. "I don't believe that the decline in defense spending has caught us unaware. We have put a plan in motion which can help us absorb losses in the defense market by selling translatable skills in new markets."

Gooden hopes that commercial contracts will account for 20 to 40 percent of business in the future. One translatable program is Zephyr, a high-altitude, ship-to-shore communications balloon which could serve commercial customers as an alternative to expensive satellites.

Entrepreneurial Lessons

Gooden suggests applying some basic business principles before attempting any new endeavor. "A well thought-out business plan will absolutely be your most valuable tool in obtaining financial backing, directing your pursuit of the market, and recruiting top talent," he says. "Everyone likes to think that everything they have done within their company is original, but the fact is, sound business practices are fairly fundamental."

Based on his own experiences, Gooden offers several other suggestions to future entrepreneurs: "Commitments for future business, made to you while you were contemplating your entrepreneurial quest, will be the least likely to occur.

If your intent is to build a sizable, sophisticated company, set that tone from the outset.

Recognize that some early employees who contribute enormously during the building phase may not have the capability to take on more sophisticated management roles in a high-growth firm. Turnover results for many reasons. Don't become overly dependent on even your most loyal employee or confidant."

And finally, Gooden says, "Pursuit of an entrepreneurial quest is an extremely demanding, lonely experience. By definition, you place yourself at the top level of risk and responsibility, and hence, you have limited resources to which you can turn when you need advice and counsel. This could be even more difficult if your spouse or family were not supportive of your efforts. Confirm this allegiance early on. It may prove to be your principal source of strength, or contribute to your demise at some critical juncture."

References

"B.E. Industrial/Service 100." *Black Enterprise,* June 1991.

Collison, Michele. "2,000 Leagues into the Future." *Black Enterprise,* June 1988.

"Integrated Systems Analysts Inc." *Inc.,* December 1987.

Magee, Harriet. "Integrated Systems Stresses Customer Contact." *EDN*, May 3, 1990.

Newton, Edmund. "The Freshman Class of 1987." *Black Enterprise*, June 1987.

Rieland, Randy. "Military Assets: A Defense Contractor's Recent Rise." *Washingtonian*, April 1988.

——B. M.

Robert Y. Greenberg

L.A. Gear, Inc.

Robert Y. Greenberg: Born 1940. Married, six children.
Venture: Manufacturer of athletic and leisure footwear, apparel and accessories.
Company: L.A. Gear, Inc.; 4221 Redwood Avenue; Los Angeles, CA 90066; (213) 822-1995
Founded: 1983.
Revenues: $902.2 million in net sales in fiscal 1990 (according to the annual report).
Employees: 1,008.
Original Investment: Unknown.
Value: $41 million net worth (1990), according to published reports.

Founder

Robert Greenberg is a self-proclaimed "fashion junkie" who grew up reading business magazines and making plans to develop his own brand of women's fashions. The son of a produce distributor, Greenberg was raised in Boston, Massachusetts. After graduating from high school, he drove across the country and spent three months attending beauty school in Los Angeles. "L.A. was everything I always dreamed of, and I vowed I would return," Greenberg remembers. Back in Boston, he opened a hair salon, and within a few years he owned five shops. Greenberg later sold the salons for what he says was "more money than I had ever seen in my life," and he began selling wigs. When the jean market boomed in the mid 1970s, Greenberg began selling his own line of jeans.

In 1979, Greenberg moved back to California with plans to pursue a new entrepreneurial venture. "I knew I wanted to start a business, and I had enough capital so I wasn't going to rush into anything," he says. Greenberg saw an opportunity in the roller-skating craze that had hit the California beaches. He opened a store that rented and sold roller skates. When a shortage developed in skate parts, Greenberg began building his own line of skates from sneakers he bought in closeout sales.

After roller skating fell out of style, Greenberg capitalized on the popularity of the movie character "E.T." by selling shoe laces bearing the character's image. In one 90-day period, that business grossed $3 million.

Business Origin

In 1983, Greenberg opened a retail shop called "L.A. Gear" on Melrose Avenue, one of Los Angeles' most fashionable streets. The store sold its own line of apparel, jeans and footwear. "I wasn't sure which of the businesses would catch on, but I was hoping that at least one would," he says. When shoes became the hottest sellers, Greenberg closed the store, sold the apparel business and declared in 1984 that he was "officially in the shoe business."

Business Growth

Greenberg found the niche that would propel L.A. Gear Inc. to rapid growth by marketing his shoes to customers concerned with fashion. "I noticed that aerobic shoes were taking off, but they were sold mainly in sporting goods stores, while department stores were waiting for shipments. I saw an opportunity for department stores and women's shoe stores to sell fashion athletic shoes," he said.

L.A. Gear began making "shoes for show," adorned with rhinestones, buckles, fringe and neon trim. The company targeted young girls ages nine to 16, a group nicknamed "the Valley Girl niche" by some. L.A. Gear's advertising and promotional campaigns tied the brand name to the Southern California lifestyle often associated with "sun, fitness and fun."

L.A. Gear sales grew from $200,000 a month in early 1985 to $1.8 million a month by mid-year. At the end of its first year, the company had reached sales of $11 million. "We were growing at a phenomenal rate and had to find additional financing," Greenberg remembers. "Since it was our preference to remain independent, we stayed away from venture capital and opted for a public offering." In July 1986 L.A. Gear stock hit the market at an offering price of $11.50 per share, and by the end of the first day of trading its value had more than doubled to $24.75. The company used the $16 million from the offering to expand the L.A. Gear product line and fund advertising and promotion. By the end of 1986, L.A. Gear had sales of $36 million.

Greenberg expanded L.A. Gear's product line in 1987 to include infant's and children's athletic footwear, sweatshirts and T-shirts. That year, the company reached sales of $70.5 million and was named one of the best small companies in the U.S. by *Business Week* magazine.

Sales mushroomed to $224 million in 1988 as L.A. Gear made the *Business Week* list of top companies once again. The company expanded its product line to include men's and junior apparel, watches and junior jeans.

In 1989, L.A. Gear stock began trading on the New York Stock Exchange and the company raised more than $68 million in a public offering. At calendar year end, L.A. Gear was recognized as NYSE's best-performing stock. Sales rose 176 percent to $617 million.

After several years of extraordinary growth, Greenberg has built L.A. Gear into the third largest domestic distributor of athletic footwear, behind Nike and Reebok. L.A. Gear products are sold in department stores, sporting goods and specialty retail outlets throughout the United States, and in more than 100 countries around the world.

Business Obstacles

While observers credit L.A. Gear as the pioneer of fashion athletic shoes, some wonder whether the company's focus on young women could prompt a downturn with a change in teen fashion trends. For instance, a $20 million deal with singer Michael Jackson to market a line of shoes did not yield the expected big sales. As one industry publication said, "L.A. Gear is definitely appealing to a fickle consumer. The challenge for [the company] is to build its business beyond teenyboppers."

In an attempt to compete with industry leaders, L.A. Gear introduced a "performance shoe" for men and hired former Los Angeles Laker basketball star Kareem Abdul-Jabbar as the product's spokesman. In 1989, the company spent 35 percent of its $35 million advertising budget on men's products, up from 10 to 15 percent in 1988.

Critics doubt that L.A. Gear can successfully promote the "technical" merit of its shoes, something the company and industry analysts agree is necessary to gain market share. As one analyst commented, "They have a long way to go to catch Nike and Reebok. It's not something L.A. Gear is likely to do in the next couple of years, but I'm not sure anything is out of Robert Greenberg's grasp."

Greenberg remains confident. "My shoes are just as performance-oriented as anyone else's. Whether they are technically fashionable or fashionably fashionable, it's all the same thing," he says. "Everybody is playing the same game. I just say it."

While many within the industry doubted L.A. Gear could continue to be successful, some outside observers did not, chiefly Trefoil Capital Investors, Inc., and Roy E. Disney, vice chairman of Walt Disney Co. In September 1991, L.A. Gear shareholders approved a stock sale that gave Trefoil a 34 percent stake in the company and L.A. Gear a $100 million boost and a new $200 million line of credit. "We believe L.A. Gear has enormous potential," Trefoil's chief strategist told *Footwear News*. Shortly thereafter, Greenberg stepped down as president as Mark R. Goldston, formerly of Reebok, joined the company to fill that position and to become COO. Greenberg remained chairman and CEO.

Keys to Success

Throughout his career, Greenberg has built businesses by anticipating and capitalizing on consumer trends. In founding L.A. Gear, he saw an opportunity to exploit the growing athletic footwear market by focusing on fashionable athletic footwear.

"We sell 'pretty' and 'good looking,'" Greenberg says. "The market I've tapped nobody even knew existed. Everybody was too busy doing their thing to realize how important fashion is to the average person," he says. An industry analyst commented that L.A. Gear, "combined great show design and powerful and impressive advertising to reach a segment of the market that nobody has ever aimed at. They've analyzed the market and come up with the perfect product."

L.A. Gear successfully tied its image to the Southern California lifestyle through flashy advertising campaigns. As *Los Angeles* magazine described it, "The company's advertising and promotion unabashedly trumpet the allure of Los Angeles: palm trees, Hollywood, fitness and pretty girls." The L.A. Gear logo features the Los Angeles city hall surrounded by palm trees. The company uses celebrity endorsers in its ads and sponsors "glitzy, celebrity-packed road shows" at industry trade exhibits around the country. Greenberg says, "It's not just the shoes or fashion we want the consumer to take home, it's the fun that goes along with that lifestyle."

L.A. Gear's advertising is created by in-house staff, something Greenberg says gives the company an edge. "Our campaigns present consumers and retailers with a consistent image of the company and its products. Our advertising staff allows us to respond to opportunities quickly and effectively, without the 'translation risk' inherent in depending on an outside agency."

Greenberg speaks freely about his business, but prefers to keep himself out of the public eye. He refuses to have his picture taken and does not include his photograph in the company's annual report. "I'm not trying out for Paramount pictures," he says. "I'm like everybody else—I come to work and do my job."

Greenberg's "job" as he describes it, is "figuring out what my consumers will want next. I'm a detective of sorts," he says. Greenberg watches his customers wherever they are. He visits shopping malls, reads "every fashion magazine I can get my hands on," and rushes out of movie theatres to watch people's feet as they exit. The CEO has spent many Saturday nights working as a shoe salesman at local retail stores.

"I listen to consumers and hear what they want. It's amazing how much I learn," he says. Greenberg gathers consumer feedback through product testing, focus groups, store and consumer interviews and surveys. "To us, every customer is important. We even allow a retailer to buy as little as four pairs of shoes without a service charge," he says.

Greenberg revels in the challenge of chasing the industry leaders. He gives credit to the competition while maintaining confidence in his ability to succeed. "Reebok and Nike do a nice job. I wouldn't want to go after somebody I didn't admire," he says. "My objective is to replace the guys who are first. When I commit to something, I do it in a big way. I don't want to be a small fry—I want to be the business." As he told *Footwear News* in an interview, "I am now a lethal weapon in the sneaker business."

The long-time entrepreneur takes pride in his past successes. "I am great at business, that's my core skill," he says. "Having been in business since I was 21, I have an innate sense of what works."

Future Vision

Even with its overwhelming success, Greenberg says that L.A. Gear has yet to reach its potential. "Eighty-year-old people and three-month-old babies wear athletic shoes now. The demographics for the market are huge," he says.

Greenberg predicts that L.A. Gear will overtake Nike and Reebok within five years. "Its only a matter of time before our sales catch up," he said. His ultimate goal is "to build the biggest brand name in the world." He believes that growth in the apparel market will push his company to the top in brand-name clothing.

Greenberg recognizes that the athletic shoe industry is constantly changing, but he says that "if the industry evolves, [L.A. Gear] will evolve with it. If everyone wakes up tomorrow and decides to wear penny loafers, who's going to make those penny loafers? We'll always evolve into the type of footwear that is selling next year," he says.

Analysts say that L.A. Gear must "make the successful transformation in management from a smaller entrepreneurially-driven firm to a larger, more institutionalized operation." Greenberg reports that he now delegates control within his company. "I'm very much a hands-on man, but now I can afford to hire the best people and leave them to do their jobs," he says. "I didn't trust anybody in the beginning. Before we went public, I was involved in all aspects of the company. Now I spend most of my time in product development. I'm still the mentor, but I'm not running L.A. Gear anymore," Greenberg says.

"I see a lot of excitement in our future. . . . [We] are hoping to become a billion-dollar company," he says. "We entered the market and have become recognized as a brand and a lifestyle. . . . [Wait] until you see what's coming next."

Entrepreneurial Lessons

"The difference between successful and unsuccessful entrepreneurs is that those who fail open up the wrong business at the wrong time and in the wrong location," Greenberg says. In building L.A. Gear, he seized an opportunity that others did not see. "Detroit missed small cars, Coke and Pepsi missed bottled mineral water and the shoe companies missed fashionable sneakers," he says.

After finding business opportunities, Greenberg says that an entrepreneur must respond to consumer wants. He uses L.A. Gear as an example: "Instead of saying, 'You can run faster, you can jump higher,' we said, 'You can look better.' It worked because everybody wants to look better," he says.

References

"The CEO 1000." *Business Week,* 1989.

Cohn, Jordan. "Rubber Soul." *Los Angeles Magazine,* November 1988.

Egan, Jack. "Will This Runner Finally Stumble?" *U.S. News and World Report,* 1989.

Kerwin, Kathleen, and Mark Candler. "L.A. Gear Is Tripping Over Its Shoelaces." *Business Week,* August 20, 1990.

"L.A. Gear Names New President, Operating Chief." *Wall Street Journal,* September 27, 1991.

Lee, P. "Fancy Footwork." *Los Angeles Daily News,* July 10, 1988.

Lev, Michael. "No. 2 Executive Departs At Struggling L.A. Gear." *New York Times,* June 14, 1991.

McAllister, Robert. "L.A. Gear Holders OK Stock Sale to Trefoil." *Footwear News,* September 16, 1991.

———. "Trefoil-L.A. Gear Proposal Stirs Conjecture." *Footwear News,* June 10, 1991.

McDaniel, J. "L.A. Gear Tries a Full Court Press." *New York Times,* July 16, 1989.

McGee, Bob. "L.A. Gear Ready for Major Shift." *Sport Style,* September 16, 1991.

Paris, Ellen. "Rhinestone Hightops, Anyone?" *Forbes,* March 7, 1988.

Rudolph, Barbara. "Foot's Paradise." *Time,* August 28, 1989.

Seckler, Valerie. "At Point Blank Range: L.A. Gear Chief Exudes All-Around Optimism." *Footwear News,* August 12, 1991.

Williams, L. "On the Right Foot." *Los Angeles Times,* July 31, 1989.

——M. J. B.

Barbara B. Grogan

Western Industrial Contractors, Inc.

Barbara B. Grogan: Born 1947. Single, two children.
Venture: An industrial construction and installation company to serve heavy and light industry.
Company: Western Industrial Contractors, Inc.; 680 Harlan Street; Denver, CO 80214; (303) 238-7900
Founded: September 1982.
Revenues: $3 million projected sales (1990), according to published reports.
Employees: 40-100 (depending on business demand).
Original Investment: Approximately $50,000.
Value: $375,800 net worth (February 1990), according to published reports.

Founder

Barbara Grogan recalls that as a child growing up in St. Louis, Missouri, she wasn't encouraged to take risks and feared failure. "I come from a very traditional, conservative, midwestern Catholic family. I was raised to be a wife and mother," she says.

After graduating from the University of Colorado with a psychology degree in 1969, Grogan began working in the research department of Mountain Bell. She later married and, as she says, "stayed home to do wifely and motherly things." Once her children reached school age, Grogan worked as general manager of her husband's truck-rental business.

189

Grogan's life changed dramatically in 1982 when she and her husband divorced after twelve years of marriage. As a 35-year-old, single mother with no job and two young children to support, Grogan describes the period as "the most painful, frightening time of my entire life. I moped for a few months, but I didn't have much moping time," she remembers. "It was my job to fix up my broken life."

Grogan started Western Industrial Contractors as a way to support herself and her children. In the last eight years, her company has grown into a multi-million dollar enterprise and Grogan has earned a reputation as one of America's successful entrepreneurs.

In addition to managing her own business, Grogan is a leader in the Denver community. In 1989, she was named the first woman chair of the board of the Denver branch of the Federal Reserve Bank of Kansas City. She is chairwoman-elect and executive committee member of the Greater Denver Chamber of Commerce, and she has served on state advisory boards at the request of two Colorado's governors. Grogan is active in civic and professional organizations including the National Civic League, the United Way, Junior Achievement, the National Association of Women Business Owners and the Rotary Club of Denver.

National magazines including *Fortune, Time* and *Esquire* have hailed Grogan's business success and her civic commitment. *Colorado Business Magazine* named her 1987 Entrepreneur of the Year. In 1989, she received the Martin Luther King Social Responsibility Award for her efforts to promote economic opportunity in Denver.

Despite the acclaim, Grogan says that her most significant success has been raising her son and daughter. She calls motherhood "my number one job."

Business Origin

When she started Western Industrial Contractors in 1982, Grogan was driven mainly by fear. "Anyone who says that fear isn't a motivating factor is dead wrong," she says. "I was scared to death, but I had to find a way to support my kids and myself."

While Grogan had never before considered owning her own business, she chose to start a company rather than work for someone else. "This was a time of overwhelming crisis in my life, and my self esteem was so low I really didn't believe anyone else would hire me," she recalled. "I had no solid experience, and I didn't think this was the time to start working with

21-year-olds. I needed a flexible schedule so that I could continue to spend time with my children. Working for myself was the only way to keep that flexibility," Grogan said.

Grogan established a millwrighting business because she was familiar with the industry after working in her ex-husband's truck and crane rental company. Millwrighting involves moving and installing heavy industrial equipment, and Grogan knew people who had equipment to move. "It was an industry that I was immersed in at the time, and I knew that I could start a millwrighting business with very little capital," she said.

While she had been raised to avoid risks, Grogan was entering a specialized, high-risk industry. At the time, friends, lawyers, accountants and other associates advised against the venture. She remembers them saying, "Barbara are you crazy? Don't you know the industrial revolution is over?" Grogan did not consider the possibility of failure. "I had to make this thing work because I had no idea what else to do. I had bet the farm— there was no 'plan B,'" she says.

Grogan began with $50,000 and a 1969 orange pickup truck. She set up her office on a dead-end street across from a junkyard and bought office furniture from the basement of a used-furniture warehouse.

Business Growth

Grogan began her business just as Denver's economy was beginning a sharp decline. It was a time when construction companies were abandoning union contracting, but Grogan quickly signed the millwrights' union to work with her. As a union contractor, she hired experienced workers on a project basis, giving her the talent she needed to service her customers while keeping overhead low.

Grogan built a team of advisers and set her strategy for going after "the big boys," national customers who would deliver a large volume of business. Her motto for maintaining a lean organization was, "Never spend a buck if you can spend a dime and get close."

Western Industrial's first big break came in its eighth month of operation, just as the business was running out of cash. "I had heard that Manville Corporation needed to move a pipe plant from Florida to Malaysia," Grogan said. "I told them that we were a real company who could do the job and that we were interested in helping them. I asked for a 10 percent 'mobilization fee', although until that time I had no idea what a mobilization fee was. I knew I needed cash. The next week a check arrived and we had our first large contract, literally just in time," Grogan said. "After that job, we had a *Fortune 500* company that loved us—it gave us immediate national credibility," Grogan says. "That was the most important job we'll ever do because it gave us our start."

Western Industrial's sales reached half a million dollars in its first year, and sales climbed to $1.5 million during the company's second year. After five years in business, the company had revenues of more than $3 million and had reported profits each year.

Among its most notable projects, Western Industrial assembled the world's largest baggage-handling system for United Airlines at Chicago's O'Hare International Airport; installed several $7 million flight simulators in the United Airlines Training Center in Denver; erected an eight-story, 200-yard wide storage system for Public Service Company; set up a four-story screen in Denver's Museum of Natural History; and is coordinating the schedule for other contractors building a terminal at Denver's new airport.

Business Obstacles

By August 1987, Western Industrial had more work in progress than at any time in its history. Then Grogan's company faced its first major obstacle. In September, city officials stopped all work in progress at the Denver airport because a new airport facility would be constructed. Western Industrial had several multi-million dollar projects planned or underway at the airport. "We lost $3-5 million in booked business in one day," Grogan recalls. The stock market collapsed in October, causing many of Western Industrial's clients to put projects on hold. "Within 60 days, we had gone from having more business than ever to having almost none," Grogan says.

Grogan was unsuccessful in her search for business to replace what the company had lost. "At the time, the Denver economy really collapsed," Grogan said. "I kept looking for construction jobs that weren't there. I was working harder, but I wasn't working smarter." She then examined her business strategy and slashed operating costs. She also established a construction consulting division as an additional profit center, and she found a market eager and willing to pay for estimating and project scheduling services. The division's success brought Western Industrial back to profitability again by the spring of 1988.

Grogan believes that in her company's early days, her presence as a woman in a male-dominated industry made some people skeptical about her business. "I just went out and danced real fast to prove that I could do it," she says. "Overall, it has been a mixed blessing. People may have been more reluctant to talk to me at first because I am a woman, but once I got a foot in the door, their curiosity made them remember me. Now, the company has developed a reputation of its own—people aren't waiting for us to fall apart," Grogan says.

Keys to Success

From the beginning, Grogan relentlessly pursued major accounts. In securing a deal with United Airlines, one of the company's largest customers, Grogan made many calls before she was able to arrange a first meeting. "I don't want you to give me a job, I just want the chance to bid," she told her potential customer. "I want you to work with me because once you do, you won't want to work with anyone else," she said.

Described as "a real dynamo," by colleagues, some profiles of Grogan call her "sharp, animated and finely dressed." Others comment on her friendliness and femininity. "I am a woman and damned proud of it, and I don't try to be less feminine," she says.

Grogan manages her business using what she calls "common sense, keeping overhead low and staff numbers small. I don't need 17 computer programs to tell me how I'm doing. Fourth-grade arithmetic will do. It's simple: I don't spend more [money] than I've got."

"Our greatest asset is our attitude about service," Grogan says of her company. "When we are asked to bid on a job, we sit down with clients and look for ways to save them money. We are extremely honest and ethical, and we build a long-term relationship of trust with our clients. We are committed above all to making our clients happy—we show them that we really care," she says.

"Once I get the clients, we service their socks off," Grogan adds. On one occasion, Grogan received a call at 6:00 A.M. that an explosion at a client's cement factory had knocked a kiln out of operation. She sent a supervisor and a team of millwrights to the site within a couple of hours, and the team worked in shifts around the clock for four days. Grogan charged the customers her regular fees. "We never take advantage of a customer in a bad position. That's how we establish long-term relationships," she says.

Grogan looks for employees who are "competent at what they do, are able to get along well with people and share the vision of the company." She believes that creating an environment where people can grow is the way to attract good employees. "I give people latitude and responsibility, and I believe that they get a great sense of personal satisfaction from their work. Around here, we don't fault anyone trying something different or new—in fact, my definition of failure is not trying," she says.

Grogan insists that Western Industrial employees care about each other. "I have fired people for not being nice," she reports. This CEO communicates her appreciation directly to staff as well, often traveling to job sites to speak with company workers. "When I'm out at a site, I'll go up and hug my guys," Grogan says. "I wear suits and dresses—even in the mud—and they warn me that I'll get myself dirty. 'I don't care,' I tell them. 'This is good dirt—its our dirt.'"

Future Vision

Grogan predicts that "the 1990s will be extraordinary, for the city of Denver, the country and our company." She plans to expand Western Industrial by increasing sales and building the company's net worth. "We'll pursue reasonable, rational growth—I'm not looking to grow for growth's sake," she says. "I would like to expand our client base outside the United States and work for companies around the world."

Grogan will continue to stay highly involved in day-to-day operations. "The people around me are a tremendous help, but ultimately 'the buck stops here,'" she says.

Someday Grogan may sell her company. "Right now, I'm very happy doing what I'm doing here, but eventually I'd like to start something else," she said. "I believe that there are bottom-line principles that apply to running any business and motivating people. I've learned these things from on-the-job-training. I'd eventually like to try them in another setting."

Grogan hopes that the 1990s will bring greater numbers of women into leadership positions. "We've come a long way, but there is certainly more room for women to lead," she says. "My bottom-line belief is that the globally-competitive nature of the work force will compel companies in the next decade to pick the best people for jobs regardless of sex, race, religion, whatever," Grogan adds. "All companies face the universal challenge of building employee loyalty. Anybody in a management position needs to understand that their employees have an infinite number of choices. The leading-edge companies of the future will use human potential to the fullest, not caring if someone is male or female, black or white or red. Leadership will come from the heart," she believes.

Entrepreneurial Lessons

As a result of her experience, Grogan's offers this advice to would-be entrepreneurs: "The most important thing when you're just starting out is not to let the 'naysayers' steal your dreams. The world is full of negative people who view entrepreneurs as crazy folks. They have a thousand reasons why your dreams won't work, and they're ready to share them with you at the drop of a hat.

"The entrepreneur must believe with all her heart that she can accomplish her dreams. To be successful, you need to possess honesty and integrity, coupled with a deep sense of commitment and caring for your employees, your clients, your community and your country," she says. "Finally, I believe that it is important to give back—to bring others along. In my office, I have hung an important reminder: 'Moving forward means leaving no one behind.'"

References

"Barbara Grogan: A Woman of Substance." *Continental Profiles,* August 1991.

Bronikowski, L. "Gazing Into the 1990s." *Rocky Mountain News,* January 21, 1990.

Caminiti, Susan."On the Rise." *Fortune,* May 9, 1988.

Castro, Janice. "She Calls All the Shots." *Time,* July 4, 1988.

DuBay, K. "Local Exec to Head Denver Fed Branch." *Rocky Mountain News,* December 2, 1989.

Goldie, Diane. "Denver Woman Makes Her Mark in Business World." *Rocky Mountain News* , November 27, 1987.

McQuay, D. "Risky Business." *Sunday Denver Post,* June 11, 1989.

"The 1987 Esquire Register." *Esquire,* December 1987.

Purdy, Penelope. "Entrepreneur Barbara Grogan: The Face of America's Business Future." *The Denver Post,* July 7, 1991.

Wright, Barbara. "How to Beat Out Big-Name Competition." *Working Woman,* May 1988.

——M. J. B.

Henry Haimsohn

PACE Membership Warehouse, Inc.

Henry Haimsohn: Born 1947. Married, two children.
Venture: General merchandise wholesale and retail company that sells merchandise through a chain of "membership warehouses."
Company: PACE Membership Warehouse, Inc.; Box 39975; Denver, CO 80239; (303) 364-0700
Founded: November 1982.
Revenues: $2.3 billion (1990), according to company sources.
Employees: 15,000.
Original Investment: $3.25 million.
Value: $107 million, according to published reports dated April 12, 1990.

Founder

It is likely that Henry Haimsohn's entrepreneurial spirit was shaped as he watched his father, Herbert, launch a successful business. In the early 1960s, the elder Haimsohn founded a chain of home improvement centers called Handyman of California, Inc.

A San Diego native, Haimsohn earned an M.B.A. from the University of Southern California in 1970. He then joined the business his father built and eventually became Handyman's vice president of sales. In that position, Haimsohn was responsible for operations, human resources, construction and maintenance of the company's 81-store chain.

Haimsohn was eager for a new challenge after 12 years at Handyman, and he decided then to start a business of his own.

Business Origin

Haimsohn saw that a six-year old San Diego-based chain of membership warehouse clubs called the Price Club had been highly successful, and he began investigating the potential for a similar chain of stores in another area of the country. Price was one of a few companies that had introduced membership warehouse shopping, requiring businesses and individuals to pay an annual fee to shop at company stores in exchange for low prices. Price outlets offered wholesale prices on merchandise including groceries, major appliances, housewares and clothing.

Haimsohn studied the Price Company extensively before deciding to open a similar chain. He researched the company's history, talked to Price employees and customers, and learned the details of how the business operated. "Committing to it wasn't a casual thing like deciding I was going to have a hamburger for lunch," he says. "The decision meant leaving a secure, high-paying corporate position and starting a company from scratch."

Haimsohn shared his idea with business associates to gather feedback and suggestions, and he enlisted their help in writing his venture's five-year plan. He then solicited the financial capital needed to launch his business. Haimsohn raised $3.25 million through a private stock placement, with much of the money coming from his family members and friends. Haimsohn invested $250,000.

Haimsohn's original business plan, which he says "never got past the first draft," called for development of 10 warehouses in Texas or Oklahoma. However, when he learned that Wal-Mart, a national discount chain, planned to open membership warehouses in Dallas and Houston, Haimsohn decided to establish his company in Denver instead.

The first PACE Membership Warehouse, Inc. store opened on July 29, 1983 in a 100,000 square foot building that was filled with merchandise. On its first day of operation, PACE had 300 members. "That morning I didn't look outside before we opened the doors," Haimsohn says. "I didn't know what was on the other side. It could have been five people or 500. When we finally rolled up the doors, I was relieved to find a crowd out there."

197

Business Growth

PACE's membership grew quickly, and it was not long before Haimsohn was considering expansion—although opening locations outside the Denver area had not been part of his original business plan. "We could sense within a matter of weeks that PACE was going to be successful," Haimsohn says. "It was clear almost immediately that if we wanted to grow, we would have to expand to a new geographic region. We determined that the Southeast had tremendous potential," he says.

In 1984, PACE raised $10 million from a second private stock placement and opened five warehouses in Denver, Atlanta, Charlotte, and Tampa Bay. Fiscal 1984 revenues were $77 million, up from $15.6 million in 1983.

In 1985, PACE's first public stock offering yielded $50 million in growth capital. That year, the company opened 10 new warehouses in Colorado, Pittsburgh, Washington DC and Baltimore. PACE raised an additional $100 million through a 1986 public offering and opened nine warehouses. In 1987, PACE opened eight outlets, as sales revenues reached nearly $1 billion.

By 1988, PACE had three million members and 34 outlets in 12 states. In March of that year, Haimsohn left the company he had founded five years earlier.

Business Obstacles

To be able to buy the brand-name merchandise offered in PACE warehouses, Haimsohn had to establish long-term relationships with manufacturers highly selective about the outlets that carried their goods. "We had to work diligently to persuade them sell to us," he says. Haimsohn also had to attract enough members to keep the warehouse in business. He targeted government employees, and employees of financial institutions, hospitals and transportation firms as prospective members. He says that his greatest challenge was explaining the warehouse shopping concept, which was relatively unknown in the region at the time. "Before we opened the first warehouse, we didn't have one to show people, so we had no frame of reference," he explains.

Haimsohn stressed that the combination of the warehouse memberships and direct purchasing from manufacturers meant that PACE could offer lower prices than any discount store. "The response varied all over the ballpark from 'Get out of here,' to 'Sounds great, I'll try it,'" Haimsohn reports. "Success wasn't overnight."

As Haimsohn expanded PACE outside of Denver, he faced management and staffing obstacles. "I couldn't be in two places at once. People were the most important factor in allowing us to expand. I clearly didn't do PACE by myself," he says.

PACE needed capital to fund rapid growth, but becoming a public company brought greater management challenges, according to the company's founder. "When you have public shareholders, you have more people to communicate with. Shareholders demand a certain level of respect because they're owners of the company. The more shareholders, the more opportunities for different opinions on what strategies are best," Haimsohn says.

Many analysts were critical of the company's rapid growth, especially when PACE posted losses in its first few years of operation. Despite multi-million dollar sales revenues, the company lost $7 million in 1985 and $1 million in 1986. PACE's stock price declined in 1987 and early 1988, prompting some Wall Street analysts to criticize the way Haimsohn had managed the business.

Haimsohn says that he expected that the company would build its way to profitability. "You have to put it in perspective. We planned for losses in the early years because of the growth."

Keys to Success

Having traded a lucrative position for the uncertainty of entrepreneurship, Haimsohn determined to make PACE a success despite early obstacles. "When I made the decision to start PACE, I had no financial resources and no employees. All I had was myself. Commitment was critical," he says.

Business associates say that Haimsohn's attention to detail is one of his greatest assets. In a September 1989 *Denver Business Magazine* profile of Haimsohn, Lorraine Warshaw, a Handyman colleague, recalled the meeting at which Haimsohn shared his plans for PACE. "I put him through an analysis of the business. I asked him who his market was, how the operation was to be run, how inventory would turn over and what kind of margins were needed," Warshaw said. "He had a ready and appropriate answer for all the questions I asked. He had already planned it in his head and understood the whole operation."

Herself a Harvard M.B.A. graduate, CPA and consultant to entrepreneurs, Warsaw told *Denver Business* that she was not surprised that Haimsohn had done his homework. "Of all of [Handyman's] vice presidents, Henry was the only one able to run his department cost-effectively without cutting people." she said. "He was able to save costs by being creative and inventive."

Modeling PACE after the successful Price Club helped Haimsohn attract investors, many of whom were familiar with the membership warehouse concept. "But it was important for me to generate the confidence of these people," Haimsohn says.

San Diego attorney Harold Small, a college friend of Haimsohn's, told *Denver Business* that his confidence in PACE's founder was the reason he invested. Small describes Haimsohn as "detail-oriented, quiet, introverted, assertive and aggressive. But usually the reason you make an investment with a start-up company is because of the person, not the business plan," he says.

PACE employees praise Haimsohn's abilities as a chief executive. Jim Vaughan, who worked with Haimsohn at Handyman and was PACE's senior vice president of operations, told *Denver Business*, "If someone was more qualified to make a decision, [Haimsohn] let that person make the decision. He might question the decision, but he would respect the person's judgement." To encourage management commitment, Haimsohn offered stock options to all company managers.

Haimsohn says that key to PACE's success was the company's unconditional guarantee the lowest prices on every item sold. He says that PACE could make the guarantee because it bought merchandise in large quantities directly from manufacturers. The "members-only" concept also kept costs low, since members were not likely then to steal from the stores or bounce checks. In addition, PACE eliminated advertising costs by relying on customer referrals to build membership.

"We believed that if you have a good base of members, word of mouth would be a good impetus for the continued growth of the company," Haimsohn says.

When Haimsohn left PACE, many speculated that he was forced out by a preference for "professional management over entrepreneurial leadership." However, industry analysts credited Haimsohn for his contribution's to PACE's growth and success. In an April 1988 *Denver Post* article, Daniel Barry, a retail analyst with Kidder, Peabody & Co. in New York said, "Henry did an excellent job in getting the company going. It required a lot of talent; he had the contacts and he knew how to get money from Wall Street."

Haimsohn says he that left PACE when he had accomplished the goals he had set for himself and believed it was time to do something else.

Future Vision

Stepping down as PACE's chief gave Haimsohn more time to spend with his wife and children. "I don't have any ideas about the next step," he said in late 1988. "I don't know if there needs to be a next step, but I feel that I still have unused resources, that I'm not using my creativity to the extent that I want to."

Entrepreneurial Lessons

While Haimsohn believes that every entrepreneur should establish concrete plans for any new business, he notes that an entrepreneur cannot expect to follow the plan exactly as it is written. He cites the fact that while he planned to open in Dallas, competition forced him to Denver. He also says that he first planned to name his company "Sabre," later settling on PACE instead.

An entrepreneur must be prepared to answer questions that others, particularly potential investors, are bound to ask, Haimsohn says. "Everyone wants to make a good investment. But they don't casually write out a check and say, 'Here's some money, be an entrepreneur,'" he says. "[My investors] asked hard-hitting questions. They wanted to know who I was professionally, how I was going to do it, and what was important to me. They wanted me to articulate my ideas regarding the operation and the market."

Haimsohn emphasizes that a business owner must hire the people who can best meet his customers' specific needs. He says that in a service-based business such as PACE, "Success requires people who will put themselves in a position of responding with their heart. Day-in and day-out, they have to be ready to live up to promises."

Haimsohn believes that "A sense of commitment to self" is what makes an entrepreneur. "One of the most important elements to success is being committed to achieve that success." The tremendous effort necessary to build a business can be costly, he cautions. Haimsohn's first marriage ended while he was developing PACE, and he says that his relationship with his two children may have suffered as well. "My commitment was very consuming, maybe to a fault. But its easier to see that in retrospect," he says.

References

Lieb, J. "Pace Fine-Tunes Warehouse Battle Plan." *Denver Post,* April 17, 1988.

Mahoney, M. "Pace Primed for Long Haul." *Denver Post,* July 10, 1989.

Riggs, R. "Haimsohn Speaks in S.D." *San Diego Union,* September 12, 1985.

Zuber, David. "Prince of Pace." *Denver Business Magazine,* September 1, 1988.

——M. J. B.

Thomas E. Haire

T² Medical, Inc.

Thomas E. Haire: Born 1944. Married, four children.
Venture: A network of physician-invested medical centers offering home infusion therapy services.
Company: T² Medical, Inc.; 1121 Alderman Dr.; Alpharetta, GA 30202; (404) 442-2160
Founded: 1984 by Thomas E. Haire and Tommy H. Carter.
Revenues: $147.5 million in fiscal 1991 (1991 annual report).
Employees: 700.
Original Investment: $18,000 from each of four friends (of Haire and Carter) toward a guaranteed bank loan.
Value: $7.9 million (1989 annual report).

Founder

Born on August 13, 1944, Thomas E. (Tom) Haire grew up in Dallas where he attended public high school. He married at 17, and he and wife Kathy subsequently had four children, now all grown. Despite his early marriage and family responsibilities, Haire went on to college at Central Michigan University, where he majored in business administration and graduated in 1966.

His first job was as a sales representative in the medical division of Dow-Corning, where he worked out of Little Rock, Arkansas, selling plastic surgery implants to doctors. He joined Dow-Corning upon the advice of his father, a former math professor, who had made quite a name for himself in the company's industrial sector. "I chose the medical division because I wanted to distance myself from my dad's accomplishments," says Haire. His mother, a homemaker, died when Haire was 19.

In 1972 Haire moved to Atlanta and for the next five years worked as a sales rep and product specialist for Baxter Healthcare, the nation's largest hospital supplier of intravenous solutions. At Baxter, Haire met Tommy H. Carter, also a sales rep, and the two became good friends. Carter later moved to California and in 1977 Haire left Baxter to realize a longtime dream—he opened a sporting goods store.

Coaching little league baseball had been a favorite hobby of Haire's for years, ever since his son was seven, and he thought it would be fun to have his own athletic supply store. It *was* fun, recalls Haire, but not profitable. He took out a second mortgage on his home ("which was money we lost") and within two years had to close up shop.

But in true entrepreneurial fashion, he started yet another venture—Medical Accessories, Inc., a medical and surgical products distribution company. Haire describes it as "a great little business" until 1984 when the company's main line of operating room equipment was bought by a major corporation. That left Haire at the helm of a distribution company with virtually nothing to distribute.

Then came a timely phone call from Carter, Haire's friend and former colleague at Baxter. Carter was moving back to Atlanta and wanted to work with Haire. When Haire explained that his company was dissolving, the two decided to form their own company. They latched upon a concept whereby physicians would be financially involved in the business of medical care. They were familiar with a physician-owned company that did CAT scans and thought that model would also work for infusion therapy.

Hence, the concept of T^2 Medical Inc. (T^2 stands for the two Toms), whereby physicians invest in the company and recommend their own patients in need of home infusion services.

When Haire and Carter founded T^2, their goal was to make a respectable profit and get out of the corporate rat race. Carter is now semi-retired, although he still serves as a director of the company. Haire, however, remains entrenched in the thick of things at T^2, which has not left him much time for civic involvement ("When you're trying to survive, you don't have time for anything but work"). With T^2's recent success, however, Haire is more relaxed about the company and is making an effort to do things outside the office. After a hiatus of many years, he has gone back to coaching little league baseball and has become an avid golfer, often sponsoring faraway golf retreats for his physician-partners.

Business Origin

When Haire and Carter decided to set up T^2 Medical, Inc., they had no money of their own to invest, so they persuaded four friends to contribute $18,000 each towards a bank loan. With that initial investment of $72,000, Haire and his partner went searching for a group of 15-18 Atlanta physicians who would each put $15,000 into T^2. Getting that first group of physician-partners was their hardest sale. "Here we were, two guys with no track record, a new concept, and asking folks to invest thousands of dollars," says Haire.

In 1984 when T^2 was established, there were already 23 home infusion companies in Atlanta. What was different about T^2, however, was the concept of physician ownership. That became the selling pitch—that physicians could maintain control. Haire emphasized that a doctor who joined the T^2 network would work with other physicians respected in their own specialties, could determine the nursing and pharmaceutical staff, and would have a built-in system of quality control, thereby assuring better patient care.

Once that first group of physicians signed on, the concept was easier to sell to others. Through word of mouth and physician recommendations, T^2 quickly expanded. In fiscal 1991, the company operated 81 centers throughout the U. S. and had 1,747 physician-partners.

T^2 infusion therapy centers consist of about 15 physicians who specialize in such areas as infectious disease, gastroenterology and medical oncology. T^2 patients generally receive intravenous feedings, blood transfusions or chemotherapy and are closely monitored by T^2 physicians and support staff. The patients themselves (or a qualified care giver) are trained to give treatments at home, which reduces the cost of medical services that otherwise would require hospitalization.

Haire acknowledges that the T^2 concept could not have worked a decade ago. A number of factors contributed to T^2's "right timing": advances in medical technology; an increasingly large elderly population; demand by consumers for more control over their medical care; and exorbitant hospital and insurance rates. Regarding those costs, Haire said in an interview in the *Atlanta Business Chronicle*, "I'd be the richest man in the world if I only had to compete with hospitals."

Business Growth

Initially, Haire hoped to establish four home infusion companies under the T² umbrella—he and Carter would both manage two. But T²'s popularity quickly grew, primarily as a result of the physicians who were involved in the network and enthusiastically passed the word to their physician-friends in other states. "Other than the first time, we never had to make a cold call," states Haire, who attributes at least half of the company's growth directly to physician referrals.

Profits in T² are split equally by ownership, not referral, and Haire thinks that such an egalitarian formula works well. The physicians in each local center receive the same return on profit, whether they refer two patients or 200.

In May 1988 T² went public (it trades on NASDAQ under the symbol TSQM). Accolades for the company were soon rolling in. It ranked twelfth among the *Inc.* 100, eighth among the *Forbes* 200 best small companies in the U.S., thirteenth on *Fortune's* "Fast 100" list, and *Business Week* cited it as the best small company for outstanding performance, based on a three-year period of sales, earnings and return on capital. Revenues were $73 million in 1990 and $147.5 million in 1991. Going public has undergirded T²'s success. Haire says that his company is well-capitalized, has $15 million in the bank, no debt and over 1,700 physician-partners in the network. "Of course, we also face a lot more competition now than when we started," he adds.

Business Obstacles

One month after T² went public, Congress passed the Catastrophic Health Act of 1988 (later repealed) which included a rider restricting physician ownership in an infusion therapy center. "We're convinced one of our competitors brought that rider on the bill," says Haire.

But T² found a way out of a potentially devastating problem. It decided to buy back the centers from the doctors, primarily using cash from the sale of stock. T²'s buyout averaged five times the pre-tax earnings of each center. T² stock has traded at about 28 times earnings after-tax. The company owns some centers and manages others, although Haire expects T² will buy all of its managed centers within three years.

Early on, Haire confronted a tremendous amount of inertia on the part of physicians, many of whom believed that doctors should not get involved in any medical enterprise. Haire had to convince them that it was in their best interest to become business persons, especially in light of soaring malpractice insurance rates, medicare cutbacks and the proliferation of Health Maintenance Organizations (HMOs). "One of the things we did best was to explain that this was an ethical, above board, high quality service," says Haire.

Haire also had to contend with the rumor mill—negative reports that T^2 was going bankrupt, was being sued by some of its physician-partners, or was under investigation by medical boards. Nervous physician-partners would call Haire, asking if the rumors were true, seeking assurance that they weren't. "The industry hated us because we strangled the competition," says Haire.

With its physician-involved concept, T^2 was considered a renegade upstart and many competitors sought to de-stabilize the new company. The strategy almost worked. Haire admits that it was difficult to allay the fears of his physician-partners during the height of the rumors. "If just one person had baled out during that first year or so, we may not have survived."

Like many small businesses, T^2 was undercapitalized. Its initial budget of $72,000 all went towards "setting up" expenses. Had it taken the company longer to show a profit or to attract physician-investors, T^2 likely would have been one of the innumerable companies which did not have sufficient starting power to stay the course.

Keys to Success

The real genius of T^2, according to Haire, is its network of over 1,000 physician-partners. They are the company's customers *and* stockholders—if they are satisfied, the company performs well. Certainly, it makes sense that a physician will refer patients to a home infusion service that he/she is familiar with and knows that the staff, pricing structure and procedures are up to standard. The fact that the doctor owns a piece of the company is yet another built-in quality control.

Haire treats his physician-partners well, frequently sponsoring educational seminars where internationally known and respected medical experts share their knowledge of the latest medical advances. Haire also organizes golf retreats, often to exotic getaways, which provide an opportunity for physician-partners in other centers to meet and talk.

Haire says that in addition to the financial rewards from T^2, doctors are committed to the company because of its reputation for quality medical care. That's one reason why, when co-founder Tommy Carter left the company, Haire brought in renown breast care specialist Dr. Joseph C. Allegra as president and chief operating officer. "That sent a clear message to our doctors that we're going to stay on track," says Haire. "If I let the quality of T^2 drop, doctors would leave overnight."

Future Vision

The $1.2 billion home infusion market is growing at a rate of 35 percent annually, and Haire expects T^2 to keep pace with the industry growth for the next several years. Despite the slow-down in the national economy, he sees the medical arena as recession-proof. "When you're really sick, you see a doctor," says Haire. He predicts that by 1993 T^2 will own all of its home-infusion centers, and in the meantime, will continue to open new centers, particularly in the western states.

T^2 is also developing a joint venture with Tokos Medical Corp., which specializes in home health care for women. The new company, Women's Homecare Inc., will have T^2's home-infusion centers and Tokos' home uterine monitoring device, the only one approved by the Federal Drug Administration, which helps detect early labor.

T^2 is also pushing a concept called IntraCare, clinic-based infusion therapy centers for patients who are not sick enough to be hospitalized, yet whose treatment is too complex to be given at home. At IntraCare clinics, patients are treated on an outpatient basis, returning home the same day. T^2 has already purchased one IntraCare facility in northern Virginia, and looks to expand the concept with its highly successful physician-involved formula. "If it works, this could be the icing on the cake," says Haire.

Entrepreneurial Lessons

The one error that Haire regrets most was giving away too much equity. He says he and Carter should have never sought the $72,000 from their four friends. He describes those original four investors as "great guys," but admits they have too big a piece of his company. Their individual investment of $18,000 in 1984 converted into 110,000 shares a piece when the company went public—equivalent to a market value of $3.3 million for each investor.

Haire says he has been in business long enough to know that the best-laid plans often go awry. It is the wise entrepreneur who recognizes that unexpected change can be an advantage; that an obstacle can turn into a benefit. Certainly, things don't always work out as planned—often, they work out better.

References

Appleby, Charles R. "Firm Aims to Nurture a Market in Obstetrical Home Services." *Health Week*, July 29, 1991.

"The Best Small Companies." *Business Week*, May 22, 1989.

Deutschman, Alan. "America's Fastest Risers." *Fortune*, October 7, 1991.

Mamis, Robert A. "The Inc. 100: The 12th Annual Ranking of America's Fastest-Growing Small Public Companies." *Inc.*, May 1990.

McKenna, Jon. "Infusion Therapy Means Blow-out Growth for T^2." *Atlanta Business Chronicle*, February 11, 1991.

Smith, F. M. "Business Achievement Award—Thomas Haire & T^2 Medical." *Business Atlanta*, July 1990.

Ticer, Scott. "Mixing Up a Rich Intravenous Solution." *Business Week*, May 22, 1989.

"200 Best Small Companies in America." *Forbes, November 12, 1990.*

——F. M. S.

Kenneth A. Hendricks

American Builders & Contractors Supply Company, Inc.

Kenneth A. Hendricks: Born 1941. Married, seven children.
Venture: Through acquisition and renovation of failing businesses, Hendricks built the nation's largest distributor of wholesale building materials for use in residential and commercial construction.
Company: American Builders & Contractors Supply Company, Inc. (ABC, Inc.); 820 Broad Street; P.O. Box 838; Beloit, WI 53511; (608) 362-7777
Founded: June 1982.
Revenues: $350 million (1990), according to published reports.
Employees: 750 (1,100 during summer).
Original Investment: Unknown.
Value: $4.4 million net worth (1989), according to published reports.

Founder

By age eight, Ken Hendricks had his first business. He began mowing lawns in his neighborhood as a way to earn extra spending money. Soon, he had more customers than he could handle and recruited other neighborhood children to help with the work. "I'd go out and drum up business, hand out the jobs to the others, give them half the money and keep the rest. It was a winning situation all around," Hendricks said.

A native of Janesville, Wisconsin and son of a local roofer and lumberyard owner, Hendricks left high school after the 11th grade to marry and start a family. Together, Hendricks and his wife, Diane, have managed several businesses and raised seven children.

210

After leaving school, Hendricks worked during the day at the local utility company and roofed houses in the evenings and on weekends. At age 21, he started his first company, International Roofing Co. Inc. Within seven years, the business grew to be the ninth largest commercial and residential roofing company in the United States with annual sales of more than $6 million and contracts in 48 states.

Hendricks calls himself a "renovator" who enjoys taking things in need of repair and restoring them to "something of value." In the early 1970s, he widened his business ventures from roofing to real estate, purchasing 200 houses and 2.5 million square feet of property in the Beloit, Wisconsin area. After restoring the homes, he rented them as apartment units to college students and others. He later became involved in renovating large commercial and industrial complexes.

Hendricks gained local attention when he purchased and restored "Stonehenge," an English Tudor manse built by George Parker, the late founder of the Parker Pen Company. The house had been abandoned and was in total disrepair when Hendricks bought it. During its restoration, he lived in a job-site trailer and personally supervised the project. While he devoted his time to Stonehenge, Diane managed the couple's successful real estate business.

Both Ken and Diane Hendricks have been recognized for entrepreneurial successes. The two were named Wisconsin's 1987 "Entrepreneurs of the Year" by Arthur Young accounting firm and *Venture* magazine. Ken Hendricks was also honored in 1987 by the Independent Business Association of Wisconsin for his contributions to the state's business climate, and he was named Beloit's "Businessman of the Year" in 1986.

Hendricks is a member of several trade organizations and a frequent speaker and lecturer. In addition to sharing his entrepreneurial success story, he has spoken to students about the disadvantages of dropping out of school. Hendricks says that while he encourages students to finish high school and seek higher education, he also tells them to follow their creative instincts. "I wish schools did more to encourage innovative thinking and entrepreneurial spirit. The more education you get, the more you read and learn about others' ideas," he said. "As a result, people tend to copy others rather than striking out with ideas of their own. I'm not a carbon-copy of anyone, and I believe that has worked to my advantage."

Business Origin

When Hendricks started ABC, ownership of building supply stores had begun to shift from small "mom-and-pop" distributors to outlets of major department store chains that sold more than building supplies. As a customer, Hendricks was displeased with the service he received. "I used to get angry when I'd shop for supplies," he said. "I'd wait for someone to help me, and when I finally did get service, the salespeople had no idea about the products I was looking for. They didn't seem to care that the time it was taking me to get what I needed was costing my business money."

Hendricks had a vision of how customers like himself could get the kind of service they needed. His answer was to establish a network of independently-managed building supply distribution centers under a corporate umbrella. Like the mom-and-pop stores, the local centers would be staffed by people who knew their customers and their products. They would also have the financial support of a national chain. Using money he had accumulated in real estate, Hendricks launched ABC by buying three Midwestern independent roofing supply distributorships in 1982. He established his company's Beloit headquarters in what had been an abandoned auto dealership/body shop before he renovated the building.

Those first three ABC outlets were failing businesses that Hendricks intended to restored to financial health. He says that he never considered opening his own store. "I simply I didn't have the capital to buy land and build a store from the ground up. Acquiring an established business gave me the advantage of that store's customer base. From the beginning, my strategy has been to apply ABC's management expertise to troubled businesses," he said.

Business Growth

ABC has grown at an extraordinary pace as a result of Hendricks' relentless acquisition. The company was included in *Inc.* magazine's list of fastest-growing, privately-held U.S. companies four years in a row from 1984-1987, and earned the number-one ranking in 1986. ABC was listed on Arthur Anderson & Company's "Wisconsin 100" of public and private companies from 1985-1987. *Venture* magazine cited the company for "stunning growth over a 10-year period" in its 1989 "Galaxy of Superstars."

ABC's 92 distribution outlets are the most owned by any company in the building supply industry. Building on his original three acquisitions, Hendricks added 13 East Coast distributors in May of 1984. The move made ABC a major player in the building supply marketplace literally overnight. The company acquired five Midwest affiliates and eight Texas wholesalers in 1985. By the end of 1986, ABC had 62 outlets. Hendricks made no acquisitions in 1987, instead taking a look inside at his now large company and developing control systems to improve productivity and profitability. Hendricks bought three centers in California in 1988, making ABC a coast-to-coast distributor. In early 1989, the company acquired eight distributors and expanded its product line.

Hendricks used profits generated by existing ABC branches to fund each new acquisition. He bought most of the businesses from failing or retiring independent owners or from major manufacturers eager to rid themselves of low-margin, high-service businesses. Hendricks says that so many distributorships are for sale as a result of changes in the building supply marketplace. "The competitive environment of the building supply industry has shifted in favor of larger owners. The independents simply can't stay ahead of the competition. Many of the privately-owned stores will only survive if a company like ours moves in."

ABC's first priority is to acquire stores in cities where it is not already located. Hendricks looks for businesses that are what he calls, "old and tired" and in need of modernization. "Managers often don't do well because they have reached a 'comfort zone' and they're no longer looking for creative ways to serve their customers. We try to inject a renewed spirit of enthusiasm and opportunity," Hendricks states. "We show them that you can't survive in business if you become too comfortable. You have to be aggressive to do well."

Business Obstacles

Hendricks remembers when many were skeptical of his expansion plans. "People told me I was crazy and that my business would be a 'flash in the pan,'" Hendricks recalls. "They insisted it wasn't possible to successfully run more than two distributorships, and I already had three."

Hendricks proved his doubters wrong, accumulating 92 outlets by 1991. He has continued to grow his business using a consistent strategy— buying failing businesses and rebuilding them the way he had renovated old houses. "Now that the business is a success, I find those same people who said I couldn't do it listening intently to what I have to say," he says.

While most of Hendricks' acquisitions have been profitable from the outset, there are exceptions. Soon after Hendricks bought distribution centers in five Texas cities, that state's economy took a downturn and the new ABC stores lost money. Similarly, operations in Denver suffered losses as a result of that city's economic setbacks. Hendricks says that both cities' stores are now profitable because ABC "responded appropriately" to the economic situation. "We didn't panic, pull out or try to sell more products by lowering prices. I've seen cases where at the first sign of trouble, businesses make the mistake of hiring salespeople to force products into a depressed economy. What you have to do is hang in there, take the cuts necessary to survive and operate a business that's right for the times," he asserts.

Keys to Success

Hendricks' ability to see value in what others have discarded or ignored has brought big dividends. Even before he started ABC, his eye for opportunity was paying off. He made nearly $1 million from the renovation and resale of modular buildings he purchased just as they were about to be demolished. He bought an abandoned railroad roadhouse for $30,000, and after selling the miles of steel rail and old fertilizer that were lying there, he was financially ahead before reselling the property. Hendricks has never been one to turn his back on opportunity. As he told *Inc.* magazine, "We've got a whole company here that's built around getting the greatest value for the least cost. We take other people's waste, stuff they don't want anymore . . . and we love it and caress it and make it good as new."

In rebuilding the businesses that form the ABC chain, Hendricks' goal is to retain acquired stores' former owners and store managers and teach them how to better manage the businesses. In many cases, Hendricks has had to reshape management's fundamental attitudes about how businesses should be run. "The people who are already working in a location have the advantage of knowing the customers and the area. Often, however, they don't understand what customer service really means or how to be profitable," he asserts. ABC sends each new manager through a rigorous five-day course at corporate headquarters, a program that costs the company a half-million dollars a year. Hendricks says it is well worth the investment. "We see former owners making twice as much money as they did when they were in business for themselves," he says.

He makes certain to take advantage of the special contributions each manager brings to the business and gives them full responsibility for managing their own locations. Branch managers decide what products they will carry, manage their own receivables, and hire their own staff. Hendricks holds managers accountable for their decisions, linking compensation, bonuses and profit sharing to how well locations are run. Top performers are recognized at an annual awards ceremony that also offers training to broaden managers' business skills. "I make it clear that the branch is theirs to run as they see fit, and they are directly responsible for its success or failure," Hendricks says. "Operating [92] stores, we've seen what works and what doesn't, so it's not difficult to judge successful performance."

Hendricks is accessible to his managers, taking their telephone calls even if it means putting something else on hold. He offers them personal guidance and creatively demonstrates what he believes to be the best ways to run a store. One method of illustration Hendricks has used asks managers to move "play" money between two shoe boxes, one marked "expenses" and one marked "budget." As managers transfer the money from one box to another, they see that poor business decisions may leave them with nothing to pay their bills. "The first criteria for a successful business is sound management, not sales," Hendricks declares. "When we enter a new market, we first look at how to run the most efficient and effective business in that economy. That's far more important than any target sales figure." He further elaborated in *Inc.*, "Making money is the *result* of good business; it's not the goal. If you make it the goal, you get into trouble."

Perhaps because he moved from laborer to owner, Hendricks has the utmost respect for the work his customers do. He demands that all who work with him respect ABC customers are much as he does. "The most important lesson I give managers is how to be accountable to their customers. Good customer service means waiting on the customer, knowing him by name, and most of all, helping him run a successful operation," he says. "If the customer needs the store to be open at 6 a.m., then it's important to open that early. After all, if your customers make money, your profit will take care of itself."

At the corporate office, Hendricks controls support services provided to the distributorships as a way to keep overhead low. Home office handles purchasing and payroll, management hiring, legal and insurance matters and offers guidance on vehicle repair. Hendricks maintains two other businesses that support the branches. One subsidiary leases trucks, forklifts and cars and helps to control costs by buying used equipment at substantial savings. A real estate division handles property leasing arrangements, often taking old commercial space and revitalizing it as a way to cut costs.

The large Hendricks family has been an integral part of ABC's growth and success. Diane Hendricks is the company's executive vice president and corporate secretary. All of Hendricks' children and a number of their spouses work in the company. "Diane has always been a critical part of the operation—she's the person who minds the details. I'm fortunate that my children decided to join us when they finished school. In each case, it seemed that just as they graduated from college, the business had grown to the point where I had a need for their specialty. I certainly never replaced anyone to make room for them, it was all just great timing," Ken Hendricks says.

Hendricks also encourages family members of ABC employees to join his team. "I know that some companies don't allow family members to work in the same locations, and I can't understand that. If I have an opening and an employee's family member has the required skills, that's the first person I want to interview," he says. "If you like your work, and trust and respect your company, why wouldn't you want family members to work there?"

Future Vision

Hendricks is comfortable with his current formula for success and doesn't envision dramatic changes within ABC. He views one of his primary challenges as keeping the entrepreneurial spirit and "small company" feeling alive within ABC as it continues to grow. "Much of my time these days is spent putting out bureaucratic fires, stopping the company from adding unnecessary red tape," Hendricks says. He is determined to keep the organization lean and has made it a practice both in the branches and at headquarters not to add staff until sales growth warrants it. "Bureaucracy is a hazard of growth, and it can stifle a company," he says.

Hendricks leaves no doubt that ABC will continue to grow as aggressively as it has in the past. He wants to expand to U.S. cities where ABC is not yet located and establish outlets in Canada, Mexico, and Europe. "Our goal is to operate 180 stores and have more than a billion dollars in sales between 1992 and 1994," he says. "People ask me why I want to get bigger, why I don't just stick with what we have? The way I see it, we're already the biggest and we're doing just fine." Hendricks asks, "Why wouldn't we grow some more?"

Entrepreneurial Lessons

While Hendricks says that he has read books on management over the years, most of his lessons have been learned "on-the-job." He has learned much from the experiences of the failed businesses he's acquired. "I have gathered a wealth of information about how not to do it. Most importantly, I see that you have to take responsibility for your business. You can't blame the customers, the market or anyone else for your mistakes."

According to Hendricks, the key to building a successful business is "knowing your product line inside and out and knowing your customer even better." That philosophy is rooted in his personal experience as a roofer who could find no supplier who understood his business needs. He has never forgotten the anger and frustration he felt as a customer, and he has built his business by treating his customers well.

Hendricks looks for employees who readily accept responsibility. "I want people here who are honest and who have a feeling in their belly that they want to get ahead. Working here is more than just a job, its an opportunity to be part of something that's growing and moving," he says. He impresses upon employees the importance of being accessible to their customers outside and inside the company. He insists that anyone who calls an ABC location with a question should only have to make one phone call. "We've limited bureaucracy so that no one is far removed from their boss and everyone is accountable," he says.

Hendricks judges how well his system is working by how few matters he must handle. "If you followed me around for a day, you'd be surprised at how little I have to do." ABC's chief says, "Everyone here knows their business and they're ready to give answers. We don't waste time on unanswered questions, we just get on with the business of serving our customers."

References

Boehne, R. "Small-Town Roofer Nails Opportunity." *The Cincinnati Post*, July 1, 1987.

"Diane, Ken Hendricks." *Corporate Report Wisconsin*, July 1, 1987.

Gendron, George, and Bo Burlingham. "Waste Not, Want Not." *Inc.*, March 1991.

Kahn, Joseph P. "Raising the Roof." *Inc.*, December 1986.

"Lessons." *Inc.*, May 1988.

——M. J. B.

John B. Henry

Crop Genetics International

John B. Henry: Born 1948. Married, one child.
Venture: The creation, production and marketing of biotechnological pesticides and disease-resistant crops.
Company: Crop Genetics International; 7170 Standard Drive; Hanover, MD 21076; (301) 621-2900
Founded: 1981.
Revenues: $2.6 million from sales of the company's Kleentex sugar cane tissue in 1989.
Employees: 90-100.
Original Investment: $1.7 million of venture capital.
Value: Approximately $16.7 million (1989), according to published sources.

Founder

"The greatest business opportunities exist where society has its biggest social needs," says John B. Henry, founder of Crop Genetics International.

In business since 1981, Crop Genetics has never shown a profit, yet Henry is certain the company is doing fine. The firm has spent more than $40 million dollars, and not yet brought its main product to market—but everything is going according to plan, he explains.

After graduating from Harvard University in 1971, Henry spent three years on the staff of the Senate Foreign Relations Committee. He then spent two years as a part-time consultant for the Mobil Corporation in the

Middle East. Later, after completing his law degree at Columbia University, he made the move to Wall Street.

Henry joined the New York firm of Cadwalder, Wickersham & Taft as a corporate securities law associate. It was there, he says, that his entrepreneurial drive became visible. "It was evident to everyone—especially me—that I was on the 'wrong' side of the table," he recalls. "When entrepreneurs were in our offices, I found myself always rooting for them, wanting them to make it." It was not long, Henry adds, before he decided to move to join the ranks of entrepreneurs.

Business Origin

In 1980 John Henry took a leave of absence from practicing law and set out to found a company of his own. "I knew there were some promising growth industries," he remembers, "mainly robotics and biotech. I quickly decided on the biotech industry, because I'm no engineer."

Having identified biotechnology as his main focus, Henry then narrowed his search to the agricultural niche of that industry. "There were already major players on the pharmaceuticals side, but relatively little was being done in agriculture," he points out. Once Henry decided to pursue building a company devoted to agricultural biotechnology, he then began searching for the right partner to help found it.

Henry began meeting with people in the biotech industry, talking with them about his plans and listening to their ideas—and asking them for referrals to others who might be interested. One of those referrals led Henry to Dr. Peter Carlson.

Henry arranged what was to be a short introductory meeting with Carlson at a Michigan airport. The meeting stretched to more than nine hours as the two discussed their visions, dreams and goals. By the end of that first meeting each knew he had found a partner.

Carlson supplied the concept for what would be the new company's flagship product. His idea was both high-tech and elegantly simple. An experienced biochemist, he envisioned using the young technology of gene-splicing to replace chemical pesticides. Carlson was convinced, and Henry agreed, that this concept could not only eliminate billions of pounds of chemicals that find their way into food and drink every year, but could also be more effective and economical. Henry was quick to realize both the social benefit and the business potential. "It fit my personal philosophy," he says.

In addition to fitting Henry's philosophy, Carlson's ideas also fit the venture capital climate. Biotechnology projects, especially recombinant DNA (gene-splicing), were popular in the investment community of the early 1980s. Henry, Carlson, and a few others mapped out their business strategy, developed a formal plan and presentation, and raised more than $1.7 million in venture capital. They opened the doors of Crop Genetics International well-prepared, well-financed, and well-equipped to create the new product they envisioned.

Business Growth

Rather than begin with what was certain to be an extremely complex effort to develop the biopesticide product, the company first turned to the less complex field of tissue culture technology to quickly get a product to market. "We wanted to prove ourselves and prove our ability," recalls Joe Kelly, the firm's vice president of operations. To do so, Crop Genetics scientists developed a disease-resistant strain of sugar cane, called Kleentex, which generates about $2.5 million in sales each year. With that product in place, and with their ability to produce genetically engineered products established, Henry focused Crop Genetics on Carlson's original concept.

John Henry credits Carlson, who became the new company's vice president of research, with the firm's focused vision. "He is a legitimate genius," explains Henry. "He not only has the knowledge and technology, but he's a real visionary as well." Carlson, who had been both a college professor and a consultant to many of the nation's largest chemical, pharmaceutical and petroleum companies, now had to make his concept a reality.

Carlson's vision was to create a safer, more effective, and more economical pesticide delivery system. By combining genes from appropriate bacteria, the company intended to create a new strain that would live only inside specific plants (corn, rice, wheat, etc.) and produce pesticides within the plant. This biopesticide would kill the plants insect enemies, but would not harm other animals, people, or the environment. In other words, Crop Genetics was going to give every corn stalk in the country the ability to defend itself.

Henry points out that the benefits of such a system would be enormous. The American corn industry alone suffers some $400 million in damage and loss every year, mainly from a single type of insect, the corn borer. The borer, which lives in the stalks of corn plants, does little but continually eat its way up and down the infected corn stalk, until the stalk is finally so weak it simply falls over. With the new biopesticide in a corn stalk, the first bite the borer took would be its last.

The new product promised other benefits as well. In addition to killing insects and greatly increasing the yield of America's corn crop, the Crop Genetics creation would be a boon to fish, wildlife, and the environment. Every year more than 1.4 billion pounds of chemical pesticides are sprayed, dumped, or dripped onto U.S. farms. Every year millions of pounds of those chemicals find their way into streams, lakes, and other unintended locations—a situation which would be vastly improved by replacing externally applied chemicals with Crop Genetic's biopesticide.

The Crop Genetics product would end farmers' intense exposure to chemicals and be cheaper than current pesticides. "The beauty of the system is that it requires virtually no manufacturing," claims Carlson. "Once our product is inside a plant, it acts like a tiny microbial factory, manufacturing pesticides around the clock. Only 20 pounds will stop the . . . corn borer from damaging Iowa's 10 million-acre corn crop."

Business Obstacles

The first obstacles Henry faced were technological. Financing was relatively stable, the venture capitalists involved were in for the long haul, and the successful introduction of Kleentex had helped prove the company's technological prowess. When the time for additional rounds of financing arrived, Henry was confident the investors would be there.

The technological aspects of creating the new product had been challenging, but it was always a straightforward challenge. With time, money, and Carlson's talents, John Henry had always been certain that Crop Genetics could meet that challenge.

By 1986, Carlson and his research teams had conquered most of the technological problems.

Crop Genetics scientists had taken a benign organism called Bt, which was harmful to insects but not to plants, animals, or people, and spliced it with another bacterium called an endophyte. The result was just what Henry and Carlson had hoped for—bacteria that lived inside a plant, and spent its life cycle creating pesticides to defend its host. The creation was promptly dubbed InCide. Now however, it was not technology but bureaucracy that threatened to stand in the way.

As "hot" as biotech was for the investment community of the 1980s, it became "hotter" still for the environmental community. The very nature of the industry—its creation of new forms of bacteria and other organisms—made it as frightening to some as it was exciting to others. In addition, the field was still so new that clearly defined lines of procedure, safety, and even government regulations had yet to be established.

Crop Genetics and John Henry had no choice but to step into the fray. The company had to obtain government approval—often from different government agencies—to conduct tests of its new product. In addition, it would need government sanction after testing to bring the final product to market. At each phase, Crop Genetics would have to provide thousands of pages of data for government scrutiny. The government, in turn, would listen to public comment. The tone of that public comment could make or break the company.

Keys to Success

From the experience of other biotech firms, Henry knew the instant Crop Genetics applied for the first test permit, the nation's environmental groups would let their opinions be known. For the most part there would be concerns on safety and side-effects. Crop Genetics, however, was prepared to answer safety questions. What worried the entrepreneur was the trouble which could be caused by extremist groups—groups opposing any biotech project regardless of its merits. Not inconceivably, they could delay Crop Genetics permits and progress for years through challenges in the courts.

With this threat in mind, Henry decided to "confront the regulatory thing head on."

Rather than view environmental groups or government agencies as enemies, Henry treated them as organizations with legitimate interests in Crop Genetics work. Both Henry and Carlson went to environmentalists' meetings to explain the concept and reality of InCide. Crop Genetics teams went to relevant federal agencies, asking about the kind of information agency scientists needed. The company even arranged to conduct some of its tests in conjunction with research farms run by the Department of Agriculture.

"Our goal was simple," recalls Henry. "We didn't want anyone to be surprised." The all-out effort eventually cost the company hundreds of thousands of dollars, but Henry thinks the money was well spent. "Without that [permit]," he points out, "we were dead meat."

With no objections from environmental groups, Crop Genetics International received its permit in record time for a biotech applicant. The company began field tests of InCide in 1989, and reported complete success in early 1990. More tests will continue and Henry says InCide will be on the market in 1993.

Future Vision

For Crop Genetics International, the main focus is to complete InCide's testing, get it to market, and begin to make money from a product that took more than ten years to create. John Henry, while remaining COB, stepped down as president and CEO in August 1990, and subsequently left Crop Genetics in June 1991 after deciding not to run for re-election as a director of the company.

Entrepreneurial Lessons

Building a company first and then trying to create a product taught John Henry a number of important lessons. First, he says, is that entrepreneurship is an on-going process, not a short-term project, or a "flash in the pan."

Equally important, Henry notes, is to know who your market is at all times. When Crop Genetics was trying to get its first test permits, the company's market consisted of environmental groups and government agencies— those were the groups the "sales effort" had to be aimed at, not the farmers who will one day use InCide.

But most of all, Henry points to two simple truths: "Make sure you get the people you need, the right people to get you from here to there," he counsels, "and more than anything else, don't let anyone talk you out of your vision."

References

Finegan, Jay. "All the President's Men. " *Inc.*, February 1990.

———. "Boring In." *Inc.*, July 1989.

Lev, Michael. "New Chief Sees Promise in Crop Genetics' Work." *New York Times*, September 3, 1990.

Smart, Tim, and Reginald Rhein, Jr. "For John Henry, Knowing the Right People May Not Be Enough." *Business Week*, April 18, 1988.

———E. C.

Frank D. Hickingbotham

TCBY Enterprises, Inc.

Frank D. Hickingbotham: Born 1936. Married, two children.

Venture: Seeking a business activity that would be less demanding of his time, in 1981 Hickingbotham opened one small frozen-yogurt shop in a suburban shopping center in Little Rock. He named it "This Can't Be Yogurt."

Company: TCBY Enterprises, Inc.; TCBY Tower Building; 425 W. Capitol; Suite 1100; Little Rock, AK 72201; (501) 688-8229

Founded: Founded in 1981 and incorporated in 1984.

Revenues: $151.2 million (1990), according to published reports.

Employees: 2,000.

Original Investment: Undisclosed.

Value: Net worth $91 million (August 1989). Market value $636 million (December 1989).

Founder

Frank D. Hickingbotham, through his frozen yogurt empire, has become one of Arkansas' most celebrated life-long residents. After receiving his bachelor's degree in business at the University of Arkansas-Monticello, he returned to his hometown of McGehee to operate an insurance agency. He also served as the town's high school principal from 1958 to 1962.

During the late 1960s, Hickingbotham moved into the food industry when he and a group of investors obtained an AQ Chicken franchise for Central Arkansas. He later purchased the franchisor company. In 1976 Hickingbotham sold AQ to Tasty Baking Company of Philadelphia, and bought Dallas-based Olde Tyme Foods, a manufacturer of frozen fruit cobblers. When he tired of the grueling commutes to Dallas from Little Rock, Hickingbotham started the process of selling the company in 1981. He sought a business opportunity closer to home.

Business Origin

During the years he ran the pie company, Hickingbotham's wife, Georgia, often accompanied him to Dallas. One day, his wife suggested he try an unusual frozen yogurt dish she had tasted at the Neiman Marcus store. Hickingbotham resisted the idea, but she insisted that he meet her for lunch. Hickingbotham accepted the invitation, tasted the yogurt, and, as the company legend goes, exclaimed, "This can't be yogurt."

Business Growth

Hickingbotham did not originally plan to expand beyond his first store, which employed his son behind the counter. But demand for the product grew, and he soon opened two more "This Can't Be Yogurt" stores. The units were managed by Hickingbotham's two sons (Herren, now president of TCBY Enterprises; and Todd, now president of a TCBY subsidiary, Riverport Equipment Company) and his brother-in-law. "I decided to franchise when I ran out of relatives," Hickingbotham remarked.

A year after opening the first store, he hired a consultant to see if anyone were building a national chain and whether he could successfully franchise the concept. He began franchising in 1982, a single unit at a time, with first franchises going to loyal customers and friends. The franchise operation did not start with polished systems manuals and training procedures. Rather, it evolved out of experiences with those early franchisees. In 1989, over 62 percent of new franchises were opened by existing owners.

Through its Riverport Equipment Company subsidiary, TCBY Enterprises offers franchisees equipment packages. All TCBY Frozen Yogurt is manufactured by the company's Americana Foods subsidiary in Dallas and sold to all TCBY stores. Outlet franchisor TCBY Systems collects a royalty of 4 percent on sales. When existing franchisees want to grow and are qualified, TCBY's American Acceptance Corp. subsidiary helps fund expansion.

Other wholly-owned subsidiaries include: TCBY International Inc., international franchisor of TCBY outlets; Creative Impressions Inc., printing company for the parent company and the public; TCBY of Georgia Inc., owns and operates 20 company co-owned stores in Atlanta; TCBY of Texas Inc., owns and operates company stores in Texas; and Carlin Manufacturing Inc., manufactures modular, mobile and restaurant equipment.

In 1985, This Can't Be Yogurt Inc. was shortened to TCBY Enterprises Inc, and the acronym was reworded to stand for "The Country's Best Yogurt." In 1988 the symbol reflected another of many company milestones as the NASDAQ "TCBY" leaped to the New York Stock Exchange as "TBY."

By 1990, the fast-growing franchisor had more than 1,600 stores (149 company-owned). TCBY's territory covered the 50 states, Canada, Bahamas, Malaysia, Singapore and Taiwan.

Business Obstacles

When Frank Hickingbotham opened his first shop, demand for frozen yogurt was practically non-existent. While people were accustomed to the tart taste of yogurt, TCBY frozen yogurt was creamy, sweet and more dessert-like. "Our thrust was to position it as an ice cream parlor," Hickingbotham recalled. "The soothsayers said it couldn't be done—that we wouldn't survive the winter." At that time, stores and delicatessens selling frozen yogurt positioned it as a side product to pizza, barbecue or sandwiches, or it was sold in health food stores. Although he was told, "You won't sell enough yogurt to survive the winter," Hickingbotham never wavered from his original plan to specialize exclusively in frozen yogurt products.

In 1984, privately-owned TCBY passed a major hurdle by going public. Hickingbotham remembers that period has one of the roughest. "Investment bankers weren't too interested in this Arkansas company. I practically had to stand on the corner and give away green stamps with the purchase of stock." With the $2.4 million raised through the public stock offering, Hickingbotham purchased his supplier, Arthur's, the company that made the yogurt he had originally tasted at Neiman Marcus.

Keys to Success

Gale Law, Senior Vice President of Finance and TCBY Enterprise CFO, describes Frank Hickingbotham's leadership style: "He surrounds himself with people who believe in hard work and loyalty to the company and its mission, and who are determined to make TCBY a continuing success story. He is a firm, but understanding leader who encourages us to do a good job. He gives people the chance to grow and develop—even to make mistakes—and counts on them to learn and achieve along the way. He is a hands-on manager, pitching in whenever help is needed. He provides guidance in all aspects of the business."

TCBY takes frozen yogurt very seriously. Much of its success can be attributed to Frank Hickingbotham's no-nonsense business style and close attention to every aspect of his operation. "Our corporate mission statement is to help our franchisees sell more frozen yogurt at a profit by following company standards," Hickingbotham says. By manufacturing its own frozen yogurt products and offering standardized equipment and decor, the company is better able to control quality throughout its far-flung franchise network. TCBY believes customers should get "the same great taste no matter where" they buy the product.

TCBY field managers locally reinforce the corporate message. "We have a field management team of 65 people. Hickingbotham maintains, "If you call any of them at 3:00 A.M., they better be able to tell you [what you need to know]; that's what their job is."

Field managers are required to live within their territories, which helps them keep abreast of local market conditions while giving franchisees quick access to advice and consultation. Armed with laptop computers, managers visit each store approximately every six weeks, and feed their findings into the mainframe system at corporate headquarters.

Hickingbotham asserts that TCBY has "taken a page out of McDonald's book. Do what you do, and do it well. Keep the menu narrow and simple. If you can keep the franchise family moving ahead, the rest will fall into place."

TCBY Enterprises Inc. is a vertically-integrated holding company with several subsidiaries. While office and headquarters space are shared, each subsidiary has its own president and board of directors and handles distinct phases of the business. By giving the subsidiaries separate entrepreneurial identities, Hickingbotham makes a profit from every subsidiary.

The company understands its market. Hickingbotham explains, "We are really competing against the ice cream chains." In a national ad campaign the company chairman declares, "Say goodbye to high calories, say goodbye to ice cream." The national concern with fat and cholesterol has been a boon for TCBY. Its original yogurt recipe uses only 4 percent butterfat compared to most ice creams' 10 to 14 percent. The company recently introduced nonfat frozen yogurts and sugar-free frozen yogurts, and offers some flavors which are both nonfat and sugar-free. A sign of the company's success is seen on the menus of major ice cream chains. Dairy Queen, Baskin-Robbins, Häagen Dazs and Breslers have all added frozen yogurt to their lines.

TCBY bolsters its "health" image through its stores' clean, natural, uncluttered interiors and its insistence on neatness.

Tabletops and floors are spotless. The company stresses cleanliness during the 10-day training session new franchisees attend at "Yogurt University" in Little Rock, TCBY's counterpart to McDonald's training facility.

Future Vision

In conjunction with adding new stores in strip malls and shopping centers, TCBY is expanding into non-traditional sites to sell frozen yogurt. In a joint venture with Marriott, the company plans to open shops in toll plazas and at airports. There are also plans to sell Mrs. Fields' Cookies in TCBY stores. "We will begin to aggressively offer franchises for development as TCBY and Mrs. Fields' together," Hickingbotham told the *Arkansas Democrat*. "We will be the only company having a double branding concept."

Competition is heightening in the lucrative frozen yogurt market. Still, TCBY's closest competitor, I Can't Believe It's Yogurt of Dallas, is just one-sixth its size. Unintimidated, TCBY clearly believes the market still has plenty of room for growth. Since 1987, the company has spent more than $25 million expanding its manufacturing plant to make it capable of supplying 3,500 TCBY stores.

Through TCBY International, the company plans to expand further its international market. In January 1990, TCBY entered into a joint venture with a Japanese company to develop 200 stores in Japan over the next 12 years.

Entrepreneurial Lessons

Reflecting on TCBY's growth and success, Hickingbotham offers his insights on what sustained the venture in its early years. "I learned early in life that hard work, honesty and determination were the ingredients for achievement. In the first years at TCBY, we all worked very hard to hold the company together, knowing that we were working toward a vision of what we believed we could achieve together. It took determination in the face of high risk to grow TCBY into a dynamic enterprise."

Maintaining growth and profitability, says Hickingbotham, depends on installing good management and operating procedures. "Consistency in our operating systems, products and management procedures is always a top priority. Experience in other business had shown me that to develop and implement a successful franchise formula, you must maintain consistency in all its applications—down to even the smallest details." Hickingbotham believes that "following this principle has allowed TCBY to offer strong business opportunities to franchises throughout the nation and the world."

Equally important to success, Hickingbotham continues, is recognizing and assembling the right employees. "Almost all of us at TCBY are Arkansans, who grew up in an environment where a strong work ethic was emphasized early on and has shaped our lives." Those are attributes he seeks in all TCBY personnel. "Bringing together people of all ages and disciplines, but who share the common characteristics of drive, loyalty, commitment to quality honesty, and willingness to work hard has been a key factor in the success of TCBY."

References

Barrier, Michael. "Cold Product, Hot Company." *Nation's Business*, September 1988.

Garrett, Echo M. "The Accidental Franchisor." *Venture*, May 1989.

Heinbockel, C.S. "TCBY Heir Apparent Named." *Arkansas Gazette*, April 3, 1988.

Moreau, Andrew. "Profits Dip, But TCBY Has Plans In the Oven." *Arkansas Democrat*, September 23, 1991.

Richman, Tom. "In the Black." *Inc.*, May 1988.

Wood, Kingsley. "Yogurt Chain Keeps Arkansas Man off of the Golf Course." *Las Vegas Sun*, March 23, 1987.

——B. M.

Samuel I. Hinote

Delta Pride Catfish, Inc.

Samuel I. Hinote: Born 1942. Married, three children.
Venture: Farmer-owned cooperative that produces and processes catfish for consumption.
Company: Delta Pride Catfish, Inc.; Indianola Industrial Park; P.O. Box 850; Indianola, MS 38751; (601) 887-5401
Founded: February 12, 1979.
Revenues: $152 million gross sales (as of July 1989), according to published reports.
Employees: 1,890.
Original Investment: Approximately $6 million.
Value: $26 million (July 1989), according to published reports.

Founder

Samuel I. Hinote combined an innovative economic strategy with aggressive marketing tactics to advance a growing "fish-farm" cooperative.

Hinote graduated from Auburn University (Alabama) with a B.S. in agricultural economics and an M.S. in administration. That training landed him positions as director of economic research and general manager of fish operations at agribusiness giant ConAgra Inc. He spent thirteen years there before taking the helm at newly-formed Delta Pride in 1980.

A catfish farm owner himself, Hinote is a director and member of the executive committee of the Catfish Farmers of America. He is a director and vice president of U.S. Farm-Raised Fish Trading Company and a past president of the American Catfish Marketing Association. Recently he was asked by the U.S. Secretary of Commerce to represent aquaculture on the newly created National Fish and Seafood Promotional Council.

After guiding Delta Pride to the forefront of the catfish processing industry, Hinote resigned as the company's chief executive officer in August 1990.

"I still have other entrepreneurial dreams to pursue," Hinote says. Remaining involved in aquaculture, Hinote formed Hinote Enterprises, Inc., with a view toward building another successful catfish processing operation (he is well underway with his new company, Bluewaters Catfish, in Demapolis, Alabama). He also has an interest in Fishbelt Feeds, Inc., a catfish feed mill in Moorhead, Mississippi.

Business Origin

In the late 1960s, Mississippi cotton and soybean farmers were facing bankruptcy. Crop prices were low and the market was unstable. Unable to withstand the ups and downs of nature and economics, the farmers converted their soil-based crops to catfish ponds. R.B. Hoke, a former Mississippi Delta cotton farmer, says of catfish farming, "It's more sure. You don't have to wait on the rain."

Catfish farming became so popular that overproduction ensued. Because large processing companies failed to expand at the same rate, farmers again found themselves selling their crop at low prices. Those same companies started farming their own fish, posing an additional threat. To combat that problem, in 1979 a group of 119 farmers formed a cooperative, Delta Catfish Processors Inc. They raised $4.5 million to build their own processing plant. The company was renamed Delta Pride Catfish Inc. in 1988.

Business Growth

Delta Pride owes its growth to shrewd economic maneuvers and effective marketing. Hinote introduced the shareholder concept. Delta farmers buy one company share—at $1,200—for each acre of catfish ponds they own. In 1981 there were 12,000 outstanding shares. By 1988 that figure was 50,000 outstanding shares, and Delta Pride had become the number one catfish producer in the United States.

Marketing transformed a lowly fish into a "yuppie" pleaser. Catfish, commonly associated with "six-packs of beer and pickup trucks," was considered *declasse*. It suffered from "that image thing," according to Bill Allen, president of the Catfish Institute.

Hinote hired a marketing firm to improve the catfish's image. A major challenge was to dispel the notion that catfish are scavenger fish. He says, "Farm-raised catfish are a far cry from their ancestors, which had a reputation [of] being a bottom-feeding scavenger fish." He points out, "Farm-raised catfish are grown in clean, fresh water; fed only a commercially prepared diet of soybean meal, corn, fish meal and vitamins and minerals. They are brought from the pond to the plant live, and kept [alive] until processing begins."

Delta Pride held approximately 40 percent of the $2 billion catfish market in 1989, and expected to process more than 140 million pounds of catfish in fiscal year 1990. Its catfish are sold in supermarkets and restaurants.

Business Obstacles

Low prices during 1987 and 1988 adversely affected catfish farmers. This situation interfered with development of new ponds, slowing growth of catfish produced. During the same period, the processing industry overbuilt. As a result, processors are caught in a market "squeeze," competing for the limited crop.

Although Delta Pride offered farmers security in an overwhelming market, the price was steep. With catfish farming being such an expensive venture—acreage costs thousands of dollars and equipment such as feeders and feed tanks run $10,000 or more—Delta Pride's share-per-acre fee is no longer as appealing as it once was. Thus Delta Pride must compete with other processors for its own farmers' product. Hinote says, "I see very tough times ahead. The farmers' condition is improving, but I see hard times for the processors because of the tremendous processing overcapacity."

Keys to Success

Hinote believes combining real product quality with strong marketing was responsible for the company's success. With health-conscious consumers concerned about seafood safety, Delta Pride let its customers know the company guaranteed a clean, safe product. A quality control staff of 20 ensured the harvested fish meet company standards.

Hinote bolstered his product's superior image by encouraging plant visitations. "If I can get the customer to come see our facility and the handling of the product, they are always convinced of our quality," he once explained to the press.

Hinote established high quality control standards which are still in effect. Catfish are fed well and each pond's crop is sampled by a "taster" to ensure "a mild, sweet odor [and] a mild, sweet flavor." According to Delta Pride "flavor-taster" Stan Marshall, "If it doesn't taste just right, I reject the fish and the pond." Hinote confirms, "Flavor-testing catfish was the most important part of our quality control."

While Hinote led Delta Pride, marketing was the banner under which the company operated. Executives attended food shows, conventions, and regional sales meetings to tout catfish's virtues. Hinote seized every promotional opportunity, once sending a ton of catfish to Moscow to establish a Cajun-style restaurant during the May 1988 Reagan-Gorbachev summit meeting.

Future Vision

In the next 10 to 15 years, Hinote predicts, 25 percent of all seafood consumed will come from aquaculture. Hinote believes catfish can capture a substantial share of that growth. He envisions farm-raised catfish becoming "to seafood what Kleenex is to tissue."

Commercial catfish processors "are only scratching the surface of what catfish consumption can become," Hinote says. " The percent per capita consumption of catfish is half a pound. I see it increasing to five or six pounds in the next 20 years."

Larry Joiner, former executive vice president and current Delta Pride chief executive officer, believes some of that increase will come from at-home consumption. While company surveys indicate consumers are "eating more seafood than ever before in restaurants," Joiner reveals, "my guess is that Americans may be less comfortable in purchasing and preparing seafood for home consumption because they may not feel confident selecting or preparing it." The company's challenge, he says, is "to help them be better informed to make those choices and feel comfortable with preparation."

Sam Hinote agrees. He thinks catfish processors can reach a broader market by promoting products through a variety of media. Future industry growth rests on effectively educating the American palate to the taste and versatility of farm-raised catfish. Hinote believes that can be done. He is willing to bet his business future on it.

Entrepreneurial Lessons

Hinote says to succeed you must have a vision, a plan, sound finances and a team of experts. "I saw the potential [of farm-raised catfish], and had the ability to build a management team to orchestrate the dream." Now, he says, he's going to go out and do it all again.

But to maintain optimum on-the-job productivity, Hinote cautions, lead a balanced life-style and retain outside interests. "You have to leave the work when you go home. I learned that early in my career."

References

"Catching up on Catfish: An Interview with Delta Pride's Sam Hinote." *Seafood Leader*, Fall 1988.

Fritz, Michael. "Catfish, Cajun Style, in Moscow." *Forbes*, December 12, 1988.

Hauck, Katharine. "Catfish Cradle." *Prepared Foods*, November 1989.

Hinote, Samuel I. "Farm-Raised Catfish Industry: Young, but Growing Like Crazy." *Quick Frozen Foods International*, January 1987.

Lingle, Rick. "Catfish Culture, Southern Style." *Prepared Foods*, November 1989.

Rice, Berkeley. "A Lowly Fish Goes Upscale." *New York Times Magazine / The Business World*, December 4, 1988.

——A. A.

H. Wayne Huizenga

Blockbuster Entertainment Corporation

H. Wayne Huizenga: Born 1937. Married, four children.
Venture: Rental and sales of videotapes and laserdiscs for home entertainment.
Company: Blockbuster Entertainment Corporation; 901 East Las Olas Boulevard; Fort Lauderdale, FL 33301; (305) 524-8200
Founded: 1985.
Revenues: Approximately $1.2 billion (1990), according to a company source.
Employees: 30,000.
Original Investment: A Huizenga-led group invested $18 million in 1987.
Value: Approximately $77 million net worth at the close of 1989, according to published sources.

Founder

H. Wayne Huizenga cut his entrepreneurial teeth in an industry where few people saw great potential—hauling garbage.

The solid waste disposal business was a fragmented industry 20 years ago when Huizenga embarked on his first venture. The industry was dominated by small family operations who were, for the most part, doing business exactly as they had been in the 1940s and 1950s. Huizenga owned such a company consisting of a truck, a list of commercial customers, and $500 in monthly revenues. But in the early 1970s he recognized opportunity.

With a relative, he founded Waste Management, Inc., and almost immediately took the company public. Using stock and funds from stock sales,

Huizenga bought dozens of waste-hauling firms, consolidating them into his company. He remembers the venture as an excellent learning experience. "The garbage business is a real good business to cut your teeth on. It's not like pest control, for example. If you are supposed to be there on Monday but don't get there until Tuesday, it isn't really a big deal. But that garbage has to be picked up every Monday or every Thursday. You've got to be there. So I grew up in a business where there were no excuses."

At the end of 1971, Waste Management had revenues of $16 million. By 1984, the companies revenues exceeded $5 billion.

In 1984 Huizenga resigned from the board of Waste Management to "pursue other business interests" without being exactly sure which interests he would pursue. He bought real estate, invested in some other companies and gave some thought to what to do next. Eventually, a friend and associate from Waste Management provided the answer—a struggling little firm called Blockbuster.

Business Origin

Blockbuster Entertainment Corporation actually had two founders, one who created the concepts which made the stores unique, and Huizenga, who created the strategy to make the company grow. In fact, the company itself really began its existence as a computer software firm.

Cook Data Services was a Dallas-based public company that supplied computer software to the oil and gas business. When the energy industry declined, the firm's founder, David Cook, began looking for new opportunities. He saw potential in video rentals.

Cook realized that existing video stores lacked adequate selection. After several months of research, he opened the first Blockbuster superstore in October 1985, with more than 8,000 tapes and 6,500 titles.

In addition, Cook added innovations in the way tapes were displayed and tracked to make it more convenient for customers to shop his store. Other stores kept tapes behind shelves to discourage theft, but that also meant customers had to wait for an employee to get the tape they wanted. In addition, most stores were writing up the rental by hand—another time-consuming process. From the start, Cook displayed Blockbuster's tapes on shelves where customers could pick them out for themselves. He also used computer equipment and a magnetic strip to track rentals and discourage theft.

"The store was wildly successful," Cook recalls. "People weren't just renting the top hits, they were renting everything. There seemed to be demand that no one had anticipated, because no one had made 8,000 tapes available before."

In less than a year, the Dallas area had three Blockbuster stores and Cook was preparing an equity offering to raise money for expansion. Then trouble struck. In September 1986, a local financial columnist wrote articles ridiculing Cook's move from oil and gas to the video business and questioning his business abilities. The equity offering fell apart, and the fledgling Blockbuster began to run out of cash.

Huizenga came to the rescue.

Huizenga, who had been busy with a variety of projects and other businesses since leaving Waste Management, was introduced to Cook and the Blockbuster situation by John Melk, a former Waste Management officer, and a Blockbuster investor. In early 1987, Huizenga, Melk and Donald Flynn (Waste Management's CFO), invested $18.6 million to buy 35 percent of Blockbuster's stock (and warrants to buy more in the future).

Business Growth

The result of blending Cook's techniques with Huizenga's strategy has been an unbroken path of growth, expansion, acquisition, and prosperity for Blockbuster. The company, under Huizenga's leadership, has grown from 19 to more than 1,600 stores across the nation, and has dozens of stores in other countries (the 1,000th store was actually opened in London). In 1991, a new store was opening every 17 hours. Prior to his involvement, in 1986 the company lost $3.2 million. In 1990, its revenues totalled approximately $1.2 billion.

To help control the growth of Blockbuster, Huizenga assembled a management team that has been called the most experienced in the industry. He hired former executives from McDonald's and kept on some of the brightest and most experienced executives from the regional chains Blockbuster has acquired. In a *New York Times* interview, Huizenga explained, "I enjoy building more than managing. What you learn from that is you ought to bring good people in."

Business Obstacles

The main obstacle facing Blockbuster was a decision on what type of future the company would have. Cook had envisioned a firm that would primarily franchise its name and computer system—a McDonald's of videos— but Huizenga wanted to grow with company-owned stores.

"I don't believe that just franchising gives you quality of earnings," Huizenga says. "If you want to build a quality company, you have to have company-owned operations (in addition to franchises)."

In addition, Huizenga sought to replicate his success at Waste Management by repeating that company's strategy of building by buying. He planned to acquire video chains that dominated local or regional markets and convert them to Blockbusters to achieve instant market dominance. The technique had worked well for Waste Management, where Huizenga had once bought more than 100 local waste companies across the nation in less than a year. He was confident it would work just as well in the fragmented video industry. Huizenga's financial strategy prevailed.

In the spring of 1989, a stock analyst wrote a report questioning some of Blockbuster's accounting procedures. As a result, Blockbuster's share price plunged. Since Blockbuster made acquisitions mainly with stock, the situation threatened the company's basic strategy. The report gave rise to a shareholder lawsuit.

Huizenga responded quickly and directly. He declared the analyst's report "wasn't worth the powder to blow it away," and issued a detailed rebuttal. He refused to change accounting policies and invited other analysts to comment on Blockbuster. The results were just what he expected. Other analysts continued to recommend Blockbuster stock. The lawsuit was dropped and Blockbuster stock rebounded, soon surpassing its previous price.

Keys to Success

When asked, Huizenga points to his experience with Waste Management as the major key to his ability to build the Blockbuster empire so quickly. "What I brought to this business from my experience at Waste Management, I think, is management through a regional concept. . . . I understand building an organization," he says.

"This is really a bunch of local businesses that we have," he explains. "We may be 1,000 stores strong . . . but if we are not doing a good job [in one store] on the corner of 5th and Main, we've got a problem."

Future Vision

Huizenga's vision for the company's future focuses on management and continued growth. "A lot of people have bitten the dust in this business; they haven't managed their inventory," he explains, noting that Blockbuster continues to improve its tracking and inventory controls constantly.

His other goal, continued growth—he wants Blockbuster to grow to 3,000 stores nationwide—is spurred as much by caution as by a desire to dominate the market. "We have the best concept in the industry, but it's not proprietary," he says. "People can copy it. That's why we have to move rapidly."

As Huizenga told *Variety,* "The industry may undergo change, but we will be at the forefront of that change, not at the end of the parade cleaning up after the elephants."

Entrepreneurial Lessons

Huizenga is straightforward about the lessons he has learned from his career. Growth and control, he says, are key. "Blockbuster is aiming for 3,000 stores nationwide because that will give us effective control of the market." He also points out that growth does not mean an entrepreneur has to do everything himself. In both the garbage industry and the video industry, Huizenga has been quick to use other smaller firms as the building blocks of his company's success.

References

Ames, Joe. "Blockbuster, Will It Live Up to Its Name." *The Miami Herald,* February 19, 1989.

Bane, Michael. "How Neat It Is." *American Way,* July 15, 1990.

Chakravarty, Subrata. "Give 'Em Variety." *Forbes,* May 2, 1988.

DeGeorge, Gail. "Blockbuster's Grainy Picture." *Business Week,* May 20, 1991.

———. "The Video King Who Won't Hit Pause." *Business Week,* January 22, 1990.

Kahn, Virginia. "Huizenga Builds a Second Growth Company." *Investor's Daily,* February 21, 1989.

Noglows, Paul. "Vid Giant Battles Stock-Busters." *Variety,* June 3, 1991.

Sandomir, Richard. "Wayne Huizenga's Growth Complex." *New York Times Magazine / The Business World,* June 9, 1991.

——E. C.

Jon M. Huntsman

Huntsman Chemical Corporation

Jon M. Huntsman: Born 1937. Married, nine children.
Venture: Founded the largest privately-held chemical corporation in America. The company manufactures styrene monomer, polystyrene resins, specialty resins and compounded petrochemical products.
Company: Huntsman Chemical Corporation; 60 E. South Temple Street; Suite 2000; Salt Lake City, UT 84111; (801) 532-5200
Founded: 1982.
Revenues: $961.2 million in fiscal 1990, according to a company source.
Employees: 1,701.
Original Investment: $1.8 million.
Value: $248 million, according to published reports.

Founder

Jon Huntsman may go down in history as the inventor of McDonald's Big Mac clamshell container, but he hopes to be remembered for much more. "Industrialist," "philanthropist," "business magnate," "lay minister," "political advisor," are all descriptions that fit, but he prefers to call himself an "entrepreneur."

Huntsman grew up in Utah and Blackfoot, Idaho, the son of a schoolteacher. His roots run deep in the Mormon church, going back to his great-great-great uncle, a scout for Brigham Young. His beginnings were modest and at an early age, Huntsman was working two after-school jobs to help put his father through graduate school. At age ten he was known for having the best lawn mower service in town.

243

His family had a firm belief in hard work and in creating something good out of a bad situation. His mother had a strong influence on his life. Etched on her tombstone is a line from Shakespeare: "Sweet are the uses of adversity." Huntsman believes that his most creative moments have come during times of struggle.

Huntsman went to the Wharton School of Finance at the University of Pennsylvania, where he graduated in 1959, with the Spoon Award for outstanding graduate. He later earned an MBA degree from the University of Southern California. He served two years as a gunnery officer in the United States Navy before taking his first business job with Olson Farms, Inc., a major egg producer in Los Angeles. It was to be Huntsman's first introduction to the petrochemical industry.

The company's experiments to develop a sturdier egg carton led to a joint-venture with Dow Chemical Company and the creation of a new company. Dolco Packaging Company developed a foam plastic container. Huntsman became president of the fledgling company at the age of 30. When he left the business three years later, Dolco's polystyrene container held 30 percent of the egg carton market.

Huntsman was then invited to serve as associate administrator in the Department of Health, Education and Welfare in the Nixon administration. He became a staff secretary to the President, but left political life after two years to head the Huntsman Container Corporation, a business that he had started with his brother.

The brothers invested $300,000 of their own money and raised $1 million in venture capital to start a company to make egg cartons, meat trays and disposable utensils out of polystyrene.

The company almost went under while Huntsman was in Washington, but when he became an active president and began calling personally on accounts, business picked up. "All my businesses have been based on personal selling. I always personally look after accounts, make sure they have my home phone, my night number," says Huntsman. The company struggled to survive the energy crunch of the early 1970s, when Huntsman's innovative bartering system kept them in raw product—but barely. At times, he bought and sold six to eight other products in order to acquire the raw material he needed.

While Huntsman was out selling containers, he had his research team working furiously to find new uses and new markets for polystyrene. They eventually came up with 80 new products. Polystyrene is now used in razors, television cabinets, pens, home appliances, auto parts, home insulation and many other items.

Huntsman credits the invention of the polystyrene clam shell container for fast food products and the selling of the idea to McDonald's as his company's greatest marketing coup.

When Huntsman grew dissatisfied with working for a company in which he only held a 25 percent interest, he sold the container corporation to Keyes Fiber in 1976 for $34 million. In what might seem a radical move for a successful CEO (but not for Huntsman, who has always thoroughly integrated his commitments to family, church and career), he spent the next three years in Washington, DC as president of the Mormon mission.

Business Origin

When he decided to go back into business, Huntsman chose a product that he knew something about—polystyrene. He was advised that the market was greatly oversupplied—the worst time to get into the industry. Through running his former company, Huntsman had learned that the chemicals-commodity business was cyclical and he saw future potential.

"In the early 1980s, I concluded that a great opportunity existed in the petrochemical industry. My strategy was to consolidate the industry into fewer hands and at the same time establish a base for Huntsman Chemical that would last over many decades. This could only be done by taking the aggressive position of expansion during a down cycle in the industry. When unusual values surfaced because the industry was going through a rare shakeout period of heavy over-production, I made my move," says Huntsman.

He managed to finance the purchase of Shell Oil Company's Belpre, Ohio plant, by taking a huge financial risk. Because of the market slump, Shell was willing to sell the $67 million plant for $42 million. Huntsman pledged $500,000 against his house and $1.3 million against his other assets and borrowed $29 million from a bank. The remaining $10 million he raised from Arco by agreeing to buy styrene monomer (the raw product for polystyrene) from their company for the next 13 years.

Huntsman knew that Shell and most industry giants expected him to fall flat on his face. Instead he quickly increased the plant output from 60 percent to 100 percent, attracting new customers by custom designing resins to suit their needs.

Business Growth

Instead of pulling in when the market continued to spiral downward, he convinced his creditors to back him as he aggressively bought other plants at advantageous prices. In 1984 he purchased Royal Dutch Shell's plant in Carrington, England. In 1986 he bought three more polystyrene plants from the German chemical firm, Hoechst A.G.

To fund further expansion, he sold 40 percent of the business to Great Lakes Chemical in 1986 for $54 million. He also expanded his operation to include the manufacturing of polypropylene, styrene monomer and packaging materials.

A year later, as Huntsman had predicted, the market took a sharp upturn. The company's income grew by 220 percent and by the end of 1988, Huntsman had paid off his debt and owned his plants free and clear.

Huntsman's move took considerable risk as well as hard work. His competitors were well-established companies such as Arco, Dow, Mobil, Chevron and Amoco. But Huntsman believes that for the most part, "corporate life is slow and inefficient." He has always enjoyed the challenge of "going up against the majors."

Today, Huntsman Chemical Corporation (HCC) is an international company, operating sixteen plants around the world from a home office in Salt Lake City. "The decision to locate in Utah was not a capricious choice. I simply decided to centralize in one locale the three greatest influences in my life—my business, my family and my church," says Huntsman.

HCC annually produces over three billion pounds of petrochemical products and is America's leading producer of polystyrene. They are also the third-largest producer of styrene monomer and the tenth-largest maker of polypropylene.

Business Obstacles

Huntsman's first major obstacle was finding the capital to get started in a market that was vastly oversupplied. He founded and expanded his business by taking financial risks that were diametrically opposed to the conventional wisdom of the time.

But Huntsman doesn't hold much with conventional wisdom. He believes a person has to see past a current situation, to look at the future, and to be inventive. "Only a visionary can be a good entrepreneur," he affirms.

In 1976, when Huntsman's capital was stretched past the limit, he took control of three polystyrene plants from Hoechst A. G. Chemical Company with no money. He convinced Hoechst to let him run the plants and pay them $45 million at the end of five years. Hoechst felt that it was worth the risk, since it saved the company the costs involved in shutting the plants down.

Continuing to expand the number of customers for his resins has been an ongoing challenge for HCC. A born salesman, Huntsman continues to increase business by moving aggressively into international markets, creating joint-ventures with other companies and pushing his research staff to create resins with the characteristics that an expanding market needs. One joint-venture, GE Plastics/Huntsman, is entering its third phase of operations and predicts its projects eventually could be worth $200-300 million.

The company has formed Huntsman-Moscow to supply polystyrene packaging to Aeroflot airlines. "We've laid down a lot of seedlings in the Soviet Union but we're not counting on a profit until the next decade," says Huntsman. While visiting there in 1991, he was quoted in *The Guardian* as speaking about "people like ourselves helping the Soviets to understand the free enterprise system. We feel a great responsibility for the private sector."

Keys to Success

Huntsman's ability to project his business into the future has been the company's greatest resource. He entered the industry in the bottom of an economic cycle, allowing him to buy plants at low prices. He then upped capacity utilization by addressing new markets.

"Clearly it involves hard work, but also a willingness to take substantial risks. Unless one is willing to accept risks, then the challenge and the excitement known to the successful entrepreneur can never be obtained and there is little, if any, reward," says Huntsman.

By "reward" Huntsman does not mean profit alone. He believes firmly that his company can make a difference in society. That philosophy is reflected on a personal level, by his spending 20 hours each week serving as a lay minister for his church.

"My religious beliefs have taught me the importance of hard work, honesty, integrity and concern for others. I consider the 1,700 Huntsman employees an extension of my own immediate family. As such I hope to always be a source of motivation and inspiration to them. I believe in being generous to my employees and I expect the very best of them. I have yet to be disappointed," Huntsman maintains. He told the *Desert News* he has "great affection" for all his employees, as was apparent a few years back when he gave each a trip to the Caribbean.

Huntsman sees the 21st century as a global century in which his company will play a major role in reaffirming the quality of life and values of all people. In keeping with that philosophy the company has donated relief funds to the homeless in America and to the victims of natural disasters around the world.

Future Vision

HCC will continue to expand its product line, but keep polystyrene as the mainstay. A $20 million capital investment in the Carrington, England plant will increase production from 25,000 to 75,000 tons annually. Huntsman expected sales to top the $50 million mark in 1990, with 55 percent of that product going to export markets in Europe.

Eventually, he would like to move into polyethylene, other thermoplastics, and feedstocks. Huntsman plans for the company to continue to expand internationally. He has new operations in China, India, Singapore and the Middle East. "The challenges we face today evolve around the need to accommodate our operations to a global economy," says Huntsman.

Although only three percent of HCC's materials are used in the totally-disposable plastics market, Huntsman recognizes that "the preservation of the environment is the single most important issue facing the world today." He donated $1 million to Utah State University in 1989 to found an environmental research center. He has pledged to give annually to that center and has donated funds for additional centers at other universities to conduct research in the areas of recycling, improved air quality, degradability and tree conservation.

Entrepreneurial Lessons

Huntsman believes that a person can become the most creative when the struggle is the greatest, a philosophy gleaned from his family and his strong faith. He cites men such as Abraham Lincoln, Dr. Armand Hammer,

Spencer W. Kimball (former Church of Jesus Christ of Latter-day Saints president) and former President Richard M. Nixon as having had an important influence in his life. However, he is also the product of a fine business education and much experience. He advises would-be entrepreneurs to ". . . find a sector of the economy that has a potential for growth and an acceptable margin of profit."

"For me, it was the petrochemical industry. For someone else, it may be some aspect of high technology, health care or some new computer or laser application. I see great opportunity for the entrepreneur who has a realistic and well-examined vision," says Huntsman.

References

Berman, Phyllis, and Dolores Latanoitis. "This Guy Is Going to Do Everything." *Forbes*, November 27, 1989.

Gaynor, Pamela. "Huntsman May Seek Aristech Takeover." *Pittsburgh Post Gazette*, June 2, 1989.

Halsall, Martyn. "A Lesson from the Mormons for Businesses Looking East." *The Guardian*, July 1, 1991.

Kimball, James. "Huntsman Chemical Corporation: Blackfoot Beginnings to Global Giant." *Utah's Business*, April 1989.

———. "Jon M. Huntsman, Chairman & CEO, Huntsman Chemical Corporation." *Sky*, July 1989.

Lythgoe, Dennis. "Jon M. Huntsman." *Desert News*, January 30, 1991.

O'Toole, Kevin. "Huntsman Interview: Making Plans for a Global Market." *European Plastics News*, June 1990.

Palmer, Anne. "Huntsman Earns Attention for Career and Money." *Salt Lake City Tribune*, December 10, 1987.

Woody, Robert H. "S. L. Is Hub of Huntsman Chemical's Global Action." *Salt Lake City Tribune*, March 30, 1986.

———L. R.

Tuan Huynh

H & A Fashions, Inc.

Tuan Huynh: Born 1936. Married, seven children.
Venture: Manufactures women's dresses and sportswear.
Company: H & A Fashions, Inc.; 3000 Irving Blvd.; Dallas, TX 75247; (214) 631-2910
Founded: 1985.
Revenues: $38 million (projected), according to March 1990 financial statement.
Employees: 50.
Original Investment: $50,000.
Value: $2.3 million, according to published reports.

Founder

From the nightmare of war to the dream of success, Tuan Huynh's life has changed dramatically in the past fifteen years. Huynh was a captain in the South Vietnamese army when the U.S. pulled out in 1975. Placed in a "re-indoctrination" camp, he served three years at hard labor. Huynh remembers his constant hunger during that time.

In 1978 he rejoined his wife Anh and their seven children. They desperately wanted freedom and planned their escape for over a year. After six months in a crowded Indonesian refugee camp, a sponsor in Dallas brought them to the U.S. in 1980. Huynh found work as an auto mechanic's assistant while Anh worked as a seamstress.

In America, Huynh saw opportunities that had never existed for him. Deep faith in the work ethic—"if you work hard, you'll do good"—runs

250

through each facet of his business and family life. He expects the best from his children and he expects the best from himself.

Business Origin

Hard work and determination have paid off for the Huynh family. Huynh's wife had been a seamstress and fabric buyer in Vietnam. In Dallas she sewed at home for local apparel manufacturers. At the end of Huynh's work day, he would deliver his wife's clothing and make business contacts at the same time. The family worked hard, saved money, and were ready to launch their own company in 1985. Huynh decided to call his company H & A Fashions after the family name and his wife's name. He started by hiring a general manager, a designer, a salesperson and a secretary. In a 3,000-square-foot warehouse, H & A Fashions began its journey toward success.

H & A Fashions manufactures women's dresses (80 percent) and women's sportswear (20 percent). H & A designs the dresses and subcontracts the sewing to others. The company's brands include American Shirtdress, Chezzam, American Creations, Pam's Closet, Kay Brandon Sport and Kay Brandon. Selling to specialty, department and chain stores, the retail price range is $35 to $65.

Business Growth

Sales came hard during the first few months after H & A introduced its first product line, the American Shirtdress. But when Huynh showed the line to J. C. Penney buyer Nancy Hillis, she saw an excellent customer value in a dress appealing to middle-America shoppers. With Penney's as a customer, business began to boom. First-year profits were about $40,000 on sales of $500,000.

According to Joe Allen, H & A vice president and general manager, "There's no law that says you have to lose money. A lot of people have a business plan saying they will lose so much in their first year or two. Our plan said we'd make money."

Today, H & A Fashions employs 50 people to create its line of six different skirts, dresses and jumpers, and Huynh projects profits of nearly $1 million on over $35 million in sales. Allen attributes the increase in sales to geographic expansion and a larger sales force. Profit has increased with higher sales coupled with continued overhead expense controls.

H & A supplies three to four thousand accounts including Sears Roebuck, Wal-Mart, J. C. Penney and other major department stores. H & A Fashions recently received J. C. Penney's top minority supplier development award. The recognition was based on criteria including quality, service and volume of business.

In 1990, H & A became the sole licensee for Cherokee's women's dresses, jumpers and rompers in the U.S. and Canada. Allen feels the acquisition of a nationally known name has been important to the company's growth.

Business Obstacles

Joe Allen says the biggest obstacles he and Huynh faced were obtaining necessary capital and establishing lines of credit. According to Allen, it took time and they had to prove themselves. Their attitude was, "If you can survive the rough times, there will be more good times than rough times."

Another on-going obstacle is the highly competitive nature of the apparel business. A well-run business and dedication to hard work serve to keep H & A Fashions ahead of the game.

Keys to Success

Huynh himself seems to be a major key to success for H & A Fashions. According to Allen, Huynh's strengths include his willingness to work exceptionally hard, a broad pragmatic streak and patience. "That mind-set helps him succeed in this country. We in this country have short-term business plans. He plans ahead," says Allen.

To get the company going, Huynh and Allen worked 12 hours a day, seven days a week, and still work 60 or more hours a week. "The Huynhs saw an opportunity to make some money; all they had to do was work hard. This was heaven for them. That extra time working put us way ahead of the competition," recalls Mr. Allen.

Huynh also recognized the need for an experienced general manager. Joe Allen's professional background provided immediate business insight and professional expertise to the fledgling company. Some of his previous positions include: founder of Sunny Isle, Inc.; co-founder and vice president of Fame Fashions, Inc.; co-founder and production manager of Fortune Designs, Inc.; founder, chairman of the board and CEO of Royal Park, Inc.; manager of Walnut Hill Industries' dress division; and a similar position with Prince Fashions.

Another element of H & A's continued success is the consolidation of the company's operations from six locations into one. According to Allen, running a lean business is important in the highly competitive apparel industry. "The apparel business has been treacherous and we believe in keeping our 'powder dry' by not over-expanding," states Allen. Its production lines are set up for quicker turn around than many companies can manage. Still, it maintains an unusually large inventory so it can fill a store's sudden needs almost overnight.

Dedication, loyalty and old fashioned hard work—what Joe Allen calls the "German and Japanese work ethic"—pays off for H & A.

Future Vision

Huynh has high hopes and grand dreams for his company. Regardless of success, however, Huynh says: "I am happy here because I have freedom. I work hard so I have money. I can sleep all night here. Why should I worry about anything?"

Future plans include reaching $100 million in sales in the next five years through internal growth and acquisitions. According to Allen, H & A will eventually seek worldwide growth opportunities. Talks are already underway with buyers in Europe. "We want to be positioned for 1992 when the European economic community becomes one market," Allen explains.

Both the Huynh and the Allen families have sons involved in H & A Fashions.

Entrepreneurial Lessons

"Their story is so encouraging to people who think opportunity has passed them by, when it's ready and waiting for people who have a good idea and work hard, like the Huynhs," Penney chairman W. R. Howell told *Nation's Business*.

According to Allen, Huynh believes the old adage of "Don't work harder—work smarter" doesn't quite ring true. He firmly believes both are important to success. Huynh and Allen also feel that to run a successful business, there is no room for greed and selfishness. Both men agree that work well done is a reward in itself.

Huynh and Allen have worked hard to make H & A Fashions a successful venture. As Allen puts it, "The harder we work, the luckier we get."

References

Bell, Sally. "Surviving—and Thriving." *Nation's Business*, March 1990.

Ricketts, Chip. "Dress Maker Relocates to W. Dallas Site." *Dallas Business Journal*, July 1989.

——C. A. C.

Joel Zylberberg Hyatt

Hyatt Legal Services

Joel Zylberberg Hyatt: Born 1950. Married, two children.

Venture: Established a nationwide chain of storefront legal clinics to make legal services accessible and affordable to middle-class Americans.

Company: Hyatt Legal Services; 1215 Superior Avenue; Cleveland, OH 44114-3249; (216) 694-4400

Founded: 1977 by Joel Hyatt and Wayne G. Willis as a partnership and law firm.

Revenues: The private company refuses to release current financial information.

Employees: 400 plus.

Original Investment: Hyatt has never disclosed the amount of private capital with which he started his first clinic. He used his and his wife's personal funds.

Value: $8.1 million (December 1987), according to published reports.

Founder

Joel Zylberberg Hyatt is the only son of David Zylberberg, a Polish immigrant who came to this country before World War II and whose family was lost in the Holocaust. Hyatt legally switched his middle and last names when he became an attorney.

He has been described as a man who fights zealously for any cause in which he believes. He credits his father for his drive, his deep-rooted belief in education and for his idealism.

"As far back as I can remember, I have been achievement-oriented. I have wanted to have an impact on the kind of society in which our kids will grow up," says Hyatt. "My Dad taught me that one person can make a difference. "

Hyatt grew up debating public policy issues with his family and by his early teens, had already decided to become a lawyer. His admiration for attorneys working in the Kennedy administration's justice department was a direct influence on his decision. He graduated Magna Cum Laude from Dartmouth College in 1972 and from Yale Law School in 1976.

He then spent a year managing the successful U. S. Senate campaign of his father-in-law, Howard Metzenbaum (D-Ohio). Hyatt proved very savvy in relation to marketing and media—a talent that has been critical to the success of Hyatt Legal Services (HLS).

Business Origin

After the campaign, Hyatt accepted a position with a well-established New York law firm. He had been practicing about six months when the U.S. Supreme Court decided *Bates and Osteen v. The State Bar ofArizona*, which held that states could no longer prohibit lawyers from advertising.

While in law school, Hyatt had researched the idea of companies and unions providing legal services for their employees the way that they provide medical plans. Although he found corporate benefits managers and union leaders interested, he encountered a major stumbling block. The delivery system was not in place to offer those services at reasonable fees.

Given the Supreme Court decision, Hyatt saw an opportunity to create an entirely new kind of law firm, one that would be available to a much larger segment of the population.

"I had just spent a year running a campaign and had come to understand the power of the media. I had also long believed that there was a great unmet need for people to have access to legal services. I felt that I could use the power of the media to inform the public how to get legal help when they needed it," said Hyatt.

To clear the way, Hyatt convinced the Ohio Supreme Court that the *Bates* decision supported the use of electronic as well as print media. Hyatt argued for the public's interest in knowing that legal services could be obtained at reasonable fees, and clinched his case by showing a taped commercial with himself as pitchman. A month later, the Ohio Supreme

Court ruled that only deceptive radio ads, or those using music or actors would be banned.

Hyatt's idea was to create a customer-oriented law firm, one with shopping center locations, extended hours and standard fees so that people would know in advance how much services would cost. With such a chain of clinics, he would then have in place a vehicle for employer-funded legal service plans.

After further consideration and talking to a number of lawyers and businessmen, Hyatt resigned his position in 1977 to begin his first store-front clinic in Cleveland.

Hyatt's initial plan was to start a network of law clinics throughout his native Ohio. Mass marketing techniques would bring in a high volume of smaller cases, and computer technology would help handle those cases in the most cost-efficient and timely matter.

By 1979, HLS had opened nine offices in Ohio and served approximately 21,000 clients. The decision to go national with the idea was made possible by the serendipitous arrival of Henry Bloch, founder of H & R Block, Inc.

Business Growth

The national tax preparation firm, looking to diversify its interests, entered into a contractual agreement with HLS in 1980. The two companies formed Block Management Company (80 percent owned by Block and 20 percent by Hyatt) to provide Hyatt's offices with a broad range of administrative services and new locations. Block's infusion of capital allowed Hyatt to expand nationally much faster than any of his competitors. With H & R Block's strategy, Hyatt's legal clinics would reduce seasonality and increase profits.

The agreement worked better on paper than in reality. Hyatt was not comfortable being part of a public company or moving the home office out of Ohio. "The synergies were never quite right in the field or the home office, and we wanted to be back in control of our own destiny," recalls Hyatt. The two companies parted amicably in 1987, when Hyatt bought out Bloch and formed Hyatt Legal Services Management Company with his three senior partners and Robert Bass, a Texas investor. Hyatt serves as board chairman of HLS Management Company.

Skyrocketing growth created some personnel and managerial problems for HLS. "My managerial style is motivational—it's based on personal contact. I want to inspire people to share in our vision. It became harder to do that as we got bigger," says Hyatt. As the number of locations and employees grew, Hyatt made adjustments. In 1987, he hired Christian Callsen, a former specialty retail manager, as president and CEO of HLS Management Company. Callsen professionalized management and set up a new organizational structure to cut the turnover rate of lawyers and allow for promotion from within.

Staff attorneys are the backbone of the company. They enter HLS at a salary range of $20-24,000, plus bonuses based on incentive programs. Staff attorneys can work up to managing attorneys (one in each office), regional partners, or a position with HLS Management. Joanne Parrino, the company's public relations coordinator, says some cutbacks in employees and locations were made in 1989 to better consolidate the firm, and some of the legal plan needs are now met by associated law offices. Hyatt believes that the clinic network now in place is adequate to handle a million new clients.

HLS is presently the largest general practice law firm in the country. It provides efficient and low-cost legal services that are frequently needed (wills, bankruptcy filings, divorces and adoptions, for example) to individuals and an increasing number of pre-paid legal plan clients. The company has 112 offices in 14 states. To date it has served over 2.25 million clients.

The company recently published the *Reader's Digest Legal Question and Answer Book*. As a co-venture with Overdrive Systems, a computer software and consulting firm, the company has developed the "Hyatt Legal Services Home Lawyer" software package.

Since 1987, Hyatt has turned his attention to the second phase of his vision—the expansion of the Hyatt Legal Services Group Legal Plans. Companies can offer legal services at about $6 a month per person. Hyatt Legal Plans now serve the employees of such major corporations as General Motors, Navistar International, American Express, PepsiCo, John Deere and AT&T. In Hyatt's opinion, "A prepaid legal plan is a wonderful concept, a real service, and it has unlimited growth potential." This segment of the company may soon become a separate entity.

Business Obstacles

Hyatt faced several ongoing obstacles in the early years. First, no models existed for the type of law office he wanted to open. He had to fight the antagonism of the public toward lawyers generally, and several Bar Associations who heartily disapproved of legal advertising. Also, he HLS with no business training. Hyatt has sought the advice of mentors when attempting something new, and then forged ahead. "We had to learn on the job how to start a small business, then how to run a company and finally, a large corporation," he said.

An early challenge was to convince former Yale classmate Wayne Willis to quit his job with a prestigious law firm on the West Coast and move to Cleveland to become his partner. Willis, with his knowledge of legal word processing equipment and law office economics, has functioned as the company's inside manager from the beginning, leaving Hyatt free to promote and market his idea.

Keys to Success

Advertising and computer technology have been the tangible keys to success for HLS. Hyatt's ability to be his own best spokesperson, to mass market his idea and appeal to thousands of clients, has made his law firm a household name.

Hyatt's client statistics prove that he is reaching people who have never before used attorneys.

From the beginning, Hyatt has relied on computers and word processing equipment to quickly and cheaply produce the legal documents the company needs. Today, the Legal Systems Department not only creates all of the forms used by HLS, but makes sure documents comply with all jurisdictions in which Hyatt has offices.

Determination has been the underlying factor, according to Hyatt. "The real key to our success is that we have understood our mission and tailored everything to building a law firm that is client-centered. The hours, the friendliness, our fee policy, the standardization of forms . . . everything has gone into making HLS a law firm that serves a segment of the population that was not being served before. That's what makes us different . . . that, and the determination to stick with it through all the obstacles we anticipated and some we didn't," says Hyatt.

Hyatt's senior partners are his wife and two of his closest friends, an arrangement that he admits wouldn't work for everyone. "There is greater pressure not to confuse the business and personal relationships, but I knew it was going to be hard work, and I also wanted it to be fun. If Susan hadn't been working beside me in the early years, I don't think we would have had much of a marriage. She's always been a real source of strength," says Hyatt of his wife.

Future Vision

Hyatt's company will continue to explore ways to help empower people, to help them protect their rights. "We will continue to have clinics and provide group plans, but there are lots of opportunities and formats to explore. We've only touched the tip of the iceberg," he maintains. He cites the home lawyer software package as one example.

Hyatt's legal clinic idea has bred many competitors, but his is still the largest network. Besides other clinics, he also competes with general practice law firms in some locations. He expects some competition from insurance companies in providing group legal plans, but with a national delivery system already in place, he believes HLS has the advantage.

Entrepreneurial Lessons

Initially, Hyatt never thought of himself as an entrepreneur. As he told *The National Jurist*, "We didn't set out to be entrepreneurs. It took me some time to overcome the embarassment in the 1980s of being a high-profile entrepreneur. That wasn't my self-image." Instead, Hyatt had a vision for providing what he saw as a much-needed public service. He now believes that entrepreneurs and new small businesses are the most important sources of growth in this country and he speaks publicly to that principle often. "I tell young people that watching something grow from nothing is the most exciting stuff there is. I left a very prestigious law firm to start a little storefront office. Now I head a large corporation," says Hyatt. He encourages young people to believe in their ideas and to take the risk while they are young. "Don't go for the status, go for the challenge," is his advice.

Hyatt clearly sees political office somewhere in his future, but isn't likely to leave HLS until he feels his vision is fully attained.

References

Atchison, Sandra D., and Bruce Nussbaum. "Hyatt: A 'Mission' to Make Legal Services Affordable." *Business Week,* January 21, 1985.

Beauchamp, Marc. "A Tale of Two Law Firms." *Forbes,* April 21, 1986.

Brill, Steven. "TV Pitchman for Cut-Rate Legal Advice." *Esquire,* May 9, 1978.

Cleesatile, Jodi. "Practicing Common Law." *The National Jurist,* September 1991.

Cohen, Laurie P. "PepsiCo Will Offer Legal Services to All Employees through Hyatt." *Wall Street Journal,* January 13, 1989.

Densford, Lynn E. "Group Legal Plans Poised for Growth." *Employee Benefit News,* January 1990.

Jervey, Gay. "Joel Hyatt." *The American Lawyer,* March 1989.

Kisner, Kathleen. "Hyatt Recruited for Job Benefit Legal Services." *Crain's Cleveland Business,* January 8-14, 1990.

Lambro, Donald. "New Entrepreneurs Showing the Way." *The Washington Times,* November 20, 1985.

Long, Victoria Sizemore. "Joel Hyatt's Zeal Is Now Flourishing Business." *Kansas City Times,* March 11, 1987.

Nuwer, Hank. "Joel Hyatt's Uncommon Law." *Success,* February 1984.

Wiegand, Virginia. "Hyatt Law Empire Topped Expectations." *Akron Beacon Journal,* October 2, 1984.

——L. R.

Steven P. Jobs

NeXT Computer, Inc.

Steven P. Jobs: Born 1955. Married, two children.
Venture: NeXT Computer, Inc. manufactures the NeXT Computer System, computer workstations and peripherals designed for the education and business markets.
Company: NeXT Computer, Inc.; 900 Chesapeake Drive; Redwood City, CA 94063; (415) 366-0900
Founded: September 1985.
Revenues: $200 million projected sales (1991), according to published reports.
Employees: 500 plus.
Original Investment: $7 million.
Value: Undetermined.

Founder

A self-taught engineer and college drop-out, Steve Jobs' success story began in the garage of his parents' home. He and fellow computer "hacker" Steve Wozniak built a machine there that launched the personal computer industry. As co-founder of Apple Computer, Jobs became one of America's most successful and most visible entrepreneurs. He was the "whiz kid" credited with bringing computer power to the individual and transforming how Americans do business. *Inc.* magazine named Jobs its "Entrepreneur of the Decade" in 1989.

Jobs was raised by adoptive parents in Santa Clara County, California. After graduating from high school, he attended Reed College in Portland, Oregon but left during his freshman year to travel. Jobs later returned to

Northern California where he worked as a video game designer for Atari. In the evenings, he attended meetings of the Homebrewer Computer Club, a group of Silicon Valley engineers and computer enthusiasts who gathered to discuss their ideas and designs. There in 1975 he met Wozniak, a Hewlett-Packard engineer.

Wozniak's plans to create a personal computer for his own use intrigued Jobs and they began developing the machine. While Wozniak was a shy, quiet and insightful engineer, Jobs was curious and creative, full of ideas and eager to implement them. In 1976, they decided to sell their computer to Homebrewer Club members. Jobs sold his Volkswagen van and Wozniak sold his Hewlett-Packard calculator to raise the money they needed to make the computers' printed circuit boards. When they received their first order from a local computer dealer, Apple Computer was born.

As head of Apple, Jobs was recognized not only for the computers he produced but for the unorthodox way he ran his company. Jobs shunned suits and ties for blue jeans and sneakers and huddled with staff for impromptu brainstorming sessions in modular cubicles. He was labeled the "Wunderkind" of the personal computer industry, and developed a reputation as brash, aggressive and cocky. Before age 27 and already a multi-millionaire, Jobs graced the cover of *Time* magazine.

In recognition of his pioneering work in technology, Jobs was awarded the National Technology Medal by President Ronald Reagan in 1985. He was awarded the Jefferson Award for Public Service in 1987.

Business Origin

Jobs oversaw Apple Computer's growth into a $2 billion company, but left in 1985 after a widely-publicized power struggle with CEO John Sculley, who Jobs had hired to run Apple. Sculley reorganized Apple management and eliminated the Macintosh Division that Jobs headed, leaving him with the chairman's title but little power.

Jobs resigned from Apple saying that he would build a new computer for higher education. His innovation was prompted by Stanford University biochemist Paul Berg, a leader in recombinant DNA research. From discussions with Berg, Jobs got the idea for a low-cost computer that could simulate expensive lab experiments. He believed that he could build a machine that was as simple to operate as a personal computer, but had the power and graphic sophistication of a computer workstation.

"[Berg] was showing me what some of his students were doing to understand how proteins fold. He asked, 'Couldn't you model this stuff on a computer if you had something more powerful than a PC?'" Jobs recalled. "It really got me thinking. What if you came up with something that was as easy to use as a Mac, or even easier, and had the power of a workstation? What if you unleashed that machine in higher education? The more I thought about it, the more excited I got," Jobs said.

Using $7 million of the fortune he accumulated by selling his Apple stock, Jobs established NeXT, Inc. (later NeXT Computer, Inc.) in Palo Alto, California.

Having learned important lessons about building computers and building a company while at Apple, Jobs had the advantage of experience as he launched NeXT. Jobs' ability to inspire employee loyalty and commitment was evident as five key Apple managers and engineers took pay cuts to join him at NeXT, giving the company the resources it needed immediately to begin product development. His success as an entrepreneurial "celebrity" meant that the industry and the public eagerly anticipated his next move.

Once he announced the formation of NeXT, Jobs and his development team slipped from public view, working in almost total seclusion for the next three years. The press and the public continued to speculate about what was being created at NeXT, but Jobs sent a message through his silence that the NeXT computer would emerge when he believed the time was right.

Business Growth

The introduction of the NeXT computer system attracted public attention and widespread press coverage. On October 12, 1988 in a packed Davis Symphony Hall in San Francisco, Jobs "unveiled" the machine in a carefully-planned performance. He appeared alone on stage with the computer and entertained the 3,000-member audience with the machine that he called "a partner in thought."

As *Time* magazine described it, "The event was vintage Jobs, a sound and light show designed to inspire the faithful and persuade the skeptical." Jobs demonstrated the machine's ability to run four stopwatches at once and give a synthetic rendition of Martin Luther King Jr.'s "I Have a Dream" speech.

After the event, industry analysts and the press gave Jobs high marks for his performance, but his computer got mixed reviews. While people raved about its innovative and dazzling capabilities, critics wondered if there was enough substance behind the "flash" to encourage people to buy the NeXT system, especially since it carried a high price tag.

Since the computer's introduction, Jobs has worked to build sales and shape NeXT into a company able to compete with industry giants. He has solicited feedback from customers and responded with system modifications. Jobs assumed leadership of NeXT's marketing effort in the fall of 1988.

In March 1989, Jobs signed an exclusive distribution alliance with Businessland Inc. With the Businessland partnership, NeXT had the advantage of a dedicated sales force working to penetrate the North American market. The deal encouraged third-party software makers to tailor their products to run on the NeXT machine. Also in 1989, Japan's Canon Inc. agreed to manage NeXT's Asian distribution and invested $100 million in the company.

After announcing the Businessland and Canon deals, Jobs abandoned his plan to sell NeXT systems only to the education market and decided to target the business market as well.

Business Obstacles

The three-year product development period of the NeXT system was filled with obstacles as Jobs worked to build a marketable product and a viable company. Success was far from guaranteed. Jobs found himself competing for attention in the thriving industry that he helped to create. While NeXT worked on its "state-of-the-art" computer, the competition was doing the same.

Apple sued Jobs for $5 million in damages in a dispute over the five key employees it had lost to NeXT. NeXT engineers experienced product development problems causing delays in the computer's release. Speculation about Jobs' likely success or failure grew more intense as promised product release dates slipped by.

Behind closed doors, Jobs and his colleagues struggled to create his vision of the perfect computer. Many co-workers say that Jobs was a perfectionist about every detail of the NeXT machine. He worked extensively with design consultants to mold the computer's distinctive exterior, insisting that it be exactly a 12-inch cube, and laboring over where the logo would be placed and what type of paint would coat the machine. Jobs was heavily involved in selecting system software, and he led company-wide retreats where NeXT personnel debated development decisions. Indeed, Jobs told *Fortune*, "My experience has been that creating a compelling new technology is so much harder than you think it will be that you're almost dead when you get to the other shore."

The computer was released in October 1988, almost 18 months past its original delivery date.

In an April 1991 article in *Business Week*, Jobs admitted "we were actually pretty lost in terms of who we were as a company until six or seven months ago."

Keys to Success

Jobs launched NeXT to bring to life his vision of the future of personal computing. Even as he was leaving Apple, Jobs touted his new venture, declaring that he would build "the best computer in the world." Time will determine whether NeXT and its machine enjoy lasting success, but Jobs' talent, charisma and determination created the company and kept it moving ahead. He told the *Washington Post*, "I'm extraordinarily happy with what we have accomplished technology-wise but we have not yet made it commercially. Things take time and I am an impatient person."

Observers agree that Jobs has dedicated himself to making NeXT a winner. He contributed $7 million of his own fortune to get the company off the ground in 1985, and he provided additional cash to support product development efforts in 1987. Jobs is a hands-on CEO who reportedly works 75 hours a week.

Fortune magazine said that at NeXT, "Steve Jobs is blending sharp technology with shrewd politicking to make his tiny startup company a well-financed force to be reckoned with." In 1987, billionaire H. Ross Perot bought a 16 percent stake in the company for $20 million after seeing Jobs on a television documentary about entrepreneurs. Jobs' ability to negotiate distribution agreements with Businessland and Canon have promoted NeXT's early success.

Jobs has been able to encourage the best and brightest minds in the computer industry to share in his vision, attracting talented employees and the assistance of technological experts. Although NeXT might have been viewed as simply another startup computer company hoping to survive, Jobs' "aura and the notice it attracts" have focused the industry's and the public's attention on NeXT.

Future Vision

Jobs says that his first goal is to create the best possible computers for individual users. He envisions NeXT to be a place where bright people have a great deal of responsibility as soon as they join the company. What's more, Jobs is determined that the employees who build NeXT will share the company's financial success.

Jobs knows that his company must grow significantly to compete in the personal computer industry. As he told *Inc.* in 1989, "Our smallest competitor is $1.75 billion these days. . . . We have to get up to a certain scale if we want to play in the sandbox, and if we want to have the effect we're looking for. . . . We're building the next billion-dollar company around here—from the ground up."

Jobs is proud of his past successes, and he looks ahead to a productive future at NeXT. "My motivation is a little different this time. The computer industry is young. I view its future and its history as one long vector. I think both the Apple II and the Macintosh contributed to setting the vector's direction . . . I hope that the NeXT machine will contribute as well.

"I want to make the most of [my opportunity], and that means providing an unobstructed path for the brightest minds in our industry. My job becomes more to help them pick the targets correctly and then get out of their way," he says.

Entrepreneurial Lessons

It has been written that Jobs has "has mellowed and matured" since his days at Apple. Signs are that Jobs may agree. At the NeXT system introduction, he chose the word "mercurial" to show-off the machine's built-in dictionary and frowned at the computer's definition: "characterized by rapid and unpredictable changes in mood." Jobs commented, "I don't really know that that's so."

At Apple, Jobs developed a reputation as a poor listener who was especially inattentive to customer suggestions. Jobs admits that when Macintosh customers requested changes in the machine, he "could have done better" in responding. Today, Jobs says that the best products are created by "melding" the customer's point of view and the developer's point of view.

Jobs says that he learned to respect customer wishes as he came to understand who his "customers" really were. He and Wozniak had designed their personal computer for Homebrewer Computer Club members. As they developed a business, the two got feedback from a small group of technical people and some dealers, but as Jobs says, "We were going on common sense. We didn't even think in terms of customer feedback. We never even used the word customer."

Jobs sees himself as "a little older and a little wiser." He told *Fortune*, "I don't sell myself as a futurist. I think of myself as a pretty-good operations person." As a manager, he has a clear sense of how he wants his company to operate. "The culture at NeXT definitely rewards independent thought, and we often have constructive disagreements at all levels," he says. "We want to be the best and [we don't] get hung up on who owns the idea. I say to my people, 'Trust the technology.' It's essential to keep going and trust your original instincts and visions. If you get confused and change directions, you can bump into a lot of walls."

References

Brandt, Richard. "So Far, So-So For Steve Job's New Machine." *Business Week*, January 29, 1990.

Buell, Barbara. "Is NeXT Finally Zeroing In On the Right Target?" *Business Week*, April 15, 1991.

Elmer-Dewitt, Philip. "Soul of the NeXT machine." *Time*, October 24, 1988.

Gendron, George, and Bo Burlingham. "The Entrepreneur of the Decade: An Interview with Steve Jobs." *Inc.*, April 1989.

Gomes, L. "Jobs' NeXT Computer Arrives." *Tribune*, October 13, 1988.

Hafner, Katherine M., and others. "Steve Jobs: Can He Do It Again?" *Business Week*, October 24, 1988.

O'Reilly, Brian. "Steve Jobs: What's Next?" *Fortune*, November 7, 1988.

Richards, Evelyn. "Jobs Evolves from 'Mercurial' to 'Matured'." *San Jose Mercury News*, October 13, 1988.

———. "Whiz Kids' Solo Shows No Sellout." *Washington Post*, September 14, 1990.

Schlender, Brenton R. "How Steve Jobs Linked up with IBM." *Fortune*, October 9, 1989.

———. "Jobs and Gates Together." *Fortune,* August 26, 1991.

Schwartz, John. "At Last: Signs of Life at NeXT." *Newsweek,* November 18, 1991.

Siegmann, Ken. "Co-founder Exits Apple." *Peninsula Times Tribune,* January 6, 1986.

Zachary, G. Pascal. "NeXT Inc. Is Enjoying Comeback, But Competitors Lurk in Wings." *Wall Street Journal,* June 27, 1991.

——M. J. B.

Judith Kaplan

Action Products International

Judith Kaplan: Born 1938. Married, two children.
Venture: Wholesale distributor of imported toys, novelties, books and soft goods.
Company: Action Products International; 344 Cypress Road; Ocala, FL 32672; (904) 687-2202
Founded: 1978.
Revenues: 1989 sales of $3.3 million, according to company reports.
Employees: 40.
Original Investment: $20,000.
Value: $1.5 million net worth, according to published reports dated March 16, 1990.

Founder

Judith Kaplan's business success story grew out of her long-time hobby of collecting souvenirs, postcards, stamps, commemorative items and other novelties. In the 1960s, she began assembling what became one of the country's largest private collections of women's suffrage memorabilia. Kaplan frequently visited museums and planetariums, always making time to browse gift shops looking for new and interesting collectibles.

Together with her husband, Warren, Kaplan today runs a multi-million dollar, international souvenir supply company. This woman entrepreneur has been called " the uncontested queen of the museum souvenir business." Her company, Action Products International, has been listed several times on *Inc.* magazine's roster of the fastest growing private and public companies. Kaplan has been honored as Florida's "Small Businessperson of the Year" by the Small Business Administration.

Kaplan says that she and her husband are "born entrepreneurs" who enjoy creating businesses and working on their own. "We've always been willing to take risks and try something new," she says.

An avowed feminist, Kaplan founded chapters of the National Organization for Women in New York City.

Business Origin

As a young mother in Queens, New York, Kaplan often took her children to local museums and planetariums and was disappointed by what was offered in their gift shops. "It seemed to me that they didn't carry items that had anything to do with the collections—those were the types of items I was looking for," she explains. "I listened to other customers and heard the same complaint."

At the time, Kaplan and her husband had established a small venture marketing first-day covers of stamps. It occurred to her that visitors to museums, planetariums and zoos would be interested in buying packets of stamps grouped by themes, such as animals, automobiles, insects and outer space.

"I asked a few shop managers if they would be interested in buying stamp packets, and they thought it was a good idea. It seemed to me that this new business would be a good way for Warren and I to augment our other ventures and make some vacation money," she says.

Kaplan's first order from a planetarium in Centerport, New York totaled just $100. That first sale motivated Kaplan to become a distributor of commemorative stamps, and using $20,000 in savings, she launched Action Packets Inc. in 1976. The company incorporated as Action Products International in 1978.

Business Growth

While Kaplan began selling stamp packets, her business soon expanded to include such novelty items as toys, rubber snakes, miniature dinosaurs, plastic airplanes, zodiac key chains, space memorabilia, and freeze-dried ice cream. Articles chronicling the company's growth have labeled Kaplan's products as everything from "whirly-gigs and doo-dads" to "gimcracks, knickknacks and whigmaleeries."

"When I started, I had no idea how the product line would grow and no real plan for the business. I guess it was more a case of 'following my nose,'" Kaplan says. "I asked the museums what they wanted to sell, and as their requests grew, so did my business."

By 1978, the company reached $100,000 in annual sales and had 100 customers. When her basement was too small to stock the company's growing inventory, Kaplan moved the business to her garage.

A major point in Action Products' history came in June 1980 when Kaplan and her husband sold their New York home and moved to Ocala, Florida. "We simply outgrew the house in New York," Kaplan remembers. "The inventory was taking over, our street wasn't zoned for the stream of delivery trucks that arrived each day, and we found that it was prohibitively expensive to operate a large company in New York City," she said.

In Ocala, the Kaplans rented a 5,000-square-foot warehouse and office to house their growing business. "We chose Florida because we knew a few people here, the taxes were lower, it wasn't congested and the weather was warm," Kaplan says. "But it wasn't an easy decision. Relocating was a big step, and it meant we were making a long-term commitment to keeping the business going," she says.

Kaplan published her first catalog in 1980 as sales rose to $120,000. In 1981 after the voyage of the first Columbia space shuttle, defense contractors who had worked on the shuttle ordered patches or shuttle replicas for their employees and customers. Eyeing an opportunity to expand her customer base, Kaplan began aggressively marketing her products to corporations for employee incentives and customer gifts.

By 1982, Action Products posted sales of almost $1 million. Looking for capital to expand, Kaplan decided to launch a stock offering. "I viewed going public as a 'rite of passage' into the world of business," Kaplan says. "It was a way for others to show that they thought our business was solid and had the potential for future success. I also wanted to establish an employee stock ownership plan to give our employees the opportunity to share in the business."

A Jacksonville investment firm with interest in emerging Florida-based companies sponsored the offering. Kaplan prepared Action Products' first business plan, which she says "gave me a good handle on where we were going and how we would use the money we raised." The company successfully completed a private stock placement in April 1984 and raised $500,000. That year, sales increased to $2.1 million.

Over the next few years, sales climbed, reaching $2.8 million in 1985. Sales in 1986 and 1987 were $3.8 million and $4.4 million respectively, dropping slightly in 1988 to $4 million. Despite the decline, however, Action Products posted after-tax profits of $105,000 versus $96,000 in 1987.

Sales fell to $3.3 million in 1989, and the company reported an after-tax loss of $145,000. Also that year, Action Products restructured its management and formed a subsidiary to manufacture its best-selling line of "astronaut" foods.

Action Products' recent 124-page catalog is filled with over 4,000 items. The company's international customer base includes corporations, museums, planetariums, zoos and aquariums.

Business Obstacles

Kaplan says that in the beginning, her greatest obstacle was establishing a market for her goods. "I'd call museum gift shops looking for business, and the managers would ask me to send them a catalog. We didn't have one, so we had to create special incentives to encourage customers to try our products without having seen them," Kaplan says. "We offered a money-back guarantee and a liberal return policy. That enticed many shops to take stamp packets on faith."

As her company grew, Kaplan had to make the transition from entrepreneur to corporate executive. "I made mistakes that sometimes put us in a difficult position," she says. "I sometimes promised our customers things that we couldn't easily deliver. I didn't focus enough on managing the size of our product line."

Kaplan faced a skeptical investment community when she decided to take her company public. "At the time, Wall Street was more interested in high-tech manufacturing firms than in our kind of company," she says. "I had no experience with public offerings, no business plan, and no idea how to prepare one. The firm that backed us gave me some sample business plans, and I copied the format of one of them to create Action Products' first long-range plan."

Kaplan says that the souvenir industry has become increasingly competitive as Action Products has grown. "There are a lot of companies that offer the same kinds of products that we do, and I know that if my customers don't buy from me, they will buy from someone else," she says. "As I look around at the competition, I see that we need to sell harder than ever before and be sure that we offer the highest-quality products."

Keys to Success

Kaplan does not hesitate in sharing her secret of success. "It is absolutely simple—just listen to the customers and give them what they want," she says. "Rather than planning a product line and then trying to sell it, I have always asked customers what they wanted and planned my product line to serve their needs."

As she has from the beginning, Kaplan continues to offer a liberal return policy, a money-back guarantee, and she allows customers to order in small quantities. In addition, Action Products discounts the price of large orders and creates custom items to meet specific customer needs.

"I don't want my customers to be stuck with merchandise that won't sell, so I give them the chance to try it before they place a large order," she says. "After all, if my customers are successful, I will be successful. My first priority is to sell them quality items that will move out of their stores."

Action Products is able to acquire quality merchandise at good prices because of the company's diversity, Kaplan says. "The beauty of our business is that we are not married to any one vendor, any one location, any one type of customer, any one product line. This allows us to look at a range of suppliers and find the right product for our customers," she says.

"Once customers place their orders, it is critical that those orders arrive complete, accurate and on time. We stay ahead of the competition by fine-tuning our delivery systems and concentrating on error-free shipping and billing," Kaplan says.

Kaplan believes that Action Products' employees are key to upholding the company's overriding commitment to customer service. "I hire people who are loyal and dedicated. I want people who are looking for a career here, and I offer them opportunity to grow with this company," she says. "These are the people who will best serve our steady client base—they will go 'the extra step' to make sure that every detail of an order is right."

Taking care of her employees is one of Kaplan's top priorities. She pays salespeople a salary plus commissions to reward excellence in customer service as well as sales volume. She established an employee stock ownership plan to give all employees the opportunity to gain a financial stake in the company. As stated in the 1985 annual report, the company's "employment philosophy" is to "develop all personnel to become flexible, motivated and involved. . . . Our company has developed innovative techniques to rapidly involve employees in all aspects of the company and to foster the development of flexibility, problem-solving, independence, conceptual thinking, accountability, pride and responsibility."

Future Vision

Kaplan is currently preparing a business plan to chart Action Products' course for the next few years. After that, she says that she may leave the business. "This plan is focused on how to best manage the business over the next five years. I intend to be here to see it through," she says. "But I would eventually like to leave the company in the hands of the stockholders and the management team we are training to take over." One of the managers who will assume responsibility for Action Products is Kaplan's son.

"I'm looking forward to the day when I have no paper work in front of me," Kaplan says. "It seems that the day-to-day is so hectic here and I'm pushing so much paper that I never get the time to reflect on what we've done to create the business. I want to have the chance to look back. I'm also eager to do some traveling," she says.

Entrepreneurial Lessons

"The hardest thing for me in learning to manage others was to accept that other people did things differently than I did," Kaplan reflects. "In some cases, they probably didn't carry out a task as well as I would have, but you have to let people learn. You simply can't do everything yourself, and if you want to build a successful team, you have to encourage people to take responsibility.

"The key is communication," Kaplan says. "I have had to work on my ability to give clear instruction and on listening closely to what my employees are telling me."

Kaplan has also had to learn to manage her own expectations for the business. "In the beginning, I wanted us to be all things to all people and I often put too much pressure on our employees. I had to learn what was reasonable and focus on what would best grow the business," she says.

Based on her experience, Kaplan offers this advice to other entrepreneurs: "Make sure that you question everything—especially in the beginning. You can't be intimidated by all the 'authorities' who will tell you what to do. You have to learn for yourself all there is to know about your business, especially the financials. It's important that you feel in control of your own destiny."

She cautions that while sound planning is important, an entrepreneur cannot predict the future. "You can't get hung up on mapping out every detail—sometimes you have to take a risk and just get going," she says. "Business is full of surprises, and it's a constant learning process. Text-books are great, but they can't always tell you what to expect."

References

Lynch, Richard A. "Museum Pieces: Judith Kaplan Built Her Company on Stamps and Dinosaurs." *Money*, April 1984.

Marth, Del. "Selling Souvenirs by the Foot." *Nation's Business*, August 1984.

Murdoch, M. "Home Grown Business That Boomed." *Ocala Star-Banner*, March 18, 1984.

Sokol, M. "One-Time Hobby Now Nets Millions." *Florida Times-Union*, April 29, 1984.

Wechsler, Jill. "The Nuts and Bolts of Going Public: How One Company Did It." *Working Woman*, October 1985.

——M. J. B.

Alan Kessman

EXECUTONE Information Systems, Inc.

Alan Kessman: Born 1947. Married, two children.
Venture: A company to manufacture and distribute telephone and other telecommunications systems and software, ISOETEC Inc. Products are designed to manage voice and data communications for small- to medium-sized organizations. A merger with two similar firms created the present corporation.
Company: EXECUTONE Information Systems, Inc.; 6 Thorndal Circle; Darien, CT 06820; (203) 655-6500
Founded: The original company, ISOETEC, was founded in 1983.
Revenues: $280.5 million in 1990 (1990 annual report).
Employees: 2,400.
Original Investment: $21 million in venture capital.
Value: $54 million net worth, according to published reports.

Founder

Alan Kessman's family always planned that he would grow up to be a doctor, and Kessman says that he never thought any different. After graduating from high school in his native Mount Vernon, New York, Kessman began pre-med studies at Lehigh University but changed his major to business after a year. He earned a business degree and became a certified public accountant.

In 1972 as an accountant with Ernst & Whinney, he worked on the case of Tele/Resources Inc. of White Plains, New York, a company headed for bankruptcy. Tele/Resources management was impressed with Kessman's recommendations and hired him to turn the company around. Kessman was successful, but left the company in 1978 to join ROLM Corporation. During his career with ROLM, Kessman was president of three company subsidiaries, and he played a major role in helping ROLM establish its first company-owned sales and services offices.

In 1983, Kessman left ROLM to start his own company—something he had dreamed of doing. Together with three partners, he launched ISOETEC Communications, Inc.

Business Origin

When Kessman started ISOETEC, the telecommunications industry was already filled with players vying for market share. But Kessman and his colleagues saw an untapped opportunity to meet the telecommunications needs of small to mid-sized companies. "These businesses weren't getting the customized attention that larger companies were getting, and they were hungry for it," Kessman says. "We figured that if we could give them the products and services they wanted at a price they could afford, we'd have ourselves a very successful business.

"People said I was crazy," Kessman remembers. "They told me that I could never make a profit because the technology was too expensive and my potential sales were too low at $20,000 or less on average. The doubters gave me incentive to go ahead. I figured, if no one believes this is possible and I'm the one who makes it go, so much the better."

While Kessman's entrepreneurial spirit was pushing him to accept the challenge, leaving ROLM was not easy. "I was giving up the comforts of a secure position and work I enjoyed, risking everything to start again," he says. "My mother was the final motivator. She called me and said, 'I don't want you to look back 20 years from now and wonder what would've happened if you had tried. You have to be able to look yourself in the mirror and know that, no matter what, you followed your instincts and gave it your best,'" Kessman recalls. "I hung up the phone, went for a three-hour walk and decided to do it."

Kessman's partners asked him to be the company's president, believing that his background and personality were best suited to lead day-to-day operations. He also raised $21 million by convincing venture capitalists that the group's business strategy was worth their investment. "I was pretty tenacious and determined. They saw that I really believed in the company's strategy and in our ability to build something significant," Kessman said.

Business Growth

Kessman led ISOETEC through exceptional growth during its five years of operation. The company became one of the ten largest companies in its industry, with annual revenues increasing from $21 million in 1984 to more than $101 million in 1988.

As ISOETEC expanded its customer base, the company added regional offices and established its Darien, Connecticut headquarters as a national customer service center. In cities where the company did not have offices, ISOETEC awarded exclusive product distributorships to independent dealers, rather than allowing a number of distributors to battle for business.

In February 1988, ISOETEC and Vodavi Technology each acquired 50 percent of competitor Executone, owned by Contel Corporation for $61 million. The three companies merged to form EXECUTONE Information Systems in July of that year. "We had an interest in Executone for its customer base, and Vodavi had also been interested in buying the company. We worked out a three-way deal that could benefit all," Kessman said. The post-merger company had combined sales of $350 million.

With the three-way merger, EXECUTONE Information Systems was instantly a company with 50 offices, a network of more than 100 dealers and more than 100,000 customers. Kessman says that in organizing the company, "Management's mission was to reduce expenses, streamline operations, improve productivity and integrate three cultures into one united force. We asked a great deal of our employees who had to continue to provide exceptional service to our customers through a period of enormous change." The new company reported a profit in less than six months, well ahead of its goals and industry expectations.

EXECUTONE products are sold and serviced by a network of more than 80 company-owned branch offices throughout the United States, Canada and Puerto Rico, and through independent distributors in the U.S., Canada, Europe, Mexico and the Dominican Republic.

Business Obstacles

From the beginning, Kessman organized ISOETEC's business like no other in his industry. Rather than selling products through a network of independent distributors, ISOETEC operated its own sales and service offices staffed by company-trained personnel. Kessman says that while this was the most expensive way to set up the company, he believed that it was the only way. "We weren't going to make money with the phones themselves, but by offering sophisticated applications software and add-on capabilities once the phones were installed. Because our primary product was software, we simply couldn't sell it the standard way. We had get to know our customers' businesses to be able to give them the software solutions they needed," he said. "It took extraordinary capital and management time to get the sales and service network off the ground, but I knew that if we didn't do it that way, we wouldn't have a company in five years."

Reflecting back on ISOETEC in its infancy, Kessman notes, "we had our setbacks, but generally it all worked well." In its early days, the company faced obstacles including a suit from a competitor, delays in product delivery caused by a manufacturer's financial woes, and labor strikes at Korean manufacturers.

Deregulation of the telecommunications industry in 1984 forced prices down by an average of 30 percent. Kessman says that this price erosion forced ISOETEC "to tighten our operation and find ways to drive our manufacturing and distribution costs down."

Since its formation, EXECUTONE Information Systems has faced its share of obstacles as well, including the enormous challenges of merging three companies with diverse identities and cultures. "We had to give ourselves time to organize for the future. We gave ourselves a year to be profitable," Kessman says.

In 1989, the U.S. Department of Commerce ruled that Japanese, South Korean and Taiwanese manufacturers were "dumping" telephone systems at less than fair value in the United States market. The ruling forced EXECUTONE to pay a small duty on the price of the several proprietary systems the company manufactured in South Korea. As a way to limit further risk, EXECUTONE has established additional manufacturing sources outside of that country.

Keys to Success

Kessman has successfully managed a company that has undergone enormous change in a short period of time. In doing so, he has not changed his original notion of how to reach his market. From the beginning, Kessman believed that the only way to serve his customers was to control every aspect of the business including manufacturing, distribution, engineering and customer service. In Kessman's opinion, having a hand in each business element allows the company to track and fix inefficiencies and continue to offer products that customers can afford.

EXECUTONE maintains 24-hour service hotlines at its two National Customer Service Centers. Through a sophisticated remote diagnostics system, customer service representatives can add features to a customer's system or check system problems with the touch of a button. If a customer's concern can not be resolved by telephone, technicians are dispatched to the customer site with solutions in hand.

Kessman encourages field offices to stay close to customers by delegating decision-making to the branch level. He also makes certain that field personnel have extensive training and fully understand the products and services they have to offer EXECUTONE customers. Kessman says his goal is for EXECUTONE "to set a new standard of national service" for its industry. "Customer service is still my top priority because our foundation for growth is in an expanding and satisfied customer base," he says.

Kessman is keenly aware of the importance of recognizing and rewarding employee efforts. EXECUTONE's sales compensation program offers bonuses, trips and other incentives to top performers. Kessman calls the program, "a big-company sales effort in a small company." "We pay our top salespeople very well, and we give them a lot of attention and love," he says. He credits employees for the company's success. "By continuing to work hard and remain dedicated, the people who work here have brought this company a long way in a short period of time," he said.

Kessman personally stands behind his commitment to customer service, offering himself as a direct resource to customers. In his 1988 annual report message, he wrote, "We want to be the best in customer support, yet I know we are not perfect . . . if we aren't providing the best in support, tell us. If our people don't react or support your organizations, call or write me and I will personally get involved."

Future Vision

Kessman predicts that EXECUTONE will see "real bottom-line benefits" from its merger.

He believes that the company is poised to capitalize on new telecommunications technology. "We know that this is a maturing industry, and overabundance of product and competitors will make it even more challenging to increase profitability. The combination of our experience, current innovations and future goals put us in a good position," he says.

As president and CEO, Kessman expects his role within the company to change in the coming years. He says that he will increasingly move away from day-to-day operations and concentrate on long-term strategy.

Kessman is proud of what he and his team have accomplished in the past, and he is excited about the future. "We've done pretty well until now competing with the 'big boys,'" Kessman believes. "We've anticipated the trends in our industry and charted our own path, and this has kept us ahead of the crowd. Now, we've spent couple of years putting our new company together and it's time to see how far we can go."

Entrepreneurial Lessons

Kessman has high respect and admiration for well-managed companies that strive for excellence. From the beginning, he had a vision of creating such a company. In fact, he named ISOETEC using the first letters of the title of one of favorite books, Tom Peters' and Robert H. Waterman Jr.'s *In Search of Excellence.*

At the time he named the company, Kessman intended the "tec" portion of the name to represent the software programmability feature of ISOETEC products that he saw as critical to success. However, as testament to Kessman's success in communicating his vision of excellence, "tec" came to mean 'Through Employee Commitment' or 'Through Effort and Commitment'" within the company.

Kessman speaks of "tenacity and commitment" as keys to his entrepreneurial success. He also says that those characteristics in his managers and employees are what has made his companies successful. "You have to have a vision to be able to attract investors, talented employees and customers," he says. "You have to know where you want to go, have a plan for getting there, and then keep pushing forward until you reach your goals."

References

"After Merger Executive Wants 'Impossible Growth'." *Intercorp*, December 23, 1988.

Garrett, Echo Montgomery. "The Strong, Silent Type." *Venture*, February 1989.

"Software and Service: Executone's Merged Market Strategy." *Procomm Enterprises Magazine*, April 1989.

——M. J. B.

W. David Kimbrell

Hall-Kimbrell Environmental Services, Inc.

W. David Kimbrell: Born 1951. Married, three children.
Venture: Architectural service and environmental engineering and consulting firm.
Company: Hall-Kimbrell Environmental Services, Inc.; Lawrence, KS
Founded: 1982.
Original Investment: $20,000.
Value: Sold to Professional Services Inc. (PSI) in 1990.

Founder

David Kimbrell says that he has "never been able to work for anybody else," and probably never will. "I tried to work in someone else's business after graduate school and lasted six months," he says. "I just knew that I was better suited to be on my own."

Kimbrell calls himself "a career student." After receiving his undergraduate degree from New Mexico Highlands University, he attended a number of graduate schools and studied a variety of subjects, including law. He earned a master's degree in environmental public health from the University of Wisconsin in 1982.

Kimbrell launched his first entrepreneurial venture as an undergraduate student, and he owned and operated a series of small businesses throughout graduate school.

Business Origin

The market opportunity for what would become Kimbrell's most successful venture emerged in the early 1980s, just as Kimbrell completed graduate school. Scientists discovered that asbestos, a material used for building insulation, posed a potential health threat when released into the air. In response, the Federal government passed legislation requiring public schools to identify and control on-site asbestos. "In 1982, the danger posed by asbestos was just beginning to come to the forefront as a national issue. Early regulations were aimed at protecting school children," Kimbrell remembers.

Having eyed an emerging business opportunity, Kimbrell and his wife formed a partnership with architect Frank Hall, and they opened Hall-Kimbrell Environmental Services, Inc. in Kimbrell's native Mississippi. The company inspected public school buildings for asbestos and developed detailed engineering plans for substance removal. Kimbrell financed his new venture with a $20,000 bank loan.

Business Growth

During the company's first year of operation, customer response was "overwhelming," according to Kimbrell. "I was surprised at how many people called us from all over Mississippi," he said. In one year, Hall-Kimbrell inspected half the school districts in Mississippi and earned a $100,000 profit.

Despite early success, Kimbrell was ready to abandon his business. "Although we had fun and did a good job that first year, I had decided not to continue to grow the company. In fact, I had accepted a job with the Federal government and was ready to start work. The weekend we were supposed to move to Pennsylvania for my new job, I went to pick up our moving truck and came home empty-handed," he says. "I told my wife that I was having second thoughts about giving up what looked like a great opportunity in a growing market. I called my new employers and told them we weren't coming."

Kimbrell decided to take his company national. In late 1983, he moved Hall-Kimbrell to Kansas, figuring that the mid-U.S. was a more central location from which to reach potential customers. Kimbrell used the company's $100,000 profit to mail letters offering a free, on-site consultation to 100,000 prospects. "In launching our direct marketing and advertising campaign, we gambled on my belief that the asbestos issue would impact hospitals and colleges and universities. For decades, Americans had been using asbestos to insulate virtually all of its buildings, and I had a gut feeling that the asbestos issue was going to gain more and more attention. It seemed to me that it was only a matter of time before asbestos testing and removal became an issue for homes, businesses, colleges and universities, offices and factories," he says. "I wanted to capture a good share of the market before competition emerged."

Over the next several years, Hall-Kimbrell grew at a blistering pace, averaging 283 percent growth each year through 1988. Kimbrell built a nationwide customer base of hospitals, educational institutions, commercial businesses and manufacturers. He expanded Hall-Kimbrell's services to include environmental issues such as toxic waste and air pollution and opened branch offices around the United States.

Revenues and profits grew as well. In 1984, Hall-Kimbrell had sales of $409,000 and posted a $37,000 a profit. Sales grew nearly ten-fold by 1986, reaching $4.4 million, and profits were $152,000 that year. In 1987, Hall-Kimbrell's revenues nearly tripled to $12.1 million and profits rose to $1.1 million.

The company grew even more dramatically in 1988, boosted by new regulations that required public school districts to survey all buildings by October. In a March newspaper article profiling Hall-Kimbrell's growth, Kimbrell noted, "Already this year, we have booked more business than we did all of last year." Hall-Kimbrell's 1988 net income reached nearly $12 million on sales of $44.5 million.

Kimbrell purposely slowed the company's growth in 1989. "I decided to put the brakes on for one year to let all of our systems and people catch up," he said.

Although 1989 revenues dipped slightly to $37 million, by year end Hall-Kimbrell was recognized as the largest asbestos-consulting company in the United States. In its first six years of operation, the company had surveyed 200,000 buildings, public schools and privately-owned commercial buildings across the U.S. Hall-Kimbrell ranked ninth on *Inc.* magazine's 1989 list of the 500 fastest growing companies in the nation. "We actually were number one in internal growth—the other eight companies grew by acquisition," Kimbrell points out. In a 1989 *Inc.* article he called his company "a big kid with a thyroid problem."

Kimbrell sold his company to Professional Services Inc. (PSI) of Chicago, Illinois in 1990. An engineering and construction company, PSI is a wholly-owned subsidiary of the Inspectorate/Adia Network of Companies, based in Switzerland. Kimbrell says that while PSI operated a "small asbestos business" before the merger, "the acquisition gave them a far better share of the market."

By the time he sold the business, Kimbrell's company had grown from five employees in 1984 to a staff of nearly 800.

Business Obstacles

From its beginnings, the enormous business potential Kimbrell had tapped posed special challenges, and forced Kimbrell to make key entrepreneurial decisions.

His initial critical decision was to continue in business after Hall-Kimbrell's highly successful first year. "I hesitated before going national because we had no business plan and we had never really considered how the future of the company would look," he remembers. "The response had been so great that first year that our resources were already pushed to the limit."

Once he had decided to "sink everything back into the business and keep going," Kimbrell continued to face the strains that accompany explosive growth. Asbestos consulting is a highly labor-intensive business that provides each client with a personalized analysis and a detailed report. Therefore, the more customers Kimbrell attracted, the more resources he needed to serve them. "It was impossible to manage that kind of growth, and it showed in our business. Although we always remained financially solid, growing almost three time our size every year put tremendous strains on our employees and our systems," Kimbrell says. "We had trouble keeping up in areas like physical plant, facilities, policies, procedures and manuals. We almost broke at the seams a couple of times. Eventually we reached the point of diminishing return on our growth and that's when I decided to sell," Kimbrell says.

Keys to Success

Kimbrell followed his hunch that asbestos detection and removal would become big business, and he tapped into a market poised for growth. In 1988, the *Kansas City Business Journal* reported that the nation spent $1 billion on asbestos removal in 1987, and said "the figure is expected to hit $10 billion by 1992."

Having carved out a unique, highly-specialized market niche, Kimbrell believed that rapid growth was the key to distancing his company from others that would enter the environmental consulting market. "My wife and I always put all profits back into the business to fund growth," he says.

Kimbrell's strategy was to anticipate which businesses would be next to seek removal of asbestos and other environmental hazards. "I looked for trends in the legal community and tried to anticipate coming regulations and liability concerns. I always relied on my gut feelings," he said. "I took a lot of chances, but my instincts usually paid off."

As a way to meet the demands of growth without significantly adding to overhead, Kimbrell developed "mass produced" products to serve his customers' needs. "I realized that there were some standard approaches to assessing properties," he told *Inc.* magazine in 1989. "If we could develop computer programs and train everyone the same way, we wouldn't have to reinvent the wheel on each project," he said.

By standardizing asbestos inspection and other environmental consulting services into packaged products, Kimbrell expanded his company from a person-to-person consulting firm to a business that distributed surveys and videotaped instruction, and offered services by mail. For example, the company supplied golf courses with a 45-minute videotape that explored environmental regulations. After viewing the tape, course officials answered a questionnaire about their facilities, and Hall-Kimbrell used the information to create a personalized compliance report.

The company also marketed a product that allowed schools and day-care centers to send water and paint samples to Hall-Kimbrell's laboratories for lead testing.

Central to Hall-Kimbrell's success was the company's reputation as a supplier of trained, experienced personnel. Kimbrell believed that the extensive training that his engineers received left them better prepared to conduct a complete inspection than people who were only Environmental Protection Agency (EPA) certified. "There's no way some kid could sit through a three- or four-day class and be expected to go out and make an adequate survey of a complex building," Kimbrell told the *Kansas City Business Journal* in 1988. "It's no simple job," he said.

When Kimbrell decided to sell his company, he looked for the buyer who would best ensure the business' continued success. "It was more than a matter of money," he said. "It was important that I sell to a company that ran well and had a bright future. I wanted my employees to have the chance for growth and development within a good company—a company with solid administrative system and technical know-how," he says. "PSI came forward saying all of the words I wanted to hear."

Future Vision

Kimbrell no longer works in the company he founded, and he acknowledges that relations between he and PSI Hall-Kimbrell management have been strained. "They fired me—it was a bad merger," he says. I'm still dealing with lawsuits between the two of us, and I'm learning quite a bit about the world of big business."

Kimbrell is also writing a book. "It's coming along slowly, but I'm enjoying it," he reports. "I guess you could call the book an authoritative guide to asbestos inspection and removal," Kimbrell says.

This career entrepreneur fully intends to launch another business some day. "Its too early to tell what the business will be, I am investigating opportunities," he says. "I definitely want to start something else eventually," he says.

Entrepreneurial Lessons

Kimbrell's experiences have taught him lessons that he eagerly passes on to other entrepreneurs. "I advise anyone to control the growth of their organization—not to try to grow too fast. I suggest that no company grow more than double its size in any given year," he says. Hall-Kimbrell's rapid growth meant that Kimbrell spent increasingly less time on engineering-related activities and more time managing the business. It was a change he did not relish. "I went from doing all of the technical work in our early days to becoming the CEO of a large company. As time went on, it was natural that I deal with the financial aspects of the business, but I had no business training, and I hated being so far away from the technical end," he says.

"I learned how important it is to surround yourself with people who have the skills that you lack," Kimbrell says. "If you're a technical person, make sure that you have good business people on your side. If business and management are your strengths, it is critical that you have people with solid technical knowledge in key positions. Don't think you can do it all yourself—you can't," he cautions. "I try to hire talented people who can keep up with my pace," Kimbrell adds. "I'm interested in people who want to build a career, not just put in their time in an 8 to 5 job. I work best with people who share my entrepreneurial spirit and ideas."

References

"Hall-Kimbrell Environmental." *Corporate Report—Kansas City*, July 1989.

Hitchcock, D. "Lawrence Firm Capitalizes on Growth of Asbestos Removal." *Kansas City Business Journal*, March 28, 1988.

Solomon, Stephen D. "Cleaning Up." *Inc.*, December 1989.

"World's Largest Service Organization Agrees to Acquire This Country's Largest Asbestos Consulting Company." *Kansas City Business Journal*, January 8, 1990.

——M. J. B.

James Koch

Boston Beer Company, Ltd.

James Koch: Born 1949. Single.
Venture: Beer microbrewery.
Company: Boston Beer Company, Ltd.; 30 Germania St.; Boston, MA 02130; (617) 522-3400
Founded: 1985.
Revenues: $15 million projected 1990 sales, according to a company source.
Employees: 50.
Original Investment: $240,000.
Value: Not available.

Founder

James Koch comes from a long line of German brewers. The family, in the United States since 1830, has seen every oldest son become a brewmaster. "It's something I consider to be my life's work," Koch says.

He started on a different career track, however. After earning a B.A., an M.B.A. and a law degree from Harvard, Koch joined the Boston Consulting Group as a management consultant in 1978. Much of his work focused on manufacturing quality control for companies like General Electric and International Paper.

Business Origin

While a consultant, the success of San Francisco's Anchor Steam Beer set Koch thinking there might be a niche in the beer market for a quality product. His father had run three small breweries, but they all went bankrupt. In the early 1980s, according to Koch, "the market was there for the first time." He modeled a financial portrait of a small brewery on a spreadsheet program. "The numbers worked," so he set up a limited partnership with himself as a corporate general partner. Any losses would flow through as tax write-offs to the investors while Koch would enjoy control, the opportunity to reap large rewards, and the protection of his personal assets through incorporation.

When he told his father he wanted to leave his $250,000 per year job after eight years as a top manager, he father replied, "Finally, someone in the family learns how to tie a tie—and he goes into the beer business."

Koch persuaded his secretary, Rhonda Kallman, to join him. "She was torn about leaving," Koch recalls. "She had an opportunity to be office adminis-trator for Boston Consulting Group's office in New York at a lot more money. She was 23 years old and willing to take a chance." Rhonda was also hesitant because she wasn't a beer drinker. Koch told her, "That's okay—you've never had great beer when it was fresh. I will make a beer that is so good that you *will* become a beer drinker." Koch continues, "When she tasted the beer, she smiled and said, 'Jim, I could sell this.'"

Koch raised $140,000 from relatives and former consulting clients to match $100,000 of his own funds. Later, he borrowed an additional $160,000 to build the company from an equity base that totaled $400,000.

Koch picked a name for the beer that would sound both American and Bostonian—"Samuel Adams." The label features a portrait of, in Koch's words, "the rabble rouser and original rebel behind the revolution. And," Koch adds, "Adams had his own brewery in Boston."

He contracted with a brewery in Pittsburgh to brew the ale while he personally supervised each batch on-site. The recipe, which has been in the family since 1870, was discovered by Koch in a trunk full of his great-grandfather's old belongings. The recipe is modeled after a Czech ale with sharper taste and fuller body than most of the ales found today.

Business Growth

Boston Beer Company started by making 500 barrels of Samuel Adams Boston Lager one day a month at the Pittsburgh brewery. Seven weeks later it won the Great American Beer Award, beating out 102 domestic contenders. The endorsement made people want to try it. The tiny company slowly added a truck driver, delivery person, and a receptionist. "My co-founder, Rhonda Kallman, and I were the only two people in a $3-million business before we had an office or a telephone," Koch recalls. "I had no idea this (success) would happen when I started. At the end of three years I thought I'd be making 500 barrels of beer a month." By 1987, Koch was brewing 500 barrels of beer every five days.

The stage was set to bring Boston Beer's brewing to Boston. Koch borrowed $5.2 million and raised another $4.7 million to renovate the aging Haffenraffer brewery that had sat unused for 10 years. "The brewery that I thought would cost $9 million, came in at $14 million," he says, "I had to cut back on what I wanted to build and return the debt money." According to Koch, to build a new brewery in the suburbs would have been cheaper, but "romance" led him to the old Haffenraffer plant.

Today, the beer is brewed in Boston, and by contracted breweries in Pittsburgh, Portland, and Germany. The German location was necessary to keep the previously exported product fresh. Koch explains, "My beers were just as stale in Germany as the German beers are in the United States."

Business Obstacles

When Koch was five weeks away from delivering his first batch from the aging tank, his uncle, an investment banker, called to see how his nephew was proceeding. Koch explained that he had been shopping for a computer system. "When he asked me why, I explained that I'd need a computer to keep track of sales, payables, and the like." "Oh yeah, sales," his uncle said. "By the way, have you got any?" "That shook me up," says Koch. "Listening to him, I realized that somehow I had gotten the whole process backward. To make my business viable, the first thing I needed was not a computer. It wasn't even an office. What I needed was a customer."

Koch packed two ice packs and seven bottles of beer in his old, brown lawyer's briefcase, and together with Rhonda Kallman, went from bar to bar. "Imagine going out tomorrow and having to make cold calls on bars, trying to convince some guy who's never heard of your beer—and handing him a bottle that isn't even labeled—to carry it." Koch continues, "The only thing standing between you and that customer's scorn is the integrity of your product. You're not talking to some demographic group. You're talking to an individual who is either going to buy your beer because he likes it or tell you to get lost."

When Koch started, the odds for success were not strong. There had been 11 bankrupt breweries in his family within the last three generations. His father had tried making the same beer and was told to dilute it for American taste. Before that his grandfather had tried making the same recipe. The American preference for light beers became an obstacle when Koch tried to sell his strong-tasting beer to 26-year-old bartenders who told him that their favorite beer was Coors Light. "I'm engaged in making a beer that 98 percent of the beer drinkers in America hate," said Koch. Fortunately, Samuel Adams Lager was a hit with beer connoisseurs. Starting the business without an office, phone or staff reduced overhead. Still, the company was losing $30,000 per month, primarily due to a fixed cost guarantee at the Pittsburgh brewery.

Koch and Kallman continued going from bar to bar. In the first year Kallman personally placed 800,000 stand-up cards on bar tables. They succeeded in getting the beer placed in Boston's finest hotels and restaurants.

Keys to Success

Koch brews a full-bodied beer with premium ingredients and no preservatives. Bottled in brown glass to prevent light from spoiling its freshness, Samuel Adams is the only American beer to meet the Reinheitsgebot, a German purity law that allows only beer brewed with malted barley, hops, yeast, and water to be imported into Germany. According to Koch, the German beers imported into the States would not pass the purity tests required back home, a point the company used extensively in its advertising until some of the radio stations were allegedly pressured to pull the ads by bigger-spending German beer importers.

Samuel Adams Lager and Koch's other beers are aimed at the four to five percent of beer drinkers now buying imports because they want the quality and sturdier taste of traditional lagers. "How well-made and how fresh my beer is are the important things to remember," says Koch. Each bottle is date-stamped for freshness. He refuses an average of three offers per week from beer distributors because his concern for fresh beer outweighs the push to blanket the market. "A lot of microbreweries have had quality problems," he says. "I felt from the very beginning, even if the brewery were small, it was necessary to meet the world-class standards of quality—things like dissolved oxygen in the tank, fill levels in the bottles, and consistency of CO_2 levels—basic technical quality-controls." Koch's background in statistical quality control was an asset. According to Koch, "it takes both technical expertise and premium ingredients brewed in small batches to put a great glass of beer in front of the consumer."

Future Vision

Koch doesn't see any major changes in the market ahead, but he will continue to produce new beers. He currently produces Samuel Adams Boston Lager, low-calorie Boston Lightship, Boston Ale (which was rated "superior in overall quality and taste" over Bass Ale in a blind taste test by the American Homebrewers Association), plus four seasonal beers—a double bock for February, an Oktoberfest beer, a winter lager, and for summer, Samuel Adams Wheat Beer.

He has also opened a brew-pub in Philadelphia, a restaurant where the beer is brewed in small quantities on the premises. Koch is not worried about competition from big brewers. "Anheuser-Busch makes as much beer in 50 seconds as I make in a week," he says. And, he welcomes the growing market for microbreweries, companies that brew less than 15,000 barrels annually. "Overall quality in microbreweries has improved because the ones that didn't make good beer went out of business and the ones that were serious about it learned how to do it," he says.

Entrepreneurial Lessons

First, says Koch, "There's nothing wrong with staying small." And second, "If you can make a big enough improvement in the quality level, the consumer will create a market for you. The consumer is equipped with an infallible product evaluator—his mouth. He can tell if something's really good."

Koch believes effective marketing is no substitute for product quality. "Marketing is all about creating, in the consumer's mind, a value that doesn't exist," he says. "After a couple of bottles, even I can't taste the difference between a Budweiser, a Miller, or a Coors. To a great extent these products are differentiated to the consumer solely through marketing."

As opposed to marketing, he says, "Selling is fundamental. It is impossible to go out and sell a product you don't believe in, particularly if, as CEO, you are directly responsible for the quality of the product." And that is what Koch does. As CEO of a $15 million company, Jim Koch now has a desk and a phone. Yet, he still spends two-thirds of his time doing what he did when he started the company—calling on clients and selling.

References

Apgar, Sally. "Made in America. Tiny Brewery Taking On the Imports." *Transcript-Telegram* (Holyoke, Massachusetts), October 7, 1986.

Castrodale, Beth. "Tiny Beer Brewer Says He's Getting Much Lager." *Cape Cod Times*, January 28, 1988.

Corman, Linda. "Home Brew." *Boston Business Journal*, February 13, 1989.

Irwin, Clark T., Jr. "Samuel Adams Lager Aims for Space in U.S. Coolers." *Portland Press Herald*, February 26, 1986.

Koch, James. "Portrait of the CEO as Salesman." *Inc.*, March 1988.

Kosan, Lisa. "Boston's Brewmaster." *Beverly (Massachusetts) Times*, October 8, 1987.

MacDonald, Bob. "Three Local Brews Top Taste Test." *Boston Globe*, August 8, 1991.

Radding, Alan. "Boston Beer Taps Domestic Market by Selling to Germany." *Northeast International Business*, April 1, 1988.

Tosto, Paul. "Beer Battle." *Connecticut Business Journal*, May 12, 1986.

——B.M.

Raymond C. Kurzweil

Kurzweil Applied Intelligence, Inc.
Kurzweil Music Systems, Inc.

Raymond C. Kurzweil: Born 1948. Married.

Venture: Companies that develop advanced electronic systems that recognize speech, read print, and realistically reproduce sounds of musical instruments.

Companies: Kurzweil Applied Intelligence, Inc. (KAI); 411 Waverly Oaks Road; Waltham, MA 02154; (617) 893-5151

Founded: Both companies were founded in 1982.

Revenues: KAI—estimated to be approximately $10 million (1988).

Employees: 85.

Original Investment: Unknown.

Value: Kurzweil Applied Intelligence (December 31, 1988)—$979,000 net worth according to published reports. Kurzweil Music Systems sold to Young Chang America in 1990.

Founder

Ray Kurzweil grew up surrounded by a family of artists and scientists in Queens, New York. His father was a concert pianist and conductor who had a passion for mathematics. His mother was a visual artist. Kurzweil's uncle invented complex automation machines, and his grandmother was a well-known chemist.

Kurzweil inherited all of the family talents. He remembers that as a child of five, he already had a keen interest in machinery and dreamed that he would be an inventor like his uncle. His love of music began at age six when he first studied piano with his father. At 12, Kurzweil became interested in computer technology—so much so that by the age of 15 he wrote a time-saving program for statistical analysis that IBM distributed to customers. He graduated from the Massachusetts Institute of Technology (MIT) in 1970 with a degree in computer science.

Kurzweil combined his love of music and science with his skill as an inventor and entrepreneur to create machines with capabilities few could have imagined. Kurzweil-developed systems have given the blind a new way to read, offered the deaf new ways to interpret speech, expanded the range of sounds produced as synthesized music and advanced the interactions of people and machines.

Kurzweil has been widely praised for his technological and entrepreneurial accomplishments. President Reagan presented him with the Computer Science Award in 1982 and the White House Award for Entrepreneurial Excellence in 1986. He was honored with the Distinguished Inventor Award from Intellectual Property Owners in 1986. He is a member of the Computer Industry Hall of Fame and has received honorary doctorates in Science, Music and Humane Letters. His 1987 film, *The Age of Intelligent Machines*, received international acclaim, and he published a book by the same name (MIT Press) in 1989. An accomplished author and lecturer, Kurzweil has also addressed congressional subcommittees on Education and Science and Technology.

Having established his companies just outside of Boston, Kurzweil actively participates in the city's educational, scientific and cultural communities. He is chairman of the Kurzweil Foundation, an organization that supports technology for the handicapped and funds projects to increase public understanding of the social impact of new technology. Kurzweil is also a trustee of Beth Israel Hospital in Boston, an incorporator of Boston's Museum of Science, an overseer of the New England Conservatory of Music, and a director of both the Massachusetts Software Council and the Boston Computer Society.

Business Origin

Kurzweil's success as an inventor began well before he launched his first business. At age 16, he developed a computer program that could create music in the style of well-known classical composers, including Mozart. "The only thing missing was the genius," Kurzweil says of his creation. "It sounded, maybe, like a second-rate student of Mozart." The discovery won him the Westinghouse Talent Search Award in 1964.

While studying at MIT, Kurzweil developed a computer system to match students and colleges. He sold to the system to Harcourt Brace Jovanovich for $100,000 plus royalties.

People began to marvel at Kurzweil's ability to link people and machines in the mid 1970s when he invented the Kurzweil Personal Reader, a machine that translated words into sounds. The Personal Reader used a small optical scanner to identify letters of the alphabet on a printed page, then read the words aloud into headphones. It was hailed as the greatest invention for the blind since Braille.

Kurzweil admits his interest in technology, not a mission to help the disabled, led him to invent the Personal Reader. He developed the machine while looking for a way to create sound through character recognition. He then searched for a market for his discovery and found the machine's application for the blind.

Kurzweil founded Kurzweil Computer Products in 1974 to manufacture and market the Personal Reader. He sold the company to Xerox Corporation in 1978 for $6 million and now heads Xerox's Kurzweil Reading Machine Division.

Later Kurzweil inventions were the impetus for Kurzweil Music Systems (KMS) and Kurzweil Applied Intelligence (KAI).

Business Growth

After he sold his first company, Kurzweil continued his work as an inventor and entrepreneur. In 1982, he invented the Kurzweil 250, a synthesizer that recreated the sound of any musical instrument played into its memory, even the complex sounds of a grand piano. Music superstar Stevie Wonder, a user of the Personal Reader and friend of Kurzweil's, offered the impetus for Kurzweil's discovery. Wonder had asked if it was possible to build a synthesizer that could recreate the sounds of acoustic instruments such as violins, saxophones and flutes. The challenge fascinated Kurzweil, who says that his aging father also influenced him to invent the machine that Wonder wanted. "My father was very excited about the application of computers to music . . . he believed that someday I would combine these two interests," Kurzweil recalls.

Before moving ahead, Kurzweil examined the market potential for the product he would develop. "The whole marketplace seemed poised for an historic transformation from what, at that time, was almost entirely acoustic technology to digital electronic technology," he said. He launched Kurzweil Music Systems to develop and market the product and two years later introduced the Kurzweil 250. KMS produces a series of computer-based musical instruments that utilize artificial intelligence, pattern recognition and signal processing technologies.

In April 1990, KMS was acquired by Young Chang America, a firm that manufactures acoustic pianos. At the same time, KMS was filing for protection under Chapter 11 bankruptcy laws. Raymond Kurzweil, who stayed on as a consultant for the KMS product line, cited the "great deal of synergy" between the two companies. While sales and administrative staffs were moved to California, KMS R&D stayed in Waltham but moved to the new Kurzweil Research and Development Institute.

Kurzweil's third company, Kurzweil Applied Intelligence, grew out of his work with voice recognition technology, the ability of a computer to respond to the spoken word. Using automatic speech recognition (ASR), the company produces voice-activated word processing machines that type words on a screen as they are spoken. Kurzweil believes that this latest invention has the power to reshape the way that people create any written document. "The spoken word is probably the most powerful mode of communication. It is the first method you learn, and human factor studies confirm that it is by far the most rapid form of communication. Creating reports with ASR combines the speed advantage of dictation with the immediate inspection and correction of handwriting," he says.

Kurzweil's voice recognition machines can aid the deaf by displaying what other people are saying. In the future, Kurzweil sees that this "artificial hearing" will also allow music and natural sounds to be translated and received through modalities such as vision and touch.

KAI now manufactures voice recognition systems comprised of printed circuit boards, application software and computer hardware. KAI sells products directly to end users and through a network of distributors and value-added resellers.

Business Obstacles

Widely credited for his technological genius, Kurzweil has been described as "a better idea man than a manager." He brought a "business" focus to the field of artificial intelligence, but questions about his ability to run those businesses were raised by slower-than-expected sales of KAI and KMS products.

Financial analysts and others have said that Kurzweil's companies suffer from misread markets, growing international competition and overpriced products. Even critics acknowledge, however, that turning advanced technologies into marketable products and profitable businesses takes time. Kurzweil calls this process the "practical realization" of a new technology, and he says that it reflects the "natural evolution" of the kinds of products his companies offer.

KAI and KMS used borrowings and capital investments from public and private sources to meet operating needs. By continuing to fund Kurzweil's businesses, investors have demonstrated a belief that his innovative technology will yield profit in the long run.

Analysts speculated that managing three large businesses and staying heavily involved in research was more than one person could handle. In an October 1989 issue of *FW,* one analyst noted, "Not everybody can be a genius inventor and a successful marketeer. Maybe Ray's problem is that he tries to do too much."

Kurzweil rejects the idea that he spreads himself too thin. "Each company has a full management team. I work closely with them but leave most of the day-to-day operations to them. I provide the kind of direction I am uniquely qualified to provide," he says.

In some cases, sales and profits have not been readily forthcoming, Kurzweil concedes. However, he continues to adhere to his strategy for planned growth as the key to ultimate profitability and success. Kurzweil's companies take what he calls "a top-down" approach to marketing and technology development, concerning themselves with product quality and performance before price. His companies focus on narrow "niche" markets before attacking what Kurzweil calls "the generic multi-billion dollar potential." He says that this is the only way to create truly end-user solutions that people are eager to buy.

Keys to Success

Kurzweil has been labeled everything from a "slightly eccentric inventor," to "a high-tech neo-Renaissance man," and even a "prophet of change." He says his goal is to create "power tools for the mind."

Kurzweil credits teamwork, not his genius, for his successes. He has high hopes for the future growth of KAI and the KMS product line. Over time, Kurzweil expects that superior products will bring the type of financial reward he is looking for.

Kurzweil says that he will work to keep the values and practices that make a small company a place where entrepreneurial ideas flourish. He says that most important are maintaining active communication within the companies and encouraging positive relationships between management, employees and investors. Kurzweil will continue to foster small business units within his companies, and he promises to split groups when they "grow too large." These "intrapreneurial" groups will be encouraged to take risks, maintain cultures of their own, and they'll be rewarded for innovation. "Large corporations tend to have slow-moving gears, while small groups have fast-moving gears. As we get larger, our management challenge will be to be an effective transducer between the two," he says.

As an entrepreneur, Kurzweil has taken his mastery of artificial intelligence technology out of the laboratory and into the marketplace. His theories on business are as clearly documented as his ideas about the connection between man and machine. Kurzweil seeks to create a work environment where creative and innovative people like himself can thrive.

Kurzweil has attracted investors without the promise of short-term financial return. One major backer described him as "a spell binder" when encouraging financial commitment. He is said to be practically-minded and keenly aware of the importance of market research and business plans. Kurzweil also clearly communicates his vision of the potential for new and advanced technologies.

Future Vision

Kurzweil articulates a vision of the world-wide impact of artificial intelligence in the years to come. He believes that computers will combine their traditional speed, accuracy and memory with newly-found intelligence to "provide us with tools that will enhance our productivity, expressiveness and creativity." He intends for his companies to have a hand in realizing that vision. He says that he may someday take KAI public, and he does not rule out acquisition as a future strategy for growth.

Entrepreneurial Lessons

Kurzweil believes that entrepreneurial ventures offer inventors the opportunity to "build something significant and to change the world." He cautions, however, that entrepreneurs must combine knowledge of technology with an understanding of the markets they are trying to reach. Otherwise, they risk creating products that nobody will buy.

He encourages entrepreneurs to enlist the support of investors, professional management, employees, the media and an early group of customer "pioneers." Noting that while any entrepreneurial venture poses risks, he says that the successful entrepreneur seeks to control and minimize risks wherever possible. "Entrepreneurs are not gamblers," Kurzweil says. "They are people who can articulate a vision and attract and lead diverse talent."

High-technology has changed significantly since Kurzweil started in business. "The pace of change is increasing, product life times are getting shorter, the technology changes so quickly," he observes. "That provides a lot of opportunity for anyone or any organization that is quick on its feet, and it provides relatively little security. Success provides the opportunity for growth, [and] growth provides the opportunity to risk at a higher level."

References

Gilder, George. "Where Are the Microchip Billionaires?" *Forbes*, October 21, 1989.

Helm, Leslie. "This Whiz Kid Isn't Such a Whiz at Business." *Business Week*, January 18, 1988.

Kozlov, Alex. "Wolf! Wolf!" *FW*, October 3, 1989.

Kurzweil, Raymond. "Beyond Pattern Recognition." *Byte*, December 1989.

———. "Life For the Handicapped in the Twenty-First Century." Excerpted from *The Age of Intelligent Machines*. Boston: MIT Press, 1989.

———. "Technology Innovation: From the Sandbox to the Showroom." Presentation to the Harvard Business School, October 1987.

"Kurzweil Completes First Year With Young Chang." *Music Trades*, August 1991.

Lander, David. "Raymond Kurzweil: Revolutionary Tradition." *Audio*, January 1989.

Melton, Louise. "Mister Impossible: Ray Kurzweil." *Computers & Electronics*, July 1984.

Minkin, T. "Speaking of the Future." *American Way*, November 1989.

"Opportunities for Risk: An Interview with Raymond Kurzweil." *Information Technology Quarterly*, Spring 1989.

Ziegler, Edward. "The Magic of Ray Kurzweil." *Reader's Digest*, February 1991.

——M. J. B.

Steven B. Leebow

Pacesetter Steel Service, Inc.

Steven B. Leebow: Born 1947. Married, three children.
Venture: Distributor of flat rolled carbon steel.
Company: Pacesetter Steel Service, Inc.; P.O. Box 1729; Woodstock, GA
30188; (404) 926-8900
Founded: 1977.
Revenues: $150 million year-end December 1989.
Employees: 150.
Original Investment: Limited personal funds.
Value: Would not release.

Founder

Steel was, for Steven Leebow, a family affair. He began working with his
father at family-owned Baldwin Steel Company in Jersey City, New
Jersey, immediately after graduating from Ohio State University. During
his eight years with Baldwin he held several positions and was exposed to
every aspect of operations.

Leebow eventually realized that his growth potential in the family business was limited. Not allowed to share in day-to-day leadership, he left
Baldwin in 1977, determined to establish his own company.

When not involved with business matters, Leebow devotes himself to
family activities. He also participates in community, state and national
projects promoting both quality education and quality anti-drug programs for young people. He admits to an "obsession" about getting the
anti-drug message across, and particularly focuses on educating young

305

elementary school children to the dangers of illegal drug use and teaching them how to say "No!"

Leebow enjoys speaking at family business workshops and seminars, sharing with other business owners his experiences in a family-owned business.

Business Origin

Leebow says he was intent on finding a niche and building a successful company in the industry he knew and loved. He found his niche in zinc-coated, flat rolled carbon steel products purchased from domestic and foreign steel producers. To deliver the product to end users, steel producers typically required a minimum of eight to ten weeks and distributors required three to five days. Using his industry knowledge and innovative marketing techniques, Leebow knew he could shorten that gap between demand and delivery to 24 hours.

Leebow gave as much thought to his start-up location as he had given to finding his niche. A vibrant economy, beautiful topography and a thriving new business environment made Atlanta particularly attractive. His headquarters city selected, he turned his attention to what he knew were essential to success: talented staff and adequate capital.

After what he describes as a "hard sell," Leebow eventually secured a bank loan. Pacesetter Steel began operations out of a small rented warehouse and office in Marietta, an Atlanta suburb. The company's lean but "talented staff" consisted of Leebow, a sales representative and secretary Margie O'Byrne. "When I first started out," Leebow remembers, "we spent a lot of time waiting for the phone to ring." But ring it did, and as orders were filled, he funneled every available cent back into the business. "We didn't have a lot of capital to start with, but we had to have inventory," says the company's founder. "So every time we would make a sale, we would buy another truckload of steel." Reflecting on those tenuous first months, Leebow says, "I never had time to be afraid. I only had time to think about what would make Pacesetter successful. Since our funds were so limited, it was critical that we were profitable from the very first month."

By the end of his company's first fiscal year, revenues totaled an unexpected $3.3 million. In retrospect, Leebow says candidly, the immediacy of his success was surprising and exciting.

Business Growth

Pacesetter Steel's customers were small to large users, and originally included primarily the sheet metal industry—heating, ventilating and air conditioning manufacturers—and other steel distributors. As the company grew, its customer base expanded, and now also includes the appliance, automotive and construction industries. By the end of its first full year in operation, enthusiastic bankers had upped the fledgling steel service center's line of credit three times and sales topped more than $6.6 million. In its next three years, the company outgrew three Marietta locations, and finally built its own facility in 1982.

Prompted by the geographical spread of its growing customer base and rising sales, Pacesetter opened its first satellite warehouse facility in Chicago in 1979. By 1985, the company had operations in Houston and Philadelphia as well. In October 1989, its Chicago operation moved into a new, 110,000 square foot, state-of-the-art distribution facility, with $3 million in new processing equipment.

In 1989, Pacesetter grew 41 percent and its revenues passed the $150 million mark. In an industry which has shrunk by over 30 percent in the last 10 years, its continuous, surging growth has made it the recipient of national media attention. In addition to detailed coverage by trade publications, the company made *Inc.* magazine's list of fastest-growing privately-owned enterprises, and for three consecutive years was one of *Venture* magazine's "Fast Track 100" companies. Leebow has himself been recognized for his business accomplishments. In 1989, the Ernst and Young accounting firm named him Georgia's "Entrepreneur of the Year," and he was one of several entrepreneurs cited by *Inc.* magazine for social responsibility.

Business Obstacles

Leebow remembers obtaining initial financing as his greatest single obstacle. The Atlanta banking community was especially tough, he reveals, because of the depressed economy in the steel industry. "We had to do an oversell job, literally turn cartwheels to get any interest. We had to explain over and over again how we wouldn't be affected by the steelmakers' problems." Finally, Fulton National Bank (later to become Bank South) took a chance and offered him a loan. The grateful entrepreneur's company continues to maintain a strong relationship with that financial institution.

In staffing his company, Leebow avoided experienced steel industry personnel. He believed the industry's problems had bred people who were neither aggressive nor risk-takers. He wanted employees who were both. To get them, he brought in talented people with no prior steel industry experience and instituted his own training programs. "As a service industry," Leebow says, "we look at people as our number one resource, and motivating them becomes the most important ingredient of success." Determined to achieve that goal, Pacesetter offers career paths, continual internal and off-site training and promotes from within. To illustrate the success of that human resource philosophy, Leebow points with pride to his first secretary, Margie O'Byrne, who is now a company vice president, and to his second secretary, Claudia Waters, who now directs daily distribution and transportation from Pacesetter's four distribution facilities to over 35 states.

Keys to Success

A large part of Pacesetter's success may be attributable to its founder's original vision. As a 1986 company profile in industry magazine *Metal Center News* reports, Leebow believed "that the strategies at work in consumer-based industries [could] be adapted to the nuts-and-bolts business of selling steel." The magazine says Leebow "borrowed management strategies from a wide range of successful companies, including Perdue Chicken, Domino's Pizza and People Express." Using techniques derived from McDonald's and Federal Express, Leebow has come up with "a steel distribution system that is exceedingly quick, ready, and responsive, providing overnight delivery to customers in 40 states."

In his satellite-based system, Pacesetter's Marietta headquarters functions as what the industry journal termed "Mission Control" for the warehouses in Chicago, Houston and Philadelphia, handling all sales, service and administrative functions. Leebow says the challenge for the satellites is then "to receive and act on information as quickly as they can from the headquarters office—whether that information concerns a mill delivery or a customer shipment." He believes the benefits of the central clearing house concept are efficiency for the company and service for the customer. "Over 90 percent of our customers receive their delivery within 24 hours of placing the order," he says.

Pacesetter's founder admits to a zealous commitment to quality control. As corporate policy, Pacesetter's aim is "to perform error-free work for ourselves, our customers, and our associates." The company strives for what outsiders might call "perfection." The philosophy encompasses both product and employees. Marketing manager Steve Lappin explains the Pacesetter view of employee performance: "The very first person who talks to the customer is the receptionist, and the last person who touches the steel is the dock loader. Those two people have to understand that they are just as important as the president of the company." Successfully meeting the demanding quality control standards requires excellent communications with employees and with customers.

While the quality philosophy is good for the company, its greatest benefit, says Pacesetter president Tom Penzone, is to the customer. He cites his company's program of mill visitation as an example of attempting to achieve error-free performance: "Since starting this program of mill visitations, we have learned to buy steel based on what each mill does best," he explains. "If, for example, a customer wants to buy seven types of prime coated steel, he does not have to go to seven different mills. He can come to Pacesetter and know he'll get the best steel from the best sources."

Leebow claims part of his success is due to his ability to delegate, a skill he believes many entrepreneurs never learn. Leebow says one of his greatest satisfactions was turning over day-to-day operations to Tom Penzone. Beginning as a sales representative with the company in 1978, Penzone rose through the ranks to become Pacesetter's president in 1987. In turning over the reins to Penzone, Leebow demonstrated his personal commitment to the company's human resource policies. "I surround myself with talented people. Being able to pass [an executive position] on to an extremely talented individual gave me the opportunity to make other people's dreams come true."

Leebow knows that his company's success does not rest solely on the excellence of his product. "It's not *what* we sell, but *how* we sell it," he claims. Leebow declares, "We probably have the best sales force of any service center in the country." To his knowledge, Pacesetter was the first steel service center to use telemarketing. Leebow explains, "Steel used to be a business of knocking on doors, but companies lose control with a traveling sales force, as well as create a huge budget expense." Pacesetter's early use of the sales technique allowed wide customer coverage, close supervision and much lower costs. Leebow doesn't rule out returning to the old sales methods now that telemarketing is so widespread, however. "We work diligently to *make* a difference and to *be* different from the rest of the industry," he says.

Future Vision

Leebow is specific about Pacesetter Steel's direction in the coming decade. In addition to opening a few new distribution centers around the country, Leebow plans to expand his international trade business substantially.

In September 1990 Pacesetter announced the opening of Encore Steel, an operation focusing on secondary and excess prime flat rolled steel distribution. "Pacesetter has specialized in prime flat rolled galvanized products, and is known for its attention to service and quality," says Tom Penzone. "Through Encore, we plan to provide the same excellent service to the secondary and excess market."

In October 1990 Pacesetter expanded its vistas further with the opening of Colortech Steel, a prepainted steel distributor.

Entrepreneurial Lessons

While Steve Leebow recognizes the vast amount of time and intensity of effort involved in achieving business success, he encourages entrepreneurs not to develop tunnel vision. "I would like to see more business owners become involved in social and civic issues," a thoughtful Leebow says. "Issues such as improving the educational system as well as educating American youth about the dangers of illegal drugs and abuse of legal drugs are perfect areas for business involvement." He feels the business community profits from involvement in such critical areas, and fulfills an ethical duty as well. Leebow strongly believes that businesses no longer can be comfortable simply supplying the community with jobs. "We owe our community much more, so much more. Everyone, not just the recipient, benefits," Leebow maintains.

References

Alter, Joy. "Rising Star on a Flatrolled Horizon." *Metal Center News*, April 1986.

Bocchino, Frank. "Keeping Pace with a Trend-Setter." *Metal Center News*, April 1990.

"Brothers in Steel." *Inc.*, May 1988.

Elgin, Peggie R. "Marietta Company Makes Obtaining Materials Easier." *Marietta Daily Journal,* March 12, 1990.

Stile, Charles. "Pacesetter Steel Opens Facility in Falls." *Trenton Times,* October 28, 1988.

Bernard Marcus

Home Depot, Inc.

Bernard Marcus: Born 1929. Married.

Venture: Nationwide chain of home improvement and building material warehouses targeting the "do-it-yourselfer" and home rebuilding markets.

Company: Home Depot, Inc.; 2727 Paces Ferry Road; Atlanta, GA 30339; (404) 433-8211

Founded: Home Depot, Inc., was incorporated in Delaware in June 1978 and opened its first store in Atlanta, Georgia, in 1979.

Revenues: $3.8 billion in net sales in fiscal 1990, according to company sources.

Employees: 26,000.

Original Investment: Not available.

Value: $360 million net worth as of January 1989.

Founder

Bernard Marcus, a New Jersey native, graduated from the Rutgers College of Pharmacy and soon after opened his own small pharmacy. Despite its success, Marcus later sold the pharmacy to the former Two Guys discount chain, and went on to manage their cosmetic and drug departments. His success later landed him the position of vice-president of hard-goods merchandising and advertising with Vornado, Inc., Two Guys' parent corporation.

Seeking a career change, Marcus left Vornado in 1972 and became president and chairman of the board of Handy Dan Home Improvement Centers, then a subsidiary of Daylin Corporation. While Daylin executives praised his performance, Marcus still lost his job in 1978 when Handy Dan was sold.

While at Daylin, Marcus began experimenting with "discounting," and developed a strategy where he could cut prices and continue to increase profits. Along with Arthur Blank, another ousted Daylin executive, and Ronald Brill, now Home Depot's chief financial officer, Marcus decided to put his strategy to the test. In 1979, Home Depot opened its first store in Atlanta, Georgia, and quickly added another store later that year. Presently, Home Depot has over 160 stores nationally, with plans to open approximately 15 new stores each year.

"I've basically been entrepreneurial all my life," Marcus told *Sky* magazine. "I've never had a corporate mentality, where you go along with whatever is in vogue and is politically proper at the moment. Being an entrepreneur is something that takes guts and a lot of character. It's not easy."

While many attribute Home Depot's tremendous growth to its ample balance sheet, others give most of the credit to Marcus' "charismatic" personality. Associates describe him as "down-to-earth," "creative," "consistent and extremely knowledgeable," "innovative and analytical." Home Depot employees describe Marcus as someone who "genuinely cares about everything and everybody he comes in contact with—a feeling customers quickly notice when they walk in the door."

Business Origin

Before Home Depot's entry into the home repair and remodeling markets in 1979, analysts describe the industry as burdened with retailers who charged outrageous prices but offered inferior products and little service. The economy was in a lull and consumers were demanding changes.

Sensing this, Marcus developed a unique mix of products and prices which would profitably allow him to offer below normal prices to his customers. He developed a three-pronged strategy geared to provide below normal prices, an extensive merchandise selection and superior customer service.

Not everyone was convinced Marcus' strategy would have long-term success. Some felt that his ideas were retailing "fads." This made finding the initial investment difficult. Powered by their convictions, Marcus and his associates sought out bankers and venture capitalists willing to take a chance. Combining venture capital with personal funds, they raised the money to open the first Home Depot.

Essentially, the Home Depot concept is a warehouse home center, a no-frills home improvement retailer. Each store averages 100,000 square feet, about the size of two football fields. A "working warehouse," the shelves are loaded with some 30,000 items including lumber, tools, lighting and plumbing supplies. Because Home Depot buys its products in unusually high volumes, unsold goods are stacked above the selling floor. This volume buying and conservation of space allows Home Depot to offer most of their products at 40 percent off the list price.

And yet, as Home Depot President Arthur Blank told *Time*, "The real difference between us and everyone else is not in the merchandise." Instead, it is the detailed attention to customer service, which competitors find hard to duplicate. Employees are required to attend product knowledge classes and are paid for their participation. Home Depot even hires experienced trades people and pays them top dollar for their talents. Employees well-versed in home repairs converse with the often less-knowledgeable shoppers, recommending products and explaining how they are used.

Business Growth

Despite Home Depot's present success, the company actually had quite a rocky start. Home Depot lost $930,000 on sales of $7 million during 1979. And while the "warehouse" approach to shopping has gained popularity, consumers were leery of the idea in 1979. The customer acceptance of warehousing was slow—Home Depot executives even tried giving away dollar bills to customers as incentives, and were surprised when money was left over at the end of the day.

Adversity made Bernard Marcus more determined. His constant involvement with various professional and civic organizations gave him the chance to espouse the Home Depot concept. He seized opportunities to acquaint business and community leaders with his management techniques and sales approaches. Eventually, customers heard his message. During 1980, Home Depot made $453,000 on sales of $22.3 million.

Despite years of success and increased profits, Home Depot was still relatively unknown in the home improvement market. Competitors with big advertising budgets dominated the radio, television and print media, practically destroying Home Depot's advertising campaigns. To compete,

Home Depot needed bigger budgets than its competitors. To raise the necessary capital, Marcus took Home Depot public in 1981, selling stock at $12 per share. The company raised $5 million which enabled them to meet their competitors head-on.

Since 1981, Home Depot has expanded in areas such as Los Angeles, Phoenix, Dallas/Ft. Worth, New Orleans, Tampa and Long Island, as well as numerous small and medium size cities. Every year since 1981, Home Depot has added five to 15 new stores to its roster.

Business Obstacles

By 1985, Home Depot's success was undeniable, with 31 thriving stores as proof. Entrance into new markets was relatively easy. A Home Depot outlet was greeted enthusiastically by other retailers hoping to benefit from the store's steady flow of customers. Small, home-improvement retailers attempted to hold on to dwindling customer bases. Ultimately, however, many succumbed.

Given his record of success, rapid expansion into new markets for Marcus was an irresistible temptation. During 1985, Home Depot enthusiastically added 19 stores, but the expansion was ill-timed, and earnings plunged nearly 42 percent.

Marcus realized his mistake early and was able to recover from the loss. This type of unchecked expansion taught the retailer a valuable lesson that he "won't soon forget." "I learned a lot of very important lessons from Two Guys," remembers Marcus. "When I worked for them they were the best retail discount store in the country, but they overexpanded and didn't have the people to carry the expansion off. I now know retail stores have to grow slowly, within their selves and their capabilities. If they do, they will be able to offer a good return to investors."

Keys to Success

"No-frills" or "warehouse" shopping has become a popular retailing tactic. Yet shoppers have come to expect little or no service while shopping at warehouses. Home Depot is quite different, hiring knowledgeable sales people and maintaining strict levels of customer service. Employees attend classes on a variety of subjects—plumbing, lawn care, construction—on a regular basis. Manufacturers are encouraged to conduct classes on the uses of their products so they can answer employee questions. Many employees also teach classes which Home Depot provides to shoppers at no charge.

Customers respond to the attention they receive. One shopper remarked, "One [employee] walked me through the complete installation of a ceiling fan. I felt like a dummy asking all those questions—I didn't even know which tools to use. But the guy really knew what he was doing. He shared some tips with me to make the installation go even smoother."

Marcus is quite vocal on the important role his employees play in Home Depot's organizational picture. They provide the service and support Home Depot customers have come to expect: a profitable niche for the company. In exchange, Home Depot offers above average wage and benefits packages. Corporate employees enjoy a wellness/fitness area at the company's headquarters in Atlanta. Programs which help employees lose weight, stop smoking or battle substance abuse are on-going.

While hiring is left to the discretion of each store manager, Marcus requires that no one be hired at minimum wage. "People earning the minimum wage don't have the commitment to the customer and the level of service we expect," comments Ronald Brill, CFO. And there are several management opportunities for employees with long-term career goals with Home Depot.

Future Vision

"The building materials growth ahead in the next 10 years will be phenomenal," says an excited Marcus. Home Depot intends to be at the forefront of that growth.

Marcus is firm in his belief that for Home Depot to survive it must continue to enter new markets, keeping an eye on even the smallest changes within the market. "I've lived through this before," says Marcus. "It's called evolution, and I guarantee that the players who do not keep up with the game won't be playing long. But there is a place for everyone, from the small store to the home center to the warehouse. The key is to change with the market."

Home Depot's five-year growth plan projects expanding the workforce to 60,000. To keep employees motivated, the company will soon have an in-house TV network to broadcast meetings and get feedback from local managers.

Entrepreneurial Lessons

The cliche "it's lonely at the top" does not apply to Bernard Marcus. On the contrary, the retail entrepreneur surrounds himself with people. His success is due, in part, to his "outgoing" nature and his need to interact with others.

Marcus credits much of his success to the "team effort" he requires of his employees. He acknowledges that no entrepreneur can maintain a business long without surrounding himself with quality people.

In 1988, Home Depot invested $150,000 in a corporate fitness/wellness program. While Marcus hopes for returns via healthier employees, it was not his motivation for developing the program: "It was the right thing to do," he says.

Employees respond to Marcus' attention with their hard work, loyalty and dedication. "You can't build a business without that," warns Marcus. "Home Depot treats its employees very well, which builds a real *esprit de corp* within the organization," comments one industry analyst.

References

Broderson, Linda C. "Wellness Programs: The Investment in Good Health for Employees Should Pay off Handily at the Bottom Line." *Atlanta Business Chronicle*, July 11, 1988.

Burritt, Chris. "Chain Sanded out Some Rough Spots." *Atlanta Journal*, March 17, 1989.

Greenwald, John. "Shelter from the Recession." *Time*, June 10, 1991.

Hawkins, Chuck. "Will Home Depot be 'The Wal-Mart of the '90s'?" *Business Week*, March 19, 1990.

Jacobs, Margaret A. "Home Depot Builds on Success." *Newark Star-Ledger*, February 5, 1989.

———. "Retail Exec Returns to New Jersey 'Roots'." *Newark Star-Ledger*, February 5, 1988.

Kamen, Robin. "Nailing Down the Home Front." *Hackensack Record*, February 3, 1989.

Nutile, Tom. "Fight for the Do-It-Yourselfer Buck." *Boston Herald*, February 28, 1989.

Shaw, Russell. "Bernard Marcus." *Sky*, April 1991.

Strickland, Bob, and others. "Home Centers Must Evolve or Die, Say Four Execs." *Building Supply & Home Centers*, May 1989.

——R. H. S.

Samuel H. Maslak

Acuson Corporation

Samuel H. Maslak: Born 1948. Married, two children.

Venture: The design, development, manufacture and marketing of ultra-sound equipment and software.

Company: Acuson Corporation; 1220 Charleston Road; Mountain View, CA 94043; (415) 969-9112

Founded: 1982.

Revenues: $300 million projected sales (1991), according to published reports.

Employees: 1,200 worldwide.

Original Investment: $10.5 million invested by a variety of venture capital firms.

Value: Approximately $102 million net worth at the close of 1989, according to published sources.

Founder

Samuel H. Maslak is among those lexicographer Samuel Johnson would have called the rarest of men—one whose business is also his pleasure. Maslak is the founder and president of Acuson Corporation, a California-based manufacturer of ultrasound equipment, and to hear him talk about his early life, it's all he ever wanted to be. "I guess you could say I really like ultrasound," says Maslak when explaining his long involvement in the field. That "like" is particularly clear when viewed in terms of his academic and business past, and even his social life. Maslak studied ultrasound, worked in ultrasound, and even married an ultrasound technician.

Described by one magazine as a "science nerd" in high school, Maslak grew up in suburban Washington, DC, and was fascinated with technology in general, and the technology of sound in particular, at an early age. He left Washington for the Massachusetts' Institute of Technology, where he majored in electrical engineering and earned his doctorate. His dissertation was on ultrasound.

After graduation, Maslak took a position with Hewlett-Packard, working with the electronics giant's ultrasound division. While there, Maslak worked on a variety of ultrasound-related projects, developing and earning a patent design on the ultrasound technology that is still the heart of Hewlett-Packard machines nearly ten years later. That design was, in part, the catalyst for his leaving the company.

Business Origin

Ultrasound technology is based on a principle discovered by the nineteenth-century physicist C. J. Doppler. Known as the "Doppler effect," the principle explains how waves (of light, sound, water, etc.) appear to change their frequency when the source of those waves is moving either toward or away from the observer. The Doppler effect describes why sirens sound higher in pitch as they approach, and lower in pitch as they move away. It also explains how radar and sonar work.

By bouncing a radio wave off of a car, airplane, or other moving object, radar can measure the changes in the frequency of reflected radio waves to determine the object's direction and speed. Likewise, a sonar system uses sound waves to accomplish the same objective under water.

An ultrasound system operates basically as a tiny sonar device, sending soundwaves into a patient's body and receiving the reflected echos. Computers then translate the echos into images on a television screen, providing an image of internal organs, fetuses and even bloodflow.

Hewlett-Packard wanted a machine to last in the marketplace for at least ten years without substantial changes. Maslak helped create that machine. But the young ultrasound engineer wanted to move on, to do more. "I was ready to think about where we could go next," Maslak recalls, "but HP was satisfied the design we had would last a decade."

Maslak could have continued to work for the firm, assured that when the time did come to redesign the company's ultrasound product, he would be called on to lead the development, and would have substantial financial and technical resources with which to work. But Maslak remembers that he had one important problem. "I did not want to wait that long," he explains.

Instead of remaining in his secure corporate position at Hewlett-Packard, Maslak joined with two other former Hewlett-Packard employees to form Acuson to develop, manufacture and market an ultrasound machine of their own design.

The new team consisted of Maslak, Robert Younge and Amin Hanafy, all three seasoned professionals and experts in their fields. But success was by no means assured.

Business Growth

Funded by venture capital, Acuson devoted the next four years to the development of a new ultrasound machine for use in hospitals and radiology labs, a machine based on both Maslak's expertise and his intuition.

Maslak's experience told him that ultrasound technology could be improved, and his intuition told him that the medical marketplace would be willing to pay a premium price for the improvements.

The goal of Maslak and his partners was for Acuson to take current ultrasound technology to a new level, and to reap the rewards of doing so, something they felt they could not do back at Hewlett-Packard. "They [Hewlett-Packard] did not have the sense of urgency I had with ultrasound," explains Maslak. "My goal was to become the world-wide leader in diagnostic equipment."

Acuson began to reach that goal when it introduced its first product in 1983, the Acuson 128. The new machine—designed completely by the company—introduced a new approach to ultrasound called computed sonography.

The Acuson 128 combined the latest electronics with the latest in software innovations. The machine doubled the number of sound transmitters (transducers) contained in competitor's machines, and its new software controlled each transmitter and the corresponding receiver with greater accuracy than anything else on the market. As a result, the device provided a clearer picture than any other ultrasound machine available.

Acuson's sales reached more than $11 million in its first year, and over $31 million in its second. By 1989, the fifth year the company was manufacturing products, total sales had climbed to more than $160 million. In addition, Acuson fulfilled Maslak's goals, becoming the world-wide industry leader and commanding more than half of the U.S. ultrasound market.

Business Obstacles

Even though Acuson's founders were willing to risk their own money to develop a new ultrasound product, development of the machine they envisioned would take years and cost millions. Their personal funds did not begin to approach the required investment.

Moreover, even if the new company managed to secure financing and develop a new machine, it would have to try to break into a thoroughly saturated market dominated by giants like Hewlett-Packard, Diasonics and Toshiba.

But Maslak and his partners were convinced of their ability to create and market a new machine, and their proposal was convincing enough to gain investments from several venture capital firms including Kleiner, Perkins, Caufield & Byers, which purchased more than three million shares of the start-up company's stock.

Keys to Success

Maslak and other Acuson personnel agree that the key to the company's success has been their understanding of the needs of the medical profession and of ultrasound's potential. "We started by introducing a system that had superior image quality when compared to anything else on the market," says Acuson's vice president Robert Gallagher. "Competitors said the system wouldn't produce superior images—now they advertise that their machines are 'almost as good' as Acuson." "People almost laughed at our original price," Gallagher adds, pointing out that the Acuson 128 entered the market at $115,000 when Diasonics was selling ultrasound units for $60,000. "They said, 'You will never sell a system for that amount.' But the reality was," he says, "that hospitals are looking for real value and are willing to pay an extra $30,000 to $40,000 to get it."

Part of the value Gallagher talks about comes from Acuson's unique software design as well as from its electronic hardware. From the beginning Acuson products have been built with up-grade ability. As new software controls are written that pull even greater performance from the machines, all past customers can take advantage of the new technology and upgrade their systems. As a result, says the company, the extra investment in an Acuson machine is actually less expensive than the alternative of buying a brand new unit every 3-5 years to keep pace with new technology.

Future Vision

Maslak's future vision is not surprising given his past. His main concern is to make sure Acuson remains the technical and market leader in every facet of ultrasound, and to make ultrasound technology as useful and practical as possible. But according to those who work with him, there is more to this vision than just greater profits. "He believes in the value of ultrasound," says an Acuson staffer. "He knows that in building this company, and in building these machines, he's helping thousands of other people."

Entrepreneurial Lessons

"I think the most important lesson I learned, early on, was how much I didn't know about what I was going to do, and how important it was to find people who knew a lot about it, who would also be willing to recognize they relied on other people," Maslak told *Nation's Business.*

The lessons of Acuson are mainly lessons the company taught to competitors. "Acuson broke the price barrier and showed that there were new tricks for old dogs to learn," says the editor of an industry magazine. "They reinvigorated the entire industry."

But along with teaching lessons to others, Maslak makes sure that Acuson doesn't forget the lessons it learned when bringing its initial product to market. The company continues to explore new markets to exploit, especially in Europe, and has undertaken developments in another type of ultrasound diagnostics—once again going head-to-head with Hewlett-Packard. In it all, Maslak remains determined to keep Acuson innovative, and to further his development of ultrasound.

References

Atkinson, Bill. "Acuson Soars to Head of Ultrasound Class." *San Jose Business Journal*, July 6, 1987.

————. "Analysts Predict Hot Response for Valley's Latest Big Offering." *San Jose Business Journal*, August 18, 1986.

Autrey, Ret. "Companies to Watch: Acuson." *Fortune*, May 6, 1991.

Barrier, Michael. "The Ultimate in Ultrasound." *Nation's Business*, September 1991.

Cone, Edward. "Ultrasound Is Probing New Markets." *Business Week*, May 2, 1983.

————. "Ultrasound Ultraprofitable." *Forbes*, October 31, 1988.

Madison, Mary. "Peninsula Firm's Ultrasound Work Making Difference." *The Peninsula Times Tribune*, September 15, 1991.

————E. C.

Alvin A. McCall, Jr.

Ryan's Family Steak Houses, Inc.

Alvin A. McCall, Jr.: Born 1927. Married, three children.
Venture: Operation of a chain of family steak restaurants.
Company: Ryan's Family Steak Houses, Inc.; 405 Lancaster Avenue; Greer, SC 29650; (803) 879-1000
Founded: 1977.
Revenues: $290 million projected sales (1991), according to a company source.
Employees: 130 in the corporate offices, 12,000 system wide.
Original Investment: Not available.
Value: $105 million, according to published reports.

Founder

Becoming a restauranteur was not the career path South Carolina native Alvin McCall, Jr. originally pursued. His business as a general contractor and subdivision developer in Greenville, South Carolina, was successful for 15 years, but in 1971 he decided to pursue other interests.

In 1971 he conceived, built, owned and operated the first Western Family Steak House in Greenville. The restaurant was so successful that the company added nine more units, expanding throughout South Carolina. Later, McCall changed the chain's name to "Quincy's Family Steak House." In 1976, McCall sold Quincy's to Trans World Corporation, which still operates the chain.

In the "here today, gone tomorrow" restaurant business, McCall's conservative and quiet nature seems almost out of place. But during intense negotiations or critical decision-making, McCall reveals his assertive and confident self.

Business Origin

When McCall sold Quincy's, many thought he would leave the restaurant business. McCall had other intentions. The enterprising entrepreneur was able to convince Trans World to waive the usual noncompete clauses, going so far as to include specific clauses granting him permission to compete. McCall says because he "left them with a good structure," they were agreeable to the terms.

McCall's experience taught him that too many restaurant operators had misplaced priorities. He felt there was too much emphasis placed on lowering labor and food costs. If the emphasis were placed instead on providing quality meals at competitive prices and superior customer service, he reasoned, the bottom line would take care of itself.

McCall incorporated Ryan's Family Steak Houses, Inc. in 1977. He chose the name Ryan's because it "had a good ring, was short and easy to identify, and was Irish."

The first Ryan's opened in Greenville in 1978. Its simple, homey decor— high ceilings, wood chairs and tables, large rooms, family atmosphere—is the same at every Ryan's. Every unit is freestanding and seats approximately 350-400 people. Upon entering, customers are directed to a long, cafeteria-style arrangement where they pick up silverware, drinks and deserts. Large signs tempt customers with descriptions of the entrees, which include beef, chicken and fish. While in line, customers place their orders. A waitress brings the meals and refreshes beverages.

Business Growth

During Ryan's early years, the company enjoyed steady growth. In 1981, the chain posted approximately $7 million in revenues, while opening seven more restaurants. To fund growth, McCall took Ryan's public in 1982. By 1985, revenues had skyrocketed to $65 million, with a total of 53 restaurants, primarily based in the Southeast.

By the mid 1980s, American's were becoming more health conscious, reducing levels of cholesterol and calories. The medical community encouraged diets with less red meat and more green vegetables. McCall anticipated a decline in beef sales and needed an idea to replace those anticipated revenue losses. Ryan's successfully shifted its strategy thanks to a young man who began his career with Ryan's as a dishwasher.

The employee's idea was the "Mega Bar," and it proved to be a stroke of marketing genius. An expansion of the popular all-you-can-eat salad bar concept, the Mega Bar lets customers choose from more than 60 food items, including soups, salads, muffins, meats, vegetables, breads and desserts. The average length of the U-shaped Mega Bar is 68 feet. An ice cream bar is part of the deal. Every Mega Bar is strategically located in the center of the dining area.

The Mega Bar offered diners an alternative to the typical fare found at most steak houses, but maintained Ryan's "meat and potatoes" image. Lunch traffic practically doubled after the Mega Bar's introduction. Many managers found some patrons who regularly ate two meals a day at Ryan's. Competitors watched closely and when the time was right, introduced their own versions of the Mega Bar. Sizzler, a primary competitor, and Wendy's, have developed similar operations.

So impressed was McCall with the Mega Bar's success that he promoted its creator, his son T. Mark McCall, to the position of president. Having worked at Ryan's part-time during college and joining the company as head of real estate and development in 1980, the younger McCall was only 26 years old when he was promoted. His father remained as chairman of the board.

Anticipated reductions in beef sales never materialized. Beef continued to account for almost 75 percent of total sales. The younger McCall commented, "Maybe in the high upper end people are eating more health consciously, but the average person out there is going to eat whatever tastes good, as long as it's a quality product. We've seen no changes whatsoever. . . . Our beef consumption has not dropped. As a percentage of sales it's lower, but total consumption at the store level has not decreased at all."

Ryan's has received a host of accolades from the business community. It was included in *Inc.* magazine's 1986 Best Managed Companies list, and in 1987, *OTC* magazine added Ryan's to its list of the 100 fastest growing companies traded over the counter.

Business Obstacles

As the company's new president and chief executive officer, Mark McCall continued Ryan's growth. He updated the company's menu to include popular chicken and fish items. His philosophy of quality service and food mirrored his father's. Yet father and son were headed for an impasse.

The younger McCall described himself as "extremely competitive and very creative," giving his all for the company. He ignored skeptics who questioned his abilities, age and lack of experience. His father was pleased with his performance.

But Mark McCall's eagerness to move into new markets and expand Ryan's menu forced his father to conclude that expansion was going too fast and costing too much. Finally, Mark resigned. The younger McCall told reporters he was "exiting from the chain to pursue personal business interests. I've always planned one day to start my own company and this seemed the appropriate time to break away and do it," he explained.

Meanwhile, Alvin McCall took control of the company, cutting expansion plans to save cash. He also launched a radio and billboard advertising campaign for the first time in company history.

While McCall reversed sales declines, rising costs in 1990 forced the first price increase in four years. Economic conditions, increased competition and diminished repeat business are making Ryan's develop new concepts to bring customers back.

Keys to Success

Despite what company officials say is a "temporary decline in business," Ryan's is still considered by many industry analysts as the leader in the family steakhouse market. Good food and good service are two of the reasons why.

Many of Ryan's patrons are from middle-income levels, but the bulk of their business is from the blue collar worker. Ryan's specifically targets their menu items—sirloin tips, hamburger, rib eye, steak sandwich, prime rib—for the middle class American. And while the cuts of beef may be inexpensive, the taste of the beef is not. Ryan's purchases beef directly from Colorado and ages it at a central location for two weeks. After shipment to the individual units, the beef is sliced by local personnel who have been trained by a skilled butcher.

Ryan's is filled with other culinary "tricks" which have set them apart from other steak houses. Each unit makes its own bread, rather than the typical "Texas toast" competitors use, and delivers it fresh to the table when the food is served.

The highly touted Mega Bar uses only top quality vegetables and fruits. McCall developed a formula to turn inventory quickly and maintains relationships with vendors that he feels comfortable can deliver products on a timely basis.

The food portions at Ryan's are somewhat larger than those of its competitors. Patrons describe the portions as "just big enough for the hearty eater, but not so much that you leave half a plate of food uneaten." Industry analysts estimate that for every $1 of food purchased, a Ryan's patron is actually receiving an estimated 45 cents in food. The industry norm is 30 to 35 cents per $1 spent.

Ryan's higher food costs are a fact which McCall considers cause for boasting. "We make less per customer than other restaurants, but we feed more customers," says McCall. "Ultimately, it all flows to the bottom line."

Maintaining these strict policies of food cost and preparation require dedicated management teams at the unit and corporate levels. Finding managers who will work 14-hour days has not been a problem for Ryan's—turnover at the unit and corporate management level is only one to three percent.

McCall maintains an "open door" policy. "Anyone can say what they think" is the rule of thumb. Unit and corporate managers use the policy to gain a certain freedom in running their operations. McCall believes the freedom he gives his managerial staff improves performance and builds loyalty.

Managers must meet goals, however. At least 50 percent of each unit manager's compensation is based on sales volume and they are penalized dollar for dollar when they do not meet cost goals.

Hourly employees enjoy benefits not typical in the industry. Part-time and full-time employees are offered full medical and dental coverage, a liberal vacation policy and a stock option plan. The average Ryan's waitress makes $20,000 annually.

Future Vision

Since returning to operating the company, McCall has focused his energies on halting Ryan's declining sales. Yet, he still plans to expand into new areas.

In 1988, Ryan's began moving into western markets in Texas, Louisiana and Oklahoma. The future includes further expansion, but at a deliberately slower pace than previous expansion plans. Adds McCall, "the steak and potato business is here to stay. Other concepts come and go, but when you can get a good steak for $5, beef is still the number one value for the dollar."

Entrepreneurial Lessons

McCall stresses the importance of people. He explains: "You can go out and buy experience and buy any top executive you want, but you can't buy enthusiasm and motivation and hard-driven people. All the people who work for us mean so much to me because of the job they do. They should get as much credit as possible. . . .No one man can make it work by himself. I don't care how good he is."

References

Carlino, Bill, and Rick Van Warner. "Ryan's Ripped by Sales Losses, Chief Exec Exits." *Nation's Restaurant News*, July 11, 1988.

Festa, Gail. "Ryan's Express." *Restaurant Hospitality*, August 1987.

Mamis, Robert A. "Meat and Potatoes." *Inc.*, July 1986.

Person, Sarah. "Ryan's Stake in Budget Beef Segment." *Restaurant Business*, October 10, 1985.

Thorp, Susan A. "Ryan's Steak Houses Offer Tasty Menu to Investors." *Memphis Business Journal*, February 20, 1989.

Van Warner, Rick. "Mark McCall Carries the Ryan's Torch." *Nation's Restaurant News*, September 7, 1987.

——R. H. S.

James M. McCoy

Maxtor Corporation

James M. McCoy: Born 1946. Married.
Venture: Manufacturer of computer disk drives and storage subsystems.
Company: Maxtor Corporation; 211 River Oaks Parkway; San Jose, CA 95134; (408) 432-1700
Founded: 1982.
Revenues: $871.3 million in fiscal 1991 (1991 annual report).
Employees: 8,000 plus worldwide.
Original Investment: $350,000 followed by three rounds of venture capital: $3 million, $5 million, and $18 million, within a year and a half of founding.
Value: $250 million estimated NASDAQ market value (March 1990), according to company sources.

Founder

James McCoy grew up in an engineering environment. His father was an aircraft and mining engineer who, according to McCoy, was a major factor in his choosing a career in electronics. In the late 1940s, the McCoy family moved from Cheyenne, Wyoming, to live in the Santa Clara Valley, which was just beginning to become the center of the country's electronics industry.

McCoy graduated from San Jose State College in 1969 with a B.A. in industrial engineering and management. While at school, he began working as a disk-drive engineer for IBM. After three years at IBM, he worked for a string of companies all involved in magnetic recording. These included Avco Cartridge Television Inc., Infomag Corporation, Verbatim

331

Corporation, and Shugart Associates. He was a co-founder of Quantum Corporation which manufactured 8-inch Winchester (hard) drives. McCoy left Quantum after a year at the company when he saw that future business would be in the 5.25 inch disk drive market.

Business Origin

McCoy and partners, Jack Swartz and Ray Niedzwiecki, developed a way to triple the amount of information storage on a 5.25-inch hard disk. The aim was to develop a niche market for high-capacity drives capable of storing large databases and for use in multi-user systems where several users share files on a host computer. The first drives packed up to 105 megabytes of storage onto the drive, the equivalent of 50,000 pages of text, by fitting six platters inside the drive. "Maxtor" was truncated from "Maximum Storage," and in 1982 the company was founded.

McCoy, his partners, and B. J. Cassin (who McCoy calls "our godfather") came up with $350,000 seed money to set the business in motion. Then McCoy and William Dobbin, vice-president of finance, located $3 million in initial venture capital. The money didn't go far. Six months later they easily raised another $5 million from investors eager for an early piece of Maxtor. "I kept trying to get to the car to get the business plan," Dobbin recalled, "but we just kept doing deals without ever having to show the plan."

Business Growth

Within a year of starting the firm, construction began on a 100,000 square foot manufacturing facility in San Jose. From the very start, though, the company's intention was to base most of its production overseas. Unlike other manufacturers that suffered the pains of employee dislocation when domestic operations were shifted offshore, Maxtor managed its hiring to avoid large-scale layoffs.

The company negotiated a long-term lease and tax-free status for nine years with the Singapore government, establishing a facility there in 1983 with 150 employees. Maxtor completed a 200,000 square foot Singapore facility in 1988 and a 100,000 square foot facility in Penang, Malaysia in 1990, and now has 6,000 overseas employees.

In 1987 Maxtor acquired U.S. Design Corporation and Storage Dimensions, Inc., both producers of high-capacity information storage systems that are externally attached to the computer. In the three years since Maxtor acquired Storage Dimensions, the subsidiary's annual sales have grown from $3 million to $100 million.

Maxtor's initial product was a 105 megabyte 5.25 inch drive. Two difficult years later it produced its second generation product, a 380 megabyte drive, and is now in the market with a 760 megabyte drive. With more than a 50 percent share, Maxtor has dominated the 760 megabyte market from the beginning. In 1989 the company entered the 3.5 inch drive market with the same high-capacity, high-performance strategy.

In 1990, Maxtor purchased Miniscribe Corporation out of bankruptcy, giving Maxtor a long-sought position in the broader market for lower-capacity hard drives used in millions of desktop computers. The acquisition doubled the company's size, making Maxtor the second largest drive manufacturer after Seagate Technology, Inc.

In 1991, Maxtor brought out a 2.5 inch drive, hailing it as the fastest in the 85-megabyte capacity range.

Business Obstacles

After successfully raising $3 million and $5 million of venture capital, the company had hoped to go public. In the company's second year however, the market for initial public offerings dropped dramatically. In the fall of 1983 Maxtor had orders totalling $150 million, but was strapped for cash. Recalls Dobbin, "The Dow dropped nine points a day while we were on the road show. I was on the phone to a major investor, and suddenly I thought he was backing out. For a minute I was literally speechless." Maxtor's original backers came up with an additional $18.3 million, but the company could count on no more.

To conserve available cash, the company instituted extreme cost-cutting measures. After hobbling through winter and spring, McCoy and Dobbin figured if they could squeeze another $500,000 from expenses, Maxtor would show a profit in the December 1984 quarter. Employees, all of whom were shareholders, were told how much cash the company had left and how fast it was being used. They were encouraged to come up with money-saving suggestions to be implemented along with management ideas. Eighty separate measures to cut costs were initiated and dubbed "Project 500." Everyone "signed up" for one or more of the tasks. Measures included cutting advertising budgets, saving on stationary, and unscrewing light bulbs. The marketing department sold books and promotional literature that the company had previously given away. The test equipment department began selling some of its proprietary test equipment to other companies.

This thrift-mindedness cut Maxtor's operating costs by $600,000 and allowed the company to show a profit. By August 1985 the market had recovered to the extent that a $20 million initial public offering was successful. The next $100 million was raised through a convertible debenture. After three-and-a-half years of surmounting hurdles, "we earned the right to be a public company," recalls McCoy.

Initially, the company also had problems obtaining key components for the 105 megabyte drive. Since the disks were so advanced in technology, vendors had tremendous difficulties in meeting Maxtor's volume and quality requirements.

Maxtor's first acquisition, U. S. Design, fell far short of expectations. External storage systems was an unfamiliar market for the disk manufacturer, and identifying and correcting problems with U.S. Design's marketing strategy cost both time and money. Eventually, Maxtor pared down the product line and merged the company into Storage Dimensions, Inc., a solid performer.

Keys to Success

According to *Dataquest* analyst Jim Moore, Maxtor's decision to focus on the high end of the hard drive market made it a strong contender. "Down in the lower megabyte storage ranges you've got a whole flock of companies going against each other."

Even though Maxtor was able to establish a lead in the high-end market, McCoy explains, "We were not like Polaroid or Xerox who stayed on top for years with a new technology. In the drive business, all you can get is a six-to-12-month lead over the competition."

One important factor that helped the company through its cash crisis in the beginning was employee-shareholders. "Every employee down to the janitors got stock options," says McCoy. Prior to going public, employees could buy stock at a very favorable price. Even today they can buy stock at the price it was listed on the date of being hired as an incentive to help build the company's value. With 8,000 employees in several different countries, the stock option program is now more difficult to implement, but remains an important incentive to employees in middle and higher management levels. The company has had a profit-sharing program since its inception, and in the early days, performance goals were also rewarded with stock and cash bonuses.

Fundamental to Maxtor's success, according to McCoy, is fostering creativity in engineering. "Engineers should be rewarded more for their initiative and creativity and be encouraged to take thought-out, calculated risks. It's a spirit that comes down from the top."

Future Vision

The computer industry was built on the ability to store information magnetically. McCoy thinks that optical storage, based on reading and writing with a laser, will not obsolete magnetic drives, but will prove to be a significant storage technology in the future. Optical disk drives are capable of much higher density storage than magnetic drives. In McCoy's opinion, the promise for the future is to record high-definition video digitally. Maxtor and Ricoh of Japan jointly developed a WORM (write once read many) drive capable of storing vast reference works.

The company also developed a removable optical erasable drive, a project that began in 1985 with the first units delivered in 1989. Maxtor's entry into the optical drive market will put them in direct competition with Japanese industrial conglomerates like Matsushita, Hitachi, and Sony. In the face of this competition, Maxtor brought in Kubota of Japan as an equity investor to help break into the Japanese market.

McCoy sees another fundamental change in the industry. Manufacturers typically have been either technologically aggressive "boutiques" or high-volume, commodity manufacturers of "mature" technology. Developing leading-edge technology is no longer enough because, says McCoy, "Even the most state-of-the-art products can be replicated relatively quickly. I feel that in the 1990s, the only way an American electronics firm will survive and grow is to become an excellent volume manufacturer while being technologically aggressive with leading edge products."

Entrepreneurial Lessons

In the face of the increasingly competitive global marketplace, McCoy has learned, "You're almost never aggressive enough in your development of new technologies, new products and new, more cost-effective manufacturing techniques." He also offers this entrepreneurial advice, "Everything starts and finishes with the best people you can possibly get."

After looking back at the early struggles of the company, McCoy reflects, "The only time to raise money is when you don't need it." This is the basis for his first commandment in starting a business: "Never, ever, run out of money."

References

Garry, Greg. "Maxtor Guns For 2.5-in. Slots." *Electronic Business News,* September 9, 1991.

McCoy, Jim. "Coupling Technology Aggression and Manufacturing Excellence." *Electronic Engineering Times,* June 9, 1986.

McLeod, Jonah. "How Maxtor Uses Passion and Leading-Edge Products to Boom." *Electronics,* June 11, 1987.

Perkowski, Mike. "Maxtor to Begin Moving Winchester Production Plant to Singapore." *Computer Systems News,* June 20, 1983.

Rapoport, Roger. "Maxtor Rides Crest of New Wave of Disk Drives." *San Jose Mercury News,* August 15, 1983.

Wiegner, Kathleen K. "Performance Under Duress." *Forbes,* April 21, 1986.

——B. M.

Scott McNealy

Sun Microsystems, Inc.

Scott McNealy: Born 1954. Single.
Venture: The development and manufacture of computer workstations.
Company: Sun Microsystems, Inc.; 2550 Garcia Avenue; Mountain View, CA 94043; (415) 960-1300
Founded: 1982.
Revenues: $3.2 billion in fiscal 1991, according to company sources.
Employees: 12,480.
Original Investment: $4 million.
Value: Sun Microsystems had a net worth of approximately $660 million at the close of 1989, according to published sources.

Founder

Scott McNealy was raised in the midst of big business. The son of former American Motors Vice Chairman William McNealy, he grew up in a family that socialized with the likes of Lee Iacocca (chairman of Chrysler Corporation) and Roger Smith (former chairman of General Motors). There was never much doubt in the family that Scott would one day enter the business world he was so accustomed to, but most of the family assumed he would enter an established Fortune 500 corporation, not build one of his own.

McNealy studied economics at Harvard, where he received a B.A. degree in 1976. He then spent two years as a sales engineer with Rockwell International in Michigan before leaving to return to school. McNealy earned an M.B.A. from Stanford University in 1980. Upon graduation, he became one of only three graduates from that year's class to accept jobs in manufacturing, joining the FMC Corporation in Chicago. The job did not last very long. "FMC put me on a strategy team and I wanted to be a plant manager—I wanted to make something," he remembers.

That desire to "make something" led him to quit FMC after just 10 months and move to California's Silicon Valley. There he joined Onyx Systems, a computer maker. After a year with Onyx, some old friends approached McNealy with some very new ideas.

Business Origin

In his business school days McNealy had made quite a few friends, among them an Indian-born computer wizard named Vinod Khosla. Khosla (and some other former classmates) wanted McNealy to help them launch a new company to manufacture computer workstations. Their idea was simple and intriguing.

Up to that point, the computer workstation field was relatively small and dominated by one firm—Apollo. Workstations are desktop machines with three or more times the processing power and speed of personal computers. In 1982, nearly all the workstations being made were based on components and technology proprietary to the individual manufacturer, and the price of an individual workstation was exorbitantly high.

What Khosla and the others wanted to do was to build lower-priced workstations by using "off-the-shelf" parts rather than developing all new components. In this way they could enter the market at a relatively low cost, win customers away from established manufacturers, and they hoped, develop new markets among buyers who could otherwise not afford workstations at all—namely small firms and colleges.

McNealy joined the others in launching Sun Microsystems in 1982. His job as head of manufacturing was two-fold. First, he had to find money to fund the manufacturing process, and then get the process up and running.

McNealy went straight to Wall Street to find venture capital for the fledgling firm. His education and family ties helped arrange some contacts. His enthusiasm about the product Sun was planning to manufacture helped win the funds. "I always felt confident calling on anyone. I wasn't intimidated."

McNealy secured roughly $4 million in venture capital for Sun and then turned his attention to his duties as "head of manufacturing." "It really meant that I built the first 25 or so Suns by hand," he recalls. "I had skinned knuckles and scrapes to prove it."

Business Growth

Giving employees the freedom to get their jobs done has paid off for Sun in phenomenal ways. The company crossed the half-billion dollar sales mark after just 5 years of operations in 1987, and sold two and one-half billion dollars worth of products in 1990. It has entered into agreements with such corporate giants as AT&T and Xerox, and long ago replaced Apollo as the largest maker of computer workstations. "We're getting sucked into the commercial marketplace like air into a vacuum," McNealy told *Business Week*.

McNealy now is working to meet the challenge of moving his company from the role of revolutionary to that of the new establishment. As part of this goal, he is working to establish Sun's SPARC microprocessor as the standard for all workstations. In 1989, he even offered to license SPARC to any competitor who wanted to clone it.

Major companies, such as AT&T, Unisys, and Fujitsu, took him up on the offer and now use SPARC for their own machines. But McNealy is not trying to give away the farm.

By licensing SPARC to other manufacturers McNealy hopes to solidify Sun as the standard for the workstation industry, much the way IBM has become the standard for personal computers. In fact, it is the threat of growing competition from IBM, Hewlett-Packard and others that helped convince him to make the move. As the workstation market continues to grow while other areas of the computer industry slump, Sun's turf looks more and more inviting to competitors. "I feel like a clay pigeon in a skeet shoot," McNealy says when talking about his rivals. But he is optimistic about selling SPARC technology to business customers. "We absolutely make general-purpose computers now. Dunkin' Donuts is a customer, and they don't use Sparcstations to engineer new donuts," McNealy told *Fortune*.

Customers seem satisfied to let Sun and McNealy set the standard. Sun Microsystems' market share, which stood at 24 percent in 1987 and 28 percent in 1988, jumped to more than 32 percent in 1989 and 39 percent in 1990.

Business Obstacles

McNealy's stint as the actual builder of Sun's products was short lived. The company took off like a rocket, stealing market share from older manufacturers and opening previously untapped markets. Its initial obstacles were few, sales and revenues grew quickly, and the company soon left the "small manufacturer" label behind. All that was according to plan. "The world didn't need another small computer company," remembers McNealy, "and we didn't intend to be small—we wanted to get as big as we could as fast as we could."

But that goal and reaching it presented two obstacles common to quickly growing companies—how to find the right people, and how to keep the entrepreneurial spirit alive.

Sun soon found that it already had the right person in Scott McNealy. The board of directors had recruited a president, but his style and personality never quite fit with the free-wheeling atmosphere that was growing at Sun. He resigned in 1984 and McNealy was appointed to fill the vacancy on an interim basis. Shortly thereafter, Khosla decided to retire (at the age of 30) from Sun's chairmanship.

The potential problems were enormous. Sun had already lost one president because he could not fit in, and now the company faced the need to find both a chairman and a new president who could successfully direct its continued growth. To solve the problem, at least for the moment, the board appointed McNealy temporary chairman as well as interim president. He has held both positions since. "I guess, at some point, I became more than interim," he says.

McNealy became more than interim president and chairman because he proved to have just the right answers for Sun's other potential obstacle: how to build a billion-dollar corporation that retains the entrepreneurial spirit and innovation that made it a success in the first place.

Keys to Success

McNealy made a point of keeping a business style that has been labeled "controlled chaos" by some. "I tell my new hires it's OK to have fun. If it's OK to have fun, that's good for the organization," he claims. McNealy backs those claims with monthly parties and special events on holidays.

Sometimes, he tries to recreate the little-company feel for certain projects or programs. Once, when a key development project got bogged down, he threw the entire team out of the office telling them to finish the project off-site in a more relaxed environment. The project was completed on schedule.

When Sun formed another division to explore entering the low-cost computer market, McNealy had it set up on the East Coast, away from corporate headquarters. "You have to fire-wall development groups and give them freedom to get their job done," he explains.

From McNealy's point of view (a view shared by others at Sun), there are two keys to the firm's success. First and foremost, the company provides a quality product at a competitive price—it meets the market's needs.

Second, and perhaps more important, Sun management from McNealy on down is dedicated to maintaining the open, inventive atmosphere of an entrepreneurial start-up even though the firm is now an industry leader. Sun continues to throw fun-filled office parties on April Fools' Day and Halloween, and a good joke is still approved of—like the time employees turned McNealy's office into a golf course or when a vice president's office was moved into an aquarium.

Future Vision

McNealy's vision of the future translates into growth and expansion for Sun. For now he concentrates on maintaining the firm's number one ranking in the workstation field as well as creating new Sun products.

He notes that there are other challenges ahead for Sun besides the threat from IBM. McNealy's offer to let competitors copy the SPARC micropro-cessor opened the door for a new generation of low cost workstations—Sun clones. "I would have liked for the clones to come a little slower," he says, but then goes on to point out that Sun invested more than $250 million in research in 1989, and is dedicated to keeping ahead of its clone competitors.

Not one to shrink from a good fight, McNealy is also preparing to invade the home turf of IBM, Apple, and Compaq. In July 1990, Sun introduced a new line of low-priced home computers based on its SPARC system, and announced that major software manufacturers had agreed to rewrite their current PC programs to make them compatible with SPARC. Also in 1990, there was talk of a Sun-Apple Computer merger. Those plans were abandoned, though, after Apple chairman John Sculley rejected the proposal that McNealy head the new company.

Entrepreneurial Lessons

McNealy has one favorite tidbit of wisdom to share with anyone looking for the lessons he's learned from his experience with Sun. "Don't set goals," he admonishes. "They only limit you."

References

Deck, Cecilia. "Small Idea, Billion Dollar Business." *Detroit Free Press,* February 10, 1989.

Fram, Jonathan. "The World According to Sun Microsystems' CEO." *PC Week,* February 6, 1989.

"Fun Days at the Sun Frat House." *Fortune,* May 23, 1990.

Ganees, Stuart. "America's Fastest-Growing Companies." *Fortune,* May 23, 1988.

Hillkirk, John. "IBM Boosts Presence in Workstations." *USA Today,* January 1, 1990.

Hof, Robert D. "Where Sun Means to Be a Bigger Fireball." *Business Week,* April 15, 1991.

Kihn, Martin. "The Underpaid: Relative Pain." *Forbes,* May 27, 1991.

Levine, Jonathan B. "Scott McNealy." *Business Week,* April 14, 1989.

Markoff, John. "The Smart Alecks at Sun Are Regrouping." *New York Times,* April 28, 1991.

Pitta, Julie. "The Trojan Horse Approach." *Forbes,* April 15, 1991.

Rayner, Bruce. "Sales-Growth Speedsters." *Electronic Business,* May 1, 1988.

Schendler, Brenton R. "The Future of the PC." *Fortune,* August 26, 1991.

"Sun and Apple Executives Battle It Out." *Computergram International,* October 4, 1991.

——E. C.

Norman Melnick

Pentech International, Inc.

Norman Melnick: Born 1931. Married, four children.
Venture: The establishment of a company to design and distribute innovative writing and drawing instruments.
Company: Pentech International, Inc.; 2 Ethel Rd.; Suite 204B; Edison, NJ 08817; (908) 287-6640
Founded: 1984.
Revenues: $35 million projected for fiscal 1991, according to published reports.
Employees: 13.
Original Investment: $200,000.
Value: $60 million (1989), according to company sources.

Founder

Norman Melnick traces his fascination with pen and ink to his teenage years when he worked as a shipping clerk in his uncle's pen business. His uncle, Harry Kaplin, invented a new product every two or three months and was the first to invent a pen that retailed for under $1. Melnick says, "Sales of the pen went wild."

His uncle had educated himself by reading countless scientific magazines. Kaplin passed these magazines on to Melnick. He also passed on an intense interest in pens and chemistry, as well as a desire to create. Kaplin felt limited by his own lack of education, and Melnick recalls his uncle urging him to "use my brain and education to surpass his own achievements."

Taking the advice to heart, Melnick earned a degree in chemical engineering from Brooklyn Polytechnical Institute (1953).

Melnick remembers his uncle as being "tenacious—never stopping until he had succeeded." Melnick inherited those qualities and describes himself as "never a great student—just one that wouldn't stop trying."

From 1953 to 1956 while employed by Union Carbide Chemical Company, Melnick spent nights and weekends working to invent the first quick-drying, non-oily ink. In 1957, he founded and headed Chemolene Industries to distribute his newly developed ink to all major pen manufacturers in the New York area. Chemolene also produced felt tip pens, plastic fine line markers and the first felt tip marker with permanent ink. Automation and the permanent ink marker's low cost enabled the company to secure a $1 million contract with the federal government's General Services Administration.

Chemolene was bought out by Magic Marker Corporation in 1971. Melnick remained as vice-president of that company until he sold his interest and resigned in 1975.

He founded Doral Industries, Inc. in 1976, and, in 1980, Doral acquired certain trademarks, inventory and equipment from bankrupt Magic Marker Corporation. The company name changed from Doral to Magic Marker Industries, Inc. with Melnick as chairman and president. Although revenues grew over the next two years, the company had net losses due to increasing costs of production in Japan. Melnick resigned and sold his interest in 1983.

Business Origin

After selling Magic Marker, Melnick wanted to use his knowledge and experience to start a company that would avoid the pitfalls he encountered in previous companies—a company that would place emphasis on innovative products rather than pricing, thus creating its own niche. He decided to avoid competition by staying away from commodity items.

With $200,000 in personal funds, Norman and his son David Melnick founded Pentech in 1984.

David, president of Pentech, received a B.S. degree in accounting from Syracuse University (1981). From 1981 to 1984 he was employed by Magic Marker Industries, Inc. as purchasing director and assistant to the president.

Father and son agreed that Norman, Pentech's chairman, would handle creative and marketing areas, while David would control financial decisions. In 1984 Pentech began operations with seven employees in Norman Melnick's basement.

Business Growth

Pentech has continuously introduced novel products, from "Fireworks" (a pen with four brilliant colors), to erasable markers, both million dollar products. The product line features an array of writing and drawing implements whose names reflect the variety and innovation Pentech products brought to the writing and drawing industry. "Grip Stix" (a pencil designed with easy-grip notches), "Hot Spot Plus" (a pack of five markers in florescent color and the first in a series of multiple packages) and "Stripes" (the first crayon that can color stripes) were followed by the "Twins," a package of 16 crayons with double ends that provide a child with 32 colors.

When the decreased value of the dollar increased Japanese production costs and competitors raised prices, Pentech expanded its product base with the introduction of inexpensive traditional writing implements (such as rolling ball markers).

Pentech initially concentrated on marketing to major domestic chains such as Wal-Mart, Target, Walgreen, Eckerd Drug and K-Mart. But in 1989, the company moved into Canadian and Mexican markets, which accounted for five percent of the company's 1989 sales.

In 1988, the company formed an alliance with a Korean manufacturer to develop and produce the majority of Pentech's products. As sales increased, a leasing and shipping agreement was negotiated with a warehouse in Trenton, New Jersey, and in 1989, the company moved its headquarters from Melnick's basement to Edison, New Jersey. In 1991, Pentech again made *Business Week*'s "Hot Growth Companies" list, coming in at No. 50.

Business Obstacles

When Pentech sought low-cost overseas manufacturers, it found itself crippled by stiff export regulations based on a company's net worth. Pentech's worth fell far short of the amount required for the merchandise ordered. To increase its value, the company offered stock to the public in 1985 and again in 1987, raising nearly $3 million.

By persuading its suppliers to absorb plant automation and product development costs in return for guaranteed minimum orders, Pentech was able to maintain its working capital.

Keys to Success

Pentech's growth is directly attributed to Norman Melnick's ability to bring excitement to a stagnant industry, creating the first new products in 25 years. Melnick says retailers "love the flow of new products because it brings people into the store."

While competitors try to emulate Pentech products, Melnick believes customers remain loyal because of his company's superior quality and service. In fact, Melnick sees increased competition as positive, promoting Pentech's name recognition and reputation among retailers. "Competitors draw attention to Pentech when they walk into a retail store and want to know 'what Pentech's doing now,'" Melnick says.

Melnick will do "whatever it takes to satisfy a customer." When Pentech entered the market, it reduced standard order requirements and allowed customers to combine styles to meet minimums. Melnick believes the resulting product mix creates far more exciting store displays. Since most Pentech products are impulse purchases, the consumer is attracted by low price (average retail $1.98), variety and novelty. David Melnick's wife Dana creates the attractive packaging.

Melnick emphasizes "doing everything right from the beginning." In his opinion, "If you avoid complaints, you don't have to hire people to handle them."

Melnick credits his son David with setting strict cost control policies which result in healthy profits and cash flow. He says, "David treats each dollar spent as if it were his own. He evaluates the smallest expenditure with the same care as a large one." In previous companies, Melnick remembers, "'yes' men let me do as I wished. David does not let me spend too much or grow too fast."

The company keeps its corporate structure lean. Although Pentech moved from Melnick's basement to its own headquarters, it remains a modest facility with few employees. Melnick says that "day-to-day operations are conducted in an informal manner, again keeping costs to a minimum."

Future Vision

Although innovation will continue to be a key word at Pentech, Melnick foresees emphasis on foreign markets. As penetration into Canada and Mexico expands, the company will pursue additional territories in South America.

David Melnick says, "The writing industry is a $2 billion industry. Pentech's goal is to generate annual revenues of $250 million."

Entrepreneurial Lessons

Melnick believes there are two basic secrets for success in any business. "Never take anything (including success) for granted. You have to keep working to improve."

Of equal importance, he says, is to "enjoy what you do. Never go into an area you don't enjoy."

References

Hager, Bruce. "Hot Growth Companies." *Business Week*, May 27, 1991.

Mamis, Robert A. "The Inc. 100." *Inc.*, May 1990.

Miller, Anita. "Innovative Products Fuel Firm's Growth." *Topeka Capital Journal*, May 15, 1988.

Osborne, Judith A. "Pentech Makes Its Mark." *Newark Star Ledger*, October 25, 1988.

"Pentech International, Inc." *Business Journal of New Jersey*, January 1, 1989.

"Pentech Is Offering to Exchange 2 Pens for 'Gold Doctor' Pencil." *Newark Star Ledger*, September 11, 1991.

Slovak, Julianne. "Companies to Watch." *Fortune*, February 13, 1989.

——A. D. K.

Robert Metcalfe

3Com Corporation

Robert Metcalfe: Born 1946. Married, two children.
Venture: The marketing of the Ethernet computer networking system and related products.
Company: 3Com Corporation; 5400 Bayfront Plaza; Santa Clara, CA 95052; (408) 764-5000
Founded: 1979.
Revenues: $398 million in fiscal 1990, according to company sources.
Employees: 1,650.
Original Investment: $1.1 million.
Value: Approximately $200 million net worth at the close of fiscal 1988, according to published sources.

Founder

Bob Metcalfe became an entrepreneur only because he was an ingenious engineer. Metcalfe's early life was one of scholarship and study, not finance and marketing. He attended the Massachusetts Institute of Technology where he received two bachelor's degrees in electrical engineering and management. He then attended Harvard College, where he earned a master of science degree in applied mathematics and a Ph.D. in computer science in 1973.

In 1972, while working on his thesis, Metcalfe joined Xerox Corporation and worked in its computer science laboratory. He served in a variety of positions at Xerox before being asked to manage the microprocessor and communications software development programs that eventually led to the creation of Ethernet. Ethernet is a technique for linking computers, their associated terminals, and peripherals together.

Metcalfe was an integral part of Ethernet's invention and was one of the early leaders in helping to establish the system as a networking standard. He holds four patents related to its development.

Unfortunately what Metcalfe had invented had little practical use. It was too far ahead of its time. In the early 1970s, no one had yet invented and popularized the personal computer, so there was no great need for the ability to network dozens of computers together in an office.

Business Origin

By 1979 personal computers were a growing fact of life, and Bob Metcalfe was convinced of their future potential, especially their potential to utilize Ethernet. He resigned from Xerox and began to work as a consultant, waiting for the change that would make Ethernet a viable product.

The change came in late 1979 as the result of his own doing. Metcalfe heard that Digital Equipment Corporation (DEC) was working to develop its own networking technology that would not infringe on the Ethernet patents. Metcalfe realized that if Xerox would agree, this was an opportunity to establish his creation as the standard for an entirely new industry. He quickly went to work as what he calls a "marriage broker," knowing that the offspring of the two companies would be his baby.

Xerox and DEC were joined in their Ethernet agreement by Intel Corporation, a maker of microchips. That was all Metcalfe needed. He and a partner incorporated 3Com corporation in 1979 (as a consulting firm, since there was still no market for Ethernet products), and waited for the giant trio to announce its agreed network standard.

In May 1980, the announcement came. The three collaborators promised to release the Ethernet standards they were creating by September of the same year. It was time for 3Com (which stands for Computer Communication Compatibility) to get into high gear.

Business Growth

The company's growth finally took off in late 1982, and it continued to expand with the personal computer boom of the 1980s. At the end of 1982, 3Com had only $1.8 million in sales. That grew to more than $19 million by the end of 1984. The company broke the $100 million dollar barrier in 1987, and achieved more than $398 million in sales in 1990.

3Com now has offices around the world, and manufactures its own workstations as well as networking hardware. Workstations are desktop computers that are three or more times as powerful as personal computers. 3Com is now the undisputed leader in the networking industry Bob Metcalfe invented.

Business Obstacles

To move from consulting to manufacturing required capital. But money was not the only serious challenge.

The company consisted mainly of engineers attracted by Metcalfe's reputation. They were not expert business managers, nor were they experts in production. In addition, 3Com was proposing to enter a market that did not really yet exist. As one investor put it, "We didn't know what kind of market 3Com was going to find itself in back then, so we didn't know what kind of business we would need."

Metcalfe was as unsure about what the company would need as anyone else. His uncertainty helped him recognize that 3Com needed someone else to run it.

Metcalfe had succeeded in raising $1.1 million of venture capital. He had created Ethernet. He had arranged for it to become the international standard. He had put together the team at 3Com. He was the obvious choice to run the company, but he was the one person arguing that he should not.

The main reason Metcalfe did not want to run his own firm was that he did want to make money. "You often hear about people who dream of saving the world," he says. "3Com, on the other hand, was more an end in itself, than a means to something more glorious." While Metcalfe knew 3Com had great potential, he also knew the company needed someone else to realize it.

But Metcalfe's vision on the subject did not go quite far enough, and the resulting arrangement led directly to some of 3Com's early struggles.

At Metcalfe's urging, 3Com hired William Krause, a former Hewlett-Packard executive. Krause became president, but Metcalfe remained chairman of the board and CEO, and the result was confusion that nearly cost 3Com its corporate life.

Krause began by doing everything he had learned was appropriate while at Hewlett-Packard. He scheduled meetings, wrote memos, created plans and spent money. He hired a vice president of sales, as well as a vice president of marketing and moved the company to new, larger offices. Trouble followed.

3Com was losing money. A second round of financing had raised $2.1 million from investors, but the company kept falling short of all its revenue forecasts. The cause was clear. The company had two heads and neither one was completely in control. If it was allowed to continue, the situation would destroy 3Com.

The final straw broke at a board meeting in June 1982. The board had to make a decision about who ran the company, Krause or Metcalfe. "I'd always intended for Bill to be the CEO one day," says Metcalfe, "the board just told me that was the day."

Keys to Success

What could have been the end of Metcalfe's involvement in 3Com turned out to be the perfect decision for both the company and him. After being demoted from CEO, Metcalfe was made vice president of sales and marketing, and proved that he had found his niche. "We doubled our sales in just three months, and we haven't lost money since," he proudly reports.

Meanwhile, Krause's plans, now the only plans for 3Com, began to pay off, and he became more adept at planning for the needs of a small company. "I didn't have enough appreciation for running a small business out of a shoebox and a checkbook [when he had first arrived]—at HP we never worried about payroll," he says. With things now in their proper place, 3Com soon stopped worrying about payroll too.

Future Vision

After being relieved of the CEO title in 1982, Metcalfe served in a variety of positions and dedicated himself to rising through the ranks of his own corporation, learning how to really run a business—not just start one. "You can't be promoted to president from being chairman," he explained. "I decided that if I wanted the job, I'd have to be an up-and-comer, not a down-and-outer . . . the stereotype [of being a deposed founder] was dangerous to my aspirations."

In June 1990, Metcalfe switched from being a manager to being a consultant for the company after he was passed over as a candidate for the presidency. "I did not agree with that decision, but I accepted it," he was quoted as saying in the *Wall Street Journal*. He went on to say, "I'm too young to retire. I have considerable experience and flair at presenting 3Com's message, but I've never viewed that as an adequate job." In October 1990, he was named chief advisor to Patriot Partners, a software development firm created by a joint venture between Metaphor Computer Systems, Inc. and IBM. In 1991, IBM tapped Patriot Partners as a licensing agent for Apple software technology. Outside of his business ventures, Metcalfe is considering writing a book or returning to university.

Entrepreneurial Lessons

Metcalfe has learned some unusual lessons from his experience with 3Com. "For one," he says, "I learned that giving up control is much harder than giving up the trappings of control," referring to giving up his title to Krause. "I also learned how to learn to run this company," he adds, noting that he had risen progressively through the corporate ranks at 3Com—and had done so based on his business success, not his stock ownership.

Most of all, Metcalfe notes that he has learned what good people and good management are really worth.

References

"Corporate Backgrounder." 3Com Corporation, January 1990.

Fisher, Lawrence M. "Founder of 3Com Plans To Become Consultant." *New York Times*, May 24, 1990.

Higgins, Steve. "3Com Founder Metcalfe Reflects on Past, Future." *PC Week*, June 18, 1990.

"IBM-Metaphor Patriot Venture Taps Ethernet Inventor As Chief Advisor." *Computergram International*, October 10, 1990.

Lapedus, Mark. "3Com Founder Loses Bid for Presidency." *Electronic News*, April 30, 1990.

Leonard, George. "Meet the Present and Future of Silicon Valley." *Esquire*, December 1985.

Quick, Gregory, and Brian Gillooly. "Summit Talks Could Help Developers." *Computer Reseller News*, June 24, 1991.

Richman, Tom. "Who's in Charge Here?" *Inc.*, June 1989.

——E. C.

Dane Alan Miller

Biomet, Inc.

Dane Alan Miller: Born 1946. Married, two children.
Venture: An orthopedic product research, design and manufacturing company.
Company: Biomet, Inc.; P. O. Box 587; Warsaw, IN 46581; (219) 267-6639
Founded: January 1977.
Revenues: $209.6 million in net sales in fiscal 1991 (1991 annual report).
Employees: 1,500 worldwide.
Original Investment: Founders' investment of $130,000; Small Business Administration loan of $500,000; and a $100,000 line of credit at a local bank.
Value: $130 million equity; $750 million market capitalization.

Founder

Dane Alan Miller was born in Bell Fontaine, Ohio in 1946. Drawn to medicine at an early age, he decided that medical school, internship and residency would take too long to complete. Instead, he received his Ph.D. in materials science/biomedical engineering from the University of Cincinnati in 1974.

From 1972 to 1975, Miller worked at Zimmer, USA, a division of Bristol Meyers and the world's largest manufacturer of orthopedic implants. As director of biomedical engineering, Miller's responsibilities included engineering, prototype design, fabrication and basic research support for all new product programs. He developed a custom and special product group, coordinating manufacturing, marketing and sales activities.

In October 1975, Miller joined Cutter Biomedical, a division of Cutter Laboratories, Inc., where he organized and staffed a complete product development group. His responsibilities, including formal budgeting and product planning, paved the way for the 1977 creation of Biomet.

Miller's entrepreneurial accomplishments have been widely recognized. He was selected Indiana's Outstanding Small Business Person and was 1989 regional winner of *Inc.*'s Entrepreneur of the Year award. He was also *Indiana Business Magazine's* Industrialist of the Year in 1989. In 1991, Miller came out on top of *Business Week's* pay-for-performance analysis of executives—those who gave shareholders the most for their pay and those whose companies did best relative to their pay.

Miller gives a great deal of time to his community. He is an elder at his church, where he has worked on the building committee. He also serves as director of the Winona Lake Preservation Association, the Winona Lake Zoning Board and the Warsaw Community Development Committee.

Business Origin

Biomet, Inc., began in 1977 when Miller, Niles Noblitt (another expert in orthopedic development), Ray Haroff (who was involved in orthopedic development) and Jerry Ferguson (an orthopedic marketing specialist) pooled their talents. Each had been frustrated with the inability of previous employers to respond quickly to technical changes and surgeons' needs. The founders of Biomet believed they could get input from orthopedic surgeons, and react more quickly than their competitors to develop improved orthopedic devices.

After intensive planning, each of the four founders left his secure job in 1978 to found Biomet. The company name was chosen to indicate the connection between biology and metals. With $130,000 of their own money, they obtained a Small Business Administration loan of $500,000, and established a $100,000 line of credit at a local bank.

The original building, described by Miller as "a glorified garage," encompassed a total of 6,000 square feet. After purchasing several specially designed sewing machines, the founders and their wives began producing "soft" orthopedic products. Among the company's first products were neck braces and arm slings.

Business Growth

Shortly after Biomet began manufacturing, rumors about new federal testing and material regulations began circulating in the orthopedic industry. While many doubted the regulations would actually become law, Miller did not. He quickly altered his product specifications and incorporated the proposed new standards. Miller was sharply criticized for "jumping the gun." When the Food and Cosmetic Act imposed strict new requirements, competitors scrambled to retool their manufacturing plants or redesign their testing procedures. Miller's foresight had turned an industry obstacle into a marketing advantage. Biomet serviced many of its unprepared competitors' clients.

The company entered the European market in 1981. An international consultant introduced Biomet to Kenneth Sugerlund, who became its distributor. Through this association, Biomet was able to corner the orthopedic device market in Denmark.

Strategic acquisitions spurred its growth. In 1985 Biomet acquired Orthopedic Equipment Company, which recorded $20 million in sales the previous year. In 1988, through a hostile takeover, the company acquired Electro Biology, Inc., whose product line complemented Biomet's. The takeover dramatically expanded the company's horizons both domestically and internationally.

A joint venture with Hercules, Inc. was formed in 1985 to produce and market high-performance orthopedic products. Subsequently, the Biomet/Ingene Partnership was initiated to jointly produce products which incorporate biologically active proteins in the formation of bone and cartilage. Acquisitions, joint ventures and European expansion resulted in 1989 revenues of $136 million, making Biomet the fourth largest manufacturer of orthopedic implants in the world.

Biomet has received significant recognition from the business community. For six years, the company has been recognized by *Forbes* magazine as one of America's 200 best small companies. Biomet was included on *Business Week*'s list of the 1,000 largest U.S. companies and *Inc.*'s list of the 100 fastest growing public companies. The National Association of Investment Clubs named Biomet as growth company of the year in 1987, and in 1988 *Dun's Business Month* listed it among the 10 best-managed companies.

Business Obstacles

By 1979 the company was ready to market its own "hard" orthopedic products (implants). Originally, Biomet designed the implants and jobbed out manufacturing. Continuing technical and quality control problems with outside manufacturers and a desire to protect its technology led the company to begin planning its own manufacturing facility.

Financing the expansion presented problems. In his search for venture capital, Miller met Kenneth and Jerry Miller (no relation), who were impressed with Biomet's management and abilities. The Miller brothers bought a third of Biomet for $500,000, enabling Miller to put his designs into production.

Keys to Success

Miller does not underestimate the significance of timing in the company's success. Biomet's founding occurred just as the demand for orthopedic products began to escalate. The company entered the market as U.S. society began to undergo the dramatic transformation commonly known as "the graying of America." As the average age of the population increases, the number of potential users of orthopedic products broadens. The fitness boom adds exercise-related joint deterioration and other injuries to normal aging problems.

The company's founder believes the most important factor in Biomet's phenomenal growth is its ability to identify opportunities and to respond quickly. Employees are expected to listen carefully to surgeons' needs and concerns, and to strive constantly for better, quicker service. Working closely with surgeons, Biomet teams have perfected implants for hospitalized patients within as little as 24 hours. Dedicated to finding innovative solutions for orthopedic needs, Biomet developed unique computer techniques to help create patient-specific implants.

The company leads the industry in developing the use of materials such as titanium alloy in implants. Biomet also introduced a knee implant system that works with ligaments, overcoming the difficulties commonly associated with such products.

Miller encourages creativity and risk-taking. He has established an environment in which employees are aware of their responsibilities and understand exactly how their jobs fit into Biomet's overall scheme. Employees with the greatest knowledge of situations make the decisions.

Future Vision

Wall Street analysts predict that sales revenues in the orthopedic implant market will grow 20 to 25 percent a year during the early 1990s. Miller plans to capture a share of that growth by continuing to research and produce innovative orthopedic products. He is also considering expanding into other medical product areas. Miller says Biomet is looking at growth in its European markets, and is currently investigating the feasibility of locating manufacturing sites in Germany and France. Negotiations also are in progress to market Biomet's products in the Soviet Union.

Miller feels that Biomet's biggest challenges lie in remembering its goals and direction. It will continue to aim for quick recognition of and response to surgeons' needs.

Entrepreneurial Lessons

Dane Miller has created a company environment that fosters creative thinking and independent action, encouraging employees to find inventive responses to opportunities. He feels strongly that retaining a small company atmosphere and entrepreneurial posture are important. Those attributes, he says are "not a function of size." Rather, he says, they are a "state of mind." To promote these qualities at Biomet, Miller's management style is informal, and he is easily accessible.

According to Miller, lean times teach valuable lessons. At Biomet, for example, limited funds in the company's early years created an atmosphere in which each financial decision was critical. The evaluation guidelines developed during that period are still applied, and help contribute to the corporation's current prosperity.

References

"Biography: Dane A. Miller, Ph.D., Biomet." *Inc.*, January 1990.

"Biomet, Inc." *Business Money*, December 1989.

Byrne, John A. "The Flap Over Executive Pay." *Business Week*, May 6, 1991.

"Distributors Lead European Sales." *European Trade Report*, December 1989.

"1st Source Corporation." *The Elkhart Truth*, May 6, 1987.

Howey, Brian. "Biomet: Bringing R&D to Market." *Indiana Business*, May 1, 1988.

Kichen, Steve. "The Best Small Company Honor Roll." *Forbes,* November 11, 1991.

Kurowski, Jeff. "Industrialist of the Year." *Indiana Business,* December 1989.

———. "Wall Street Sees Growth in Biomet's Future." *SouthBend Tribune,* October 3, 1989.

Rosato, Donna. "Biomet Growing Quickly." *USA Today,* November 8, 1989.

Smith, Geoffrey, and James E. Ellis. "Pay That Was Justified—And Pay That Just Mystified." *Business Week,* May 6, 1991.

—A. D. K.

Josie Cruz Natori

The Natori Company, Inc.

Josie Cruz Natori: Born 1947. Married, one child.
Venture: Started a company that manufactures women's nightwear, bedding, fragrances and bath accessories.
Company: The Natori Company, Inc.; 40 East 34th Street; New York, NY 10016; (212) 532-7796
Founded: Incorporated in New York, 1977.
Revenues: $25 million in 1990, according to published reports.
Employees: 130.
Original Investment: $150,000 to $200,000.
Value: Not disclosed.

Founder

Born and raised in the Philippines, Josie Cruz Natori came to the United States at age 17 to attend college. She studied economics at Manhattanville College and graduated with honors in 1968. "Business just seemed the most logical thing for me to study. I was exposed to it early through the family business, and through the culture of my country. The Philippine people are very resourceful and always looking for ways to improve their situation. It's a very entrepreneurial culture," says Natori.

After graduation she joined the corporate-finance department of the Bache Group, who soon moved her to Manila to start a branch office. She became a registered stockbroker and managed a staff of twenty people. Two years later, a disagreement developed between the government and her company, forcing the office to close.

In 1971, Natori switched companies and returned to Wall Street. She entered the corporate-finance department of Merrill, Lynch, Pierce, Fenner & Smith and within five years became the first woman vice president in the company's investment banking division. Natori was promoted quickly at a time when women executives were rare in the financial world. "When I left Merrill Lynch in 1977, they had about 20,000 employees and only six women vice presidents," says Natori.

Two men—her father, a successful construction company owner, and her boss at Merrill Lynch—get partial credit for her success. "I had my father's example—he's a self-made man—and my boss at Merrill Lynch was a great mentor. He really believed in me. I also worked very hard, because I wanted to learn everything," says Natori. She considered her years on Wall Street an apprenticeship for what she really intended to do, have her own company. "That was my vision all along, and I never faltered from it. I still work long hours and I'm obsessive about the business, but I love it," Natori relates.

Natori is well suited to the type of company she chose because it allows her to use both her creativity and her business skills. She views the company as a combination of business and art and describes herself as a businesswoman who "happens to be artistic," as she told the *International Herald Tribune*. An accomplished musician, Natori has played piano with the Philippine Symphony. Although she now has a staff of designers, she is on the ground floor of any creative decisions and routinely draws her own design suggestions. When she is not working on new designs, she devotes her time to making sales.

Business Origin

At age 30, Natori believed that she had the know-how and the necessary capital to make it on her own. "When you start a business, you have to have an advantage. My own heritage made me different from other business owners," says Natori. She began looking at products native to the Philippines that she thought would be marketable in the United States. "I tried baskets, furniture and several other things before ending up by accident in intimate apparel," states Natori.

In 1977, Natori tried selling blouses embroidered with the delicate stitchery and applique work of Philippine craftswomen to New York department stores. A friendly buyer at Bloomingdale's didn't want blouses, but suggested that there might be a market for the same fine needlework on nightshirts. "I would never in a million years have put one of those things on my body," she told *Mirabella* magazine. "I thought, 'Who the heck would want to wear that ethnic stuff?'"

Despite that, within a few months Natori and a friend designed a full line of upscale lingerie and contracted with small factories in the Philippines to produce the line. She sold $150,000 worth to major department stores in the first three months.

Business Growth

The early days were chaotic. Natori soon learned that the fashion industry had a whole different language than Wall Street. Moreover, the industry seemed to have almost no rules. "Not being born into the rag trade, I had to learn everything from the ground up. I was lucky to find extremely helpful people along the way. I was making cold calls, with no introduction, but I found people very receptive to me. I was a fresh face, a sort of oddity," she recalls. As she told *Cosmopolitan*, even today "I make it work for me. Being female and Filipino . . . have been my greatest assets."

In the beginning she worked out of her home, taking orders from racks of samples in her living room. She also traveled regularly to the Philippines to secure the labor to fill her orders.

By 1978, she opened a small showroom in New York's garment district. With financial help from her family, Natori built her own factory in the Philippines a year later. The factory now employs over 600 people.

In a market dominated by huge apparel companies and well-known designers such as Christian Dior and Calvin Klein, Natori carved out a niche and managed to expand her company 25 percent a year for the first ten years. She attributes that both to having a good product and to smart marketing. "When I first came into this business, lingerie was still considered one of two things—kinky or something your grandmother wears," remembers Natori. Natori's products are neither. "A Natori garment equals quality and craftsmanship first of all. These are very luxurious, very desirable kinds of garments that a woman buys to pamper herself," says Natori. Much of the work is done by hand on fabrics such as silk, cashmere, cotton and polyester satin. "'Natori' isn't just a name on a label, it's a state of mind . . . a lifestyle." She finds it difficult to put into words, but when pressed describes her designs as "luxurious, very sophisticated, somewhat exotic and yet modern. There is nothing revival or Victoriana about us. We are today and tomorrow."

Traditionally, lingerie was considered a gift bought by men for women. But Natori markets to career women who are tired of the work-day uniform and want something softer and more feminine to wear after hours. While other designers were concentrating on dress-for-success wardrobes, Natori targeted the woman who could afford to buy herself something special for her leisure time. Having been a career woman herself, she totally understood her market.

To reinforce the "lifestyle aspect" and to increase sales, she has added new product lines along the way. Natori manufactures a full line of bedroom and bath accessories and table linens with the same fine needlework that is the trademark of the company. She also has a fragrance and a new line of evening wear. However, lingerie still makes up 80 percent of the company's revenues. Natori fashions and accessories range in price from $9 to $3,000.

Natori sells her products to major retailers from her showroom in New York and at five market fairs annually held in Atlanta, Los Angeles, Chicago, Miami and Paris. She also has a retail store in Paris and a growing international market.

In 1986, when the business grew too large for Natori to manage alone, her husband Kenneth Natori quit his job as an executive vice president with Shearson Lehman to join the company. He serves as chairman of the board of directors. "I had to bring in someone in order for us to keep growing, and Ken's coming into the business has been fabulous," says Natori. "After a few initial adjustments, we found that we work quite well together," she adds.

Business Obstacles

"I had a lot of learning to do in the beginning. I knew nothing about the rag trade when I started. But I never really considered that an obstacle, just an intense learning process," says Natori. "Our major early obstacle was not having control over production," she reflects. "We were having to take our designs to sub-contractors in the Philippines, and we weren't their first priority. There were problems in quality and delivery and it involved a lot of traveling, which we really didn't have the resources for," Natori recalls.

By 1979, she knew that she needed her own factory. Natori learned from all the mistakes that had gone before and organized the factory to suit her needs, with inspection checkpoints to control quality.

Filling orders takes five or six months because of the detailed workmanship. "By the time a garment gets on the racks, it has probably gone through 25 pairs of hands. That much handling can be a real headache," relates Natori. She describes the garment industry as a crisis business where something is always going wrong, a situation she has learned to take in stride.

Even with her own factory, Natori believes manufacturing overseas will never be trouble-free. The instability of the political situation in the Philippines has caused her to lose production time due to protests and strikes. At one time Natori tried moving some of her operations to Antigua, but could not find the skilled seamstresses that she needed to make her garments distinctive. Embroidery is a talent that is passed from one generation to the next in the Philippines, explains Natori, not something that can be learned overnight.

Since Natori products are sold in many countries, the company must also contend with many different languages, trade rules and regulations. "We haven't had to change the product for the foreign markets. It caught on very well, but all the red tape makes it harder to do business," Natori explains.

Keys to Success

One of the major factors to Natori's success has been the way she markets her products. Natori maintains that she is selling a "total concept" and that for it to work, all of the products must be placed together on the showroom floor.

In her own showroom, the products are displayed against black lacquer shelves and backgrounds. "That was a design decision that reflects my own taste. I always wear black myself—it's very matter-of-fact and also a good contrast for the colors in the clothing," says Natori.

In a large department store, clustering the clothing against a bold background serves to clearly define Natori space and separates her products from the competition. Having a mini-boutique within a department store also means more sales. Customers are more likely to buy accessories when they can see how well they match the garments.

Contrary to normal department store layout where everything is compartmentalized, Natori wants to see her bedding and bath linens also displayed together. "As much as possible, we control how the product is going to be sold. We started with a good product and the timing for it was right, but we were successful largely because we were able to present a clear image of what a Natori garment is and what it stands for," maintains Natori.

Future Vision

"Obviously we would like the company to grow bigger and better and solidify its position in the market place. We would like to see more retail stores," says Natori. She also intends to keep adding new products and to run the risk of making some errors in judgment. Not all of her ideas have gained acceptance. A line of sportswear was abandoned in 1986 after dismal sales. "When you're an entrepreneur, you're going to make mistakes. What's important is learning from each one. With the sportswear I had to realize that the line was too far removed from our concept. Women don't buy casual clothes to pamper themselves. But without risks you can't grow," says Natori. As she told *Savvy Woman* magazine, "I'm a gambler at heart—I have to keep doing something new. That's important to me. I don't want to lose the entrepreneurial spirit."

Natori plans to continue growing internationally. She now sells in 40 countries and her European markets account for about 20 percent of total sales. "My goal is to be recognized as an important fashion house internationally," says Natori.

Entrepreneurial Lessons

Having a strong vision is the most important thing in starting a business, advises Natori. "You need to know clearly who you are, what you want and where you're going. After that it's a matter of tenacity and capital," she relates.

Financing is often the most difficult part of a business to plan and a most crucial ingredient to a company's success. "If we hadn't had savings and help from my family we would have gone bankrupt. It seemed like we needed a bottomless pit of money in the beginning," Natori says. "You have to have a good product, but you also have to fill a void in the marketplace. The reason we're so successful is that we're different from the next guy—our styling, our marketing, our whole concept is different," explains Natori.

References

Ballen, Kate. "Josie Cruz Natori." *Fortune*, February 2, 1987.

Better, Nancy Marx. "The Pajama Game." *Savvy Woman*, February 1991.

Greenberg, F. "Good Setting for Sales." *Working Woman*, September 1986.

Haynes, Kevin. "Three SA Women: How They Built Their Business Niches." *Women's Wear Daily*, April 10, 1987.

Konrad, Walecia. "The Luminary of Luxury Lingerie." *Working Woman*, November 1987.

Menkes, Suzy. "From Burning the Bra to Flaunting It." *International Herald Tribune*, July 16, 1991.

Monget, Karyn. "Jose Natori: Breaking Out Of the Boudoir." *Women's Wear Daily*, July 11, 1991.

Monroe, Valerie. "The Natori Story." *Mirabella*, March 1991.

Rosenblum, Anne. "Josie Natori: Queen of the Night(gown)." *Cosmopolitan*, December 1991.

Weisman, Katherine. "Cementing a Marriage." *Forbes*, July 22, 1991.

——L. R.

Raymond L. Nelson, Jr.

Allwaste, Inc.

Raymond L. Nelson, Jr.: Born 1938. Single, one child.
Venture: Industrial waste removal for refining, petrochemical, utility, steel and paper industries.
Company: Allwaste, Inc.; 3040 Post Oak Blvd.; Suite 1300; Houston, TX 77056; (713) 623-8777
Founded: January 1978.
Revenues: $235 million projected sales for 1990, according to a company source.
Employees: 1,784.
Original Investment: $100,000.
Value: $60 million book value; $340 million market value.

Founder

Raymond L. Nelson has been in the garbage business most of his life. Bubba, as he prefers to be called, began by driving a garbage truck for his family's thriving garbage service in Sulphur, Louisiana. He speaks proudly of that heritage, giving credit to his father for instilling values that continue to serve him well. "I got my work ethic from my father," says Nelson. "The principles of integrity I built my business on, I learned from him. That's something you can't put a value on." That paternal influence, he believes, played a role in his present success.

Nelson earned a degree in industrial management from McNeese University in Lake Charles, Louisiana. He then returned home to the family business.

In 1971, the family sold its company to Browning-Ferris Industries. As a condition of the sale, Nelson stayed on. When he had learned all that Browning-Ferris could teach him about building a business, he says, "I decided to do it on my own."

Business Origin

Nelson opted to move into industrial waste management. He researched the Gulf Coast to determine whether competitors were operating in the air moving business, and found none. An air mover collects industrial waste through use of a heavy-duty, powerful vacuum. Its use cuts job time and personnel by more than half. Beginning his business with one $85,000 air moving truck and $15,000 in working capital, Nelson drove to job sites at steel mills, refineries and electrical utilities.

Business Growth

For two years, until he was able to hire and train other workers, Nelson continued to drive the company's truck. As he expanded his customer base, he acquired additional air movers. With 14 trucks serving the petrochemical industry throughout Texas, the company was vulnerable when the bottom fell out of the oil industry. The economic downturn left him with a mountain of debt and forced him to re-evaluate his growth strategy.

Although the economy slowly improved, Allwaste didn't begin to grow until its public offering in December of 1986. With $9 million raised from sales of stock, Nelson began to buy other small clean-up companies. He used stock swaps in lieu of cash and insisted that the entrepreneur come aboard along with his company.

The strategy allowed Allwaste to expand into related cleanup fields like railroad tank car cleaning, asbestos removal and recycling. Asbestos removal and air moving at one time each accounted for one-third of Allwaste's sales. In August 1991, the company sold the entire Asbestos Abatement Division to IAM/Environmental, Inc. so management could "focus on the continued growth of Allwaste's core business," said Nelson.

For a time, the company also moved into manufacturing. Through its Guzzler Manufacturing, Inc. subsidiary, Allwaste assembled air moving equipment for sale to contractors, municipalities and industrial companies. Allwaste sold its Guzzler Manufacturing division to Powerscreen International PLC in September 1990 in order to concentrate on service rather than producing air moving equipment.

Allwaste has become the largest independent transport tank cleaner and the largest glass recycler in the United States. "Glass is only about two percent of our business. We could sell more glass than we can get. We don't have any problem using it, just getting it. We sell it back to glass manufacturers who use it in processing other glass. The insulation industry is also a heavy user. So are paint manufacturers who mix ground glass into paint to make the stripes reflect on the highway at night."

Business Obstacles

When Nelson began Allwaste, the petrochemical industry was booming. To survive the domestic oil bust that followed, Nelson cut 25 percent of his workers, went further into debt and returned to calling on customers himself.

An ongoing challenge is meeting the constantly changing environmental regulations for handling and disposing of waste products. Allwaste is careful to monitor itself for compliance with the stringent requirements for cleaning tankers and handling hazardous materials.

Keys to Success

"In growing by acquisition, we acquire only successful companies that fit in with our business and we acquire the entrepreneurs with the company," said Nelson. "We keep the entrepreneurial spirit alive. In this company, everyone is encouraged to think as an entrepreneur and I think that is what makes the company successful."

Entrepreneurial thinking produces profitable ideas, Nelson finds. "One way is to find new uses for equipment. One of our pieces of air moving equipment, the ramrodder, is used to clean out sewer lines. One of our entrepreneurs came up with the idea of running telephone cable through while it is being cleaned, to save time doing it later."

Nelson emphasizes giving the customer full value for his money. "We have a very, very focused work ethic. We work very long and hard, and smartly. We tell the people in the field that they are key to our success. We continually tell them that the corporate office exists to serve them, not the other way around. They're the best asset we've got."

A combination of a number of right decisions, strong management and willingness to take prudent risks characterize Allwaste, according to Nelson. "I think a company should listen as much as it directs. It's really a two-way street—we're willing to take risks and we're inviting all kinds of input to help make decisions."

Future Vision

Allwaste plans to continue to expand into new opportunities in the environmental industry and grow in its current operations. A combination of acquisitions and good management should continue to facilitate growth, Nelson believes.

"Management succession is always a concern. Although we're only three and a half years old, we're working toward enlightened succession at every level," said Nelson. "Everybody should have a fair idea of who would succeed them in their management position and get those people ready to take on their position.

"I see some things that we don't do in all locations, and I see new horizons that we'll focus on. We try to address a special niche. One area we're looking at is de-watering, taking water out of waste. It has a long term potential because much waste has a high liquid content. We see all kinds of potential if we can remove and process it so it becomes acceptable to dispose of in a conventional way."

Nelson foresees greater recycling efforts. "I think in years to come recycling will be major part of industry. It will take the support of everyone— local and state government, citizens, the President. Corporate America is facing the fact that they've got to work with regulations."

Entrepreneurial Lessons

"Our philosophy is work simple but hard. The character of this company to a large degree is my character. Number one is hard work; number two is how you conduct yourself in business. This company has the highest integrity and principles. Our goal is to be a responsible corporate citizen wherever we operate," Nelson says. "In our acquisition strategy, we have been totally honest. I don't think we've disappointed anybody. It's a matter of people sharing the dream, and at the same time sharing our performance and our growth."

Nelson places strong emphasis on the value of retaining entrepreneurial thinking. "I think the youth of our organization, the entrepreneurial spirit and teamwork help us succeed. I want people to be receptive to 'How can I best get from here to there' as opposed to circling the wagons."

The corporate philosophy formalizes that stance: ". . . grow internally and . . . by acquiring successful entities and retaining the entrepreneurs who conceived and managed them. The entrepreneurial spirit is encouraged and nurtured within the corporation to the mutual benefit of all. The successful teaming of entrepreneurs provides a forum for continued progress and growth plus the benefit of sharing and learning from other entrepreneurs."

References

"Allwaste: Turning Garbage into Gold." *Business Week*, September 7, 1987.

Klempin, Raymond. "Allwaste Follows Offering with Initial Acquisition." *Houston Business Journal*, March 23, 1987.

———. "Allwaste, Inc. Acquisitions Total 27—and Counting." *Houston Business Journal*, February 27, 1989.

———. "Allwaste, Inc. Registers for Stock Sale." *Houston Business Journal*, May 9, 1988.

Simon, R. "An Air Moving Experience." *Forbes*, March 5, 1990.

Vogel, Todd. "Bubba Nelson Fights for the Dirty Jobs." *Business Week*, May 22, 1989.

———S. B.

Lane Nemeth

Discovery Toys

Lane Nemeth: Born 1947. Married, one child.
Venture: Direct sales of educational toys for children.
Company: Discovery Toys; 2530 Arnold Drive; Suite 400; Martinez, CA 94553; (415) 370-7575
Founded: 1977.
Revenues: $90 million in projected sales (1991), according to published reports.
Employees: 180 in the corporate offices.
Original Investment: $50,000.
Value: The privately held company does not release financial information.

Founder

At one time, Lane Nemeth supplemented her family's income with food stamps. Now she heads a multi-million dollar corporation.

With a master's degree in education from New Jersey's Seton Hall University, Nemeth directed a state-funded day-care center in Concord, California for three years. Through training and experience, she developed high standards for the quality of children's toys. When her daughter was born, Nemeth found herself increasingly frustrated that she could not find educational toys that met her standards. She had been able to buy quality playthings from school supply houses when she worked at the day-care center, but found these items were not available to the public. Nemeth established Discovery Toys as a solution to that problem.

Making a success of her business is only a secondary goal, according to

372

Nemeth—her first is to be a good wife and mother. Despite her years in business, Nemeth does not see herself or her family separately from Discovery Toys. Her husband works for the firm, and Nemeth says she hopes her daughter will someday succeed her as company CEO. "I never lose sight that my child comes first," she says.

In 1984 Nemeth was chosen by *Esquire* magazine as one of some 270 people under the age of 40 who are changing America. That was exactly what Nemeth originally set out to do. "I was going to make kids better with good toys. I was going to make society better," she reflects.

Business Origin

Nemeth initially thought she would open an educational toy store. Her husband suggested she imitate Tupperware instead, selling toys through home demonstrations. Nemeth took his advice. In 1977, she launched the business from her garage, funded by $50,000 borrowed from family and friends.

Discovery Toys' concept to sell medium-priced educational toys, books and games, most of which are unavailable from any other source, is realized by a staff of engineers, designers and child-development specialists. The playthings are designed to teach such motor skills as hand-eye coordination and to develop such cognitive abilities as spatial and cause-and-effect relationships. Colors are bright, designs are eye-catching, and materials are nontoxic.

Discovery Toys' educational qualities, Nemeth says, "can't be explained on a box." She chose the Tupperware-type approach because she believed the relaxed party atmosphere would allow her to discuss with parents how they could become more involved in their children's play. She could "take a more complex toy and explain how to utilize it to their child's best advantage."

Under the company's party-plan arrangement, each sales consultant purchases exclusive rights to a territory and finances inventory. The consultant goes through a standard two-day training seminar and receives brochures detailing toy demonstration techniques and suggested narratives.

Business Growth

By 1985, Discovery Toys was one of the fastest-growing direct sales companies in America. Nemeth's sales force had grown from three independent contractors to nearly 10,000 "educational consultants" across the United States, and racked up an estimated $35-40 million in sales.

In 1988, Nemeth put about $2 million into a children's book club division, and in 1989 entered into a joint venture with a Japanese firm to market a portion of the Discovery toy line in Japan. "The Japanese venture is the realization of a long-term goal," says Nemeth. "I like the idea of blending American entrepreneurism and Japanese management."

The privately held company markets roughly 135 toy products throughout the United States and Canada. Discovery Toys designs many of its own playthings and contracts for exclusive American distribution rights with European toymakers.

With 1990 revenues of $83 million, Nemeth finds herself heading a profitable direct sales toy business that has become one of the nation's top grossing companies of its kind.

Business Obstacles

Without business training, Lane Nemeth describes herself as both inexperienced and naive. She made several "beginner's mistakes." Nemeth under-ordered her first year, and over-ordered the next year. She borrowed money at the exorbitant rate of 27.5 percent, and her business nearly failed three times when funds ran out. According to Nemeth, bankers originally would not even talk with her because she was a woman and had little collateral. "Educational toys are not exactly the greatest asset in the world for a bank," she says.

Nemeth must continually contend with keeping her mostly female sales force pleased and motivated. Annual turnover of direct-sales field agents averages 100 per cent.

The seasonal nature of the toy business also presents a problem. Sixty percent of the company's annual sales are generated during the three months preceding Christmas. Discovery borrows on a $9 million revolving credit line and dips into retained earnings to operate in the off season, which to Nemeth is "very scary."

A lawsuit brought against her by eight minority shareholders has been her toughest obstacle yet. Her troubles stemmed from a deal several years back with venture capitalist Philip Greer's firm. In exchange for stock (20 percent of the company), Greer bailed out financially floundering Discovery Toys. But despite the success that followed, the company never paid dividends. According to *Inc.*, Greer wanted to sell his holdings, but his original contract with Nemeth failed to specify a way to do that. His suit (later joined by seven other minority stockholders) sought Discovery's involuntary dissolution. In June 1991 the issue was settled out of court when the minority stockholders were bought out, said Nemeth.

Keys to Success

Nemeth attributes Discovery Toys' success to several key factors. Of primary importance is product quality. In addition to its educational features, Nemeth demands each toy be safe, well-constructed and reasonably priced.

Using in-home, direct sales methods had a decisive impact on consumer acceptance. Nemeth candidly admits her toys need explanation. "If they were in a store you'd probably walk right by them," she told *Advertising Age* about one of Discovery's best-selling items. "But you can do about 100 different things with them—you wouldn't have an idea of what those were unless you were told."

The company's ability to attract a high caliber sales force also plays a role. Many sales representatives are teachers or other professionals and most have college degrees. Nemeth says would-be reps do not first ask about income potential—they have instead what she calls a "giant desire to help kids."

She feels direct contact with her sales representatives is essential. "If you get too many layers between you and the field, your message doesn't get through," Nemeth says. Believing that "the direct sales company will fail or succeed directly on what the field needs," she spends ten days out of every month on the road visiting with and listening to her salespeople.

Future Vision

What's next for Lane Nemeth and Discovery Toys, which is close to breaking the $100 million mark? "Two hundred million," she told the *Martinez News-Gazette*. But while she expects to see an expansion of

Discovery Toys around the world over the next few years, she hasn't lost sight of her real aim in selling toys. As she told the *News-Gazette,* "Our children deserve the very best as they begin to explore their capability, meet fresh challenges and discover new opportunities in their lives. After all, the skills they learn as children are the skills that will encourage them to build a more peaceful, loving world."

Entrepreneurial Lessons

Nemeth urges would-be entrepreneurs to take an idea and go for it. "The worst thing that can happen is it doesn't work. So what? You just go on to the next idea. You just take the first step and put one foot after the other, and suddenly," she maintains, "you're there."

Nemeth says making mistakes in business is inevitable. The important thing is to learn from them. "I never make the same mistake twice," she says. Moreover, she believes in sharing her hard-won knowledge with her sales representatives. Numerous educational seminars and twice yearly conventions, she comments, are part of her "campaign not to have them make the mistakes I made."

Don't lose sight of your mission, Nemeth cautions. She recalls that her own lapse "almost killed the company. I forgot what we were here for, and when you lose sight of that, you get into lots of trouble."

References

Bekey, Michelle. "How to Succeed by Doing Everything Wrong." *Working Woman,* August 1985.

"Discovery Toys: One Smart Mom's Little Marketing Miracle." *California Business,* June 1991.

Fitch, Ed. "Discovering the Fun and Games in Direct Sales." *Advertising Age,* October 17, 1985.

Garr, Doug. "Power of a Great Idea." *Reader's Digest,* October 1990.

Greim, Lisa. "Discovery Toys Enters Listing of Private Firms." *San Francisco Business Times,* September 6, 1991.

Kathman, Janice. "Toy Company Discovers Key To Learning." *Martinez News-Gazette,* October 1, 1991.

Kelley, Jack. "Lane Nemeth Made a Discovery When She Toyed with Success—the Game's Up if You Leave Your Friends Behind." *People,* December 2, 1985.

Neal, Roger. "Knock on Any Door." *Forbes*, November 21, 1983.

Nelton, Sharon. "Toying with Running a Conglomerate." *Nation's Business*, May 1985.

Rutter, Nancy. "Greer vs. Nemeth." *Inc.*, July 1990.

Shaw, Jan. "Discovery Toys Heads for Japan in Joint Venture." *San Francisco Business Times*, July 24, 1989.

Silver, A. David. "Lane Nemeth." *Entrepreneurial Megabucks: The 100 Greatest Entrepreneurs of the Last 25 Years and How They Did It*, New York: Wiley, 1985.

"Toy Makers See a Rising Demand For No-Frills Toys." *San Francisco Business Times*, September 17, 1990.

——C. A. C.

Dorothy Cole Noe

Dorothy's Ruffled Originals, Inc.

Dorothy Cole Noe: Born 1943. Married, two children.
Venture: Establishment of several home furnishings retail outlets and a mail-order division.
Company: Dorothy's Ruffled Originals, Inc.; 6786 Market Street; Wilmington, NC 28405; (919) 791-1296
Founded: Begun as a cottage industry in 1973; incorporated in 1978.
Revenues: $13 million estimated 1989 sales, according to published reports.
Employees: 150.
Original Investment: $10,000 in personal funds and antique sale profits.
Value: The privately-owned company releases no financial information.

Founder

With no business background and no formal training, Dorothy Noe maintains that her own desire to achieve has been the simple driving force behind her success. Noe says her mother was a strong influence in her life, and is responsible for her desire to succeed.

After her parents divorced when she was 12, Noe's mother took on the role of both mother and father, raising her five children alone. "She was a very strong-willed and determined person," says Noe, "and is still that way today."

Noe earned a liberal arts degree from North Carolina's Mount Olive Junior College.

Not long after graduation she met another great influence in her life, her husband, James B. "Chuck" Noe. She credits Chuck's support of her ideas as a primary reason for the start of her business. Chuck currently serves as chief executive officer of Dorothy's Ruffled Originals.

Noe is still very active within the company, but devotes much of her time to community service. She served on the steering committee of the North Carolina White House Conference on Small Business. In 1987, the New Hanover County Museum inducted her into its Superstar's Hall of Fame along with Sugar Ray Leonard, Meadowlark Lemon and David Brinkley.

Business Origin

What began as a home decorating task almost 20 years ago has flourished into a multi-million dollar entrepreneurial venture. In 1971, the Noes became homeowners. Eager to decorate her new Dutch Colonial-style residence, Dorothy quickly became displeased and frustrated when she could not find suitable quality curtains to complement her new home. Although she had never sewn a stitch, Noe decided to take on the job herself. She took lessons and began designing her own curtains. "I wanted something uniform, as picture perfect from the outside as from the inside," she recalls.

Her designs were unique, rich and formal—yet casual. Guests quickly took notice of the window treatments and began requesting them for their homes. Even strangers from the street stopped to inquire about the unusual decor. Oddly enough, that first effort was Noe's only attempt at sewing curtains herself. The initial idea, however, unleashed her entrepreneurial spirit. Popular response to her drapery designs opened the door to filling a very distinct home decorating need.

At the same time, Noe maintained an extensive antique collection. When the collection outgrew her space, she decided to sell some of the pieces. Again, people responded to her taste in decor. She sold out in one day.

Intrigued by the interest the antiques had aroused, Noe began taking orders for pieces. She set about to locate and purchase antiques from other dealers, flea markets and antique shops.

Her antique business produced a first-year profit of $50,000. Noe used a portion of the profits to invest in her cottage curtain industry. She employed an installer and two seamstresses who worked out of their homes. Meanwhile Noe began an aggressive marketing and advertising campaign. She visited real estate, pediatric and dental offices and offered them a commercial discount to buy and use the curtains in their offices. "I knew that's where the women would be," explains Noe. As orders came in, Noe found the fabric and arranged and boxed the orders—often working 17-hour days.

In 1975, she decided to expand the operation through mail-order. She placed an ad in *Early American Life* and orders poured in.

Business Growth

Noe incorporated her business in 1978, opening her first retail shop on the same site with the manufacturing operation. That same year, Dorothy's Ruffled Originals opened an outlet in Goldsboro, North Carolina.

When Noe began to feel competition from the larger retailers like J. C. Penney and Spiegel, she developed The Original Curtain Makers, a separate wholesale division with a New York City showroom. This division was cited as one of the fastest growing privately-owned companies in the United States by *Inc.* magazine in 1986. Today the wholesaler services many of her former competitors.

Dorothy's Ruffled Originals has experienced steady growth since 1978. Showroom and production facilities now include more than 30,000 square feet. The manufacturing operation consists of 15 buildings housing a photography and art studio, shipping, telemarketing operations, a maintenance center warehouse and executive office space. Nine showrooms exist: Charlotte, Raleigh, Goldsboro and Wilmington, North Carolina; Newport News and Richmond, Virginia; Myrtle Beach, South Carolina; Roswell, Georgia; and Cincinnati, Ohio.

Between 1978 and 1990, overall sales grew 3,277 percent, equally distributed between retail and mail-order sales. While the firm's basic product line remains custom, ruffled, tailored and ready-made curtains, additional product lines have been added, including antiques and various decorative accessories. The company also offers a free home consultation service, maintains a national mail-order company and produces a 100-plus-page catalog.

Business Obstacles

In the company's early days, Noe experienced problems with her fabric suppliers. Although Noe felt she had already proven the demand for her products and services existed, suppliers refused to believe her projections and limited the quantities of fabric she could order. Some suppliers refused to fill her orders at all. "They would laugh when I would call in my orders," says Noe.

She believes the fabric companies held her back for two reasons—"I was a woman and they thought I was a fly-by-night." Her own stubbornness and determination eventually enabled Noe to overcome the resistance. "When they [the companies] refused to listen to me or I couldn't get answers, I would simply ask for someone who could deal with me. If I had been a softie, I would have said 'forget it.'"

When changing from a cottage industry to a fully integrated manufacturing organization became critical to survival, Noe responded by designing, building, staffing and managing a complete manufacturing facility. The company reinvested profits for several years to finance the facility. Noe personally supervised the new project, touring office sites, developing production schedules and interviewing key management personnel.

When cash flow became a problem during an expansionary period, Noe instituted new purchasing procedures. The company bought huge volumes of fabric and materials, gaining substantial price discounts. She paid bills up front, reducing charges another six to eight per cent.

Keys to Success

Noe attributes most of her success to strong customer service policies. Since the company's inception, Noe has personally responded to each order and inquiry with a handwritten letter. She explained the value and quality of her product, and the volume of fabric used. She assured customers that if for any reason they were not happy with the product, she would happily refund their money.

Those customer-oriented attitudes still rule today. "I place myself in the position of the customer and treat them as I would like to be treated," she says. She is confident that her product quality and customer service remain unequaled in the industry.

Future Vision

Noe sees the company's future business environment as positive. She expects continued growth in company-owned retail shops and is also considering franchising. Other plans include the development of her wholesale division in Canada and expansion into international markets. "The challenge will be to find out what your customers want and provide it," Noe stresses. "That's what it's all about—you've got to fill a need."

Entrepreneurial Lessons

Noe lets her personal philosophies and beliefs guide her business practices. "The Golden Rule is so practical," she says. "God has to be first in the elements of a person's life and family second." She believes in acting on time-honored adages like 'be honest with yourself and others,' 'be a doer, not a complainer' and 'set daily goals.' "Nothing brings more joy in life than a goal achieved," she notes. "It takes great concentration and patience to complete goals worth achieving."

Noe suggests that entrepreneurs who have a business idea need to "market it and believe in it. Research and make sure that it is viable. Then take action." But, she cautions, success requires self-discipline, a trait not always easy to acquire. "You're going to have to do some things that you don't want to do," she stresses.

Perhaps the most important ingredient in making an entrepreneurial venture successful, Noe says, is a willingness to work hard. "The only time success comes before work is in the dictionary," she quips.

References

Dennis, Bob. "Winning Small Business Ideas: Curtains, Bows and Concrete." *Charlotte Observer*, April 22, 1985.

Ford, Rita. "Finding Riches in Ruffles." *Nation's Business*, September 1986.

Johnston, Steve. "Riding High on Ruffles." *Charlotte Observer*, November 23, 1987.

Polson, Jim. "Cashing in on Frills." *Business North Carolina*, September 1986.

——L. P.

Ward D. Parkinson

Micron Technology, Inc.

Ward D. Parkinson: Born 1945. Married, two children.
Venture: The founding of a company to develop a 64K microchip.
Company: Micron Technology, Inc.; 2805 E. Columbia Road; Boise, ID 83706; (208) 383-4000
Founded: 1978.
Revenues: $425.4 million for fiscal 1991, according to company sources.
Employees: 4,100.
Original Investment: $300,000.
Value: $550 million, according to the 1989 annual report.

Founder

Ward Parkinson, principal founder of Micron Technology, Inc., was born in San Antonio, Texas, in 1945. He holds a B.S. degree in engineering from Utah State University (1969) and an M.S. degree in engineering from Stanford University (1972). Parkinson worked in various capacities in engineering and management for Intel (1972-1973), Motorola (1973-1976) and Mostek Corporation (1976-1978). In 1978 he founded Micron Technology, Inc.

Business Origin

Micron was founded to develop a 64K DRAM (Dynamic Random Access Memory) chip, a key component of computer and technology systems for Mostek Corporation (at that time a powerful company in memory design).

The 64K chip holds 64 kilobits (the smallest unit of information in a computer) as opposed to the previous generation of chips which held 16 kilobits. When Mostek was acquired by United Technologies Corporation in 1979, the contract was cancelled. Parkinson continued to work on the 64K chip in the basement of a dentist's office in Boise. Parkinson, Doug Pitman (a circuitry and layout designer recognized as the top layout man in the profession) and Dennis Wilson (another engineer) developed a 64K chip that was 40 percent smaller than Motorola's chip and 15 percent smaller than Hitachi's. The first products were shipped in 1981.

Although most of the research to develop the 64K chip was funded by Mostek Corporation, Micron needed additional financing to begin production. Parkinson was turned down by many potential investors who thought the odds were against the company. In late 1979 three Idaho businessmen, Ron Yanke (a machine shop owner), Allen Noble (a potato farmer) and Tom Nicholson (a sheep rancher) invested in Micron.

Business Growth

As Micron grew, Ward brought his brother, Joseph Parkinson, into the company in 1980 to serve as president. In 1982, J. R. Simplot, the Idaho potato king, invested $9 million in Micron for additional research and development. Due to the resulting expansion, Micron shipped over 1.5 million chips (1.25 percent of the market) in 1982.

After successfully marketing the 64K chip, Micron licensed manufacturing of the chip to several companies including Storage Technology, ITC and Commodore. By the end of 1984, the company had sales of $87 million with net profits of $29 million, making Micron's profit margin among the highest of any electronics company in the world.

While growth and profits suffered in 1984 and 1985, the company returned to earlier profit trends in 1986 and 1987. Higher prices, yield improvements, diversified product base and more efficient manufacturing processes resulted in a profitable year in 1988.

In June 1989, *Electronic Business* rated Micron the most profitable U.S. electronics company (with a profit of 32.6 percent on sales of $300.5 million). It is the only major seller of DRAMs manufactured almost entirely in the United States. In addition to the 64K and 256K DRAM, 256K VRAM (Video Random Access Memory) and 256K SRAM (Static Random Access Memory), the company manufactures and markets a variety of memory intensive board products and video and color board level products.

Under an agreement with IBM, Micron will be licensed to use certain IBM process technology designs. The company also signed agreements with Sanyo Electric Company granting Sanyo exclusive distribution rights in Japan for all Micron's component products as well as allowing Sanyo use of Micron design and process technology in return for royalty payments.

Ward Parkinson no longer plays an active management role in the company he founded, having stepped down as board chairman. A 1989 *Forbes* article describes him as currently "on sabbatical." *Forbes* comments that brother Joseph, now Micron CEO and chairman of the board, "has his work cut out for him" catching up with rivals who are well ahead of Micron in developing next-generation DRAMs.

Business Obstacles

In 1984, when Japanese manufacturers began "dumping" (selling below production cost) 64K chips on the market, Micron's stock lost 40 percent of its value. The quarter that ended November, 1985 showed losses of $11.6 million.

In 1985, Micron filed a 64K DRAM "anti-dumping petition" with the U. S. Department of Commerce and International Trade Commission. Because of Japan's illegal "dumping," Micron was forced to scale down operations, reduce prices and shut down one of its two production lines. Employment was reduced from 1,400 to 700. Micron CEO, Joseph Parkinson, explained, "Instead of making serial layoffs, we decided to cut back to the bare bones right away. We told them, 'this is the crew, this is the boat. We're going to make it or sink together.'" All salaries were reduced. Additional payroll was saved by offering employees optional stock purchases of up to 25 percent of their salary. Pension plans, life insurance, disability and dental coverage were eliminated. Medical coverage was reduced.

Despite its struggle, the company improved its product, broadened its customer base and developed a new generation of DRAMs. "The whole thrust of the strategy was to use the down time to prepare for a comeback. Micron's production performance and quality today is a direct result of those dark days," Joseph Parkinson says.

In 1986 severe penalties were imposed against the Japanese for unfair trade practices. Under the terms of the August 1986 U.S./Japan Semiconductor Trade Agreement, Japanese suppliers agreed to sell certain types of memory chips at fair market prices. Supply tightened and drove the price of the chips back up. This paved the way for Micron to regain profitability and to continue expansion.

Keys to Success

Ward Parkinson says that Micron succeeded "by doing what other companies wouldn't. Fast trackers want to do more advanced things, and it's usually a crowded field." When the Japanese flooded the market with low-cost chips, most companies gave up and went into more specialized areas. "It's not hard to succeed when your competition gives up," Parkinson noted.

Known for high quality, the company believes its 64K chip is the best combination of size and cell (slots that hold information) capacity. In each generation of DRAMs, Micron developed the smallest chip. Smaller chips aid quality control because the smaller the chip is, the smaller the chance of defects.

Micron's 256K chip has 50 percent more cells than others being produced. This permits electrical impulses to switch automatically from malfunctioning cells, enormously increasing the chip's reliability.

By being the lowest-cost DRAM producer, Micron maintains a healthy profit margin. At its founding, Micron cut expenses by using carefully maintained, second-hand equipment.

Manufacturing in Boise (instead of Japan) saves on transportation costs. Boise construction costs are lower than Silicon Valley's. Micron achieves the highest possible utilization by running its plants 24 hours a day, seven days a week. The company's reduced chip size also helps control costs. As the chip shrinks, manufacturing costs drop and the amount produced increases. The company also reduced the number of process steps necessary to make its 256K DRAM.

Joseph Parkinson credits Micron's success to the company's "strategy of establishing long-term customer relationships by offering an expanded product line, by differentiating our products . . . and by stressing quality and on-time delivery."

Micron's corporate culture promotes loyalty and innovation. More than half Micron's employees own stock or have purchase options. Through the company's profit sharing plan, ten percent of monthly profits are distributed to employees. The company's education and training program offers on-site classes to all employees. Micron also has a tuition assistance program and a unique sabbatical leave benefit.

Future Vision

Micron's long-term goals include offering electronics manufacturers the highest quality and most advanced memory products, expanding into other memory related fields and helping to reinstate the United States as a leader in the production of memory semiconductors. To accomplish these goals, Micron will continue to focus on improving manufacturing efficiencies, accelerating product development, increasing quality and strengthening customer relationships.

Kipp A. Bedard, company spokesman, says, "Micron will become the technological leader in the development and manufacturing of DRAMs, SRAMs and VRAMs and will lead the industry in the introduction of future generations of RAMs."

Entrepreneurial Lessons

In Ward Parkinson's opinion, "It is important for companies to keep goals in mind, but remain flexible in the way they reach them. We were right on target with our five-year business plan, but the way we hit it was different than the way we thought."

Parkinson goes on to say, "We should all do what we can to create opportunities for the next generation. States are competing with each other to create a climate where people want to stay. In founding Micron, we created thousands of jobs in Idaho."

Perhaps reflecting on tough times in the company's past, Joseph Parkinson suggests that "People need to stay in condition, in shape and be prepared to fight when they're losing as well as when they're winning."

References

Beebe, Paul. "Micron Posts Earnings Rise in Second Quarter." *Idaho Statesman,* March 16, 1989.

Chakravaraty, Subrata N. "We've All Heard That Before." *Forbes*, December 31, 1984.

Gilder, George. "Idaho's New Breed of RAMS." *Forbes*, March 14, 1983.

Micron Technology, Annual Report, 1989.

Pewitt, Jana. "Agreement Lets Sanyo Use Micron Chip Design," *Idaho Statesman,* July 2, 1991.

"Semiconductor Entrepreneur, Joseph Parkinson." *Inc.*, July 1988.

Silver, A. David. "Ward Parkinson and Joseph Parkinson." *Entrepreneurial Mega-bucks: The 100 Greatest Entrepreneurs of the Last 25 Years and How They Did It.* New York: Wiley, 1985.

Wise, Ray. "Coining It: Top U.S. Firms Show 12 Percent Profits Gain." *Electronic Business*, June 12, 1989.

—A. D. K.

John William Poduska, Sr.

Stardent Computer, Inc.

John William Poduska, Sr.: Born 1937. Married, five children.

Venture: Company to develop and manufacture computer workstations for computer-aided design, molecular modeling and finite element analysis. The present company results from a 1989 merger with a major competitor; Poduska heads the combined company.

Company: Stardent Computer, Inc.; 6 New England Tech Center; 521 Virginia Rd.; Concord, MA 01742; (508) 287-0100

Founded: Stellar Computer Inc. was founded in 1985, as was merger partner Ardent Computer Corporation.

Revenues: $30 million projected sales (1990), according to company management.

Employees: 400.

Original Investment: Approximately $8.5 million to launch Stellar Computer Inc.

Value: $12.2 million net worth as of September 1989, according to company management.

Founder

Bill Poduska has been described as "a computer guru who just can't resist a good idea." Known as a "high-tech visionary" with a talent for creating successful businesses out of technological advances, Poduska has built two *Fortune 500* companies and currently heads his third Massachusetts-based venture. In addition to running his own company, Poduska funds other high-tech startup companies. He is a director of Xyvision of Wakefield,

Massachusetts, Javelin Software of Cambridge, Massachusetts and Safeguard Scientific of King of Prussia, Pennsylvania.

Poduska is committed to cultural organizations and actively supports Boston's Computer Museum, the Boston Ballet and Boston's Museum of Science. He is also affiliated with higher education institutions including Bentley College, Northeastern University, Rice University and Pine Manor College, and he served on the National Academic Advisory Committee of the Wang Institute of Graduate Studies.

Poduska has received awards from many organizations including the Boy Scouts of America, the North Middlesex (County) Chamber of Commerce, the Computer Museum and the Massachusetts Institute of Technology (MIT). In 1987, he was named New England Entrepreneur of the Year. Poduska has spoken on successful entrepreneurship to audiences around the world, and he co-hosted the first U.S./German entrepreneurial conference held in West Germany in 1984. In October 1985, Poduska hosted a computer conference at the Great Wall of China.

Born and raised in Memphis, Tennessee, Poduska developed an interest in electronics in his father's radio-television repair shop. He attended West Point for a year, then left to study physics at MIT. Poduska earned his bachelors, masters and doctoral degrees at MIT and joined the Institute's electrical engineering faculty in 1964. From 1966 to 1970, he directed an 18-person research team at the National Aeronautics and Space Administration's (NASA) Cambridge laboratory, designing computers for use in the Apollo moon project. When NASA closed the lab, Poduska moved from research to business, joining the Honeywell Information Science Center in Framingham, Massachusetts.

His involvement in entrepreneurship came unexpectedly in 1972 when a Honeywell vice president asked Poduska to be part of a new venture. "My boss asked me to come out to his house and proposed the idea of starting a company to develop a new minicomputer," Poduska remembered. "He said that he needed someone to head the R&D organization and asked if I was interested. There was a meeting of the founders the next day, and I immediately threw my hat into the ring. I figured when the dice are that hot, you've got to pick them up," he said.

Poduska had never before considered owning his own business. "It was the technology and the people that motivated me to do it," he says. With money supplied by his father-in-law, Poduska became part of the birth of Prime Computer, Inc. As vice president of engineering, Poduska led Prime's development of an affordable interactive minicomputer for engineers and scientists. The company's sales grew steadily from $6.5 million in 1974 to nearly $153 million in 1979.

Poduska left Prime as a result of what he calls "serious business differences" with Prime's president. "We had a different view of where the company should be headed—his focus was on sales and marketing and I wanted to spend more money on development. It was a business debate that we weren't going to resolve," Poduska said. "A company can only have one leader, so we agreed that I would leave by the end of 1979. It was a gentle way of being fired, I guess."

Poduska says that he intended to "take a few months to decompress" after leaving Prime, but within days he was planning his second venture, Apollo Computer. "Venture capitalists had been asking me to start something new, and they invited me to come to California for a meeting. I left Prime on December 31st, and on January 9th I was writing Apollo's business plan on a plane to the West Coast," Poduska recalled.

With $15 million in venture capital, Poduska launched Apollo, naming the company for the NASA program he had been involved with years earlier. The company developed a new type of desktop workstation for engineers. Poduska had again anticipated a market opportunity, and Apollo enjoyed great success. From sales of $3.4 million and a net loss of $2.9 million in its first year of operation, the company grew to post $80 million in revenues and $13 million in profits two years later. Poduska took Apollo public in 1983.

In 1984, Poduska gave up daily management of Apollo, hiring former GTE executive Thomas Vanderslice as the company's president. Poduska assumed the role of chairman of the board.

Business Origin

As Apollo's chairman, Poduska had an idea for a machine that would give scientists in genetics and molecular biology the ability to model "live" pictures of their experiments on a computer screen. Poduska asked the Apollo board to fund the project. He hoped to form a spin-off company to develop the new superworkstation, remaining as Apollo's chairman while Vanderslice became chairman of the new company. Poduska says that Securities and Exchange Commission (SEC) regulations blocked the new venture. Others have speculated that Apollo was not willing to invest the $12 million necessary to develop Poduska's idea.

Determined to build the new machine, Poduska says that he "reluctantly" left Apollo in November 1985 to establish Stellar Computer. Poduska vowed that Stellar would cover a part of the graphics and computer market that no one had covered. "And we will be first," he said.

Poduska was already a multi-millionaire, and many people wondered why he would start another company less than six months after leaving Apollo. "People ask me why one or even two companies isn't enough," Poduska said at the time. "My mother told me I had to keep doing it until I got it right."

In 1989, Stellar merged with California-based Ardent Computer Inc. to form Stardent Computer Inc. The two companies had been rivals in the desktop supercomputer market, each earning annual revenues of approximately $12 million at the time of the merger. "We were beating each other's brains out and spending huge amounts for development of competing machines. It made perfect sense to merge development dollars and see what we could create together," Poduska says.

Business Growth

"Following our merger, we are in a startup situation all over again," Poduska says. Stardent is developing its own line of supercomputers and visualization software for advanced scientific and technical engineering applications. The company's customers reached through Stardent's direct sales force and third-party distributors, include government organizations, commercial companies and research firms.

Business Obstacles

While Poduska is widely credited as a brilliant engineer and an accomplished company-starter, some have questioned his ability to manage the companies he founds. Critics say that once Poduska's companies pass the startup stage, he has difficulty operating within a large corporate structure. Some have attributed this to Poduska's "natural restlessness." *Boston Magazine* said of Poduska, "He is a technophile with an almost visionary sense of where the next bend in the high-tech river will be. And he is often impatient to get there."

Poduska admits that at Prime he was often "heavy-handed" in dealing with engineers who wanted to make changes in old products once he considered the projects to be finished. "I was an ogre about that," he says. "I felt that when something was done, it was done."

At Apollo, Poduska shared control of product design and delegated greater responsibility to others. He says, however, that he "backed off a little too far. I gave the engineers so much freedom that it got to the point where anarchy reigned," he comments. Poduska says that it was always his intention to hire a professional executive to head Apollo. "I'm not short on ego, but I know there are things I can't do. I can't be a brain surgeon, either," he said.

Investors insisted that Poduska appoint a seasoned executive as Stellar's president before they would fund the venture. One investor commented, "He had a good idea, but he needed a strong CEO."

Poduska rates himself "a passable, tolerable executive of a company," but says that he prefers to leave operational details to others. At Stardent, he is content to concentrate on activities that take advantage of his capabilities. Fellow high-tech entrepreneur Phillipe Villers said of Poduska, "Bill is one of those rare individuals who has well understood his areas of weakness and has taken steps to compensate for them."

Keys to Success

Poduska credits timing for much of his success. "If ever a man was lucky enough to be born at the right time, I chose my birthday real well," he says. He joined the computer industry just as it was beginning its boom and anticipated the technological trends that would shape the growth of computing in the 1970s and 1980s.

Those who have worked with him say that Poduska has a rare ability to combine technological innovation with attention to bottom-line costs, marketing strategies and profits. As Poduska explains, "I don't invent methods of changing lead to gold. What I do is watch what other people have done and say, 'It's time to take that technology and build that product and propel it into that marketplace.'"

Poduska has attracted talented and loyal employees, many of whom have been part of more than one of his ventures. He has also attracted the backing of venture capitalists. One investor calls Poduska "the kind of guy you want to follow," and a *Business Week* article categorized him as one of a few "graybearded" entrepreneurs—"industry veterans whose depth of experience makes them a good risk."

Although he left his first two venture companies to be run by others, Poduska says that he made certain there was an "orderly transition" within the organizations. "I cleaned up what I was doing, and I left without anger," he says "I firmly believe in the saying, 'you can agree to disagree' without being disagreeable."

Future Vision

Poduska has confidence in Stardent's ability to market its new line of computers. "We want to get people into a feeding frenzy so everyone wants one of these," he says. "In the short-term, I want to get the company profitable, and if all goes well, I'd like to take the company to the public market sometime next year. After that, who knows what will happen?" he says.

As COB and CEO Poduska focuses on technology and remains actively involved in research and development activities. He travels to Europe and the Far East to view emerging technologies, and he continues to look for new market opportunities.

If Stardent grows as large as he hopes it will, Poduska says that he will step down as company head. "I much prefer the startup of companies. I get bored when a company gets to about the $300 million mark," he admits. "But just as I wanted to stay at Apollo, I would like to stay involved at Stardent. I am also looking forward to devoting more time to my other interests, including my two-year-old daughter," Poduska says.

In August 1991, Poduska stepped down as president. But while staying on as Stardent's COB and CEO, he also formed AVS, Inc. to market the Application Visual System, Stardent's visualization software environment.

Entrepreneurial Lessons

Having successfully launched more than one venture, Poduska has gained confidence in his ability to succeed. He encourages other entrepreneurs to be confident as they start out, but he cautions that past accomplishments do not guarantee future success. "Every entrepreneur expects his company to be a big success, and when you win, it helps make the next venture a little easier," Poduska remarks. "But you can't count last Saturday's score in this Saturday's ball game. You have to have a sound business plan for each new venture you try." He adds, "When it gets scary as hell, you have to have enough faith in what you're doing and the courage to stick it out and execute your plan."

Poduska stresses the importance of hiring good people. When choosing executives, he says he looks for "a fire in the belly and steel in the eye. I want someone who really cares about making the company go and who won't flinch when bad things happen, " he says. "But I don't look for people who work 100-hour weeks," Poduska stresses. "I'd rather have a person that works smart and hard, not long." "The successful entrepreneur doesn't need awesome intelligence," Poduska adds. "Simply showing people you care yields the type of loyalty, commitment and dedication that managers never dreamed of."

References

Beam, Alex. "Banking on the Graybeard's Savvy." *Business Week*, May 12, 1986.

Guterl, Fred V. "Bill Poduska's On the Move Again." *Dun's Business Month*, April 1986.

Kiely, Tom. "Rich and Restless." *Boston Magazine*, July 1989.

Nulty, Peter. "Computerdom's Heavenly Brawl." *Fortune*, February 4, 1985.

"A Quantum Leap in Workstation Wizardry." *Business Week*, March 7, 1988.

Solomon, R. "Poduska Starts Yet Another Firm." *Middlesex News*, May 4, 1986.
——M. J. B.

Sheri Poe

Rykä, Inc.

Sheri Poe: Born 1952. Single, two children.
Venture: Women's athletic shoes.
Company: Rykä, Inc.; 36 Finnell Dr.; Weymouth, MA 02188; (617) 331-8800
Founded: 1987.
Revenues: $4.7 million in net sales (1990), according to company sources.
Employees: 13.
Original Investment: $100,000.
Value: $17 million (September 1990).

Founder

Sheri Poe dabbled in philosophy and psychology in her early twenties, and supported herself making jewelry. She never expected to command her own manufacturing company one day. "I thought I would be an artisan. I was selling my jewelry and counseling young teens in drug abuse prevention," said Poe.

Her father dreamed of owning his own business but never did. He is now seeing his dream come alive through his daughter's success. "I think because my father worked for someone else and because he worked so much, I grew up with our whole environment focused around business. We talked business at the dinner table every night. It was really a priority in life."

The "baby sister" of the family, Poe has two brothers. One owns a human resource company for teachers in the classroom, and the other is a graphic designer (he designed Rykä's logo).

After studying philosophy, psychology and English literature at several colleges, Poe says "I was restless. I wanted to get out on my own and was pretty rebellious." She heard repeatedly that she had a natural ability to sell. Instead of pursuing a career in sales, however, she married and had two children. After her second child was born, "the whole business aspect of my life kicked in."

She became the highest volume sales person in her area for Mary Kay cosmetics, then started working for her husband's company. Poe started in telemarketing and rapidly took over the work and territories of all three regional sales managers. "I had a good feel for marketing," she modestly states.

Business Origin

Poe was putting in a lot of hours with two small children and not making nearly as much as she thought she could, so she started looking for a product to develop and sell. About this time, she began working out to get in shape and started having tremendous pain. She discovered her aerobic shoes were to blame.

Poe learned that women's athletic shoes were simply scaled-down versions of men's shoes, even though women's bodies respond differently to exercise and are built differently than men's.

Poe decided to develop a shoe designed especially for women. "I said, 'why can't we make athletic shoes—we're in the middle of the footwear capital.' I was told I was crazy."

Poe came up with Rykä after noticing the popularity of European-sounding products and discovering her first choice, the family name Riker, already belonged to another shoe company. Her husband at the time, Martin Birrittella, worked on designing a woman's athletic shoe and helped Poe develop Rykä's business plan.

Taking on the exercise giants Reebok and Nike would be suicide, according to doubters. Poe and Birrittella put $50,000 of their money into the fledgling venture and went out to raise another $50,000. Friends and family, persuaded by Poe's determined passion for the venture, contributed all they could to start the business.

It was not enough. Enthusiasm alone failed to convince the investment bankers. "They laughed us out of their offices," says Poe.

A Denver-based investment firm, R. B. Marich, became Rykä's fairy godmother. Poe discovered that the "B" stood for Betty Marich, an aerobics buff herself. Marich convinced the males at the firm that a women's athletic market existed and Rykä gained the working capital needed to get started.

Business Growth

Bartering when she did not have cash, Poe gained suppliers and manufacturers who would take a chance on the young company.

Persuasiveness helped her lure Reebok's director of public relations to Rykä. Poe convinced him and 21 employees to come aboard, using stock options as incentives. During the two years Poe took to gather her staff, not one shoe was shipped. In March 1988 her first shipment of 50 pair of aerobic shoes went to Nordstrom's department store in Los Angeles.

Rykä's products are positioned as medium priced, high-performance athletic shoes and are distributed through major footwear and department store chains. Poe believes her customers are open to trying a new footwear company, especially one headed by a woman.

Rykä is in a critical stage of growth, says Poe, who thinks store-level merchandising efforts will help sales. Her ads run in fitness-oriented magazines that reach Rykä's target market: women who need correctly designed athletic shoes. But she expects the most effective way of reaching customers will be through the 8,000 aerobics instructors currently wearing Rykä shoes. "The fact that we've accumulated that many instructors is a major plus for us," says Poe. "They're the most critical fitness enthusiasts and the fact that they believe in us is really a testament to our shoes. People look at their instructor and say 'If it's good enough for her. . . .'"

Business Obstacles

Money was the company's biggest obstacle. "We went public from the beginning and raised $12.5 million in two years," said Poe. "We knew we couldn't even get into this business unless we had the funds to advertise and manufacture our product." Rykä went public in March of 1987, with another public offering a year afterward.

Another problem was the fact that Poe was a woman. "There had not been a woman in athletic footwear. I had to talk to big buyers and they had a hard time taking us seriously." "When you stand in front of a group of investment bankers, if you're attractive at all they look at you like you don't have a brain in your head. It's just like the Dark Ages. It has been very frustrating to get them to really respect me," says Poe.

The single most insulting incident occurred during a private venture capitalists meeting. One of first groups Poe approached wanted to give her a million dollars—but they also wanted 90 percent of the company. They told her she was out of her mind to think she could do it.

Poe regrets the long hours and traveling necessary in getting the company up and running. "I have not been able to be around my kids as much as I have wanted to and have had to employ someone to help me bring them up. I always make time for them, though. If I'm in a meeting, I will stop if they call and find out what they need. I also schedule my travel around their special events."

Keys to Success

Rykä feels more like a California company than an East Coast firm. Most employees are wear-testing aerobic shoes on any given day, including Poe.

She tries to keep a hands-off management approach. "I like people to feel that they have control over the outcome of their effort," she says. "If you get a talented manager, or any talented employee, and try to corral them and tell them every single thing that is to be done, they don't have room to breathe. People like to be free, to make their own impact." Poe describes the management as "informal—both relaxed and intense."

Her persistence helps her overcome obstacles. "As a kid, I was relentless. My parents told me if I kept that trait in business, I would be very successful."

Future Vision

Rykä is coming out with the lightest weight, most inexpensively priced aerobic shoe ever. "It is revolutionary in our business to have a shoe that weighs less and to deliver it first," Poe explains.

The Ultralight shoe is performance oriented, but still fashionable in the hot colors that make Rykäs attractive on and off the aerobic floor. "There's a lot of excitement that we could be the next L. A. Gear or Reebok," says Poe.

One of the smallest companies in athletic footwear, Rykä has expanded into walking shoes and enlarged the existing product line.

Poe expects Rykä's shoes to be available in more outlets within the next three years. Although carried in many important sports shoe stores, distribution is still incomplete.

Entrepreneurial Lessons

"If you're going to start your own business, you need to have a real burning desire because the time and energy that goes into it is massive," warns Poe. "You've got to know what you're getting into. "Would I do it again? Yes. Would I do it differently? Yes. I had to learn the hard way about time management," she laments.

For her, the single most important thing is to have support mechanisms in place to be able to make sure all the bases are covered. "I need to spend time with my husband and children—keep the home maintained. My life has to be really well managed." Despite such efforts, Poe and her husband recently divorced. Yet as she warns, it's not just the kids and the relationship with your mate that can be hurt. The stress level can be physically devastating. Studies about women who are professionals and very successful show the types of health ailments they suffer from—heart attacks, cancer—are stress related. "You have to make sure to take care of yourself and your own needs. You have to be able to say 'This has to wait. *I* have to come first right now.'"

Poe suffered a bout with mononucleosis a couple of years ago and had to pay more attention to her health. "I had to have one of my kids say to me 'I never see you anymore,' and had to regroup. I have to work out to release stress. I really believe you can have it all—I believe you can have everything. I don't know how you measure how successful everything is, but you can keep everyone happy. It really takes attention."

References

Huffman, F., and P. Korzeniowski. "One Step Beyond." *Entrepreneurial Woman,* September 1990.

McCune, Jenny C. "Hit the Ground Running." *Success,* June 1990.

Touby, Laurel Allison. "Creativity vs. Cash." *Working Woman,* November 1991.

——S. B.

Safi U. Qureshey
Thomas C. K. Yuen

AST Research, Inc.

Safi U. Qureshey: Born 1951. Married, three children.
Thomas C. K. Yuen: Born 1952. Married, two children.
Venture: An electronic design consulting firm, which expanded into complete production of computer enhancement products and personal computers.
Company: AST Research, Inc.; 16215 Alton Parkway; Irvine, CA 92713-9658; (714) 727-4141
Founded: July 25, 1980.
Revenues: $688.5 million in fiscal 1991, according to company sources.
Employees: 2,700.
Original Investment: $40,000.
Value: $106 million.

Founders

Safi Qureshey, Thomas Yuen, and Albert Wong personify the American dream. Three immigrants—Qureshey from Pakistan, Yuen and Wong from Hong Kong—turned a simple consulting business into a half-billion dollar computer manufacturing company.

Qureshey graduated from the University of Karachi, Pakistan, with a B.S. in physics. He came to the United States in the early 1970s and received an electrical engineering degree at the University of Texas-Austin. His work experiences included serving as a project and design engineer at Telefile

Computer Products, a minicomputer and mainframe manufacturer. Later he worked as a test engineer for Computer Automation—where he met Yuen—and A.M. International, both manufacturers of point-of-sale terminals.

Yuen, who was born in Shanghai, Hong Kong, came to the United States in 1969. He attended Orange Coast College (Costa Mesa, California), and graduated with honors from the University of California-Irvine, receiving a B.S. in electrical engineering. Yuen held various engineering and project-management positions at Sperry Univac, Hughes Aircraft and Computer Automation before co-founding AST.

Wong also came to the U.S. from Hong Kong in 1969. He and Yuen met as students at Orange Coast College. Wong graduated from California State University-Fullerton with a degree in engineering. He worked for Datum, Inc. and Technology Marketing Inc. before co-founding AST. Wong is credited with transforming AST into a complete computer systems manufacturer, as well as with expanding into international markets.

Qureshey became president of AST through the luck of the draw—they literally drew straws—but he was president in name only. In a 1989 *Los Angeles Times* article, David Olmos wrote, "From the start, AST's founders shared in managing the company and divided up their responsibilities according to respective skill and interest. Yuen focused on marketing and sales. Wong oversaw engineering and manufacturing. Qureshey divided his time among several areas."

They were called "The Three Musketeers," and were well-known for their "free-spirited" company atmosphere. Although the corporate culture was "cool" and relaxed, tensions began to arise among the founders. In November 1988, Wong abruptly resigned, citing, "disagreement over the company's management style." At that time he was co-chairman and chief technology officer and retained 17 percent of AST's stock. Eventually he founded Amkey Systems. Yuen told *Business Week*, "The outside perceived romance of the three partners was always largely an illusion."

Business Origin

In 1980, Qureshey, Yuen, and Wong started AST, an acronym representing the first letters of their first names, as a "high-tech consulting firm." It was Yuen who offered the breakthrough idea. After seeing a news story (1981) about IBM introducing its first personal computer, he suggested that AST develop products to work with the new computer. By December 1981 the company was shipping "enhancement" products, including a 64k to 256k expansion memory board, a multiprotocol communications board, and an asynchronous communications card.

Qureshey remembers that period. "We sold our first board to a customer in Orange County. They sent us a check for $82, and the check bounced. It was not a good feeling," he recalls. But the company rebounded and grew.

Business Growth

From 1981 to 1986 AST's accessory market was successful. In 1982, it developed the first asynchronous communication card which allowed users to communicate with their mainframes via a personal computer. In 1983 the company introduced the first multiprotocol communication board, which permitted interaction between personal computers and more advanced minicomputers. In that same year AST introduced the AST SixPakPlus, a "100 percent IBM-compatible memory/multifunctional enhancement board."

AST introduced its first line of personal computers in 1986. By 1987, four models of a more advanced line, the Premium/386, were selling. The new, "diversified microcomputer supplier" had gained a place in the competitive computer market. AST was sixth on *Inc.* magazine's list of fastest growing small companies in May 1987.

The next two years saw continued expansion of the corporation's personal computer line—accounting for 70 percent of revenues—as well as development of memory/multifunctional boards and other upgrades. At the end of fiscal year 1990, AST had introduced 12 new PC systems and three new enhancement board products. In 1991, the company shipped out computer number one million, which was presented to the President of the United States.

AST went from $71,000 in sales in 1981 to $688.5 million in fiscal 1991. Its product is manufactured in Fountain Valley, California, London, Hong Kong, and Taiwan, and is sold in 89 countries.

Business Obstacles

When IBM started producing its own line of enhancement products in 1986, AST profits plummeted. SixPak sales, which once accounted for 60 percent of revenues, slowed dramatically. AST recovered by introducing its own line of personal computers, selling $412 million worth by June 1988. But that success was short-lived.

In 1986 the company began to suffer because of increased personal computer competition. Profit margins were "squeezed." Also, AST was slow in designing new computers. Its introduction of Apple and Digital Equipment Corporation (DEC) enhancement products was unsuccessful, draining resources and failing to boost revenues. In January 1989 it announced an $8.9 million loss for the quarter ending December 31, 1988. The company was forced to lay off 120 employees, and Wong abruptly quit.

Qureshey and Yuen used Wong's departure to reevaluate the past goals of AST. Says Yuen, "When Albert left, it provided us with a golden moment to re-examine ourselves and why we went through a slump." AST improved its position by eliminating overlapping product lines and by combining engineering, sales and marketing, which had been separate divisions. It sold its Apple and DEC divisions, and paid off $30 million in short-term debt. It also replaced Wong with a five-member executive committee made up of veterans in the field.

As the corporation emerged from that turbulent year, Qureshey said, "AST is getting ready to become a mature company, to find its place in a group of very established companies." He told *Business Week* that because of AST's pricing, tough economic times can hit those "established companies" harder than AST. "Customers have less money to spend, but they're still looking for value and a quality product. . . . [They] are judging us with their pocketbooks."

Keys to Success

AST's success is tied to two characteristics: being humane and being enterprising. Joel Kotkin, West Coast editor for *Inc.* magazine, says AST gave "Orange County a business soul." At AST, he says, "they don't have a hit and run business philosophy." Qureshey clarifies, "We have a very long-term view of our company and the business we're in. We're not a flashy company, but we are aggressive. We are not here to make money fast and get out." The company's management, Kotkin adds, "are humane and genuinely nice people." Until 1988 AST sponsored pancake breakfasts with employees and held impromptu meetings to discuss company successes and obstacles.

Yuen attributes AST's success to hard work saying, "Some people wait for fortunes to befall them, but we worked hard."

Future Vision

AST predicts its growth will be nourished by international expansion. "We look at countries with no real competitive industry now, maybe only some PCs from Korea or Taiwan sold on price but not name. We want to establish AST as the brand name," Qureshey explains. The company is investigating opportunities in Japan, the Soviet Union, Central America, and the Middle East.

In 1990, AST introduced the Dual SX/16, the first dual-compatible personal computer for the Japanese marketplace. According to the company, compatibility presented special problems due to the graphic complexity of the Japanese language compared to the Latin-based Industry Standard Architecture (ISA). The American Standard Computer Information Interchange (ASCII) character-coding system, for example, uses only 256 characters and graphic symbols based on the Latin alphabet, and a few kilobytes of memory. In comparison, the Japanese language needs a minimum of 3,000 high-resolution characters which require up to half a megabyte of memory. A single Japanese computer company (NEC PC-9801) holds approximately 50 percent of the Japanese microcomputer market .

Jim Ashbrook, senior vice president of marketing, explains the significance of the Dual SX/16, "The dual-compatible architecture provided a bridge between the NEC standard, popular in Japan, and the ISA standard that dominates the worldwide personal computer marketplace. A company can use software developed for both standards without the expense of a second PC." Qureshey adds, "It [Dual SX/16] demonstrates that an American company can develop and manufacture new, innovative technology that brings unique computing capability to the Japanese marketplace."

In April 1990, AST expanded into Mexico, licensing SIGA Corporativo of Mexico City to distribute AST computers and computer enhancement products. In May 1990, the Hong Kong government bought 1,500 386-based systems. AST signed a sales and distribution agreement with Robotron, East Germany's largest computer and electronics company in July 1990. And, there are AST PCs in the Soviet Union, sold through

Computerland, the U.S.S.R.'s first computer store, which opened in March 1990.

Entrepreneurial Lessons

Qureshey credits teamwork with AST's progress. "The larger we grow the more we recognize the each of us could not have accomplished what AST has as individuals." He adds, "The challenge as we become larger and more successful is to suppress the ego."

References

Anderson, Stephanie. "PC Slump? What PC Slump? *Business Week*, July 1, 1991.

Armstrong, Larry. "This 12-Year-Old Has Come of Age." *Business Week*, May 6, 1991.

Kramer, Matt. "AST, a PC-Compatible Market Old Timer." *PC Week*, November 29, 1983.

Lazzareschi, Carla. "'Nice Guys' at AST Planning for the Long Haul." *Los Angeles Times*, May 3, 1990.

Olmos, David. "Albert Wong, a Founder of AST to Resign." *Los Angeles Times*, (Orange County Edition), November 9, 1988.

———. "AST Struggling Back Following Founders' Rift." *Los Angeles Times*, May 28, 1989.

———. "Ex-AST Partner Wong Weighs Idea of Returning to Computers." *Los Angeles Times*, (Orange County Edition), May 28, 1989.

Stroud, Ruth. "Growth Rages on at AST." *Orange County Register*, May 7, 1987.

Takahashi, Dean. "AST Challenges the Skeptics." *Los Angeles Times*, April 22, 1990.

Vranizan, Michelle. "AST Gets Serious." *Orange County Register*, November 12, 1989.

———. "Wong, AST Co-Founder Leaves Firm." *Orange County Register*, November 8, 1988.

———A. A.

Joyce Rice
Ted Rice

T. J. Cinnamons

Joyce Rice: Born 1945.
Ted Rice: Born 1932. Married, five children.
Venture: A nationwide chain of bakeries specializing in such foods as cinnamon rolls, muffins, cupcakes and pies.
Company: T. J. Cinnamons; c/o Signature Foods, Inc.; 1010 West 39th Street; Kansas City, MO 64111; (816) 931-9341
Founded: T. J. Cinnamons was developed as a part-time business in 1982. The venture became a full-time business in 1985.
Revenues: $32 million projected sales (1991), according to a company source.
Employees: 15 in the corporate offices.
Original Investment: $36,000.
Value: Would not release.

Founders

Described by husband Ted as "the sweetest and dearest person you will ever meet," Joyce Rice was raised in the small town of Slater, Missouri, the daughter of a minister. As a member of a large family, she learned to coexist with several sisters and a brother. She received an education degree from Central Missouri State University (CMSU) and taught elementary school for 17 years. "There was really nothing out of the ordinary about Joyce's childhood," says Ted Rice, "except that she always had a traditional family to depend on."

408

His own childhood was somewhat different. His parents divorced, Rice and his brother were raised by their mother in Jefferson City, Missouri. While working day and night to support them, the youngsters' mother was always optimistic about the future. Rice recalls that his mother encouraged him to look for opportunities anywhere he could.

He took his mother's advice. A neighborhood wading pool provided him with his first entrepreneurial opportunity. There were no concessions available at the pool. During hot summer days young Rice would buy graham crackers, ice cream, wax paper and dry ice from the local grocer. The youth would make ice cream sandwiches, pack them in dry ice and sell them for 35 cents a piece. "I had less than a dollar to buy all my materials with, but by the end of the day I had as much as $15 or $18 profit," remembers Rice.

To earn extra money, Rice was a delivery boy for the city newspaper. One day he noticed a local merchant delivering handbills. "I had to deliver my newspapers at 5:00 A.M. in the morning," he says. "So I went to the merchant and told him I would deliver his handbills with my newspapers, so people would get them first thing in the morning. He agreed, and I was able to increase my profits without increasing my workload."

Like many youngsters in his neighborhood, Rice shoveled snow during the wintertime. "The going rate was $1.50 and no one thought about asking for more," he remembers. "But one day, after a heavy snowfall, a guy asked me to shovel his driveway. I asked him how much would he pay me. He said $4. Of course, I shoveled his driveway. But I made it a point to let the adult set the price, and it was always over $1.50. I learned that $4 to an adult didn't mean as much as $4 did to a kid." The youngster never worried about the "competition" undercutting his price because "I provided a much better product. Those sidewalks didn't have a snowflake left on them when I was finished," laughs Rice.

Business Origin

After they married in 1970, Joyce Rice continued her job as teacher and Ted as cameraman for a local television station. Neither was looking for entrepreneurial opportunities when a tragic event completely changed Ted Rice's outlook on life.

As a cameraman, he witnessed dramatic, often fatal, incidents such as airplane crashes, fires and tornados. Never had any incident disturbed him more than a 1981 disaster in which two aerial walkways collapsed in a

Kansas City hotel, killing over 100 people. "There was death all around, and not a thing I could do about it," Rice recalls. For him, the tragedy's suddenness and magnitude underscored life's fragility and the importance of appreciating each day.

Rice arranged a leave of absence from his job and the couple spent four months sailing on Lake Superior. The temporary change of venue was so calming, both wondered if they could ever go back to their old jobs. Rice remembers "having so much fun, that we didn't want to go back to work. So we looked for a way to supplement our income and support our habit of sailing."

Carpentry and charter sailing were a few of the part-time ventures the Rices considered. Neither remembers how the idea of cinnamon rolls originated, but the couple recalls their enthusiasm over the idea spurred them to pursue it further.

Being a typical small town bakery—a cozy shop with a cute store front— was not what the couple envisioned. They wanted a niche, not just a mouth-watering recipe. The solution was a $50,000 mobile bakery. Ted Rice felt, "if we [added] showmanship, letting our customers see the people who [were] handling their food, and the equipment it [was] being made in, we could make a go of it."

Still working full-time, the Rices began driving their mobile bakery during the summer of 1983. They traveled the midwest, visiting state fairs and rodeos. The bakery was an instant success—so much so, that several months later Joyce quit her teaching job to drive the mobile bakery full-time. "Where is your permanent bakery?" Joyce answered that question hundreds of times a day. It prompted the Rices to think, "Why not?" In January 1985 they opened their first T. J. Cinnamons (named for Ted and Joyce) in a Kansas City shopping mall. In March, Ted quit his job to devote his energy to their thriving business.

Business Growth

Colorful, airy and spacious describes every T. J. Cinnamons bakery. The original bakery in Kansas City has a glass roof and is positioned between two escalators so that it attracts the attention of hungry shoppers. No walls separate the baking equipment and the sales floor. Customers watch as pans of nine-ounce cinnamon rolls and other bakery items are pulled from ovens. Other T. J. Cinnamon bakeries contain almost 50 items on their menus.

Such details catapulted T. J. Cinnamons into franchising. After the success of their first bakery, the Rices were flooded with requests for franchising information. Would-be competition was also following the bakery's success, attempting to copy their recipes and store decor. "It was at that point that we went to our lawyers and said, 'We think we have something that's a little more than a one-bakery operation,'" says Joyce Rice.

With the assistance of two Kansas City businessmen, Kenneth Hill and Roger Cohen, Signature Foods, Inc. was formed to serve as the franchising arm of T. J. Cinnamons. The first franchised bakery opened in late 1985. As of January 1990, Signature Foods had franchised approximately 238 T. J. Cinnamons bakeries nationwide. In 1988, *Venture* magazine ranked the franchise the 35th most successful among the 50 it rated.

Business Obstacles

Many people stay away from "sweets"; calories and extra pounds are the usual objections. The attitude is so prevalent, many would-be customers avoid bakeries at any cost, especially in today's fitness and diet-conscious world.

With such a "sinful" stigma attached to their product, the Rices developed their bakery products with "health" in mind. When available, only natural ingredients are used, especially those low in cholesterol and fat. A majority of the baked goods do not contain any sugar, suitable for diabetics. "We use margarine, not butter, because butter is different in different parts of the country," says Joyce. Nutritional information is available on every menu item. "Our cinnamon rolls, which weigh eight to nine ounces, have the same amount of calories as a piece of fried chicken," explains Ted. "But people just don't believe that anything that tastes that good can possibly be good for them. It is a very difficult attitude to overcome, one which we have to fight in almost every type of marketing we do."

Keys to Success

Ted and Joyce Rice added a certain level of excitement to an industry which was stagnant for many years—and customers are taking notice. Their bakeries are not typically cute and quaint, but rather bold and striking. Hungry customers are first attracted by the decor, then lured by aromas of fresh bakery fare. The bakeries are more than inviting—they are a temptation some customers find hard to satisfy elsewhere. Rice claims the "bakery experience" at his store is unlike similar experiences at the neighborhood bakery, which he describes as "hum-drum and sort of matter of fact."

The Rices regarded this approach as so vital to T. J. Cinnamons' success that the couple wrote their own franchise agreement to maintain consistency within the chain. They refused typical franchise agreements, which they thought gave some franchisees too much freedom. Comments Ted, "We only sell franchises to individuals who we feel will maintain our image. We don't want to tell someone how to run each detail of their store. But our image must be preserved. It is what has made us successful and is what our customers have come to expect."

Future Vision

"What do you do when the new wears off?" asks Ted Rice. It is the one question he feels he must answer successfully to guarantee a future for his company. While the Rices have proven their baked goods are more than "fads," the couple has found they must change their menu often to satisfy customer demands.

The company founders carefully watch sales on individual menu items. Slow-to-sell items are quickly pulled from the menu. New recipes are regularly developed and test-marketed. But the Rices claims it is difficult to know what to do. "Do you maintain an image of a gourmet bakery with one product and lose sales, or do you go along with the blending of menus that's going on these days, and wind up not knowing who you are?"

Signature Foods president Kenneth Hill hopes to diversify the franchise branch into full-service restaurants and other franchised food operations. International markets such as Canada and Japan are also a possibility.

Entrepreneurial Lessons

The Rices describe themselves as "convicted." They operate their business and personal lives with a deep conviction, stemming from the morals with which they were raised. "I shall lead a guilt free life," proclaims Ted Rice. This philosophy, he says, allows him to make better, and kinder decisions. Rice cites numerous individuals he has chosen to hire, sometimes against the advice of others. "I felt better knowing I had given that person a job, money in their pocket—money so they could buy their kid a toy or put a down payment on the house they wanted." He acknowledges he has been taken advantage of, but knowing he did "the right thing" made him feel less angry.

Rice warns up-and-coming entrepreneurs that they may be called upon to make difficult choices, some of which may compromise their morals or ethics. "You have to do the right thing," he advises. "It may cost you money, [or] it may put you out of business. But if you don't do what you think is right, I guarantee you many sleepless nights."

References

Appelbaum, Cara. "T.J. Cinnamons Makes the Sticky Bun as Down Home as Apple Pie." *Adweek's Marketing Week*, February 19, 1990.

Barrier, Michael. "Rolling in Dough." *Nation's Business*, February 1990.

Bertagnoli, Lisa. "T.J. Cinnamons Adds New Markets, New Products." *Restaurants and Institutions*, November 11, 1988.

Frydman, Ken. "Cinnamon Roll Sales Heat Up." *Nation's Restaurant News*, January 13, 1986.

——R. H. S.

Walter Riley

G. O. D., Inc.

Walter Riley: Born 1955. Married, three children.
Venture: Overnight delivery of freight in the Mid-Atlantic region via truck.
Company: G. O. D., Inc.; P.O. Box 100; Kearny, NJ 07032; (201) 344-3013
Founded: 1983.
Revenues: $21 million (1990), according to a company source.
Employees: 270.
Original Investment: Unknown.
Value: Approximately $2.7 million net worth at the close of fiscal 1989, according to published sources.

Founder

Walter Riley began his career at the age of eight, helping around his father's company, Seigle's Express. He learned trucking from the inside out, not knowing he would one day turn it inside out himself.

Riley joined Seigle's Express full-time immediately after graduating from high school. His presence had an instant impact on the company. A relatively small, local cartage company that had rarely seen a profit experienced increased sales and revenues as the younger Riley found new markets and customers for the company. Soon, pretax profits of about eight percent were the norm at Seigle's. Rather than contentment, however, the situation led to conflict.

Though Riley is not proud of it, he admits the main trouble was between him and his father Richard. Their views differed on the future of the company and when the elder Riley would let his son participate in

414

ownership. "I wanted to grow, grow, grow," remembers Riley, noting his father did not share his growth mentality.

Things finally came to a head in 1979, when the two Rileys erupted into a shouting match with each other in Richard Riley's office. Walter left the company and the country, moving to St. Thomas.

In St. Thomas, Riley went into business for himself for the first time, renting mopeds to tourists (as well as to locals). He was as successful at that as he had been in spurring Seigle's growth. That success put him in the right place at the right time.

In 1981, the trucking industry underwent a fundamental change. Highly regulated by federal and state governments since the 1930s, the new Motor Carrier Act released companies from almost all economic and rate controls. Trucking companies would now compete in the open market on the basis of price and service. Many companies would not survive the new competition, and it looked as if Seigle's would be one of them.

Riley returned from St. Thomas with one thing in mind: to buy the ailing Seigle's Express from his father and run it his way. "If I hadn't given my best shot to buy that company, I don't think I could have looked myself in the mirror," he says.

Riley bought the business from his father, paying a price that he considered "a little on the high side," and then got down to business.

Business Origin

Riley focused on Seigle's growth. The company was growing when another change in the laws opened an opportunity to expand in an entirely new direction—and Riley went after it without hesitation.

In 1982, Congress passed the Surface Transportation Act. In a trade-off for raising the tax on fuel, Congress mandated that all states allow two-trailer "tandem trucks." This was the opportunity Riley had been awaiting.

Two months before the act was passed, Riley purchased 30 tandem-size trailers and seven new tractors to put his idea into action. His plan was to become a land-based Federal Express. Riley copied and adapted the Fedex hub-and-spoke system to provide overnight delivery with trucks.

Riley's system used single small trailers in an assigned area to make package pick-ups. That trailer was then linked to another and the two were then hauled to the central hub in North Jersey where the packages were reassigned to trailers that would then take them to their destination. Riley bet Seigle's future on the concept.

The last element in Riley's plan was to make sure that potential customers knew his company and its services existed. "Seigle's Express" neither described what the company was going to do, nor helped sell the firm's new services. Riley and his employees began to kick around other possible names for the new service. Suggestions included Guaranteed Overnight Service, Overnight Express, Guaranteed Overnight Delivery, and others. Guaranteed Overnight Delivery sounded good to everyone, but it was too close to another company's registered name to be used. The acronym, however, wasn't being used by any company—G. O. D.

Riley was certain the new name would get attention. In 1983, the large red and black letters G. O. D. went on the side of his trucks and the new company was officially born. "The name has been great," Riley says. "When we enter a new market people know our name within weeks."

Business Growth

Riley's new company made a powerful impact with both its name and its system. The overnight concept was just what the market wanted, and soon the firm was servicing such major clients as General Foods, Mercedes-Benz, Johnson & Johnson, NEC, Mita, and Volvo. The company was growing, and Riley pushed growth just as hard as he had with Seigle's Express.

G.O.D. has experienced rapid growth since its inception. The firm started with four employees in 1983, and grew to more than 270 employees and $21 million in sales by 1990. G. O. D. has been profitable in every year but one, and is expanding beyond its original New Jersey based, Mid-Atlantic market.

In 1991, G.O.D. formed a partnership with McQuaide Freight Lines of Pennsylvania to reach previously unreachable markets through second-day delivery. "Our customers wanted us to expand west into Pennsylvania, Ohio and part of New York. And we thought it would be quicker, easier and just as good if we were able to do that with a partner carrier, . . ." Riley told *Transport Topics.*

Business Obstacles

Riley had always been a fan of incentive plans for workers. He thought of it as a way to get them as excited about growth and profit as he was. G. O. D. was loaded with incentive plans for every area of the company—all geared to productivity—and always aimed toward growth. Instead, the company began to suffer serious internal setbacks—employee morale and productivity were plummeting.

Problems that surfaced were twofold. First the incentive plans did not recognize that the ability of many employees to be productive, drivers for instance, was directly related to the productivity of others. The second problem was that in too many cases, the easiest way to earn money under the incentive plan turned out to have nothing to do with growth.

In one case, when Riley hired an outside consultant to review his drivers' performance, he found that they were making only 80 percent of their assigned stops each day. "You know what," he recalls telling one of his vice presidents, "we've got a lazy bunch of drivers around here."

His conclusion was wrong. What Riley finally realized after his vice president researched the situation was that the drivers' failure to make stops resulted from the trucks being loaded wrong by dockworkers (who were being paid to load as fast as they could).

Other examples of the failure of Riley's incentives came flooding in from every area of the company. Workers refused to help each other because incentives and bonuses only came as a result of the work assigned to each person, not for helping someone else. Supervisors on the loading docks were falsifying records to give extra bonuses to dockworkers of their choice, and one salesman was spending much of his time each day auditing the prior day's shipping reports to put his name on any shipment he could, because even the smallest shipment added to his bonus.

As the company grew, the internal problems and poor attitudes grew faster. "I tried to let everyone win," says Riley, "but it seemed like I had created a company with too many losers."

The final evidence of the firm's personnel troubles came when G.O.D. received notice from the IRS that it had to file tax information by magnetic tape, since it had more than 500 employees. In fact, the company had less than 200. Riley wanted to know what was going on, and the answer was astounding. In one year, 1987, G. O. D. had employed more than 700 different people to keep less than 200 jobs filled. It was the final straw for Riley. "I was hoping to have a positive influence on peoples lives, and I could see we just weren't moving in that direction. I realized we were not a great company," he recalls.

Keys to Success

Riley knew the company needed to change, but the change would not come overnight. It would not come at all without a change in his attitude as a leader. He attended management conferences with the famous quality consultant W. Edwards Deming. He took his senior management on trips and outings where everyone could not only speak frankly, but also just relax and get to know each other. Most important of all, he scrapped his incentive plans.

With the help of an outside consultant who had studied under Deming, Riley and the senior management drafted a set of values under which G. O. D. would operate. The top value listed sums up the metamorphosis of both Riley and the company. The company will seek "to provide an environment for its people that promotes joy at work, achievement of personal goals, and an opportunity to share in the prosperity of the company."

Along with changes in philosophy, Riley sought changes in actions as well. "I decided to crush what we had and start from scratch," he says. Instead of firing people on a moment's notice, company management spends time looking at its systems to make sure they allow employees to do their best work. Instead of incentives that are counterproductive or unfair, the company shares overall profits and devotes greater resources to providing the best equipment and support to employees.

"Sure we want to get bigger and better businesswise," Riley told *New Jersey Monthly*, "But what excites me the most is the possibility to get our people to get the most they can out of their lives. . . ."

Future Vision

Riley maintains his vision of growth for the company, and his long-term goal of reaching $200 million in sales. But he is quick to point out that his vision now includes other things as well. "I like trucking, but what I really like is people. I have a vision of a place where people find a lot of compelling reasons to be the best they can be."

Even if his company grows a little slower, Walter Riley is convinced he has found a better way to build it. "This feels good," he says, when talking about the goals and environment of G. O. D. today. "More than that. This feels right."

Entrepreneurial Lessons

Riley is among the first to point out that the lessons he learned from the early years of G. O. D. were "people" lessons, and not strictly business lessons. "I learned that it takes more than the promise of money to make a team," he says, "that investments in helping people to work better and work happier pay off both inside and outside the workplace."

He illustrates his lesson with an incident from the company's loading docks, where workers used to fight over equipment, or steal it from each other in the middle of a job. For ages Riley refused to buy more of the expensive tools, such as pallet jacks, because the "numbers didn't add up." But when he finally broke down and made the investment—more to satisfy workers than to increase productivity—productivity on the loading dock skyrocketed, and freight damage fell.

References

Brokaw, Leslie. "G.O.D.: Sitting Comfortably in Overnight Shipping Heaven." *Business Journal of New Jersey*, September 1, 1987.

———. "The Miracle of the Name." *Inc.*, April 1988.

Gilroy, Roger. "McQuaide and G.O.D. Team Up." *Transport Topics*, May 6, 1991.

Hyatt, Joshua. "Growing Up as CEO." *Inc.*, July 1989.

Petrick, John. "Walter Riley: G.O.D." *New Jersey Monthly*, February 1990.

——E. C.

Thurman John Rodgers

Cypress Semiconductor Corporation

Thurman John (T. J.) Rodgers: Born 1948. Single.
Venture: Manufacturer of high-performance integrated circuits.
Company: Cypress Semiconductor Corporation; 3901 N. First St.; San
  Jose, CA 95134; (408) 943-2600
Founded: 1983.
Revenues: $295 million in 1991, according to published reports.
Employees: 1,925.
Original Investment: $7.5 million by T. J. Rodgers with the backing of six
  venture capital firms.
Value: $219 million net worth (1990, company figures). $417 million market
  value (1989, NYSE).

Founder

T. J. Rodgers grew up in Oshkosh, Wisconsin, with a younger brother,
James. His mother always complimented his achievements and taught him
to accentuate the positive. A "straight-A" student accustomed to being
number one in his class, Rodgers' lessons on the high school football field
helped prepare him for the challenges he would later encounter in business. "I ran into a defensive tackle who knocked me flat on my butt,"
recalls Rodgers. "It was the first time in my life I ran into something that
was very difficult to do, very unforgiving, and the coach, rather than
telling me what a great guy I was, told me how stupid I was." Years later,
the fiercely competitive Rodgers derived one of his corporate maxims from
the experience: "Life is unfair."

Rodgers received an A.B. in physics and chemistry from Dartmouth (1970).

He received both his M.S. (1973) and his Ph.D. (1975) from Stanford. Just 26 years old, the freshly graduated doctor of electrical engineering had invented VMOS (V-shaped metal oxide semiconductor), an exotic technology for making high-performance semiconductor chips by etching silicon wafers with chemicals. Rodgers brought the license to develop VMOS with him to American Microsystems Inc. (AMI).

The VMOS project failed. AMI figured that good technology would sell, but it underestimated the marketing strength needed to unseat entrenched existing technology. While VMOS floundered, Rodgers and Mike Starnes, who headed up manufacturing, began to talk about a new technology called CMOS (complementary metal-oxide semiconductor). CMOS chips could be built faster, cooler, smaller, and with less power usage than existing technology. The two believed that CMOS would be the technology of the future, but they were unsuccessful in pitching the idea to potential investors who questioned their ability to market the chip in such a competitive industry.

Business Origin

In 1980, after the VMOS project was halted, Rodgers went to Advanced Micro Devices (AMD) and Starnes landed at Intel. AMD's marketing expertise gave Rodgers insight in how to bring a new product to market. Now he was ready for a second attempt to sell his CMOS idea.

Rodgers' second business plan positioned his technology in niche markets—static RAM memory chips, programmable logic devices, and programmable read-only memories. This avoided head-to-head competition with the semiconductor giants who favored high-volume markets. The big companies felt it was premature to bring CMOS, a difficult and costly process, to the market.

Despite their apprehension about the competitiveness of the semiconductor industry, six venture capital firms committed $7.5 million to Rodgers' niche concept. Cypress was launched in April 1983.

Business Growth

Right from the start the company was lean and aggressive. Rodgers called all the shots. "We didn't have a chief financial officer for the first three years of the company," recalls Rodgers. "I raised the money for our company in the four rounds of private financing we had that totaled $40 million. I had to learn how venture capital worked, how rounds of financing were put together, how pricing and valuation of shares were established, and how consortia of venture capitalists are put together."

Cypress grew quickly, even by Silicon Valley standards. In 1984 revenues were $4 million. The next year, they reached $20 million despite an industry-wide slump. By 1986, the company was ready to go public. Again, Rodgers was a hands-on CEO. "I literally wrote important parts of our prospectus and participated in the feeding frenzy you have to go through if you want to get a good price for your company."

Rodgers' all-consuming management style reached its limit at the $100 million mark. "I stopped having a company where 200 people pretty much reported to me. We shifted over to much more delegation where I managed, where I created systems to monitor progress, and the vice-presidents really started running the day-to-day activities in the company. It was a typical system, and I started to see the typical failure modes of that system. I started hearing excuses for lack of performance that sounded just like two large companies I had worked for before Cypress. There were squabbles between groups instead of cooperation. I began to believe that I would end up growing just another big, arteriosclerotic company if I didn't do something different."

Rodgers reorganized the company and established four wholly-owned subsidiaries to tap the creative energy of start-up organizations: Cypress Semiconductor (Texas) Inc., Aspen Semiconductor Corp., Multichip Technology Inc., and Ross Technologies, Inc.

Rodgers cites four major benefits from the start-up approach: it is creatively cheap; people who like the small company environment and who might have been tapped by other start-ups end up staying with the company; the tremendous product focus of start-ups is much more efficient in bringing new products to the market; and finally, start-ups attract talented people who would be otherwise unavailable.

Cypress Semiconductor produces random access memories, programmable logic devices, programmable read only memories, RISC (Reduced Instruction Set Computer) microprocessors, and other logic and memory chips. Major end-use markets include computers, telecommunications, instrumentation/industrial, and the military.

Business Obstacles

With funding in place, Rodgers had to find the talent to run a sophisticated fabrication plant. He felt the key player needed for the team was his old partner, Mike Starnes. Rodgers waged an intensive phone campaign to recruit Starnes from Intel, and succeeded by selling the idea to Starnes' wife.

Rodgers, who had agreed not to hire anyone from AMD for nine months, crisscrossed the country setting up interviews, making twelve trips to Dallas alone. Rodgers recalls, "We'd screen 500 people, to interview 100, to make offers to 20, to get 18 acceptances. And that was a good trip."

Making matters more difficult, when employees change employers in Silicon Valley, lawsuits often follow alleging that trade secrets have been stolen. "I frame lawsuit or threatened lawsuit letters," Rodgers said. "I have hung them on my wall, and they run the length of my office. The lawsuits always ask for a lot of money and then they settle out of court in return for not hiring their people, so they should be really viewed as a warning shot over the bow."

Keys to Success

Attracting and keeping talented people within the company is vital in an industry whose growth is sustained by innovation. Cypress was able to gain a competitive edge in RISC technology by recruiting Roger Ross, a leading designer of this new microprocessor technology. Ross was set to start his own company, but Rodgers was able to attract him to Cypress by forming Ross Technologies as a Cypress subsidiary.

Keeping turnover low and morale high has been accomplished with a system of motivational goals and rewards. "Our buddies think of us as the Marine Corps," Rodgers explains. As he roams the company, he carries a tape recorder and dictates memos that he calls "action requests," demanding weekly updates on the status of his requests.

The management uses a comprehensive computerized evaluation system to track the company's goals and progress. Each employee, from secretary to executive, must meet a series of goals set by a supervisor. Short-term goals have one-to-three week deadlines. Quarterly goals are more ambitious, and every employee has three. Every Tuesday at 4:00 P.M. employees must file a progress report into a data base. Rodgers takes a few hours every week to review all those goals. Delinquent goals may result in disciplinary action. Employees, though, are rewarded through a quarterly profit sharing plan. Each employee—"from the receptionist to myself"— receives an identical sum that has been as high as $800 per quarter.

While this tough-minded approach may sound extreme, with tens of millions of dollars tied up in chip fabrication equipment, Rodgers recognizes that profitability is tied to efficiency. Rodgers concedes, "This management style is a lot of work, but it's the only successful way to bring in the numbers." He told *Upside* magazine that Cypress' corporate culture could be summed up in one sentence. "I work at Cypress, I work hard and I'm competent, who are you?"

Rodgers is well-versed in the numbers that support his marketing strategy. The company is founded on a niche strategy of 160 products, in seven product lines, sold to four major end-user areas, generating an average of $1.5 million per product each year. No product commands more than ten percent of sales, nor does any of its 1,600 customers exceed six percent of sales. As a result of this market diversity, Cypress usually has an eight percent share of the many markets in which they participate, in contrast to typical niche strategies that command up to 50 percent of one or two markets.

With its diversification, the company is much less susceptible to economic dislocations than, for instance, a high-volume chip manufacturer of dynamic RAMs with 200 customers.

Future Vision

Cypress's next battlefield is the market for the coming generation of microprocessors based on the RISC technology. Cypress will be competing head-to-head with IBM, Hewlett-Packard, Fujitsu, and Texas Instruments. Rodgers refutes those who claim the company is untested in such a highly competitive arena. "We've been competing against the Japanese with static RAMs for several years and we do just fine," he explains.

Another factor in the future marketplace will be Sematech, a government-sponsored consortium of U.S. chip makers designed to compete against what is claimed to be an unfair advantage enjoyed by Japanese manufacturers. Rodgers feels that Sematech will benefit the industry giants at the expense of smaller manufacturers, like Cypress, who have been competing effectively all along. Writing in *Computerworld*, he called such a consortium "the most dangerous threat to U.S. entrepreneurs today."

Entrepreneurial Lessons

"A good entrepreneur is someone with a headstrong nature," Rodgers explains, "He knows what he wants, and goes for it." But, as he learned, "People who are very headstrong and self-directed don't want to take advice. When I first started Cypress I was virtually immune to the advice of our board of directors. One thing I've learned over seven years is that the wisdom of the elders does matter. The old guys who have been through the wars and have scars all over from having done that really have some valuable lessons."

References

Brandt, Richard. "The Bad Boy of Silicon Valley." *Business Week*, December 9, 1991.

"The CEO 100." *Business Week*, October 20, 1989.

Dumaine, Brian. "The Bureaucracy Busters." *Fortune*, June 17, 1991.

Finegan, Jay. "Do You See What I See?" *Inc.*, April 1990.

Gemperlein, Joyce. "Mr. Right." *San Jose Mercury News/West*, May 12, 1991.

Karlgaard, Rich. "An Interview With T. J. Rodgers." *Upside*, December 1990.

Kaufman, Steve. "Passion for Perfection." *San Jose Mercury News*, March 3, 1986.

Kraar, Louis. "25 Who Help the U.S. Win." *Fortune/The New American Century*, Spring/Summer 1991.

McLeod, Jonah. "'You Don't Need Mass Resources to Win'." *Electronics*, August 1990.

Pitta, Julie. "Rodgers Regiment." *Venture*, April 1989.

Postrel, Virginia I., and Steven R. Postrel. "The New Mr. Chips: Speaking for Silicon Valley's Upstarts." *Reason*, July 1990.

Rodgers, T. J. "Battling the Technology Giants." *Computerworld*, January 14, 1991.

"Ten Top U.S. Chief Executives." *Electronic Business*, September 3, 1990.

——B. M.

Richard D. Sanford

Intelligent Electronics, Inc.

Richard D. Sanford: Born 1944. Married, five children.
Venture: A successful network of retail microcomputer outlets housed in department stores.
Company: Intelligent Electronics, Inc.; 411 Eagleview Boulevard; Exton, PA 19341; (215) 458-5500
Founded: May 1982; incorporated in Pennsylvania in 1982.
Revenues: Approximately $1.5 billion in fiscal 1990, according to company sources.
Employees: 3,000.
Original Investment: Initial capitalization from proceeds of private placements sales. In June 1987, Intelligent Electronics became a public company, offering shares of common stock for $10 per share.
Value: $700-750 million estimated sales in fiscal 1989, with net earnings of $10.6 million (December 1989).

Founder

A native of New York City, Richard D. Sanford founded Intelligent Electronics (IE) in 1982 and has served as the company's chairman and chief executive officer since that time. He was also IE's president from its founding until July 1989. Under his leadership, IE has grown to over 1,100 stores.

Sanford is a former executive vice president of Commodore International, Ltd., where he also served as vice president of finance and general manager of the U.S. personal computer group. During his five-year

426

association with Commodore, he saw revenues grow from $45 to $700 million. A CPA, Sanford also worked at Arthur Anderson & Co. for five years.

A Hofstra University graduate, he is a member of the board of directors of the Kennett Symphony, chairman of The Sanford Foundation, and a recipient of the Delaware Valley "Entrepreneur of the Year" award for 1989.

Sanford says Commodore founder Jack Tramiel is perhaps his greatest mentor. While Tramiel "had no formal education, he's the guy you like to have on your side—he stands head and shoulders above the rest," Sanford said. Sanford says he learned many lessons from Tramiel as he led Commodore through a phenomenal growth period.

Another role model in his life is his father, who worked for a large organization and always gave his all to his job, his church, and his wife and family, Sanford said.

Business Origin

Dick Sanford thought he was ready for retirement at the age of 38. "I had had enough at Commodore, I wasn't really learning anything new, and I was relatively wealthy," he explains. But after four months, Sanford realized retirement was not for him. "When I realized that the most serious thing I was accomplishing was taking my tennis lesson, I knew I was having a very non-productive lifestyle."

Sanford's dream throughout his young career was to start his own company. He admits that idea was nurtured while at Commodore when he saw that department store customers were interested in the microelectronics phenomenon. "I wasn't sure they (computers) would sell in that environment, but I talked to department store executives to understand that culture," Sanford said.

He had seen all the problems encountered by a burgeoning business at Commodore, and he thought he wanted out. "It's like walking off a spinning merry-go-round. But, yet, sailing around in boats and enjoying the leisure life wasn't what I wanted either." He was ready to put his entrepreneurial instincts to work to build his own business in what he knew best—microcomputers.

427

Business Growth

Sanford cites two important acquisitions as milestones in leading IE along the road to success. In January 1989 he bought Entre Computer Centers for $62 million. A franchised network of about 185 centers in North America, Entre generated $559 million in end-user sales in fiscal 1988. In August 1989, he acquired the chain Connecting Point of America, Inc., with 245 stores. An additional acquisition was made in June 1991 when IE bought the office supply superstore chain Biz Mart, planning to sell personal computers directly to the public from their 57 stores.

Another major decision for Sanford came in July 1989 when he turned over the operational controls of the corporation to a new team which included Michael Shabazian, a former president of ComputerLand who serves as IE's president and chief operating officer. "That was a tough decision because, in order to allow the organization to grow and prosper, I felt I had to keep my hands in it," Sanford admitted.

In 1991, IE distributed microcomputer systems and related products and services in the United States and Canada through its network 1,125 franchisees and 66 company-owned stores. A 120,000-square-foot distribution center near Washington, DC ships an average of $3 million of product per day to centers in the U. S. and Canada. According to *Forbes*, IE is the biggest distributor of Apple computers.

Business Obstacles

Sanford founded Todays Computers Business Centers (TCBC) in 1982—retail computer outlets in department stores. His first partner was Philadelphia-based store chain Strawbridge & Clothier. By 1984, he had a simple formula—provide franchises with inventory and employees and rent was a percentage of sales. Then the ground was pulled out from under him when a competitor undercut his prices. While Sanford paid department stores a 4.5 percent royalty on everything he sold, the competitor offered nine percent. "Our phones rang off the hook asking if we would meet the competitors' percentage, and I refused to do it," Sanford said. "It handed over too much control to the stores." The setback destroyed his growth opportunities, but did not deter Sanford's entrepreneurial spirit. "I had three choices—continue on and be swallowed up by my competition; sell out immediately; or find a solution allowing me to unite others on a common front." He chose the latter.

Sanford joined the National Office Machine Dealers of America, an association of about 12,000 sellers of copiers, facsimile machines and phone equipment. Instead of competing in the "big city," he went for established small-town dealers who would welcome his technology and expertise. Under a standard royalty arrangement, stores pay a percentage of their gross sales to the parent company in exchange for services such as marketing assistance and technical support.

Sanford attributes much of his success to this redirection of the organization away from his competition and into a new marketing area. "You normally meet your competition head on," Sanford said, noting his critics said he'd be bankrupt after 18 months. His main competitor filed Chapter 11 bankruptcy after six months.

By 1987, Sanford had 100 TCBC franchises. In June of that year, IE earned a place on *Business Week's* list of "Best Small Companies."

Keys to Success

Flexibility and the ability to react to changes in the marketplace are key factors in Sanford's success. He believes that entrepreneurs often make the dangerous mistake of falling in love with their ideas. "You have to be flexible enough to change your ideas," Sanford said. "Many entrepreneurs develop an idea that makes sense, but when they try it out, it doesn't work. Yet they refuse to change that idea to fit the new model or marketplace, and that refusal often means the demise of the business." One IE executive said that, while Sanford has a reputation for being a tough boss who asks tough questions and delegates authority, "he isn't afraid to roll up his sleeves and do what has to be done."

Sanford keeps the company as lean as possible. "You can't be a financial burden to franchisees," Sanford commented. "They must be involved as partners because they are our sales force." He told *Philadelphia Business Journal* that he helps his franchisees stay competitive by keeping product stocked--94 percent of the time IE has what the dealer ordered and can ship the product out in five hours. Sanford also said that it would be easy to make ego-based decisions and never visit his dealer locations throughout many isolated parts of the U.S. "but you can't grow organizations in ivory towers," Sanford stressed. "You must listen to problems and strategies."

Sanford is known to be a manager concerned about people and not just the bottom line. He went from a company with 55 employees to almost 800 employees within a year, yet he was sensitive to how the mergers would affect people. "I was concerned that people would keep their jobs or that we would at least offer them alternative positions," Sanford said.

He believes it is essential for entrepreneurs to reward loyal employees who stick it out through the hard times. "It's hard to attract good people who will dedicate themselves to building the company," Sanford says, adding he rewards his staff with stock options, making them equity partners in the business.

Future Vision

Sanford's goal for IE was to become the largest reseller of Intelligence-based products in North America—and he has seen that goal become a reality. He continues to champion the cause of dealers, seeking to increase their profitability. While some in the microcomputer industry now charge a royalty for use of a brand name product, Sanford charges on a sales-based, cost-plus agreement. Under a standard royalty agreement, stores pay a percentage of their gross sales in exchange for marketing and technical support. IE allows franchisees to pay the cost of the product purchased plus a percentage markup. This strategy allows more of the profits to be shared, with less emphasis placed on royalties.

He envisions beginning "Intelligent Electronics University," where his firm can attract college-bound persons to an education center for the microcomputer industry. An M.B.A. in micro-electronics would include working at a dealer for two or three years of field training.

Sanford also sees challenges in the microcomputer industry because of a shake-out of store types. "The weak will go and the strong will survive," he notes, adding segmentation of product lines will continue and technologies will merge together to offer the customer the best service.

Entrepreneurial Lessons

One lesson Sanford learned during his entrepreneurial trek is that there is no luck or guesswork involved. "I believe you create your own luck by spending a lot of time researching your opportunity," he said. "There is always a strong element of risk, but you should never bet the ranch. After all, there are a lot of people depending on me. I have a sense of responsibility to them and I can't let them down."

That sense of "responsibility" has also carried over to Sanford's civic involvement. Sanford said he began to share his financial success with those less fortunate than himself—namely terminally ill children. He founded the Sanford Foundation, where fundraising projects match what he contributes to various causes. Recently, $100,000 was given to the "Make A Wish Foundation" for terminally ill children. "I have two children of my own, but I also feel a corporate responsibility to my community," Sanford said.

References

Armstrong, Michael W. "A Fast Entry Into the Area's $1 Billion Club." *Philadelphia Business Journal,* December 17-23, 1990.

Benoit, Ellen. "To Nirvana: Intelligent Electronics Grows Six Times Faster than the Market; For How Long?" *FW,* May 29, 1990.

DeMarzo, Camille. "IE's Power, Approach Send Ripples." *Computer Reseller News,* May 22, 1989.

———. "The Rise of Dick Sanford." *Computer Reseller News,* May 22, 1989.

"Firm Acquires Biz Mart Inc. in a $16.50-a-Share Offer." *Wall Street Journal,* June 18, 1991.

Hilgen, David. "Sanford Has Taken Intelligent Electronics to Largest Computer Network in America." *West Chester Sunday Local News,* January 28, 1990.

Jaffe, Thomas. "Goodwill to All." *Forbes,* June 10, 1991.

Leonard, Bernadette. "Power People: Richard D. Sanford." *Advertising/Communications Times,* March 1991.

Weinstein, Bob. "Smart Moves." *Entrepreneur,* November 1989.

——D. E.

Richard M. Scrushy

HealthSouth Rehabilitation Corporation

Richard M. Scrushy: Born 1952. Married, four children.
Venture: Chain of independent centers offering medical rehabilitation services.
Company: HealthSouth Rehabilitation Corporation; Two Perimeter Park South; Birmingham, AL 35243; (205) 967-7116
Founded: 1984.
Revenues: $180 million in 1990 (1990 annual report).
Employees: 3,800.
Original Investment: $1.3 million.
Value: $224 million, according to *Forbes* magazine, June 1990.

Founder

As a child growing up in Selma, Alabama, Richard Scrushy was motivated by his father's drive for excellence. "Whatever Dad did, he did perfectly. After two decades, people still talk about the Little League team he coached," Scrushy says.

Scrushy was a member of that baseball team, and like his father, he is a high achiever. After earning a degree in respiratory therapy from the University of Alabama at Birmingham (UAB), Scrushy became a UAB instructor. Within 18 months of graduation, he was named director of the program. Scrushy joined Lifemark Corporation, a Houston-based, publicly-owned health care corporation in 1979. He became one of the youngest vice presidents in the company's history and at age 29, he was responsible for more than 2,000 employees and 128 profit centers.

432

Scrushy launched his own business in 1984, and in six years built a multi-million dollar corporation. Today he lives in an antebellum mansion in Alabama and spends much of his free time playing keyboards for a local rock band.

Scrushy serves on the board of directors of Integrated Health Services of Baltimore and he is a member of the Board of Trustees of the Leukemia Society of America, Alabama Chapter. He is also a member of Birmingham's King's Ranch advisory board and an advisor to the board of National Health Industries in Louisville.

Business Origin

Scrushy first considered launching the chain of rehabilitation centers that would become HealthSouth Rehabilitation Corporation in 1983 when a federal prospective pay system began limiting Medicare's reimbursement to hospitals.

In response to the new limits on Medicare funding, hospitals began discharging patients sooner while still in need of sophisticated medical services. Because rehabilitation care was exempt from the prospective pay system, Scrushy believed that he could build a profitable business by organizing fragmented rehabilitation services to meet the increased demand for outpatient care. "I saw the squeezing of reimbursement in the health care system, and I wanted to take advantage of that change," he says. "My idea was to provide high-quality, comprehensive, hospital-type rehab services in a low-cost setting. I believed that by unifying rehabilitation services, we could provide economies of scale that reduced costs and the need for expensive hospitalization, while giving our patients comprehensive service."

When Lifemark merged with Los Angeles-based American Medical International Inc. in 1984, Scrushy brought his idea for rehabilitation clinics to the attention of American Medical management, but the company was not interested. Scrushy decided to pursue his vision on his own.

He left Lifemark on a Friday, and by the following Monday he had moved his family to Birmingham and begun assembling his new company. To fund the venture, Scrushy used $55,000 in savings and $1 million from a venture capital division of Citicorp. Four Lifemark executives moved to Birmingham to join him, and together they opened Amcare Inc. in late 1983. The company changed its name to HealthSouth Rehabilitation in 1985.

When they began, Scrushy and his colleagues shared a one-room office that housed two desks, one telephone and four chairs, making it necessary for one of the five men to work at home each day. "People think I'm joking when I tell that story, but it's the truth," Scrushy says.

Business Growth

Scrushy structured HealthSouth to serve entire communities by providing them with a range of services not offered by other rehabilitation centers. HealthSouth facilities offered specialized rehabilitation services to people with disabilities caused by illness or injury, as well as specialized services in sports medicine, work injury prevention, head injury and spinal cord injury.

The first HealthSouth facility opened in September 1984 in Little Rock, Arkansas. Within 90 days, HealthSouth opened its second facility in Birmingham.

In May 1985, HealthSouth acquired an 88-bed facility in South Carolina and began offering inpatient services. While the cost of rapid early growth brought financial losses to HealthSouth in its first few years of operation, by the end of 1985 the company generated revenues of $4.7 million and managed seven rehabilitation facilities in six states.

In 1986, HealthSouth's first public offering raised $15 million and company revenues rose to $19.7 million that year. Revenues more than doubled to $51.8 million in 1987, and HealthSouth raised $24 million through a second stock offering.

HealthSouth's revenues reached nearly $90 million in 1988 and rose sharply to $149 million in 1989. In early 1989, the company raised $52 million in a convertible subordinated debenture offering. In May of that year, HealthSouth was listed for the first time on the New York Stock Exchange, making it one of only 13 health care companies on the "Big Board." Also in 1989, the company purchased South Highlands Hospital, a 219-bed facility in Birmingham specializing in sports medicine. According to *Hospital News*, the new HealthSouth Medical Center is "palatial," resembling a "towering glass palace."

In seven years, HealthSouth has provided services to more than 100,000 patients. The company operates 60 inpatient and outpatient rehabilitation centers in 23 states. HealthSouth is considered the nation's largest independent provider of medical and rehabilitation services and was eleventh on the 1989 *Inc.* magazine list of the 100 fastest-growing small public companies in America.

Forbes magazine described HealthSouth facilities as "more like high-priced health clubs than hospitals," noting that "some patients peddle exercise bikes while rock music blares. Old and young people work out side by side on exercise machines, some alone and others supervised by therapists. There are private treatment rooms and physical, occupational and speech therapy departments. Computers are linked to testing machines that send reports to doctors on how their patients are responding to treatment," the magazine reports.

Business Obstacles

In May 1988, a report critical of HealthSouth was released by the investment firm Drexel Burnham Lambert. The report raised concerns about HealthSouth's financial stability and lead to a sharp decline in the price of HealthSouth stock. In the report, Drexel Burnham said that HealthSouth's rapid expansion had meant significant "growing pains" for the company. The firm cited HealthSouth for "inadequate management controls" that caused a "serious collections problem" for the company.

CEO Scrushy publicly disagreed with the Drexel Burnham report, saying that it was compiled by "a not very smart, aggressive young analyst," and was filled with "inaccuracies." He said, "What we've done here is meet or surpass everything we set out to do in our original five-year plan. We've done everything we said we were going to do and more."

Scrushy calls the report an "inconvenience. It was like I was driving along and I had to take my eyes off the road for a minute," he says. "But you have to accept the fact that when you live in a fishbowl, people are going to shoot at you."

To fund its growth, HealthSouth relied on funds from investors and a $50 million convertible debenture offering. Despite the company's indebtedness, not all analysts believed that HealthSouth was troubled. Frank G. Morgan, a securities analyst with First Birmingham Securities Corporation, observed in May 1988 that HealthSouth's operations were beginning to generate sufficient cash to meet the company's operational needs. "I think they've turned the corner, if you could say there was ever a corner there," he said. "Operationally, the company is doing very well."

HealthSouth remains highly leveraged, according to a June 1990 *Forbes* article. However, the magazine also reports that "HealthSouth has $32 million in cash and marketable securities, $50 million available on a credit line and more than $10 million in estimated cash flow available from operations this year. The chances are that HealthSouth will be able to continue its rapid rate of expansion for as long as the insurance companies remain willing to foot the rehabilitation bills," the article says.

Scrushy says that the company is prepared to handle rapid growth because it was "built right."

Keys to Success

Scrushy carved a market niche for HealthSouth by providing affordable outpatient rehabilitation services in areas where few other providers existed. He expanded the services offered by HealthSouth facilities by listening to customer needs. "We're set up to serve entire communities, help more patients, offer better equipment and more varied programs," Scrushy says.

Although skeptics doubted his potential for success, Scrushy remained confident. "I never thought it was anything but a great idea," he says. "Early on, I actually had visions of these facilities operating all over the country. I believed in the idea enough to convince other people to help me pursue it. Some people thought I was crazy, but some in the business knew it wasn't," Scrushy says.

Industry analysts agree that Scrushy tapped a market ripe for success. "HealthSouth was in the right industry at the right time," Sterne, Agee & Leach securities analyst Steve Huffines told *The Birmingham News* in May 1989. "They perceived the need for rehabilitation services and cornered a major market share very rapidly," he said. "We have always had a very clear direction," Scrushy says. "Nobody has any question about where the company is going. We don't spend a whole lot of time talking about what we're going to do. We spend a lot of time doing it. That's one thing that's made us successful."

Scrushy strives to keep "bureaucracy at a minimum" at HealthSouth and to discuss new ideas as they are raised. "We don't have a single committee in this company. You don't need a committee to tell you if an idea is good or not," he says. "If somebody wants to discuss an idea, we'll do it right there and then, even if its in the hallway."

Scrushy calls HealthSouth employees the key to the company's success. "I hire people who know how to make things happen. As a result, there's a lot of energy and enthusiasm in this company. We all work hard and have fun doing it. If we didn't enjoy working here, I don't think HealthSouth would work," he says.

HealthSouth's sports medicine therapists, many of whom are former athletes, coaches or trainers, volunteer at high school and college athletic practices to treat injuries and educate young athletes about preventing injuries.

More than 80 percent of HealthSouth's top management are former therapists or other types of clinicians. According to Scrushy, this gives them a keen understanding of the company's service mission, great patient empathy and a strong sense of what the company can accomplish.

Scrushy has commented that his clinical background was of more benefit to him than an MBA. "An MBA would have been one of the biggest mistakes of my career," he told *Rehabilitation Today*. "I feel that having been 'in the trenches' and having had on-the-job training has given me a better perspective than a business degree would have—and certainly an earlier start in getting my real career underway."

Scrushy says that one of his greatest challenges is finding experienced managers in a relatively young industry. He has established an extensive in-house management training program as a way to develop quality management talent. "He has been a kind of visionary through all this," one of Scrushy's associates told *The Birmingham News*. HealthSouth staff say that their CEO's vision is reflected in the "look and feel" within each HealthSouth facility.

Future Vision

In a 1988 *Birmingham News* article, Huffines of Sterne, Agee said that while "HealthSouth can't keep up its historic growth rates indefinitely," he believes the rehabilitation industry will continue to grow at least for the next few years. Huffines says that HealthSouth put itself ahead of the competition by expanding quickly, but he predicts that competitors will enter the market. "It's the law of the jungle. You put a big piece of meat out there and a cave man here and a cave man there comes out and wants a piece of it," he says. "But HealthSouth already has a tremendous jump on everybody else."

Scrushy intends to stay well ahead of the competition. "I expect we're on track to be a 500-billion-dollar company," he says. "I don't see any end to the business potential in outpatient services, but I believe that in another eight to 10 years, we'll see a slowdown in inpatient hospitals. We are already the nation's largest provider of rehabilitation services and we want to be America's brand-name rehabilitation company," Scrushy says.

While Scrushy has big plans for HealthSouth, he holds strong ties to the small-town atmosphere in which he was raised. "You know what I'd really like some day?" he says. "I want to coach Little League and build the best baseball team in Alabama."

Entrepreneurial Lessons

Scrushy's entrepreneurial success has brought him significant personal wealth, and he uses his success as a way to motivate HealthSouth management. "I own the best Mercedes there is so my young executives have something to look forward to," he told *Esquire* magazine in 1987.

Scrushy models his management philosophy on that of legendary University of Alabama football coach Paul "Bear" Bryant—"There ain't nothing like a winner. Feel good, have class, and always be number one."

References

Deutschman, Alan. "America's Fastest Risers." *Fortune*, October 7, 1991.

Gill, Mark. "Turning Health into Wealth." *Esquire*, September 1987.

"HealthSouth Rehabilitation." *Bama Chatter*, February/March 1990.

Ingram, C. "HealthSouth Is Running 'Right Track,' Chief Says." *The Birmingham News*, May 28, 1989.

Kilpatrick, A. "HealthSouth Rehabilitated Health Care." *Birmingham Post Herald*, May 30, 1989.

Mamis, Robert A. "The Inc. 100." *Inc.*, May 1990.

"Palatial Expansion Is Centerpiece of HealthSouth's Nationwide Growth." *Hospital News*, September 1991.

Singleton, Vince. "HealthSouth Holds Grand Opening." *Kingsport Time-News*, September 25, 1991.

Taravella, Steve. "Rehabilitation Providers Expect Radical Change Following Rapid Industry Growth." *Modern Healthcare*, June 3, 1988.

Wallace, Cynthia. "Rehabilitative Care Moving to Lower-Cost Treatment Centers." *Modern Healthcare*, January 15, 1988.

Wilder, Marvin. "Richard Scrushy: The Powerhouse Behind HealthSouth." *Rehabilitation Today*, May 1991.

——M. J. B.

G. Arthur Seelbinder

Cooker Restaurant Corporation

G. Arthur Seelbinder: Born 1943. Married.
Venture: Restaurant chain specializing in traditional American fare and excellent service.
Company: Cooker Restaurant Corporation; 1530 Bethel Road; Columbus, OH 43220; (614) 457-8500
Founded: 1986.
Revenues: $33.8 million (1990), according to a company source.
Employees: 1,264.
Original Investment: $500 to start corporation.
Value: $32 million (1989).

Founder

G. Arthur Seelbinder can chuckle as he recounts an incident from his past. In 1968, with youthful naivete, a negative net worth and no collateral, he approached a bank officer for a loan of $7 million to help finance his first real estate project. The officer laughed, Seelbinder's project never got off the ground, and he learned a valuable lesson. "I didn't realized then that you needed to have money to make money," he said. "Having money" presents no problem for Seelbinder now. Starting with nothing, he built his first million by the time he was 30.

Seelbinder put himself through Ohio State University by working with computers from 4:00 A.M. until noon everyday, then attending afternoon classes. A diving/gymnastics scholarship helped fund the remainder of his education. He graduated in 1965 with a B.S. degree in finance.

He formed Arthur Seelbinder & Company, Inc., an independent mortgage and real estate brokerage firm in 1970. For more than 15 years Seelbinder's firm specialized in commercial real estate financing and development. That corporation has since merged with CTI Restaurants, Inc., the forerunner of Cooker Restaurant Corporation.

In addition to his diverse business pursuits, Seelbinder's varied personal interests include racing thoroughbred horses and reading. He particularly enjoys biographies of entrepreneurs and other businessmen, professing special admiration for the business acumen and management skills of Leslie Wexner, founder of The Limited.

Business Origin

Cooker Restaurant Corporation was organized in 1986 by Seelbinder and three business associates. The company initially operated four restaurants, developing the Cooker name and operating concept. Early operations and growth were financed by limited public stock offerings to Ohio residents. Plans called for steady expansion.

Cooker emphasizes service, quality and value. Its menu features well-prepared, moderately priced food items served in a comfortable atmosphere. The company focuses its resources on providing superior service to existing customers, and relies on word-of-mouth advertising and the reputation of the restaurants to attract new and repeat business.

Located in Tennessee, Ohio, Indiana and most recently Michigan, Cooker Restaurants typically have seating for about 230 customers in a facility of 7,800 square feet. Kitchens are large and designed for quality and speed of food preparation. Wood, brass and framed graphic art create a casual and contemporary decor.

Business Growth

Thirteen restaurants have been added since Cooker's inception. The company's revenues increased nearly tenfold in three years.

In 1989 Cooker Restaurant Corporation went public, its NASDAQ-listed stock raising about $12.2 million. The funds were used to retire $7.8 million of bank debt and to fund further expansion.

According to Seelbinder, even in a year (1989) which was far from one of the restaurant industry's best, Cooker Restaurant Corporation continued to grow. "Increases in profitability outpace our gains in sales," he said.

Business Obstacles

In his early years in business, Seelbinder's greatest problem was a lack of capital. At twenty-four, he says, he looked "more like twelve," and had difficulty convincing banks to take him seriously. Eventually he secured small loans and took his first steps on the road to success.

Seelbinder now finds debt to be motivating. "No matter how much money I make, I always manage to accrue enough debt to have to work a little harder," he says.

Cooker must constantly deal with the intensely competitive nature of the restaurant industry. The food business is often affected by changes in consumer tastes, economic conditions, demographics, traffic patterns, availability of employees and cost increases. Cooker battles back by constant monitoring of quality, value and service.

The corporation also suffered a major conflict among its top executives. Shortly after its 1989 stock offering, Cooker president Philip J. Hickey led an outside group's buyout attempt of Seelbinder's 16 percent stake in the company. He failed, was ousted by the board, and Seelbinder became president and chairman. Hickey sold his 530,536 shares to a newly formed employees stock ownership plan. Gerald Hornbeck, Cooker's vice president of development, also resigned and sold his shares to the ESOP.

While Seelbinder does not discuss details of the conflict, he does say, "These things happen. People disagree and someone had to leave—it certainly wasn't going to be me. There was a minor setback because of the incident, but we've moved on."

In the opinion of securities analyst Barry M. Stouffer of J. C. Bradford, "Obviously, it's highly unusual for something like this to transpire this soon after a public offering. If you lose the guy who's in charge of operation, there has to be a void. As long as the company is able to fill that void in a reasonable time frame, then there's no reason to expect that the company will have any long-term problems as a result of this."

Keys to Success

Seelbinder attributes his success to several significant factors. He believes that his attitude toward debt has played an important role in all his business achievements. "As long as you're committed to repaying your debts, you have to continue to work. There have been many times when I was in a position in which other men would have thrown in the towel, but I didn't," says Seelbinder. "We live in a time when many people feel it isn't important to pay one's debts," he continues, "but for reasons partly of pride and partly because it makes good business sense, I get tougher in that kind of corner. Through sheer ingenuity alone, I have always paid my debts."

Seelbinder's ability to adjust to the difference between real estate and the restaurant business has been a strong factor in Cooker's growth. "In real estate," he says, "you have to perform independently, whereas in the restaurant business it is possible to delegate responsibility to the right people."

Seelbinder actually prefers the restaurant business, because he likes the people who work with him, and who themselves are excited by the business. Success, he says, comes from letting those people do their jobs.

In 1989, the company formed an employee stock ownership plan. The plan allows employees at all company levels to take a personal interest in and share in the rewards of Cooker Restaurants' future successes. "We have a team of dedicated hardworking employees, led by a management team who have made Cooker restaurants the success we are today. It is fitting that these past and future efforts be rewarded with the opportunity to establish a significant ownership state in the company," Seelbinder says.

Future Vision

The company's founder sees Cooker Restaurant Corporation growing indefinitely. It has a 30 to 40 percent growth rate yearly, compounded, and still funds itself. "It's the first business I've found that will do that consistently," Seelbinder observes.

He thinks Cooker is well-positioned for the long term. The restaurants take advantage of changing demographics—more aging "baby boomers" who, with more discretionary income, increasingly seek reasonably-priced dinner houses rather than fast-food restaurants.

The company anticipates that further expansion will be in medium to large metropolitan areas in the Midwest and the East, or in certain markets in which the company already profitably operates units.

Entrepreneurial Lessons

During his years in business, Arthur Seelbinder has learned several significant lessons. For 20 years, he was a real estate and mortgage broker and dabbled in many different businesses. Had he realized earlier that a single ongoing business could be as profitable and exciting as many, he reveals, he would have concentrated on finding that one business. "I always thought that diversity was the key," he says. "But now I think that *focus* on the best opportunities is the better route." Although Seelbinder admits he'll always be intrigued by an interesting new venture, he plans to stay with and expand the restaurant business.

Seelbinder uses a personal example to illustrate what he believes are essential entrepreneurial qualities: "When I place a two dollar bet," says the horse fancier, "I don't believe it's the potential money that's important—its the winning and the risktaking."

"If money is what you want," Seelbinder advises would-be entrepreneurs, "you can make it by being a high-paid employee. Entrepreneurship is primarily about controlling your life and your time—making money is only secondary."

References

Chaudry, Rajan. "Cooker Prexy Exits After Failed Buyout Try." *Nation's Restaurant News*, October 2, 1989.

———. "Cooker's IPO Nets $12.2 Million." *Nation's Restaurant News*, June 26, 1989.

Cooker Restaurant Corporation Prospectus, June 13, 1989.

Kimmins, Dick. "Cooker Pursues Offering Despite Market Slump." *Business First-Columbus*, November 2, 1987.

———C. A. C.

Alan F. Shugart

Seagate Technology, Inc.

Alan F. Shugart: Born 1930. Married, five children.
Venture: Manufacturer of magnetic hard disk drives for personal computers.
Company: Seagate Technology, Inc.; 920 Disc Drive, Bldg. 1; Scotts Valley, CA 95066; (408) 438-6550
Founded: 1978.
Revenues: $2.6 billion in net sales in fiscal 1991, according to company sources.
Employees: 40,000 worldwide.
Original Investment: $850,000.
Value: Net worth $442 million (June 30, 1989). Market value $641 million.

Founder

Alan F. Shugart, a native of Los Angeles, received a bachelor degree in engineering/physics from the University of Redlands (California) in 1951. Shugart got his start at IBM and eventually worked his way up to become director of engineering. In 1969 Shugart became vice-president of Memorex Corporation, a leader in magnetic data storage products. In 1973 he founded Shugart Associates, a pioneer of the small disk drive. A year later, he was forced out after a fundamental disagreement with the board of directors on company financing.

For the next five years, Shugart shunned the Silicon Valley pressures and chose to live in a beach house on Monterey Bay. He found a variety of ways to "enjoy himself," including running a commercial fishing boat in search of salmon and albacore. He even tended bar at a Santa Cruz drinking establishment called "The Castaways" that he and a friend bought. During his beach-house period, however, Shugart kept current with the computer industry by consulting with computer disk drive companies.

Business Origin

In 1978, Finis Conner, a former associate, called Shugart at the beach house to tell him his idea for a 5 1/4 inch winchester disk drive using a hard, non-removable disk. Other companies, including Shugart Associates, made bigger ones, but nobody had one that would fit in personal computers. Shugart and Conner decided to build it and Seagate Technology was born. "There was no altruism involved," says Shugart. "Everybody wanted to get rich."

Shugart and Conner also brought in David T. Mitchell and Syed Iftikar. Six weeks after the business plan was finished, and after being turned down by ten venture capitalists, the four founders were funded by C. Norman Dion of Dysan Corporation, maker of the magnetic disks inside the drives. Dion put in $450,000, lent $100,000 to each of the founders and committed more.

Shugart, Conner, Iftikar, and Dion had worked together at Memorex Corporation in the early 1970s. Previously, many of them had been at IBM's disk drive plant. Shugart had been dubbed the "Pied Piper" in the industry as he led engineers from IBM to Memorex to Shugart Associates and finally to Seagate.

Business Growth

Seagate opened its doors December 1, 1979 and delivered the industry's first 5 1/4 winchester disk drive the following July. Seagate's rapid growth followed the explosive growth of the personal computer industry which was still in its early stages.

By 1984 Seagate was clearly the industry leader with annual sales of $344 million. Seagate's command of the market was largely due to its low manufacturing costs. That changed when competitors dropped their prices and Japanese manufacturers entered the market. In a series of dramatic moves, Seagate moved its manufacturing to Singapore, lowered its costs for manufacturing and components, and regained its market share. "You ride the roller coaster by hanging on real tightly," Shugart told *Forbes*. "If you loosen your grip, it's all over."

By 1987 Seagate had 60 percent of the 5 1/4 hard-disk market and revenues approaching $1 billion. Sales continued to grow through the late 1980s, in large part due to an increased percentage of computers sold at the retail level with hard drives installed. The continuing trend toward larger and more sophisticated software requiring larger and more expensive drives also boosted revenues.

In the early days, the Seagate management team would "meet practically continually to discuss the management of the company," Shugart says. "Each person in the management team has an equal voice at meetings. It's like a jury," he says. "We keep working until we agree."

In 1983, Shugart gave up his spot as president to the firm's co-founder, David Mitchell. While Shugart wasn't involved in the day-to-day operations of the company, he would still start work at 7:00 A.M. and coordinate marketing, tradeshows, annual reports and corporate communications. However, in September 1991 Mitchell resigned and Shugart, stepping down as chairman, was once again president of Seagate.

Controlling costs has been a prime focus of Seagate management in the cost-driven disk-drive market. Most disk-drive makers are really assemblers, buying disks from one source, printed circuit boards from another, motors from a third. Seagate has done this as well, but since the mid-1980s it has been making more of its components to lower its manufacturing costs. In 1985 the company purchased Grenex, a California maker of computer disks. It also began making its own printed circuit boards which control the motors and heads in the drive. "We wanted to be in control of our own destiny," says Shugart.

Only 1,400 of 40,000 employees are at the Scotts Valley headquarters. The rest work mainly at overseas manufacturing facilities in Singapore and Thailand. The company also maintains sales offices throughout Europe and the Far East.

Business Obstacles

The key to Seagate's rapid growth was IBM's decision to house Seagate drives in the IBM PC-XT in the early 1980s. At one point, IBM accounted for 70 percent of Seagate's sales. This dependency brought serious trouble to the company when IBM cancelled its orders with Seagate in late 1984. In one quarter, Seagate's revenue dropped from $100 million to $50 million. As the company stumbled through three straight quarters of disappointing sales, Shugart and Mitchell had to act fast. Seagate fired about 1,000 employees, moved its manufacturing offshore, and widened its customer base. "We were going from a significant profit to an insignificant profit very quickly, and we needed to avoid that," Shugart said. In addition, other manufacturers were starting to set up offshore operations. According to Shugart, if Seagate didn't cut its costs, it could die.

The firings created a lot of animosity in Silicon Valley. A year later, a county job placement officer remarked, "I've worked with people who say they won't go back to Seagate, even when I say Seagate needs 60 people right now." "Layoffs are never easy," says Shugart, "But you're damned if you do, and damned if you don't." Most of the Seagate workers were able to find new jobs in the industry, including many who were offered new jobs at Seagate.

IBM, ironically, also suffered from the Seagate cancellation. The computer-maker switched to Computer Memories Inc. (CMI) as its hard disk-drive source. Problems with the CMI drives forced IBM eventually to shift back to Seagate. By 1986, Seagate had diversified its customer base, with IBM accounting for only 16 percent of sales. In 1987, Shugart helped strike a $200 million deal with IBM to supply high-end disk drives for IBM's new PS/2 line of computers.

Keys to Success

"In the beginning, timing was everything as evidenced by the 40 or 50 competitors that came in," says Shugart of Seagate's leap to the top in the early days of the industry. "Shugart is one of the few people in this industry who has ever succeeded twice," said industry analyst, William Frank, of Shugart's success with Seagate after being forced out of Shugart Associates.

True to his fishing boat days, Shugart has managed to navigate the stormy ups and downs of the industry. When Seagate's stock dropped due to nervous reaction by investors to IBM's unveiling of the PS/2 line, he personally took all the phone calls to calm the fears of troubled investors. "He just jumps right into things when they're critical to the company," Frank continues. "He's a manager who runs a very tight ship, and he's very intimately involved with what's going on."

Shugart spends much of his time meeting with customers and analysts at a staggering pace. During one week in 1987, he visited 60 different customers across Europe.

He brings this tenacity to all aspects of his work. Co-founder Doug Mahon says Shugart got to where he is because he grasps issues quickly. "You don't have to spend any amount of time explaining a problem, just hit the highlights. And, he mitigates what he does with humor, even if what you're doing is unpleasant. Most people who are quick are abrasive. He's not." A typical Shugart retort, according to Mahon, would go, "That's not the worst idea I've ever heard, but it's close."

Future Vision

In 1989 the company acquired Imprimis Technology Incorporated, a manufacturer of high-capacity drives used in multi-user systems, scientific workstations, and other high-end computer systems. The acquisition of Imprimis boosted Seagate's sales from $1.3 billion to $2.5 billion, and gives the company a 45 percent share of the market.

The high-end Imprimis drives will complement Seagate's previous product line of low-cost, lower-capacity drives used in desk-top computers. Following industry trends, Seagate also plans to continue developing ever-higher storage capacities in its low-cost 5 1/4 inch and 3 1/2 inch drives.

Entrepreneurial Lessons

Roger Smith, a Silicon Valley banker who has known Shugart since his early days, describes him as "a smart, hard-working guy who learned his lessons and continues to." Shugart, Smith says succinctly, is "a realist."

Reflecting on the lessons learned when Seagate's survival was at stake, Shugart says, "It was a good learning experience. Going through those times made us lean and mean."

Shugart has distilled his lessons into four rules which he says he tries to follow: "Treat other companies the way you'd like to be treated." "If it's not broken, don't fix it." "Keep it simple." "Cash is more important than your mother."

References

Arnett, Nick. "Shugart Didn't Like the Easy Life, So He Decided to Get Rich." *The Business Journal-San Jose*, December 31, 1984.

"The CEO 1000." *Business Week*, October 20, 1989.

Greer, Jonathan. "The Fall and Rise of Seagate Technology." *San Jose Mercury News*, May 12, 1986.

Jones, Stephen. "From a Fishing Boat to 'Disc Drive,' Shugart Enjoys Life." *San Jose Business Journal*, June 15, 1987.

McGee, Marianne Kolbasuk. "Seagate President Resigns As Vendor Tries New Formula." *Computer Systems News*, September 23, 1991.

Oppenheimer, Cris. "For Disk-Drive Maker Seagate, 1986 Was a Very Good Year." *San Jose Mercury News*, June 8, 1987.

Pitta, Julie. "The Survivor." *Forbes*, July 8, 1991.

"Ten Top U.S. Chief Executives." *Electronic Business*, September 3, 1990.

———B. M.

Roy M. Speer

Home Shopping Network, Inc.

Roy M. Speer: Born 1932. Married, three children.
Venture: Twenty-four-hour television shopping program broadcast over cable systems and company-owned UHF stations.
Company: Home Shopping Network, Inc.; P.O. Box 9090; Clearwater, FL 34618-9090; (813) 572-8585
Founded: 1982.
Revenues: $1 billion in fiscal 1990, according to a company source.
Employees: 5,000 plus.
Original Investment: $2 million.
Value: $273 million (ASE, May 1990).

Founder

"I've never worked for anyone else, and I never will," says entrepreneur Roy Speer. Described by others as a "climber," who is "never short on drive," Speer has made his fortune by investing in everything from real estate to radio stations.

Raised by his mother in Key West, Florida, Speer left home after high school and earned a business degree from Southern Methodist University and a law degree from Florida's Stetson University. Speer was more interested in business than law, however. "I didn't want to spend my life working on other peoples' problems," he says.

From the late 1960s to the mid 1970s, Speer invested in real estate, developing 4,000 acres and building 15,000 homes. Speer says that the business earned him profits of $30 to $40 million. When the real estate market softened in the 1970s, Speer diversified his business holdings. In the past two decades, he has invested in a beauty parlor, a boat dealership, restaurants, Texas oil wells, mobile home parks, TV and radio stations, and a Caribbean pineapple farm. He has financial interests in more than 15 ventures.

Business Origin

The idea for Speer's most successful venture, Home Shopping Network (HSN), originated at Speer's Clearwater, Florida, radio station. In 1977, the station's co-owner Lowell Paxson accepted 120 can openers as payment from an advertiser. Paxson sold the can openers over the air at discount prices. The public responded so well that Paxson created "The Bargaineers," a show dedicated to on-air merchandise sales.

Speer and Paxson believed that a Bargaineers-type show for television would be a great success. Once the Clearwater area was wired for cable television in 1982, they began broadcasting their "Home Shopping Channel" to 10,000 area homes. Speer's $500,000 investment gave him a 60 percent stake in the local venture.

Business Growth

The Home Shopping Channel was profitable within three months of going on the air. Convinced that the concept would work on a national scale, Speer launched the Home Shopping Network in 1985. HSN's around-the-clock shopping program reached a nation-wide audience via local cable stations.

HSN sales grew to $160 million in 1986. That year, Speer took HSN public in an overwhelmingly successful initial public offering. HSN stock debuted at a price of $18 a share and rose to $43.63 a share by the end of the first day of trading. In the months that followed, the stock price climbed to more than $100 a share, and HSN stock split 3-for-1 in September 1986. In October, HSN sold 1.5 million shares in a second public offering. The stock split 2-for-1 in December. Speer had become a multi-billionaire in what the *St. Petersburg* (Florida) *Times* called "one of the greatest stock-buying frenzies in Wall Street history."

By April 1987, HSN sales reached of $582 million. The company had 4,300 employees and was sending out 60,000 pieces of merchandise a day. To expand its audience to people without access to cable television, HSN bought eight UHF stations and built two others, launching a second HSN network for broadcast television.

Home Shopping's combination of broadcast TV stations and cable stations gave the Network the ability to reach 50 percent of American homes by 1988. Sales rose to $730 million that year and $1 billion in fiscal 1990.

From 1987 to 1989, Speer diversified HSN operations and purchased a pharmaceutical company, an electronic ticketing company and a financial planning firm. He saw that these companies' products would add to the variety of merchandise available to HSN viewers. Many of these business were divested in 1989 as part of a shift in the company's business strategy.

In 1991, HSN formed a joint venture with an L.A.-based music promoter to merchandise T-shirts, tapes and musical paraphernalia, "a sort of MTV with price tags," according to *Forbes* magazine. HSN also made plans to launch Home Shopping Network Entertainment, a 24-hour-a-day channel showing infomercials (long commercials) and live programming. A deal with NBC for a daytime shopping show was in the works and plans for HSN 800/900 telephone services were in the offing.

Business Obstacles

Although HSN enjoyed overwhelming growth in net sales, profits declined steadily from 1987 to 1989. Analysts have attributed the fall to many factors including increased competition, a lack of management depth at HSN and viewer boredom with HSN product offerings. According to a February 1989 article in the *St. Petersburg Times*, HSN critics believed that "An ingenious marketing tool has been wasted selling imitation diamonds, inexpensive porcelain and kewpie dolls to an audience of hard-core devotees and shut-ins."

Since its initial offering, HSN's stock price has fluctuated, dropping to as low as $4 a share in 1989. Many HSN investors have either made or lost significant amounts of money depending on when they bought their shares. A group of shareholders sued HSN, charging that Speer and Paxson had manipulated the stock market to inflate share prices and enrich themselves.

Analysts say that a stock like HSN, which had a great rise in price after offering, is subject to wide price swings. Robert Sobel, a professor at New York's Hofstra University told the *St. Petersburg Times*, "It happens with every concept stock. The concept made sense, but the projections made no sense." Others like Boston stock analyst Mark Friedman have called HSN a "story" stock. "They had a great story to tell: Each TV was a store," Friedman told the *St. Petersburg Times*.

Speer was convinced that problems with HSN's telephone system cost the Network business and profits. Questions about the telephone system resulted in a billion-dollar lawsuit with between HSN and GTE Corporation. HSN claimed that GTE sold the company inadequate telephone systems and tried to hide the error. GTE countersued for slander and libel and was awarded $100 million in damages. After considering appeal, HSN settled the suit and paid GTE a cash award.

Speer attributes HSN's profit decline to the cost associated with the company's divestiture of subsidiaries. In his 1989 message to shareholders, he says that the company's net loss of $14.9 million in 1989 came "as a result of taking $28 million in special, non-recurring write-offs primarily associated with discontinuing or reducing certain of the company's subsidiary operations." Speer says that HSN will "rededicate itself to the financial success of its core business."

Keys to Success

"I knew how big a success this was going to be the second we were on TV," Speer says. "We combined the influence of television, the solid backbone of retailing and the natural need to get something for nothing and created one of the greatest business relationships ever conceived. "The whole concept is driven by television—an immensely powerful medium," he adds. "All we ask people to do is reach for their telephone—they don't have to get up and go anywhere to buy our merchandise. We're offering them convenience and service."

Speer's program formula is much the same today as it was in the early days of the Home Shopping Channel. Items appear on the viewer's television screen with a toll-free telephone number that shoppers call to make purchases. On-air hosts describe the items and take calls from viewers. New merchandise is introduced about every seven minutes, and the show runs 14-hours-a-day, 365 days a year.

HSN's $100 million computerized telemarketing center manages customer orders and viewer telephone calls. "That's our secret ingredient," Speer says. "We spent five years developing an infrastructure so solid no amount of volume can faze us. Home Shopping is the 'world's largest telemarketing operation.'"

In the beginning, Speer interested cable stations in airing HSN programming by offering them commissions on HSN sales and the option to buy company stock. He bought discounted merchandise in volume and was able to sell items at lower prices than consumers would find in retail stores. The Network's start-up costs included computers, satellite rentals and cable commissions.

HSN has developed a loyal following of viewers eager to take advantage of TV bargains. One viewer told the *St. Petersburg Times*, "You can very easily become addicted. It's almost like I have to have it. In all my years of shopping, I've never felt an urge like that."

Home Shopping is a form of entertainment to many viewers. "I watch in the morning before I go to work and then for an hour or so at night," a viewer said in a recent *Florida Magazine* article. "I'm not a television freak, and I really don't watch any other television shows—but you get addicted to this one. The hosts are like family; you get to know them."

Speer admits that he does not watch his own program. "I only turn it on late at night, if twenty ideas are chasing each other around in my head and I can't sleep," he says.

Speer regularly works 12 to 14 hours a day, six days a week. He conducts business even while exercising in his home gym or traveling in his car. "I guess I am the personification of the work ethic," Speer says. "I love my work, so the hours fly by."

Future Vision

In his 1989 message to shareholders, Speer outlined his goals for HSN. "Nationwide consumer response to electronic retailing continues to be strong," he says, citing an analyst's estimate that the industry will achieve sales of $2.5 billion in 1993. "Through the cable and broadcast media, HSN reaches a majority of the 90 million television households in the United States, and we are working vigorously to expand our television reach," he continues. "[Our] greatest challenge is to increase the level of penetration in each of our markets."

"The company is in transition from a stock-market phenomenon to becoming a real business," said Andrew Racz, director of a New York investment firm in a February 1989 *St. Petersburg Times* article. "If they touch the right merchandise, things will be dramatically better," he said.

Speer intends to continue heading the Network. "I never plan more than three to five years ahead of time, and I expect to be here for at least that long. If you're inquisitive, ingenious and love to work hard, this is like plugging into a hotline," he says.

Entrepreneurial Lessons

Although Speer's success has brought him great wealth, he says money has not changed him. "I've always been very fortunate and made a lot of money. It doesn't make a whole lot of difference if you go from $50 million to $1 billion. You can only drive one car. You can only wear one or two suits of clothes."

Through HSN, Speer shares his good fortune with the local community. HSN has donated millions of dollars worth of goods and services to orphanages in the Tampa Bay, Florida area. The company sponsored St. Petersburg's Martin Luther King Day parade in January 1990. HSN also sponsored a telethon to raise money for a drug treatment program headquartered in St. Petersburg. "When you have success, you owe it to the community to share it," Speer says.

References

Corvini, M. "Success Brought Riches, More Work." *Tampa Tribune*, January 4, 1987.

Gill, Mark. "The Rise and Rise of HSN." *Esquire*, April 1987.

Greiff, J. "At the Controls." *St. Petersburg Times*, February 7, 1989.

———. "Criticism Hits Home." *St. Petersburg Times*, February 6, 1989.

———. "Stock's Story Fueled Frenzy on Wall Street." *St. Petersburg Times*, February 8, 1989.

Higgins, John M. "HSN Developing Show for NBC." *Multichannel News*, May 27, 1991.

"HSN's Expansion Team." *Tampa Tribune*, May 12, 1991.

James, E. "So What's a Billion to Roy Speer?" *Venture*, May 1987.

Newcomb, Peter. "Shop Along With Doc." *Forbes,* July 8, 1991.

Thompson, Rachel W. "HSN to Hawk T-Shirts, Music with L.A. Promoter." *Multichannel News,* May 13, 1991.

——M. J. B.

Thomas G. Stemberg

Staples, Inc.

Thomas G. Stemberg: Born 1949. Married, four children.
Venture: A retail chain of deep-discounted office products and furniture in a no frills supermarket-style setting.
Company: Staples, Inc.; 100 Penn Ave.; P.O. Box 9328; Framingham, MA 01701-9328; (508) 370-8500
Founded: November 1985; first store opened in May 1986.
Revenues: $299 million in fiscal 1991, according to published reports.
Employees: 3,000.
Original Investment: $4.5 million in venture capital, according to company sources.
Value: $66 million in stockholder's equity, according to company sources.

Founder

Tom Stemberg, the son of Austrian restauranteurs, was born in Orange, New Jersey. At the age of 13 with the loss of his father, Stemberg moved to Vienna with his mother. He later returned to the United States to attend Harvard College, graduating in 1971. In 1973 he graduated from the Harvard Business School as a George F. Baker Scholar.

Before founding Staples, Stemberg had already proven himself in discount supermarket stores, rising to vice president for sales and merchandising at Jewel's Star Markets. He developed and launched the first line of generic foods to be sold in the U.S. He also introduced warehouse specials on selected items. Stemberg's innovations raised Star Markets' sales ranking in the competitive Boston market from fourth to a tie for first place.

As president of the Edwards-Finast division of First National Supermarkets, Stemberg established the Edwards Food Warehouse chain. The success formula for this network of high volume megastores: cut costs, buy in volume and slash selling prices.

A member of the National Office Products Association's Member Services Advisory Committee, Stemberg participates and speaks at office products industry seminars and conferences. He serves as a director of Petsmart, deep-discount retailer of pet supplies. He is an active alumnus of his alma mater, and serves as president of Friends of Harvard Basketball.

Business Origin

The idea for Staples originated while Stemberg was interviewing for the position of chairman of a wholesale club. He noticed the office products department was one of the busiest even with its limited product selection. After a complete analysis of the office products market he wrote a business plan which would redefine the office products industry. His concept was Staples-The Office Superstore: a chain of discount office-product stores serving businesses with fewer than 100 employees by providing a broad selection of products with discounts averaging 50 percent from catalog list prices and convenient stores hours.

Leo Kahn, one of Stemberg's fiercest supermarket competitors, is co-founder of Staples. The two first met in 1980 when they debated marketing concepts on WBZ-TV in Boston. Kahn, an entrepreneur in his own right, virtually invented the idea of no-frills, deep discount supermarket retailing. Kahn admired Stemberg and was interested in backing him in a business venture. During a conversation at a Harvard basketball game the Staples idea developed.

Kahn was only one of the original investors. Stemberg's business plan was extremely well received in the venture capital market and he received an abundance of offers. The group of blue chip investors backing Staples in its early stages included Bain Capital, Hambro International Ventures, Chancellor Investment Management, Alex. Brown Ventures, Harvard Management, Bessemer Ventures, Adler & Company and Trust Investment Management.

Business Growth

The first Staples store opened in Brighton, Massachusetts in 1986. Since then, Staples has continued to grow steadily in a very methodical manner. During its first year of operations, the company concentrated its efforts on assessing the interest of various target audiences in the deep discount retail format, evaluating the performance of product categories and suppliers, improving store merchandising and refining its store design, procedures and systems.

One of the company's initial strategic decisions was to focus growth in the northeast quadrant of the U.S. This territory included the Boston-to-Washington corridor, which has the highest concentration of office workers in the country. The second important decision was the establishment of centralized distribution centers. Initially facing opposition from some company management, this important strategic move has given Staples the lowest average dollar value of inventory in the industry, a long-term competitive edge in merchandise pricing.

Staples completed its initial public offering in April 1989. A total of 3,250,000 shares were offered, 2,050,000 by the company and 1,200,000 by selling shareholders, at $19.00 per share.

With the opening or acquisition of 21 stores and a distribution center, Staples has entered the Los Angeles market. The company also plans to enter the center city markets with the opening of smaller stores known as Staples Express.

In 1991, an agreement was reached with Dell Computer Corp. to supply Staples with a line of personal computers for stores nationwide. Stemberg said he was "delighted" with the agreement, adding that both companies offer high quality products at low cost.

Staples anticipates having 124 stores in operation at the close of fiscal 1992. Future growth is projected at 30 to 35 new stores per year.

Business Obstacles

As the pioneer in the office superstore concept, Staples needed to get the customer into the stores. This proved to be a difficult task. With the opening of the first store, Stemberg could not even pay people to visit the store. Staples sent merchandise coupons to office managers in the area; it took more than a month for the first one to visit the store. Persuading the office manager who is accustomed to traditional purchasing methods may require several months and personalized direct marketing. Once persuaded, they become loyal customers.

Getting the merchandise into the stores was another obstacle. Staples had to educate the manufacturers into the new retailing concept. Fracturing the industry and cutting out the traditional wholesaler middleman, Staples sought to purchase direct and receive volume discounts. Manufacturers were pressured from all sides and reluctant to change.

Once the products reached the stores, boxes and shelves were being torn apart because different products were packaged in virtually identical packaging. In an effort to "see" what they were purchasing, consumers opened the boxes. Staples launched a campaign to convince the suppliers to change their packaging. If they refused, the product was purchased from some other supplier.

Keys to Success

Stemberg learned from his grocery store experience the challenges of rapid growth and the necessity of infrastructure. It is vital to plan from the start for the successful operation of a larger company, especially having a capable management organization in place. Staples has made such a commitment and continues to build store management and senior executives. "What you always want to have in business is to be able to achieve profitability at a price level where others have difficulty making money," says Stemberg. For Staples, this has meant operations in the northeast markets which are notorious for high rent and labor and expensive marketing.

Future Vision

Staples was the first office superstore. As a compliment to Stemberg's innovative idea, more than a dozen other chains have quickly emerged. As the chains saturate their individual territories and expand nationally, they will be forced to face competition head on. Stemberg has carefully laid the foundation for Staples' success and welcomes the challenge. "We will win only because we have better execution, not because there's this huge wall that keeps other people out of the industry. We knew that from Day One."

Entrepreneurial Lesson

Stemberg is a retail man. His formula for retail success: "Devote your career to developing and implementing bold new ways for customers to save money."

References

Barrier, Michael. "Tom Stemberg Calls the Office." *Nation's Business*, July 1990.

Caminiti, Susan. "Seeking Big Money in Paper and Pens." *Fortune*, July 31, 1989.

Charm, Robert E. "Thomas G. Stemberg of Staples Inc.: Sacrificing Earnings to Build the Right Way." *New England Business*, May 2, 1988.

Flax, Steven. "Perils of the Paper Clip Trade." *New York Times Magazine*, June 11, 1989.

Selz, Michael. "Office Supply Firms Take Different Paths to Success." *Wall Street Journal*, May 30, 1991.

Solomon, Stephen D. "Born to Be Big." *Inc.*, June 1989.

"Staples' Big Plans In Office Supplies." *New York Times*, August 14, 1991.

Staples, Inc., Prospectus, 1989.

Stern, Aimee. "The Toys 'R' Us of Office Supplies." *Adweek's Marketing Week*, August 15, 1988.

——K. S. M.

Carolyn J. Stradley

C & S Paving, Inc.

Carolyn J. Stradley: Born 1946. Married, one child.

Venture: Asphalt paving and grading business, specializing in difficult jobs other contractors often refuse.

Company: C & S Paving, Inc.; 786 Ruby Street; Marietta, GA 30066; (404) 422-9124

Founded: January 1979.

Revenues: $2.6 million (December 1989).

Employees: 30.

Original Investment: $25,000 in personal funds.

Value: $1 million (September 1990), according to the company's accounting firm.

Founder

Born near the small mountain town of Blairsville, Georgia, Carolyn Jones Stradley grew up in a poverty-ridden region with an alcoholic father. Their mother dead, she and 15-year-old brother Eldon were abandoned by their father when Stradley was 11. Eldon moved to Atlanta a short time later, leaving Carolyn alone in the family's two-room house.

Maternal and paternal relatives "quietly feuded," unable to agree on responsibility for the young child's care. Ultimately, Carolyn remained alone in the family home and raised herself, receiving visits from family members on Sundays or special occasions. "It wasn't total isolation, but as far as a day-in, day-out routine. . . . I had to maintain my own schedule," recalls Stradley. Odd jobs such as cleaning the school lunchroom or picking green beans, provided her with money or an occasional hot meal.

At 13, the teenager joined Eldon in Atlanta and began working as a waitress. She soon met 26-year-old Arthur Stradley, who made her "typical American dreams of a house and family" seem attainable. She quit high school at 15 to marry Arthur, and shortly after her 17th birthday, the Stradleys' first child was born.

In 1968, Carolyn Stradley was hired by Bankhead Enterprises, a small asphalt paving company. Her job as secretary/bookkeeper supplemented the family's income until Arthur became ill with kidney disease and lost his job. Stradley cleaned offices and did bookkeeping on the side to earn money to pay for Arthur's increasing medical bills. She also earned her GED (Graduation Equivalency Degree) and took civil engineering courses at Georgia Tech to gain a promotion to division manager at Bankhead Enterprises.

Arthur died in 1973. Stradley continued working with Bankhead until 1979, when she formed C & S Paving. Remarried in 1984, her subsequent success has enabled her to pursue many life-long dreams, like world travel. When not at the office, charity functions or business meetings, Stradley can sometimes be found at Six Flags Over Georgia, "living the childhood I never had."

Business Origin

After Arthur's death, Stradley focused her attention on her job and nine year-old daughter. The hard work was "therapeutic," she says. More importantly, she gained an inside view of the asphalt paving business. After advancing to division manager at Bankhead, she realized that while reasonably successful and secure, she was not happy. "I looked at my life," recalls Stradley. "I had made steps in personal achievement. But I knew a division manager position was as high as I could ever dream, working for someone else." Still with Bankhead, Stradley optimistically began plans for her own paving business. Her first step was to secure a bank loan.

The banks she talked with did not share Stradley's optimism. Neither did her boss. He fired her on-the-spot when he learned of her plans, but they soon reached an agreement that let her keep her job. Within a month, however, another disagreement resulted in her leaving the company. Stradley viewed this break with Bankhead as the motivation she needed throw her total energy into pursuing her own business.

The next day, January 16, 1979, Stradley landed her first paving job.

Equipped with a pickup truck and a few rented tools, she tackled the job—shoveling and setting forms at the Atlanta Botanical Gardens.

Turning to family members, Stradley linked with brother Eldon Jones and his wife Shirley to form C & S Paving (C & S stands for Carolyn and Shirley). A mechanic by trade, Eldon gradually learned the business and helped Stradley at job sites. Shirley served as the company secretary. Eldon and Shirley each owned 25 percent of the company, with Stradley owning the rest.

Business Growth

C & S Paving's growth was modest, at best, during its early years. Stradley's office was her kitchen table and her equipment was rented. Without bank credit, she had to use personal funds for capital. But one of the greatest constraints on company growth came from men reluctant to accept a woman in the asphalt business. "Men certainly hassled me, like locking me in "Job Johnnys" (portable restrooms on job sites) to see if I was tough enough to accept the jokes. They made bets that I couldn't operate the equipment," Stradley reflects. But Stradley claims she "earned" the respect of her male associates, never "asking that it just be given." She insisted on being "equal" with men, performing most of the physical labor herself. She shoveled asphalt, gravel and dirt, and operated the heavy equipment such as tractors, rollers and dump trucks. Gradually, the jokes ceased. Contractors began noticing Stradley's attention to critical details. Still others were impressed by her obvious physical stamina. According to Stradley, contractors "noticed the quality work we were doing and realized this was not a school-girl dream. C & S Paving was in this for the long-term."

C & S Paving sought the jobs "nobody wanted"—smaller, complex jobs not profitable for larger companies with expensive equipment and heavy debt. Stradley devoted her energy to asphalt repair and small road projects like parking lots and subdivision roads. With her growing reputation for "perfectionism," Stradley's business grew. She was able to hire much-needed laborers and purchase new equipment. The growth also permitted her to compete for bigger contracts. In 1986, Stradley's C & S Paving landed the largest government contract ever awarded to a female contractor, repairing the roads and runways at Dobbins Air Force Base in Marietta, Georgia.

As Stradley's business flourished, so did the media recognition she commanded. Her "rags to riches" story was published in several business publications. In 1982, she was selected by *U.S. News and World Report* as one of eight U.S. women most likely to succeed. At business or charity functions, she was quickly recognized—even sought out.

Carolyn Stradley still receives tremendous media attention as well as many business honors and awards. In 1987 she was selected as entrepreneur of the year by *Venture* magazine. Her local chamber of commerce chose her as Small Businessperson of the Year in 1988. In 1989 Stradley really hit her stride. She was among 12 Georgia Entrepreneurs of the Year, named by accounting firm Arthur Young and brokerage house Robinson-Humphrey. Avon Products included her as one of six Women of Enterprise national award winners. Finally, President George Bush presented her with the Small Business Administration's National Businessperson of the Year (second runner-up) award.

In 1986, Stradley became the sole owner of C & S, purchasing Eldon's and Shirley's interest.

Business Obstacles

When she began her asphalt business, Stradley expected resistance from men in the industry. However, she never expected the cool reception she received from women. "Women have discriminated against me probably three-fold more than men," the contractor claims. On many occasions receptionists made rude comments about her clothes—boots, jeans, hard-hat and T-shirt. Quite often Stradley was kept endlessly waiting for an owner or a contractor by a receptionist who would "turn her nose up" at her. She endured comments such as "don't you dislike that stuff [the asphalt] because it stinks so bad," or "my husband wouldn't like it if I was out there doing that . . . it's not very ladylike."

Today, Stradley sports silk blouses rather than messy work clothes, but continues to encounter women, as well as men, who are somewhat negative about her profession. Stradley handles the situation by letting her company's reputation speak for itself. "Of course there are closed-minded people who can not accept a woman in the contracting business," says Stradley. "But when a contractor needs a job done right, he should be concerned about workers' abilities, not whether they are male or female. Our excellent work record speaks for itself." As for dealing with narrow-minded women, Stradley takes it all in stride and does not get "too concerned about their inability to accept my chosen profession."

An additional obstacle has been the effect of the Supreme Court decision in *Richmond v. Croson*, which caused the city of Atlanta to suspend a set-aside minority contracting program. Most of the C&S paving contracts stopped "midstream," Stradley told *Newsweek;* she hopes a new city plan will remedy the situation.

Keys to Success

Stradley credits much of her success to her difficult childhood. Growing up in poverty taught Stradley to survive without money. She began her business in much the same fashion. Even today, she maintains a modest office, preferring to invest the company's profits in better machinery and equipment.

Stradley's childhood also taught her to "find solutions" in apparently hopeless situations. She extends that philosophy to her clients, finding ways to accomplish difficult paving jobs—the jobs her competitors avoid. To win a contract with Underground Atlanta (a major entertainment and shopping district), Stradley cut the tops off two dump trucks. The alteration let the trucks maneuver in tight underground areas, winning C & S Paving a $130,000 contract.

Future Vision

Stradley does not consider herself successful. "I haven't yet seen the light at the end of the tunnel," she quips. Therein lies Stradley's primary goal for the future. She hopes to add new names to the company's client list and increase revenues. Stradley claims the planned business expansion is not solely to increase profits. "I do not relate success to dollars. Rather, success is the total journey you take, not merely the destination," she says. She also hopes to phase in an employee ownership program, and in time make the company totally employee-owned. "We work as a team here," says Stradley, "and every employee is like a member of my family. This way C & S Paving will continue long after I am gone."

One of Stradley's problems on job sites led her to envision a new opportunity. While male counterparts could conveniently relieve themselves, clothing and facilities made a woman's effort much more problematic. Stradley has never forgotten that feeling of "unequalness." She has developed a new line of clothing called "Equalizers," slacks which contain a unique zipper that allows women to use restroom facilities with efficiency and ease. Stradley cites the case of a female police officer carrying a gun, radio, handcuffs and a multitude of other items. The officer must remove all of the items from her belt before using the restroom. Wearing Stradley's new design, the officer would simply unzip the zipper. "Sure, people are laughing and snickering," says Stradley. "But when you consider that in the year 2000, some 47.5 percent of the work force in the construction industry will be women, you realize there is a need for this type of clothing." Stradley has presented samples to the Department of Forestry, Department of Defense, the Georgia State Patrol and the Atlanta Police Department. Each is seriously considering her product. "Equalizers will give women of the future, employed in non-traditional roles, some equality," says Stradley. "I believe Equalizers will be the next Coca-Cola of Atlanta."

Entrepreneurial Lessons

Carolyn Stradley's pain-filled childhood could easily have turned her into a bitter and resentful woman. Instead, she views her experiences in a positive light. A devout Christian, Stradley believes every life experience should be viewed as a "lesson," a tool to learn from. She relates several incidents which she believes strengthened her personal and professional life.

Shortly after her mother's death and her father's abandonment, the young Carolyn's classmates drew names to exchange Christmas gifts. Because she had no money, her name was not included and she did not expect a present from any of her classmates. But one little girl gave Carolyn a bar of soap. "I had been making my own lye soap to bathe with and I knew she was just trying to make fun of me for not always looking so nice or smelling good," remembers Stradley. At first, she recalls, "I wanted to kill her. But [then] I thought, 'No, this is a beautiful bar of soap and it smells good.' I decided that I would find good in her gift." Stradley claims she has learned to find good in everything. Doing so allows her to find positive solutions to both business and personal problems. Her positive outlook "serves our clients better than a negative one," she believes, finding that in many instances, "attitude is better than aptitude."

The self-sufficient, independent entrepreneur recalls another incident which she says, "taught me never to depend on other people for my needs." One Christmas day, expecting to spend time with relatives, 11-

year-old Carolyn did not build a fire or cook any food. When those plans fell through, she went to her minister's home. The house was filled with wonderful food aromas and she could not help but think about sitting down to eat. But before the meal was served, the minister told Carolyn to go home because he wanted to spend time with his family. Cold and hungry, she left. From that experience, Stradley says, "I learned that whatever my wants and desires, *I* am responsible for my own happiness."

As she reached adulthood, Stradley's philosophical approach to life and business continued to evolve from hardship. When she married Arthur, Stradley felt she had everything—a husband, a baby and a home. But when Arthur died she initially thought she had lost it all. "Afraid I would go back to the poverty I had known as a child, I began to question God," recalls Stradley. "I would ask 'why are you doing this to me—haven't I suffered enough?' But I realized I had my health and I had a beautiful baby girl." From Arthur's tragic early death, Carolyn Stradley learned to value what she has.

She applies that philosophy to C & S Paving. Criticized by some for maintaining her humble office, Stradley refuses to invest attention in exterior trappings. While admitting that a new office would be "nice," she continues to focus instead on maintaining what she sees as the company's most important assets and attributes: good machinery, hard-working employees, satisfied clients and substantial cash flow.

More than anything else, Stradley has learned to persevere. "If I, a dirt-poor farm girl from the north Georgia hills can be successful, anyone can," she declares. "Human beings can do almost anything in the world we want to if we are willing to set priorities and make sacrifices."

References

"Carolyn Stradley." *The View*, September 1989.

"Carolyn Stradley Paves Her Way All the Way to the White House." *Inside Cobb Magazine*, Summer 1989.

Ezell, Hank. "Entrepreneur's Road to the Top Was Not a Well-Paved Freeway." *Atlanta Journal and Constitution*, July 10, 1989.

Feuerstein, Adam. "When Women Wear the Pants: Freedom's Just Another Name for New Business." *Atlanta Business Chronicle*, April 1990.

Lawson-Beerman, Anne. "Woman's Road to Success Paved with Lots of Asphalt." *Atlanta Business Chronicle*, October 6, 1986.

Morris, Chris. "Stradley's Road to Success Paved with Risks." *Atlanta Business Chronicle*, April 30, 1990.

Smith, Vern E. "A Second Look at Set-Asides." *Newsweek*, July 1, 1991.

"Women in Charge: Eight Who Made It." *U.S. News & World Report*, March 24, 1980.

——R. H. S.

David W. Thompson

Orbital Sciences Corporation

David W. Thompson: Born 1954. Married.
Venture: Commercial space technology company that designs, manufactures, tests and markets space vehicles, propulsion units and satellite systems.
Company: Orbital Sciences Corporation; 12500 Fairlakes Circle; Fairfax, VA 22033; (703) 631-3600
Founded: 1982.
Revenues: $100.4 million (1990), according to company sources.
Employees: 780.
Original Investment: $2 million.
Value: $8.3 million book value as of December 31, 1989, according to a prospectus dated April 24, 1990.

Founder

David Thompson has been fascinated by space for as long as he can remember. "I think it was pretty clear from an early age that I was going to do something with rockets or satellites when I grew up," he recalls. "I always wanted my own little space program."

Thompson was building and launching small rockets by age five. In high school, he built a six-foot, 50-pound rocket and began sending monkeys into the air.

Thompson studied aeronautics and astronautics at the Massachusetts Institute of Technology (MIT) and worked summers at the National Aeronautics and Space Administration's (NASA) Draper Laboratory in

Cambridge, Massachusetts. He received a Master of Science degree in Aeronautics from the California Institute of Technology in 1977 and joined NASA as a project manager and engineer on the Space Shuttle project.

While he worked with NASA, Thompson began planning his own space company. "I noticed that an enormous amount of technology had been developed by the government for a small number of programs. The technology worked well in those programs, but it really wasn't being used in many other areas where it could be," he says. "It occurred to me that perhaps a private company would be more effective than either a government agency or a large aerospace company that viewed space as a sideline to its primary business."

Recognizing that he "needed to learn a lot about business in a hurry" if he wanted to start his own company, Thompson entered Harvard Business School in 1979. After he earned an M.B.A. in 1981, he became Special Assistant to the president at Hughes Aircraft Company in Los Angeles.

Thompson has received awards from NASA, the American Institute of Aeronautics and Astronauts (AAIA), and the Space Foundation for his work in space-related projects. He was the founding chairman of the Washington Space Business Roundtable, and he is affiliated with a number of space-related organizations including the American Astronautical Society, the Space Foundation, the National Space Club, the Foundation for Space Business Research and the NASA Advisory Council Commercial Programs Advisory Committee. He is also a member of the Young Presidents' Organization. In 1989, Thompson was named the Washington, DC-area "High-Tech Entrepreneur of the Year."

Business Origin

At Harvard Business School, Thompson met Scott Webster, a mechanical and electrical engineer, and Bruce Ferguson, a law and business student who had once dreamed of becoming an astronaut. The three conducted a Harvard-sponsored study of business opportunities for commercial space ventures.

After they graduated from Harvard, Thompson, Webster and Ferguson went their separate ways but continued to discuss the possibility of capitalizing on their research. They were reunited in late 1981 when the Space Foundation presented them with an award for their Harvard study.

At the Foundation awards dinner, Thompson, Ferguson and Webster met

Texas oilman and space enthusiast Fred Alcorn. Alcorn and Thomas O. Paine, former NASA administrator and president of Northrop Corporation, agreed to invest $500,000 to get Orbital Sciences Corporation (OSC) off the ground.

Business Growth

OSC was incorporated in April 1982. Initially, the company concentrated on developing and marketing the Transfer Orbit Stage (TOS), an orbit transfer vehicle designed to launch satellites from the Space Shuttle and the Titan unmanned rocket. OSC's aim was to develop a "space-perfected rocket" by 1986.

By September 1983, OSC was $1.3 million in debt and needed additional funding to continue the TOS project. In 1984 OSC raised $50 million through a private investment of capital that created a research and development limited partnership among the investors. The bid was the largest private investment in space transportation history.

In January 1986, NASA placed the first purchase orders for the TOS. However, the explosion of the Space Shuttle Challenger a few weeks later put the purchases on hold.

Recognizing that the Shuttle disaster might limit future TOS sales, OSC began planning a second product in 1987. Dr. Antonio Elias, the company's vice president of engineering, approached Thompson with the idea for an airplane rocket that would carry satellites into space. "I told him it was an absolutely crazy idea," Thompson recalls. After reconsidering, Thompson suggested modifications to Elias' project, and the concept for the Pegasus winged rocket booster was born.

OSC began developing Pegasus in 1987. That year, the company earned revenues of $25 million.

Nineteen eighty-eight was a significant year in OSC's growth. The company established a joint venture with Hercules Aerospace Company to develop Pegasus and acquired Space Data Corporation of Tempe, Arizona, significantly expanding its product lines and manufacturing capability. *Inc.* magazine named OSC the fastest-growing private high-technology company in the nation, and *Business Week* reported that OSC had the greatest employee growth of any U.S. high-tech firm that year. A December 1988 *Fortune* article called the Thompson, Ferguson and Webster trio "potential billionaires of the 21st century." OSC's 1988 revenues totaled $35 million and the company had $150 million backlog by year end.

Inc. magazine named OSC the nation's fastest-growing private high-tech company again in 1989, and that year the company posted revenues of more than $80 million. "We've always had an important growth objective," Thompson says. "We felt that to be a significant company in the space business we couldn't be a $20 million company for very long."

OSC's Pegasus vehicle was successfully launched in April 1990. In September 1991, the Pegasus rocket team was awarded the National Medal of Technology, the United States' highest honor for technological advancement and engineering achievement.

OSC is the country's leading small company providing space products and services to the United States government and to commercial and international customers. To expand its marketing, technical and financial capabilities, OSC regularly invests in project-related research, forming strategic business alliances and joint ventures with compatible partners.

Business Obstacles

When they began OSC, Thompson and his partners were not certain that their venture would survive. *Washington Business* commented in 1989 that the three started with "little more than credit cards, a telephone answering machine and a lifetime romance with space."

During its first five years, OSC's greatest challenge was to stay in business. Because Thompson and his partners were running a small company marketing a highly-specialized, expensive product, they knew that OSC would only be profitable over the long term.

The Challenger disaster in 1986 underscored the unpredictable nature of the space industry and its impact on space contractors such as OSC. The company acknowledged in its April 1990 prospectus that "launch vehicle programs typically experience some failure, and these setbacks vary in their impact on the mission's overall success." Space experts agree that the industry faces the danger of rocket explosions, changes in national policies and the elimination of funding for space technologies. Because space projects typically undergo a lengthy development cycle, investors often do not realize a financial return on their investment for many years.

Thompson and his associates faced a space community skeptical about the possible success of a commercial space company managed by three young Harvard MBAs. *Forbes* magazine commented in March 1984 that "Youth and inexperience do not disqualify one as an entrepreneur, but this venture would be risky even for experienced managers." Each of the three partners was 31 or younger when they founded OSC.

To win their first contract, OSC persuaded NASA to fund the TOS project with private, rather than public funds. Once NASA accepted OSC's proposal, the company had just six weeks to find contractor to engineer, manufacture and test TOS.

Keys to Success

Thompson and his co-founders believed that new technologies and changes in national space policy created opportunities to sell space products and services to government, commercial and educational markets. To capitalize on this opportunity, they designed advanced space products that were less expensive and more adaptable to customer needs than existing products.

From its beginning, OSC operated differently than other companies competing for space-related contracts, ignoring long-standing business traditions. To bring products to market more quickly, OSC favored private financing over government funding. The company also took advantage of existing aerospace, computer and other high-tech industry technologies, rather than engaging in costly and time-consuming basic research.

Thompson, Ferguson and Webster were able to convince private investors to gamble on their ability to create meaningful projects for space. Douglas S. Luke, managing director of Rothschild Ventures Inc., which invested $2 million in OSC, says, "They were three young, bright, energetic people who sold themselves well. We bought their story. They were totally unproven and half the age of most of the venture capitalists that would have been interested in investing in them, but they were able to persuade us that they were a good bet," he says.

Investors were convinced that the three had a solid business plan that was based on the evolution of technology. Paine, a founding investor and OSC board member says, "They weren't trying to so something so far out that the engineering would be impossible. Investors liked their style. These guys are listeners . . . that's rare in young guys moving this fast," he says.

As OSC grew, Ferguson, Thompson and Webster assumed different roles within the organization. Thompson is the company's chairman, president and CEO. "Everyone has one vote and Dave has two," Ferguson says. Ferguson is the company's vice president of finance and senior counsel. Webster serves as senior vice president for marketing and business development.

As the company's CEO, Thompson plans OSC's business strategy and directs day-to-day operations, including the work of three major space product operating divisions. He is responsible for the company's engineering, manufacturing marketing and administrative staff of more than 600 people located at facilities in six states.

Those who have observed OSC say that the company reflects the founders' entrepreneurial spirit and energy. As *Washington Business* reported in 1989, "employees at OSC, where the average age is little more than 30, talk exuberantly about the intelligence of their colleagues and bosses, about the freedom and lack of bureaucracy, and about their wonder at seeing vice presidents and other executives pitching in to do things like working on assembling the rockets."

Future Vision

Thompson plans to develop OSC into a $350 million company by 1992. "That's the size we need to have the engineering and industrial capability to conduct the kind of projects we would like to in the future," he says. Thompson predicts that "the ten-year future for both communications and transportation to space is quite good. After that, everything is kind of hazy," he says.

Board member Paine says of Thompson and his co-founders, "If they continue to be as confident, as entrepreneurial, as smart and as lucky, they may have a great future. But they face an awful lot of hazards."

As for his personal future, Thompson says, "Before I retire from OSC in 45 years or so, I want to be operating a passenger-carrying cargo line to space," he says. "There will be an enormous market of people that would like to see the Earth rotate below them."

Entrepreneurial Lessons

Thompson says that the work he and his partners completed at Harvard was "very useful" as they launched OSC. "Not only did we find out that we worked quite well together as a team and that we had some of the same objectives for the future, but we got a lot of the groundwork done that formed the basis for our future business," he says.

As the first corporation in 30 years to enter the aerospace industry as a prime contractor, OSC's founders proved that an entrepreneurial company can thrive in a traditionally non-entrepreneurial industry.

Thompson and his partners have remained firm in their belief that there is room for private industry in space. A product like Pegasus—which not only offers existing services at significantly lower cost, but also introduces new services—observes Thompson, "is probably the best manifestation of what this company is all about."

References

Brokaw, Leslie. "Rocket Man." *Inc.*, March 1990.

Brown, Stuart F. "Winging It into Space." *Popular Science*, May 1989.

Mack, Toni. "Pies in the Sky." *Forbes*, March 26, 1984.

"OSC's High-Flying Plans No Pie-in-the-Sky Dream." *Washington Business*, October 1989.

Perry, N. "From HBS to Outer Space." *Harvard Business School Bulletin*, June 1989.

Sugawara, S. "OSC, a Successful Company Still Trying to Get Off the Ground." *Washington Post*, October 23, 1989.

——M. J. B.

Index

Index